BROTHERS OF LIGHT,
BROTHERS OF BLOOD

BROTHERS OF LIGHT, BROTHERS OF BLOOD

The Penitentes of the Southwest

Marta Weigle

Ancient City Press
Santa Fe, New Mexico

Second Printing

International Standard Book Number:
0-941270-58-0 paperback
Library of Congress Catalogue Number:
88-072048

Cover Design by Stephen Tongier

Cover photograph: A Penitente Morada in Northern New Mexico. (Photograph by Thomas R. Lyons. Courtesy of the Albuquerque Museum.)

To
Brotherhood
Community
Faith

Contents

List of Illustrations

Photographs following page 102

Preface

The Brothers of Our Father Jesus, commonly known as the Penitentes, are men of Hispanic descent who belong to a lay religious society of the Roman Catholic Church. Membership requires sincere faith and unstinting commitment to Christian charity through mutual aid and unobtrusive good deeds for all neighbors and fellow citizens. The Brotherhood's headquarters are in Santa Fe, and the organization's greatest strength is in northern New Mexico and southern Colorado. Local chapters or moradas are governed by elected officials headed by an *Hermano Mayor,* or Elder Brother. Most moradas belong to larger councils which are organized into districts under the Archbishop's Supreme Council, headed by the *Hermano Supremo Arzobispal,* or Archbishop's Supreme Brother.

The pious observances of these Brothers are centered around the Passion of Jesus and the spirit of penance. During Lent and Holy Week they worship in retreat as well as in certain public rituals which devout members of the community may join. They also sponsor wakes for the dead and wakes for the saints. Both the Brotherhood's ritual practices and its social commitments have spiritually and substantively benefitted long-isolated communities. These benefits have too often been overlooked by superficial observers and apprehensive newcomers.

Penitente rites formerly involved closely supervised expressions of the penitential spirit through self-flagellation, cross-bearing, and other forms of discipline. Sometimes, in the past, a Brother was tied to a large cross in a short simulation of the Crucifixion on Good Friday. These more "spectacular" aspects of Penitente worship unfortunately attracted a disproportionate amount of attention from the media and from casual, uncomprehending observers. Their unwelcome scrutiny did and still does violate the religious freedom of the Brotherhood and desecrate a genuine devotional expression which has a long tradition in Spanish Catholicism.

Since the first thorough scholarly investigation of the Brotherhood by Dorothy Woodward in the early 1930s, workers on the New Mexico Writers' Program of the W.P.A. have assembled additional valuable data. More importantly, the Spanish, Mexican, and Territorial Archives of New Mexico, as well as the Archives of the Archdiocese of Santa Fe through 1900, have become available. It is now possible to write a general history of the Brotherhood through the post-World War I period. This book builds on the sound scholarship of Dorothy Woodward, Fray Angelico Chavez, and E. Boyd and synthesizes other relevant published and unpublished sources to provide just such a reference. A more definitive rendering of recent Brotherhood history must await official authorization and the opening of Church archives from the twentieth century. Nevertheless, the account for this period is as accurate and conservative as possible.

Part I sketches the physical setting with a brief history of settlement patterns in New Mexico and southern Colorado. Descriptions of Brotherhood meetinghouses or *moradas* and their locations are necessarily imprecise. Sadly, many of these structures have suffered from disrepair and vandalism during the past decade or so.

The historical background and development of the Brotherhood is traced in Part II. A chronology of important ecclesiastical and secular dates in Southwestern history introduces this material. The appendixes, which are transcriptions of key documents and newspaper articles, follow the sequence of the text. (Note that these transcriptions follow the original documents as closely as possible. This means that both the Spanish and the English appear awkward and faulty in many places.)

Part III provides an overview of Brotherhood organization and rituals. Both the councils and the local chapters are discussed. Basic ritual patterns are elucidated, *not* particular Holy Week observances at a specific morada. The explanation relies on standard Church sources with non-Catholics in mind. The final chapter, "The Legends and the Sacred," is an attempt to analyze the folklore about ghostly penitents and to indicate some more general significance to penance, rites of passage, and the experience of the sacred.

Throughout the text, no accents have been used on Spanish place names except in quoted material. All such names are treated as if they were completely Anglicized. The decision about accenting personal names is much more difficult and has been resolved arbitrarily in order to be consistent throughout. Names of persons from the Spanish and Mexican periods have their appropriate accents. Names of persons from 1846 on have not been accented because the practice of doing so or not is decidedly inconsistent in the literature as well as in personal use. The name of Don Antonio José Martínez of Taos, a transitional figure between the Mexican and American periods, appears with proper accents in Part II, chapter 1, but without accents in subsequent chapters.

All names, except place names, retain their proper accents in the Chronology, Notes, and Bibliographical Essay, as well as in quoted material. The exception is Fray Angélico Chávez, who in recent years has ceased to use accents on what is now his accepted pen name. His name is therefore never accented herein, regardless of the way it appears on his earlier writings.

Spanish words are defined when they first appear in the text. The reader should refer to the Index for further examples of usage and the like. Most Spanish words appear in italics, except titles and subsequent instances of previously defined terms.

The Bibliographical Essay which concludes this volume summarizes only the most notable materials relating to the Brotherhood. An exhaustive, annotated listing of well over one thousand items forms the contents of *A Penitente Bibliography: Supplement to Brothers of Light, Brothers of Blood: The Penitentes of the Southwest,* bibliographical supplement to this work. Virtually all available resources, from sensational, derivative stories in pulp and prestige journals to serious, sensitive historical and descriptive studies of documents and actual ceremonies, have been surveyed. Hopefully, this companion volume will become the obituary for any further accounts ·of the Penitentes which purport "at last" to reveal the "truth" and report "bloody" contemporary rites and questionable secular involvements.

Both these volumes should provide an essential resource for anyone interested in the Brotherhood. From now on, serious field or ethnohistorical studies of particular villages or chapters, or the rigorous interpretation of new documentation and substantial data would seem to constitute acceptable publications. However, it is hoped that Brotherhood permission will always be obtained first.

*   *   *

This book germinated in Dr. Don Yoder's stimulating course on folk religion at the University of Pennsylvania, Philadelphia. Mr. Robert Kadlec of Santa Fe urged that I elaborate my class work and encouraged me immeasurably by publishing a brief preliminary volume at his Ancient City Press. The research eventually grew into a dissertation which was carefully supervised by Dr. Dan Ben-Amos and Dr. Kenneth S. Goldstein, Department of Folklore and Folklife, and Dr. Samuel G. Armistead, Department of Romance Languages, University of Pennsylvania. Dr. Armistead has been especially generous with his extensive knowledge of the Spanish language and Hispanic folklore.

Various librarians now or formerly associated with the libraries of the Museum of New Mexico, Santa Fe; the Southwest Room of the New Mexico State Library, Santa Fe; St. John's College Library, Santa Fe; and Zimmerman Library, University of New Mexico, Albuquerque, have been most courteous and helpful in all my research. Mrs. Eileen Eshner of Carnegie Public Library, Las Vegas, New Mexico, has assembled a notable collection of Brotherhood materials, and she has always been willing to make allowances for my infrequent trips to Las Vegas. The original research also profited as a result of prompt attention from Mrs. Marion Murra, Reference Librarian, Pueblo Regional Library, Pueblo, Colorado; Mrs. Alys Freeze, Head, Western History Department, The Denver Public Library, Colorado; Mrs. Enid T. Thompson, Librarian, The State Historical Society of Colorado, Denver; and Mrs. Ruth M. Christensen, Librarian, Southwest Museum, Los Angeles, California. My sister and brother-in-law, Connie and Tom Mann, located needed materials in the Yale University libraries, for which I am most grateful.

Any number of people generously contributed information. Among Santa Fe residents I would gratefully note: Mr. Robert Bright, Mr. Charles DuTant, Mr. Charles Hagerman, Mrs. Jo Roybal Hogue, Dr. Rudolph Kieve, Mrs. Farona Konopak, Mrs. Sallie Wagner, and especially the late Mr. W. Thetford LeViness.

Claudia and Sam Larcombe have shared many ideas and experiences. The original work was aided by Dr. Louisa Stark, Department of Anthropology, University of Wisconsin, and Dr. Jack E. Holmes, Department of Political Science, University of Tennessee. I would also like to thank Mr. Richard Stark and Dr. Yvonne Lange of the Museum of International Folk Art, Santa Fe. Dr. Paul Kutsche of Colorado College made extensive and substantial criticisms of the dissertation which helped shape this volume.

All the people in the Historical Services Division of the New Mexico State Records Center and Archives, Santa Fe, have always extended me every courtesy and demonstrated unfailing good humor. I note especially Mrs. Arlene Padilla, Mr. James H. Purdy, and Mr. J. Richard Salazar, as well as former staff member Mr. Michael Cox.

Documents from the Archives of the Archdiocese of Santa Fe have been included with the kind permission of the Archbishop of Santa Fe, the Most Rev. Robert F. Sanchez. Many of these documents were skillfully transcribed by Mr. J. Richard Salazar of the New Mexico State Records Center and Archives. The Henry E. Huntington Library, San Marino, California, has granted permission to publish items from the Mary Austin Collection and the W. G. Ritch Collection; these important materials are designated by the prefix "HM," indicating Huntington Manuscripts. The photographs are included by courtesy of Dr. and Mrs. Thomas R. Lyons of the Chaco Center, National Park Service, University of New Mexico, and Chief Justice John B. McManus, Jr., of the Supreme Court, State of New Mexico.

Mr. M. Santos Melendez, Hermano Supremo Arzobispal of the Brotherhood of Our Father Jesus, honors this book with his Afterword. I am deeply grateful for his criticisms of the manuscript and for his counsel.

I would like to single out several people whose special knowledge and generous spirit have strengthened both the study and my own spirit. They are not, of course, responsible for any shortcomings. Mr. Lorin W. Brown, formerly and still spiritually of Cordova, shared his reminiscences and his abiding feeling for New Mexico and New Mexicans. Both Tom and Margil Lyons have constantly encouraged and enlightened me with their quiet enthusiasm and longstanding familiarity with these aspects of New Mexico. Two women have shown me much about academic and human excellence. The late E. Boyd was a primary source of information and inspiration; we are all the poorer for her passing and very much the richer for having known her. Dr. Myra Ellen Jenkins, historian and Chief of the Historical Services Division of the New Mexico State Records Center and Archives, Santa Fe, permitted me access to the Dorothy Woodward Penitente Papers, taught me to appreciate the complexities of New Mexico and its historical resources, and herself exemplifies the highest standards in scholarship and humanity.

Finally, I have been supported throughout by my parents, my grandfather, and my friends, Bob Kadlec, Barby and Brian Anderson, and Chuck and Nan Perdue.

Introduction

La Fraternidad Piadosa de Nuestro Padre Jesús Nazareno, the Pious Fraternity of Our Father Jesus Nazarite, is a lay religious organization related to the Roman Catholic Church in the southwestern United States, primarily northern New Mexico and southern Colorado. Members of this *Cofradía,* Confraternity, or *Hermandad,* Brotherhood—commonly known as *Los Hermanos Penitentes,* the Penitent Brothers, *Los Hermanos,* the Brothers, or simply, and not infrequently pejoratively, *Los Penitentes,* the Penitent Ones—are almost exclusively men of Hispanic descent. Their fraternities are organized to support pious observances and to render mutual aid. The Society as a whole has evolved through different phases, but it has long played an appreciable role in the history of the region and of Hispanic culture on this remote frontier.

Sometime during the late eighteenth century, a religious force which later came to be known as the Brotherhood of Our Father Jesus emerged among the Spanish pioneers in northern New Mexico. Isolated from southern centers of Spanish New World administration and plagued by natural adversities and hostile nomadic Indians, these settlers evolved sociocultural forms adaptive to their frontier situation. Variant forms of worship were among these.

The Franciscan Order virtually monopolized New Mexican Church administration until late in the eighteenth century. Both before (1598–1680) and after de Vargas's reconquest (1692–96), a chronically inadequate number of *frailes* ("friars") set up missions among the Indian pueblos and ministered to the Spaniards in the Custodia de la Conversión de San Pablo, or Custody of the Conversion of St. Paul, governed by the Franciscan Province of the

Holy Gospel in Mexico City. Even when the missions and parishes were gradually secularized, the various bishops of Durango were unable to supply sufficient *curas* (secular priests) to meet the religious needs of the colonists, and some Franciscans stayed. The resources of the Church were insufficient, however, and by 1833 an identifiable folk religion had evolved, particularly in communities relatively isolated from the tenuous control of Santa Fe officialdom.

This folk religion was by no means aberrant. The brotherhoods' observances involved rituals, such as *rosarios* (extended rosary services), *Via Crucis* (Way of the Cross processions), Tenebrae services, and penitential devotions, primarily flagellation and cross-bearing, with clear precedents in the history of Spanish Catholicism and its mystical, penitential and especially Franciscan traditions. Various lay associations of the pious were also common in Spain from the twelfth century, and many were established in the New World colonies. In addition, the Third Order of St. Francis, for fervent lay believers in Franciscan ideals, was a popular affiliation. Rather than a result of selective borrowing from Indian religion, then, the New Mexico penitential brotherhoods formed a movement clearly within Spanish Roman Catholic tradition.

Whatever its origins, the Brotherhood took root because it fulfilled vital needs for social integration and individual spiritual security. This was further complicated during the so-called Secular Period (ca. 1790–1850), when the Franciscans were gradually replaced by the secular priests. Many Hispanos may thus have felt an increased need to preserve the familiar Franciscan traditions. In the early stages of the Brotherhood, then, intracultural and intra-Church tensions predominated.

Although the Santa Fe Trail was opened in 1821, the influx of Americans was relatively insignificant until after Kearny claimed New Mexico for the United States in 1846. As residents of a Territory of the United States, the Hispanic populace had to adjust to a new regime which separated the powers of church and state, to a new language, to important changes in Catholic Church administration, and to a growing influx of Anglo-American settlers who were largely Protestant. Most immediately felt were changes within the Church itself. Santa Fe was elevated to the see city for a new southwestern vicariate apostolic, which became a diocese in

1853, and an archdiocese in 1875. Church administration was placed in the hands of Bishop John B. Lamy, a Frenchman. Three of the seven native priests left or were suspended, and Franciscans did not return to the area until 1899. There was some bitterness against the new French and American clergy, as well as the Jesuits, who arrived in 1867 at Lamy's request.

During the latter part of the nineteenth century, the Brotherhood's strength increased as the various moradas or chapters became more organized and independent. *Concilios* (councils) of local chapters were formally recognized by Territorial law, and the Brothers acquired considerable political and legal expertise. Annual Brotherhood rituals, especially the all-important Holy Week observances, provided a familiar haven for those of the faithful who were bewildered by the religious and political changes.

After World War I, Brotherhood affiliation was more prevalent in rural and poorer urban areas. Hispanic village life grew more heterogeneous, and fewer males would become Brothers. Outsiders intruded more and more on the sanctity of Holy Week observances, and severe rites were generally modified or conducted more covertly. In 1947, through the efforts of Don Miguel Archibeque and several others, a systematic organization of councils and chapters was officially reinstated into the Catholic Church by Archbishop Edwin V. Byrne, who proclaimed that the Brotherhood was "a pious association of men joined in charity to commemorate the passion and death of the Redeemer." It continues so today, albeit with a drastically reduced membership.

The adaptability of the Penitente movement as a whole and the variability of individual chapters within it has assured its survival. Nonetheless, Brotherhood beliefs and rituals have suffered symbolic and literal desecration by uncomprehending outsiders. Details of these beliefs and rituals remain partly secret, but certain patterns are discernible in reliable and available documents and reports. If the resultant picture appears incomplete, this is as it should be. In the end, the Brothers must speak for themselves, if they so choose.

That the Brothers have persisted attests to their social strength and religious integrity. The history of the Brotherhood is part of the history of the American Southwest and of Hispanic culture there and elsewhere. Most important, Penitente beliefs and rituals are part of the varied religious experiences of mankind.

PART I
A Geographical Sketch

Meanwhile, the sun sinking at our backs had turned the cliffs across the valley into splendid cathedral shapes of rose and saffron beauty—a beauty that is touched here in this country with a sometimes terrible sense of eternity, loneliness, and futility. For all the gay laughter of youth on the hillside, the stark parable of the Crucifixion is close to the country's soul. It eats into the heart, this terror; and it is not difficult to imagine how the early Franciscans felt, as they gazed upon this terrible afternoon light on bare mesa and peak, and felt the thorns of this eternal loneliness pressing into their souls. Actual mortification of the flesh is perhaps less poignant.

—Alice Corbin Henderson,
Brothers of Light, 1937, p. 49.

At the end of the eighteenth century, New Mexico was still a remote province of New Spain. Except for the El Paso del Norte communities some two hundred miles to the south, most New Mexico settlements were clustered near the various Indian Pueblos in the Rio Grande Valley from Belen to Taos. The Villa of Santa Fe (established 1610) was the provincial capital, with an administrative center for the north, or Rio Arriba, at the Villa of Santa Cruz de la Cañada (established 1695) and one for the south, or Rio Abajo, at the Villa of Albuquerque (established 1706). Bancroft estimates the Hispanic and Hispanicized population in 1799 to have numbered 18,826 persons, with about 9,732 Pueblo Indians.[1] Isolated in a semiarid environment far from New World cultural, economic, and administrative centers, and subject to the depredations of nomadic Indians, these inhabitants formed an insular enclave on a harsh frontier.

The Rio Grande, eighteen hundred miles long from its source in southern Colorado to its mouth in the Gulf of Mexico, passes through a series of narrow alluvial valleys in the provincial area. Bottomlands on the valley floor quickly give way on either side to non-arable benchlands, mesas, plains, foothills, and mountains. By irrigating, the pioneers managed to raise wheat, beans, corn, chili, and some other vegetables and fruits. They grazed sheep, some cattle, goats, and horses on common lands. Self-sufficiency was vital because limited trade was possible and permissible only with Comanches to the east and Chihuahua about five hundred miles to the south over the perilous Camino Real.

The Rio Grande Valley became crowded by the end of the eighteenth century, and irrigable land scarce. Outpost or "buffer" settlements had been established from the early part of the century, but hostile Indians made life on these grants arduous and uncertain. Comanches and other Plains Indians posed a threat from the east, while Apaches, Navajos, and Utes threatened from the south, west, and north. Nonetheless, expansion continued, slowly and almost elliptically from the core area.

The signing of the Treaty of Córdoba on August 24, 1821, marked the beginning of a Mexican nation independent of Spain. That fall, William Becknell, a trader from Missouri, was welcomed to the newly opened territory. Thus began a steadily increasing traffic over the Santa Fe Trail, which eventually extended to

Chihuahua. In 1829, Antonio Armijo and a party of traders blazed the Spanish Trail to California, trading woolens for horses and mules at San Gabriel Mission near Los Angeles.[2] So-called "Mountain Men"—French-Canadian and Anglo-American fur trappers—had already infiltrated the Rocky Mountains to the north, sometimes even settling in the northern communities. Santa Fe gradually assumed international status, with towns such as Abiquiu, Taos, Las Vegas, San Miguel del Vado, and others gaining stature as trading centers.

Meanwhile, settlement had begun in the Mora Valley east of the Sangre de Cristo Mountains.[3] Other groups moved eastward toward the Ceja ("Eyebrow") or Cap Rock on the northern and western rim of the Llano Estacado ("Staked Plains"), the giant plateau bounded on the west by the Pecos and Canadian Rivers, and on the east by Palo Duro Canyon and present-day Amarillo, Texas.[4] Settler pushed south along the Rio Grande to Socorro and below, and moved east into the Estancia Valley, while others from El Paso entered the Mesilla Valley still farther south.[5] West of the Rio Grande, hardy families established *placitas* (small settlements) near the San Mateo Mountains, in the vicinity of Laguna and Acoma Pueblos.[6] To the northwest, groups slowly pioneered the Chama Valley.[7] Still, peripheral and even established communities were often difficult to maintain in the face of natural adversities and Indian raids.

On August 18, 1846, Brigadier-General Stephen Watts Kearny led the Army of the West into Santa Fe and claimed New Mexico for the United States. The 1848 Treaty of Guadalupe Hidalgo officially ceded New Mexico and other southwestern lands to the United States, although the present boundary between the two countries was not established until the Gadsden Purchase in 1853. The Territory of New Mexico created by Congress on September 9, 1850, included land east of the Rio Grande claimed by Texas (which was compensated for the loss by a payment of ten million dollars), present-day Arizona (made a Territory in 1863), the southern tip of Nevada (separated from Arizona in 1866), and southern Colorado from the Continental Divide along the 38th parallel east to the 103d meridian (incorporated into the Territory of Colorado in 1861). The first Territorial census, in April 1851, reported a population of 56,984, excluding Indians, while 1852 estimates of the Anglo portion of this figure ranged from 538 to 1,200.[8]

The Hispanic population pushed northward into the San Luis Valley of present-day southern Colorado soon after the United States occupation. Most of these early settlements are difficult to date.[9] Initially, they were administered politically and ecclesiastically from Taos and Santa Fe.

West of the Culebra Mountains, along the Rio de las Animas Perdidas en Purgatorio (Purgatoire River), the area of present-day Trinidad, Colorado, became a popular rest stop along the northern branch of the Santa Fe Trail. New Mexicans scouted the region in 1859 and 1860, and Felipe Baca returned with settlers from the Mora area in 1861.[10] At first, most communities were Hispanic placitas, but burgeoning railroad and mining operations quickly brought many other settlers.

After the Civil War, movement east, south, and west was facilitated by the subjugation of hostile Indians, the extension of stage lines, and the advent of the railroads, with major construction carried out between 1879 and 1881. Sheep-raising, an important part of the New Mexico economy since early Spanish times, throve, and "soon, western flocks were being driven on to range in Arizona and Hispano stockmen from the Las Vegas region moved into the Llano Estacado and established the traditional settlement placitas."[11] Hispanic communities in the San Juan Basin of northwest New Mexico and southwest Colorado were established from the 1870s by settlers from the Chama and San Luis Valleys.[12]

The Church always played an important part in Spanish colonization, and New Mexico was no exception. However, the remote northern frontier barely supported a chronically understaffed clergy. Before 1851, the religious were governed from administrative centers far to the south. After United States occupation, Pope Pius IX established New Mexico as a Vicariate Apostolic attached to the Archdiocese of St. Louis in 1850, and it was elevated to a see, the Diocese of Santa Fe, in 1853. Nonetheless, despite a growing ecclesiastical structure, the population continued to expand, and Church ministrations long remained inadequate.

Santa Fe was elevated to an archdiocese in 1875, with the

Vicariates Apostolic of Colorado and of Arizona, which included southern New Mexico, as suffragans. A Church memorial publication shows priests at Cimarrón, Taos, Picurís, Santa Cruz, Mora, La Junta, Sapelló, Las Vegas, Pecos, San Miguél, Antonchico, Santa Fé, El Rito, Abiquiú, San Juan, San Ildefonso, Jémez, Peña Blanca, Bernalillo, Albuquerque, Cebolleta, Isleta, Tomé, Manzano, Belén, Sabinal, Socorro, and Paraje at this time.[13] In Colorado, Jesuits performed mission work in the San Luis Valley. During Father Salvatore Personé's first visitation of his Conejos mission in 1872, he "found about 3,000 souls in the twenty-five different villages extending north as far as Saguache and San Luís, some 15 miles, south to Los Pinos, about 6 miles, east as far as Los Sauces, some 25 miles, and west as far as Las Mesitas, about 7 miles."[14] Jesuits also set up a parish at Pueblo in 1872, and in 1875, took over at Trinidad, which had had a priest, Father Munnecom, since about 1866.[15]

The Penitentes developed during the early nineteenth century, probably in the heart of the northern sector of the Province of New Mexico. In 1833, Bishop Zubiría's letter, the earliest definite mention of *"una Hermandad de Penitentes,"* a Brotherhood of Penitentes, cites a group at Santa Cruz which maintained a *"Piesa,"* or room, to keep their paraphernalia.[16] Apparently, either the use of such a room and/or the local church or chapel itself was common until increasing ecclesiastical intolerance, as well as pressure from non-Hispano immigrants after the Civil War, forced local chapters to build separate meeting houses. These structures came to be known as *moradas,* a Spanish word current in the English vernacular of the region by the beginning of the twentieth century.[17]

After the 1860s, then, the construction of moradas in long- and recently established Hispanic communities served to identify and focus such settlements. Buildings, often windowless at first or with irregular small or high windows, were placed to insure privacy and integrity. The history and distribution of the local structures can thus provide evidence for the Brotherhood's development, as well as indications of the strength and/or isolation of the Hispanic areas.

Moradas at Upper Arroyo Hondo, Abiquiu, and Las Trampas have been carefully documented in notable studies by Bainbridge

Bunting, Richard Ahlborn, and E. Boyd, respectively.[18] According to the latter scholar:

> Equally valid examples elsewhere indicate that the average New Mexico morada is scarcely one hundred years old. Many were built between the 1870s and the 1920s, according to their charters. As in domestic dwellings, locally found building materials were used; a morada was made of adobe, undressed stone, jacál, or logs, depending on its location. While some were placed in a village or at its edge, others were hidden in canyons. Older moradas were often partly below the surface level so that their flat roofs were only four or five feet above the ground.[19]

More recent builders may modify existing houses and utilize such modern materials as cinderblock and stucco.

As yet, no reliable historic-geographic study of Penitente moradas, either from documentary sources or from contemporary material culture evidence and informants' accounts, is available.[20] There is general agreement that the Brothers were, and to a very limited extent still are, strongest in the more isolated areas of the older core of Hispanic settlements, i.e., in the San Luis Valley, the Chama Valley, the Taos Valley, the Embudo Watershed, the Mora Valley, and the Upper Pecos Watershed. Smaller areas of former vitality are indicated in the Sandia and Manzano Mountains, near the San Mateo and Cebolleta Mountains, and in parts of southeastern Colorado.

Since the concept of a Brotherhood organized for penance and mutual aid could have been carried anywhere Hispano settlers migrated from the original core area, the actual extent of Penitente activity is impossible to ascertain. Woodward shows moradas as far northeast as Clapham in Union County.[21] Cabeza de Baca reports a morada serving the Llano Estacado built at Saladito in 1880, but there are no Texas chapters mentioned.[22] Lamb photographed a Lincoln County Penitente cemetery which a local informant said had been in use until the turn of the century.[23] Woods describes a morada at Doña Ana.[24] Woodward's map indicates another morada in Doña Ana County, and she also notes Penitente activity in southwestern settlements in the Pinos Altos Mountains of Grant County.[25] Barker claims that there were Penitentes in southeastern

Utah and northeastern Arizona, but there are no further references to this.[26] More recently, field workers have identified chapters as far north as Denver.[27] Hogue, who worked with the late Hermano Supremo Miguel Archibeque, maintains that "there are also Penitentes and moradas in Wyoming, Montana, and wherever people from Northern New Mexico have emigrated to work."[28] This would seem plausible and likely, provided the emigrants were unable to return to their home communities during Holy Week.

Perhaps the most interesting report of penitential rites outside the northern New Mexico-southern Colorado area is found in the Hugo Reid Letters. E. Boyd has edited a short 1852 manuscript in which Reid briefly describes self-flagellation rituals in San Gabriel, California.[29] Since San Gabriel was once at the end of the Spanish Trail from New Mexico, it is just possible that these were indeed Penitentes aware of the new Brotherhood. On the other hand, penitential practices involving self-flagellation have certainly been part of Spanish Catholicism throughout the world. Nonetheless, the possibility of an early communication of a growing organization remains a provocative speculation.

Until more extensive and intensive cultural geographical studies are available, then, the present sketch provides only a minimal background for the historical evidence that follows. The Brotherhood was one of many responses to a variable, long, and difficult frontier situation. The organization probably originated in the northern sector and soon spread throughout the original core of settlements. It proved adaptable and useful enough to be established in many places of later Hispanic migration, and to be maintained in core communities attempting to cope with the encroachment of new ways of life.

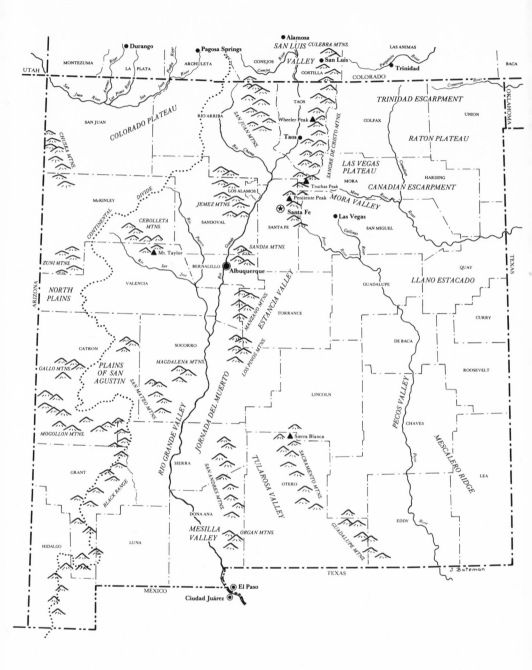

FIGURE 1. Certain Topographical Features of New Mexico and Southern Colorado.

Selected landforms and rivers are shown on the map to indicate the nature of the original frontier and as a reference for later settlement patterns.

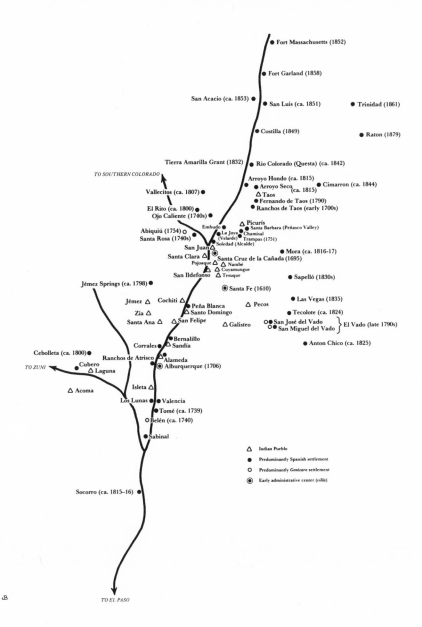

FIGURE 2. A Schematic Diagram of Selected Hispanic Settlements.

Relative locations of Indian Pueblos and selected Hispanic settlements present a general picture of the expansion pattern in New Mexico. Most dates are approximate because the intricacies of land grant, Church, and actual occupation records require specialized study for each community. Nonetheless, this diagram may be compared with the map in Figure 3 showing moradas.[30]

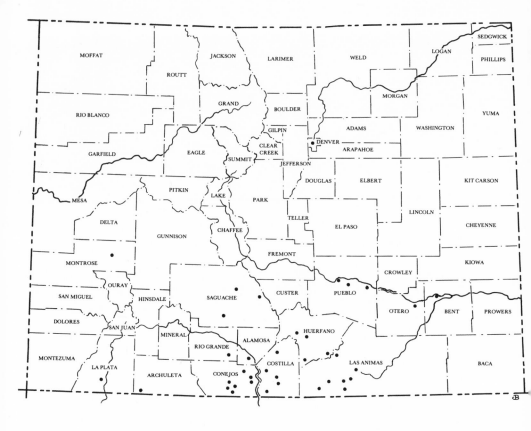

FIGURE 3.   Penitente Moradas from Published Sources.

Approximate locations of communities supporting one or more moradas
are indicated. The information was obtained from available references
in documents and the literature. The map is partial and descriptive; it
does not show the full extent of past or present Brotherhood chapters.
It is intended solely to illustrate the area of primary concentration of
Penitente activity.

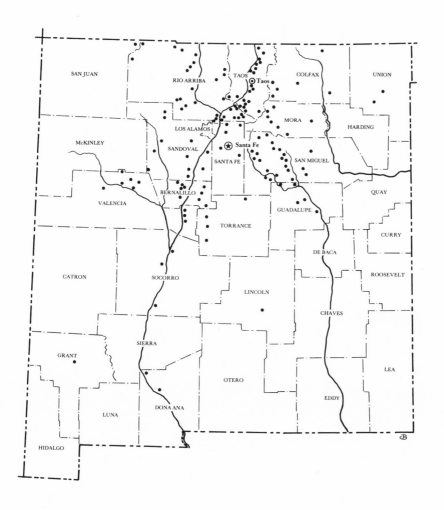

PART II
The Historical Evidence

En conclucion de este art? para atajar otro grande mal que puede
ser mallor en adelante proibo esas hermandades de penitencia ó
mas bien de carniceria, que há ido tomando cresimiento ál abrigo
de una tolerancia indebida.

> —Bishop José Antonio Laureano de
> Zubiría y Escalante, October 19, 1833.

It has become necessary for us to make a definite declaration
regarding the Brothers of Jesus of Nazareth (commonly called the
Penitentes), in order to clarify their status both to Catholics as
well as to non-Catholics. These Brothers or Brethren constitute a
pious association of men joined in charity to commemorate the
passion and death of the Redeemer. This society, like many
others in the Catholic church, is part of that church and therefore
deserves her protection and guidance so long as it keeps and
practices the teachings of the Church.

> —Archbishop Edwin Vincent Byrne,
> January 28, 1947.

Chronology

11

somewhere south of present-day Ciudad Juárez, Mexico.

July 11   Oñate's party settles at the Indian village Ohke, renamed San Juan de los Caballeros.

1610   Villa of Santa Fe established.

1616   New Mexican missions designated the Franciscan Custody of the Conversion of St. Paul.

1620   Diocese of Durango erected.

1626–29   Fray Alonso de Benavides serves as Custos and Commissary of the Inquisition in New Mexico.

1627   Benavides is upbraided by an Indian for Christians' flagellation.

1630   Benavides's *Memorial,* addressed to King Philip IV of Spain.

1634   Revised *Memorial,* addressed to Pope Urban VIII.

1680   Pueblo Revolt forces colonists' retreat to the Guadalupe del Paso area in the Rio Abajo.

1692–96   Captain-General Diego de Vargas Zapata Luján Ponce de León y Contreras reconquers New Mexico.

1695   Villa of Santa Cruz de la Cañada established.

1706   Villa of Alburquerque established.

1710   Confraternity of Carmel founded in New Mexico.

1723–34   Benito Crespo is Bishop of Durango.

1729   Franciscan Custody officially annexed to the Diocese of Durango.

1730   First episcopal visitation of interior New Mexico.

1736–47   Martín de Elizacoechea is Bishop of Durango.

1737   Episcopal visitation of New Mexico.

1747–57   Anselmo Sánchez de Tagle is Bishop of Durango.

1758–68   Pedro Tamarón y Romeral is Bishop of Durango.

April-July, 1760   Episcopal visitation of New Mexico. Confraternity of Our Lady of Light founded in Santa Fe.

1769–72   Fray Vicente Díaz Bravo is Bishop of Durango.

1773–82   Antonio Macarulla is Bishop of Durango.

1775   Fray Francisco Atanasio Domínguez appointed canonical visitor to New Mexico from the Mexican Province of the Holy Gospel.

March 22, 1776   Domínguez arrives in Santa Fe.

April-June Domínguez compiles a detailed visitation report on conditions in New Mexico.

July-November Domínguez and Fray Sylvestre Vélez Escalante explore a possible northern route to California.

1783–93 Estéban Lorenzo de Tristán is Bishop of Durango.

1794 Fray José Joaquín Granados is Bishop of Durango.

1795 Francisco Gabriel Olivares y Benito is Bishop of Durango.

1797 Secularization of villa churches at Santa Fe, Santa Cruz, Alburquerque, and El Paso.

1806 Zebulon Montgomery Pike arrested by Spanish authorities and released the following year.

1810 Spanish constitutional Cortes convoked.

Official report of Pike's expedition. The first account of the Hispanic Southwest available in the United States.

1812 Pedro Bautista Pino, belated New Mexico delegate to the Cortes, publishes his *Exposición sucinta y sencilla de la provincia del Nuevo México* in Spain.

1815–28 Juan Francisco Marquéz de Castañiza is Bishop of Durango.

1817–20 Juan Bautista Ladrón del Niño de Guevara makes a visitation of New Mexico for Bishop Castañiza.

1821 Treaty of Córdoba signed, August 24. Mexican independence from Spain.

William Becknell welcomed to New Mexico in the fall, thus officially opening the Santa Fe Trail and the Mexican territory.

1826 Agustín Fernández San Vicente makes a visitation of New Mexico for Bishop Castañiza.

Secularization of Abiquiu, Taos, San Juan, Vado, and Belen.

1828 Juan Rafael Rascón appointed Visitor General and Vicar of New Mexico by the Cathedral Chapter of Durango.

1829–33 Rascón's visitation of New Mexico.

1829 St. Francis of Assisi officially adopted by city govern-

ment and clergy as Patron of the City of Santa Fe,
June 29.

1831   José Antonio Laureano de Zubiría y Escalante begins
his service as Bishop of Durango.

1832   Lawyer Antonio Barreiro completes his *Ojeada sobre
Nuevo México.*

1833   Zubiría's first episcopal visitation of New Mexico.

July 21   Zubiría issues a special decree from Santa Cruz
de la Cañada condemning the Penitentes.

October 19 Zubiría concludes his visitation with a pastoral
letter, which includes a further warning against
the Penitentes.

1834   First printing press brought to New Mexico by
Josiah Gregg and purchased by Ramón Abreú. Later
acquired by Don Antonio José Martínez of Taos.

1835   Texas Revolution begins.

March 2, 1836 Texas declares its independence from
Mexico.

1837   Brief Rio Arriba rebellion in New Mexico suppressed by
Manuel Armijo.

1841   Colonel Hugh McLeod's Texas expedition to occupy
Santa Fe defeated by Armijo.

1844   First edition of Josiah Gregg's *Commerce of the Prairies,*
describing his 1831–40 experiences along the Santa Fe
Trail. Reports Good Friday Penitente procession at
Tome, New Mexico.

1845   Zubiría's second episcopal visitation of New Mexico.
Texas admitted as the 28th state, December 31.

1846   President James K. Polk asks Congress for a declara-
tion of war on Mexico, May 13.
Brigadier-General Stephen Watts Kearny leads the
Army of the West into Santa Fe, August 18. New
Mexico surrendered by acting Governor Juan Bautista
Vigil y Alaríd.

1847   Revolts at Taos and Mora quickly suppressed.

1848   Treaty of Guadalupe Hidalgo signed, February 2. Ratified by United States Senate, March 10, and by Mexican Congress, May 26.

Death of Fray Mariano de Jesús López, the last Franciscan in New Mexico, at Isleta Pueblo.

1850   Pope Pius IX creates the Vicariate Apostolic of New Mexico, attached to the Archdiocese of St. Louis, July 19.

Compromise Bill passed, including Organic Act of the Territory of New Mexico, September 9.

Zubiría's third episcopal visitation of New Mexico.

1851   First Legislative Assembly of the Territory of New Mexico convened.

Jean Baptiste Lamy, newly consecrated Bishop, arrives in Santa Fe during the summer and immediately departs for Durango to receive Bishop Zubiría's acceptance of the new division.

1853   New Mexico elevated to a see, the Diocese of Santa Fe, a suffragan of the Archdiocese of St. Louis, July 28.

Earliest record of a Penitente booklet, approved by Bishop Lamy.

Gadsden Purchase, December 30.

1856   Bishop Lamy issues rules for the Penitentes.

1857   Vicar Joseph Projectus Machebeuf excommunicates Don Antonio José Martínez at Taos, April.

1861   Act to incorporate *La Fraternidad Piadosa del Condado de Taos* approved by the Legislative Assembly of the Territory of New Mexico, January 30.

1861–65   United States Civil War.

1867   Death of unreconciled Antonio José Martínez in Taos, July 27.

Jesuits from the Neapolitan Province arrive in New Mexico, August 15.

1868   Vicariates Apostolic of Arizona and Colorado established and attached to the Diocese of Santa Fe.

1869   Cornerstone laid for the new cathedral at Santa Fe, July 14.

1875   Pope Pius IX elevates Santa Fe to an archdiocese with the Vicariates Apostolic of Arizona and Colorado as suffragans, February 12.

Lamy consecrated as the first Archbishop of Santa Fe, June 16.

1876	Colorado admitted as the 38th state, August 1.
1880	First locomotive enters Santa Fe, February 9.
1885	Lamy resigns as Archbishop, July 18.
	Jean Baptiste Salpointe consecrated as second Archbishop of Santa Fe, November 21.
1886	Salpointe issues his first Circular on the Penitentes, March.
1887	Diocese of Denver erected, August 16.
1888	Death of Lamy, February 14.
	Charles Fletcher Lummis takes the first photographs of Penitente rites, at San Mateo, New Mexico, March 29, 30.
	First Synod of the Archdiocese of Santa Fe, June 26-July 1.
1889	Salpointe issues his second Circular on the Penitentes, March 31.
1890	Rev. Alexander M. Darley's controversial Penitente number of *La Hermandad* published in Pueblo, Colorado, April.
	Alleged meeting of a General Council of the Brotherhood at Mora, New Mexico, June 7.
1892	Salpointe's final Circular on the Penitentes, February 7.
1894	Salpointe resigns as Archbishop, January 7.
1895	Placide Louis Chapelle consecrated as third Archbishop of Santa Fe, October 17.
1897	Diocese of Tucson erected as suffragan see of the Archdiocese of Santa Fe.
	Archbishop Chapelle reassigned to the Archdiocese of New Orleans, December 1.
1899	Pierre Bourgade consecrated as fourth Archbishop of Santa Fe, October 4. Franciscans return to New Mexico.
1908	Death of Bourgade, May 17.
1909	Jean Baptiste Pitaval consecrated as fifth Archbishop of Santa Fe, January 3.
1912	New Mexico admitted as the 47th state, February 12.
	Arizona admitted as the 48th state, February 14.
1914	Diocese of El Paso erected as suffragan see of the Archdiocese of Santa Fe.
1915	An act to define libel against fraternal and religious

orders or societies passed by the Legislature of the State of New Mexico, February 20.

Case No. 1107, District Court of Taos County: *Fraternal Brotherhood of Our Father Jesus of Nazareth* v. *Rev. F. F. Thomas,* June.

1918   Pitaval resigns as Archbishop, February.

1919   Fr. Albert Thomas Daeger, O.F.M., consecrated as sixth Archbishop of Santa Fe, May 7.

Jesuit New Mexico-Colorado Mission divided and dissolved, August 15.

1932   Death of Archbishop Daeger, December 2.

1933   Rudolph Aloysius Gerken consecrated as seventh Archbishop of Santa Fe, August 23.

1935   Dorothy Woodward's Yale University doctoral dissertation, "The Penitentes of New Mexico," the first scholarly study of the Brotherhood, is completed.

1936   Murder of Carl N. Taylor, free-lance writer, near Cedar Crest, New Mexico. Penitentes wrongly implicated in the subsequent nationwide sensationalism.

1937   Publication of *Brothers of Light,* by Alice Corbin Henderson, one of the most sensitive outsider's accounts of Penitente rituals (at Abiquiu, New Mexico) available.

1939   Diocese of Gallup erected as suffragan see of Archdiocese of Santa Fe. Diocese of Tucson reassigned to Archdiocese of Los Angeles.

1941   Archdiocese of Denver erected, with the Diocese of Pueblo as one of its suffragan sees.

1943   Death of Archbishop Gerken, March 2.

Edwin Vincent Byrne consecrated as eighth Archbishop of Santa Fe, June.

1946   Case No. 13761, Fourth Judicial District Court of San Miguel County, Las Vegas, New Mexico: *La Fraternidad de Nuestro Padre Jesús de Nazareno del Condado de San Miguel, Territorio de Nuevo México* v. *Concilio Original de Nuestro Padre Jesús Nazareno de Sheridan, Condado de San Miguel, Nuevo México,* February.

Miguel Archibeque begins a seven-year term as the first Hermano Supremo Arzobispal, June.

1947   Archbishop Byrne signs a statement officially recognizing the Brotherhood of Our Father Jesus of Nazareth and the organizational work of Archibeque, January 28.

1953   Roman Aranda becomes the second Hermano Supremo Arzobispal, serving for one year, June.

1954   Miguel Archibeque begins a second term as Hermano Supremo Arzobispal, this time serving for six years, June.

1960   M. Santos Melendez becomes the third Hermano Supremo Arzobispal, serving until the present, June.

1963   Death of Archbishop Byrne, July 25.

1964   James Peter Davis consecrated as ninth Archbishop of Santa Fe, February 25.

1968   Rededication of the remodeled and restored Cathedral at Santa Fe, October 2.

1970   Death of Miguel Archibeque, first Hermano Supremo Arzobispal, June 16.

1974   Resignation of Archbishop Davis.
       Robert Fortune Sanchez ordained as tenth Archbishop of Santa Fe, July 25.

CHAPTER 1

The Germinal Period, 1776-1850

Don José Antonio Laureano de Zubiría's episcopal visitation to interior New Mexico in 1833 marked the first time frontier provincials had entertained a bishop since Tamarón's inspection of 1760. Indeed, in 1812, New Mexico's delegate to the Spanish Cortes, Pedro Bautista Pino, lamented that "I, an old man, did not know how bishops dressed until I came to Cádiz."[1] His and other lay and clerical sentiments regarding the sorry state of spiritual affairs in New Mexico were also voiced by the few official visitors from administrative centers in Durango, Mexico City, and elsewhere.

Spiritual and civil administration of the northern frontier was difficult at best.[2] The government, the military, the missions, and the churches did not attract sufficient numbers of dedicated, qualified, and competent men. Distances between supply centers and the interior made service uncertain. Insofar as possible, important decisions and policy changes were effected months and sometimes years after the original decrees. Besides these common tribulations, there were specific ecclesiastic and civil problems as well as disputes between the two authorities.

Secularization of the missions was at the crux of Church affairs in the late eighteenth and early nineteenth centuries. New Mexico had been designated the Franciscan Custody of the Conversion of St. Paul in 1616 and remained so, never attaining the status of a province. The local Franciscan prelate was a *Custodio* (Custos) responsible to superiors in the capital of the Province of the Holy Gospel at Mexico City. Like his later counterpart from among the secular clergy, the *Vicario* (Vicar), he held limited episcopal powers at various times. Although Bishops of Durango could exercise rights of visitation, they did not do so until 1725, and then only to El Paso.

The Diocese of Durango was part of the expanding Mexican ecclesiastical structure. At first suffragans of Seville, the New World diocese were detached and, in 1545, formed into the Archdiocese of Mexico with a Metropolitan See in Mexico City. The See of Durango was erected in 1620, and attempted shortly thereafter to include New Mexico and Arizona within its jurisdiction. However, the Franciscans jealously guarded their Custody while a battle between the Order and the Bishop of Durango ensued to the south.[3]

Criticisms against the friars, which included attacks on their spiritual integrity, their assumptions of power, their neglect of Spanish settlers, and the quality of their missionary work among the Indians, were sometimes justified and sometimes dictated by self-interested vindictiveness on the part of civil and secular clerical officials. Adams emphasizes the rigors of the ministry, which exaggerated "all the ordinary human failings and many human virtues."[4] A Church publication attributes "the decline and death of the Franciscan Custody" to the inability of the Province to supply a full quota of missionaries, claiming that "there had been two centuries of dissension within the Order between friars born in Spain and those born in the New World; they also had been loathe to accept vocations from among the Indians and those known to have mixed blood; the result was a steady decline in spirit as well as manpower in the Province of the Holy Gospel."[5] Constant quarrels between the secular clergy and the religious orders are also cited. In general, then, differences between the friars (*frailes*) and the secular clergy (*curas*) in New Mexico were further manifestations of longtime rivalries elsewhere.[6]

Fray Alonso de Benavides had proposed a bishopric for remote New Mexico as early as 1630, but no action was taken until 1850. Don Benito Crespo finally made the first episcopal visitation of interior New Mexico in 1730. At that time, he appointed one secular priest, Don Santiago Roibal, to be his vicar and ecclesiastical judge at Santa Fe. Crespo's successor, Don Martín de Elizacoechea, continued to press the suit against the Franciscans and visited the interior himself in 1737. Bishop Francisco Anselmo Sánchez never visited New Mexico, but his successor, Don Pedro Tamarón y Romeral made an enterprising visitation in the early summer of 1760.[7] His was the last such episcopal inspection until Zubiría's, during the Mexican period.

In 1775, Fray Francisco Atanasio Domínguez was appointed canonical visitor from the Province of the Holy Gospel to prepare a detailed survey of the New Mexican missions. Besides compiling invaluable geographical, ethnological, sociological, and religious data, he also explored, with Fray Sylvestre Vélez de Escalante, a possible northern route to Monterey, California. Domínguez reports twenty-two friars serving the northern frontier in 1776. Only those at the villas of Santa Fe, Santa Cruz, and Albuquerque were not paid a royal stipend, relying instead on obventions and offerings. Nowhere does he find evidence of wealth and strength, let alone adequate facilities.[8] The situation had not changed appreciably by the 1800s, although treasury records indicate some thirty friars in 1788.[9]

The Diocese of Durango had been nominally and technically in charge of New Mexico since 1729, but it began actual administration only in 1797, when villa churches at Santa Fe, Santa Cruz, Albuquerque, and El Paso were secularized. The first curas did not always stay long, and their departure taxed the dwindling resources of the remaining Franciscans. "Other priests came from Durango later on, some native New Mexicans were ordained, but these were never near enough to cover a vast primitive territory which the Franciscans had left vacant, and whose population had increased and spread out in many new villages and hamlets away from the Rio Grande Valley."[10] Persons in peripheral communities, as well as many inhabitants, especially the poorer ones, of core settlements, were thus left largely to their own devices in religious matters.

Pedro Bautista Pino's *Exposición sucinta y sencilla de la provincia del Nuevo México* of 1812, states that the 26 Indian Pueblos and 102 Spanish settlements were served by twenty-two Franciscan missionaries and two secular priests. Most of his pleas regarding the

Church center around the establishment of a bishopric (*"obispado"*) and a seminary (*"colegio de religiosos"*) in New Mexico. He attributes many ills to the lack of a resident bishop:

> Consequently, the sovereign provisions and the instructions of ecclesiastical discipline have not been fulfilled. . . . Persons who have been born during these fifty years have not been confirmed. The poor people who wish, by means of a dispensation, to get married to relatives cannot do so because of the great cost of traveling a distance of more than 400 leagues to Durango. Consequently, many people, compelled by love, live and rear families in adultery.[11]

Pino suggests that the proposed bishop could live as well as the governor, whose salary was 4,000 pesos, a sum which was but part of the annual 9,000 to 10,000 pesos produced by tithes in New Mexico. Unfortunately, according to Ryan, "when the Spanish Government finally did decree, on January 26, 1818, the establishment of the long-desired See, her power had become almost extinct in that part of the world and the decree was ineffective."[12]

At the time of Don Juan Bautista Ladrón del Niño de Guevara's visitation (1817–20), twenty-three friars, four secular priests, and an assistant served in New Mexico, which included El Paso. Guevara's report to Bishop Juan Francisco Marquéz de Castañiza, dated October 23, 1820, describes "el deplorable estado en que se halla aquella tan recomendable parte de Su obispado" ("the deplorable state in which that so commendable part of your Bishopric exists").[13]

Don Agustín Fernández de San Vicente, Bishop Castañiza's Vicar and second Visitor General, ordered Abiquiu, Belen, Taos, San Juan, and Vado secularized in April 1826. His First Book of Administration lists only nine Franciscans and five secular priests. An entry in his Book of Acts for July 1826, takes up the "question of friars giving up secularized missions, or administering them *ad interim* for lack of secular priests."[14]

The Franciscans were never actually expelled from New Mexico; many stayed at the posts assigned them, mostly Indian missions, until they died in service. Only two friars were theoretically affected in 1828, when all Spaniards were ordered to leave Mexico, but they remained anyway and died in the late 1830s.[15]

Bishop Zubiría tried to revive Franciscanism in New Mexico, but the Province of the Holy Gospel was able to send only one man, Fray Mariano de Jesús López, who arrived in 1845, to administer missions at Isleta, Laguna, Acoma, and Zuni. His accidental death, mentioned in February 1848, in Vicar Juan Felipe Ortiz's Log of Official Acts, marks the end of Hispanic Franciscanism in New Mexico.[16]

The next Vicar and Visitor General, Don Juan Rafael Rascón, was appointed by the Chapter of Durango on November 1, 1828. Details of his visitation (1829–33) are "rather perfunctory, or at least poorly recorded."[17] However, Rascón's records may be supplemented by Barreiro's gloomy and more vivid overview of New Mexico's religious and temporal affairs in the early 1830s.

Licenciado Antonio Barreiro arrived in New Mexico during the spring of 1831, to assume duties as *asesor* (legal adviser) to the local authorities. He completed his *Ojeada sobre Nuevo México* in June 1832. In it, his sketch of spiritual conditions is altogether cheerless:

> Spiritual administration in New Mexico is in a truly doleful condition. Nothing is more common than to see an infinite number of the sick die without confession or extreme unction. It is indeed unusual to see the eucharist administered to the sick. Corpses remain unburied for many days, and children are baptized at the cost of a thousand hardships. A great many unfortunate people spend most of the Sundays of the year without hearing mass. Churches are in a state of near ruin, and most of them are unworthy of being called the temple of God.[18]

Barreiro blames the lack of ministers on the poverty and remoteness of the territory. Most priests, he claims, aspire to a life of luxury which they cannot possibly attain in New Mexico, and so try to avoid assignment there. Barreiro suggests limiting their duty to ten years. He too recommends the establishment of a bishopric and a seminary. At the conclusion of this discussion of ecclesiastical matters, Barreiro emphasizes the somber picture by stating: "that Christian piety revolts on seeing the abuses committed in New Mexico with regard to the care of souls. Charity demands that a veil be thrown over many things which would, if they were narrated, create a scandal. . . . The harvest is great, but the reapers are few. Let us pray that the Lord may send His reapers into that province."[19]

Neither the Spanish nor the Mexican Church ever persevered to persuade authorities to elevate New Mexico to a see. Whether this would have assuaged New Mexicans' demonstrably acute needs for spiritual ministrations and temporal benefits is debatable. In any case, the chronic and even desperate inadequacies came to be partially remedied by the developing lay brotherhoods. Under the circumstances, it is perhaps inconceivable that a devoutly Catholic and of necessity stoutly independent pioneer people would do otherwise.

Bishop Zubiría and the Brotherhoods of Penance

Until Bishop Zubiría finally toured the isolated frontier of his large diocese, official visitors had not specifically noted the existence of brotherhoods organized for penance and mutual aid, at least in available records. Whether this omission was due to judicious oversight, to the unremarkable familiarity of such groups, to simple ignorance of their existence, or to the fact that the organization was as yet nascent must remain a matter of conjecture, barring further documentary evidence. The bishop, however, felt no constraints against the admonition of an existing, named society.

Don José Antonio Laureano de Zubiría y Escalante became Bishop of Durango in 1831, and three times, in 1833, 1845, and 1850, made episcopal visitations of interior New Mexico. During his first tour of inspection, he discovered a lay association of penitents whose excessive zeal disturbed and concerned him, both as a danger to the brothers themselves and as a potential threat to the Church. His special letter, dated July 21, 1833, from Santa Cruz de la Cañada, is the first unequivocal instance of Church opposition to Penitente groups, and his pastoral letter of October 19, 1833, at the conclusion of his visitation, clearly states the official position of the Hispanic Church.

Zubiría's special letter contains the first extant, definite record of the "Penitentes," as they were apparently already known by that time. He states that the *"Hermandad de Penitentes"* in the Villa of Santa Cruz had been in existence for a number of years without authorization or knowledge of the bishops.[20] On certain days of the year, the Brothers (*"Hermanos"*) practiced immoderate corporal penances, sometimes publicly, using crosses and other unspecified instruments of mortification. These were kept in a room, which may also have been used for the meetings (*"reuniones"*) which the bishop deplores and prohibits, noting that moderate penitential mortification was appropriate either at home or in a church, but not in separate congregations.

In an October pastoral letter at the end of his stay, Zubiría concludes a section on the sacrament of penance with another warning against the brotherhoods of penance, or, as he prefers to describe them, of carnage.[21] Again, he bans their large crosses (*"grandes maderos"*) and other instruments of mortification, *not* the practice of self-discipline. Moderate penance employing the usual instruments, presumably whips or uncomfortable clothing, in private, is proclaimed to be beneficial to the soul. Unauthorized congregations and destruction (*"distrucion"* [*sic*]) rather than self-mortification are condemned.

Zubiría's charge to the Rio Arriba clergy that further abuses of this sort (*"abusos de esta clase"*) be stopped was apparently ineffective. Soon after, Josiah Gregg witnessed a Good Friday procession of three penitents with their companions at Tome in the Rio Abajo.[22] It is impossible to date this event precisely, but it would have occurred during one of the trader's several trips to New Mexico between 1831 and 1840.

Gregg's is the first Anglo-American report of Penitente activities, and it also confirms the rapid diffusion of the Brotherhood despite official ecclesiastical opposition. In fact, on February 21, 1845, Cura Trujillo of Santa Cruz wrote to Albuquerque's Cura Gallegos reminding him of the 1833 decree.[23] That year, during his second visitation, Bishop Zubiría himself ordered his pastoral letter again read in the churches. This too had little effect, particularly after United States occupation. During Zubiría's final visitation in 1850, there were other matters to confront, and he "issued an exhortation to his people to stand firm in the Faith now that it was endangered by contact with heretics."[24]

Some Theories of Origin

Bishop Zubiría evidently felt no need to account for the unacceptable brotherhoods. He was familiar with the traditional elements involved and objected only to excessive penances and unsupervised meetings. What was to prove sensational and unfathomable to outsiders unfamiliar with Hispanic Catholicism was merely unsurprising and troublesome to the ecclesiastics initially concerned.

Only later, when the French clergy attempted to renovate and restore the Church in the Southwest, did the question of the Penitentes' origins become important in the formulation of official policy regarding attitudes toward and rules for the Brotherhood. Still later, the influx of non-Catholic immigrants, as well as journalist observers, forced both ecclesiastic and civil authorities to attempt to explain the strange and by then flourishing brotherhoods. Although many of these explanations were ludicrously and sometimes viciously inaccurate, certain of the origins proposed deserve review because they show an awareness of European, Iberian, Mexican, or even native American traditions which seem to provide likely antecedents for Penitente practices.

The various names used by Brothers and nonmembers to designate Penitente chapters offer no particular help in establishing either an identity or a genealogy for the Brotherhood, as Woodward demonstrates.[25] Recorded instances of one trait or another, such as self-flagellation or passion plays, also do not constitute substantial proof of historical relationship. Strictly speaking, a pious society to provide mutual aid for its members and to observe rituals centered on penance and Christ's Passion would be a likely progenitor for the New Mexico Brotherhood. Early New World references to such a conjunction of attributes are scarce and difficult to connect directly with the New Mexican groups. Nevertheless, the following subsections provide a brief review of the major traditional elements which may have been known to or recalled by the early settlers and which have been seriously proposed as possible sources for the configuration of traits associated with the Penitentes. Successive sections then elaborate a likely theory of the Brotherhood's evolution from lay interpretations of Franciscanism.

Indian Influence

Isolation and hardship are key factors in the various proposals of Indian origins for or contributions to Penitente rites.[26] Harsh frontier conditions supposedly precipitated a "regression" to or borrowing from religions with expressive elements more satisfactory for worship under extreme circumstances. Ross Calvin, for example, a clergyman and avowed environmental determinist, claims that "popular ignorance, left without the guidance of the Church, relapsed naturally into fanaticism, and the Mexican zealot inheriting from the Spaniard a tragic interpretation of Christianity, and from his Indian forebears a recent and thinly covered savagery, evolved presently a cruel and schismatic cult of the scourge."[27]

Others, such as Charles Fletcher Lummis, who cites the work of Adolph F. Bandelier on penances among the Pueblo Indians, and Albert B. Reagan, have reported local Indian practices which were similar enough to Penitente ones that they could have been incorporated into patterns of Hispanic worship.[28] In fact, documents later available indicate that even precolonial Spanish explorers witnessed Indian rites superficially somewhat familiar to them. Hernán Gallegos, official notary for the 1581–82 Rodríguez-Chamuscado expedition, describes a December dance at a Galisteo Valley Pueblo in which dancers flagellated an Indian in their midst. "These lashes are given in such a manner that they draw blood, making him look like a Disciplinant."[29]

Neither the ethnocentric recourse to a subjective notion of the primitive nor the discovery of a single identical trait such as flagellation constitutes substantial evidence for Indian influence on Penitente rites. Actually, as Woodward demonstrates, the systems of ritual and belief were profoundly incompatible. Even in settlements near Indian Pueblos, borrowing culture traits necessary for survival did not also mean a mingling of fundamental religious ideas and practices, especially in situations where the dominant Spanish culture felt so spiritually superior to the dominated Indian groups.[30] As recently as the 1960s, Taos Hispanos caught in what Bodine terms a "tri-ethnic trap" resented Anglos glorifying Indian observances while ignoring, belittling, or outraging the "True Faith" of the Spanish, including their Penitente rituals.[31]

27

Few Indians ever became Hermanos. Ritch cites Pedro José Medina from Zia(?), who in the 1870s "never heard of an Indian belonging to them." However, one of Parsons' Indian informants told of a pure-blooded San Juan Pueblo man who became Hermano Mayor at Alcalde in the nineteenth century. Lange claims that "no Cochití is currently [1940s and 1950s] a member, and, from all information, it seems that José Antonio Montoya was the only Cochití who ever joined this group." For the northwest, Swadesh's statements that "although the Animas Valley Utes were fairly observant Catholics, they stayed away from the morada," and that "few people with strong Indian connections of any kind were active in the Brotherhood," are telling.[32]

Although Indians did not as a rule join the Brotherhood, they did occasionally walk in Penitente processions and ask Brothers to sing at wakes. María of San Ildefonso Pueblo told Alice Marriott that her father was invited to accompany Brothers in Chimayo during Holy Week of 1890. Mary Austin saw an Indian walking in a Penitente procession at Ranchitas, near Taos. The famous Taos Indian, Tony Luhan, is supposed to have told his wife that "over in Picuris Pueblo, sometimes Indians walk in parade with Penitentes. I don't know what for they do that, unless they all mixed up with Mexicans, now." Both Woodward and Lange report Penitentes singing during wakes for dead Indians, at Santa Clara and Cochiti Pueblos respectively.[33]

Neither walking in Penitente processions nor requesting Brothers' leadership in song and prayer constitutes more than respect for a different mode of conduct and worship. When asked if Penitentes were Catholics like themselves, María's father is alleged to have replied: "Yes, they're Catholics . . . but this is something besides that belief, the way the kiva is with us."[34] Later, he is supposed to have answered his daughter's query about flagellation with the following incisive remarks:

> It's their religion. . . . It's different from the dances, in that way. The Indian religion is to be happy, but the Spanish religion is to be sad. That's why they are two different people.[35]

A significant religious influence of the subordinate over the dominant of these "two different people," particularly when the latter had ample historical precedent for its religious complex, is highly unlikely.

Medieval Flagellants

Father Inigo Deane, a Jesuit who witnessed Penitente rites in 1883, was the first to propose a medieval origin for the practices, claiming that "the Flagellants, I think have their lineal descendants in the Penitentes of New Mexico."[36] Both he and later theorists are referring to the flagellant sects which twice emerged in Europe as powerful and schismatic enough to provoke Church denunciation. The processions and practices of these fervent groups, which included cross-bearing, flagellation of self and others, hymn-singing, and praying—all superficially similar to Penitente rites—are vividly described elsewhere.[37]

Neither movement appears to have appreciably affected Spain. The first outbreak originated in Perugia, Italy, about May of 1260, following the plague of 1259, and during the wars of the Guelfs and Ghibellines. An Umbrian hermit, Raniero Fasani, organized processions of self-punishing *disciplinati,* and the idea spread rapidly through Italy and into Alsace, Bavaria, Hungary, Bohemia, and Poland. Such processions were prohibited in 1261, and abated until their reemergence in Germany at the time of the Black Death in the fourteenth century.[38] Pope Clement VI forebade the demonstrations on October 20, 1349, but they continued to reappear—at Münster during the 1384 plague, and in Italy during the 1399 plague. In 1417, the Council of Constance decreed against them, but "for many years later the sect persisted in Thuringia and other regions, allying itself with chiliastic expectations and joining with many sporadic types of heresy . . . [and] did not wholly pass away before the Reformation."[39]

Until 1492, the Spanish were involved in their crusades against the Moslem infidels, and these absorbed much religious zeal. Public disciplines were not common until the end of the fourteenth century, when the apocalyptic preachings of St. Vincent Ferrer (ca. 1350–1419; canonized, 1455) contributed to their rise in cities such as Valencia, Barcelona, and Seville.[40] These penitents were, however, by no means the "lineal descendants" of or even directly related to earlier heretical sects in other parts of Europe.

Religious Dramas

Penitente rituals are frequently termed passion plays, with some writers even suggesting they are the American counterpart of Oberammergau.[41] This appellation would seem to imply that the Brotherhood's Lenten and Holy Week observances evolved from composed dramas which were enacted with increasing realism. The difficulty in proving such a theory lies in establishing a connection between specific New World passion plays and New Mexico communities in the early nineteenth century.

Religious theatre in Spain had its florescence during the sixteenth and seventeenth centuries. When the first Franciscan missionaries arrived in Mexico in 1523, "being familiar with the liturgical drama of the Church, even to its latest developments just before their departure from Spain, they were obviously able to adapt, translate, and direct all types of plays, from the simple pantomimic sermon plays to the elaborate pageants like *The Conquest of Jerusalem.*"[42] These and other missionaries used such dramatizations to convert and educate New World Indians. In addition, the Spanish colonials themselves maintained certain traditional *autos,* or religious dramas.

Passion plays were among the dramas which became entrenched in the religious life of the New World:

> Towards the end of the sixteenth century Fray Francisco Gamboa, who was in charge of the Chapel of San José in Mexico, and was greatly devoted to the Passion of Christ, instituted special devotions for the Fridays in Lent. On Palm Sunday of each year he produced a *Passion Play* which drew large crowds. This friar also wrote little sermon-plays, like those of Fray Torquemada and Fray Juan Bautista, to accompany his instructions on the Passion of Our Lord each Friday, for the Confraternity of Our Lady of Sorrows. Icazbalceta says the Passion plays by Fray Gamboa continued throughout the next century and had even come down to his own day, the late nineteenth century. He recalls having seen *The Capture and Trial of Jesus, The Three Falls,* and *Jesus Taken down from the Cross,* not only in the Capital, but also in the small towns.[43]

It is conceivable that an immigrant or a traveler could have witnessed such performances and brought the idea to New Mexico. However, it is improbable that groups organized to perform a passion play became nuclei for the Brotherhood. More likely, groups already formed to practice penance appropriated various dramatized episodes, possibly in response to community needs during the important Lenten and Holy Week season, especially if no priest were available. McCrossan concludes that "passion plays were undoubtedly used by the missionaries in the Colonial days, then were taken over by the Folk, and later made part of the expiatory practices of the *Penitent Brothers.*"[44]

Passion play performances recorded in New Mexico have not necessarily been associated with the Penitentes. Olibama López describes San Luis Valley communities where "the entire story of the capture, trial, and crucifixion of Christ" was enacted by nonmember villagers, some of whom paid a fee to the church to sponsor the ceremony and were then given the most important role, the Centurion's. In at least one village—Costilla, New Mexico—the concluding Tinieblas services were observed separately from the Brothers' Tinieblas.[45] The Talpa play is enacted by the Penitentes, but, in the past, the procession of the famous Tome community passion play was only joined by the Brothers.[46] In addition, Penitentes have been instrumental in preserving and producing other plays, such as *El Niño Perdido* in Taos.[47]

A specific link between early missionary or later Mexican passion plays and New Mexico Penitente rites cannot be established. The rituals and the benevolent activities of the Brothers are more than the elaboration of a composed drama.[48] Barring further evidence to the contrary, it seems reasonable to conclude that the Brotherhood's fundamental worship complex of realistic enactment, intimate participation, and solemn penance is a deeper, more pervasive dramatic and religious configuration.

Iberian Penitential and Confraternal Traditions

Spanish Catholicism, especially during the fifteenth, sixteenth, and seventeenth centuries, is generally characterized as nationalistic and persistently medieval, particularly with regard to the sacrament of penance.[49] In describing the great Spanish mystics of

31

the sixteenth century—St. Ignatius of Loyola (ca. 1491–1556), St. Peter of Alcántara (1499–1562), St. Teresa of Ávila (1515–82), and St. John of the Cross (1542–91), Underhill states that "if we wish to define the peculiar character of Spanish spirituality, we shall find it perhaps in an intensely austere, practical, indeed militant, temper; an outlook on realism which leaves small space for mere religious emotionalism; a tendency, once the principles of the spiritual life have been accepted, to push them at all costs to their logical end."[50] The elaboration of organized, public, dramatic, realistic, and severe penitential expressions substantiates this pervasive tenor, which missionaries and Conquistadores alike carried to the New World.

The penitential tradition on the Iberian Peninsula is closely connected with the *cofradías* ("religious brotherhoods"). These developed in Spain during the twelfth century, somewhat later than in other parts of Europe, and wielded their greatest power during the sixteenth and seventeenth centuries. Cofradías and related *gremios* ("trade guilds") were governed by rules in *ordenanzas* (charters) issued by Church, royal, or municipal authorities. These documents, the earliest known of which dates from 1151, specified the organizational structure, the sickness and death benefits members could expect, and the nature of their patron saint celebrations and of their participation in public religious observances. Both external controls over the sodalities and internal regulations governing the members, generally in the form of monetary fines, were exacting and rigorously enforced.[51]

Although flagellation became a popular form of penance in Spain as a result of St. Vincent Ferrer's preaching, Puyol dates "los disciplinantes de Semana Santa" ("Holy Week flagellants") only from the first third of the sixteenth century. The practice diffused rapidly, and a 1565–66 canon in the Valencia provincial council mentions the Holy Thursday and Good Friday abuses of these penitents. Puyol claims the apogee of such cofradías came during the early seventeenth century. A civil law of 1777 prohibited public disciplines, but suppression was never complete until the nineteenth century.[52]

Spanish penitential processions have been extensively described elsewhere.[53] Certain Sevillian brotherhoods are notable, however, because of their similarity to New Mexico groups. Both Woodward and Chavez have delineated analogies between the Cofradía de Nuestro Padre Jesús Nazareno de Sevilla y Santa Cruz en Jerusalém, with their Via Crucis processions involving Brothers of Light and self-scourging Brothers of Blood, and New Mexico Brotherhoods.[54] Only "the *Nazarenos* with their long gowns and wigs are missing in New Mexico, and their heavy burden of cross-bearing is taken up by the brothers of blood."[55]

Another society, the Escuela de Cristo, for the religious as well as laymen, was very popular during the sixteenth and seventeenth centuries. A Spanish friend wrote Aurelio M. Espinosa describing early twentieth century activities of the group in his village of Tudela in Zaragoza:

> The confraternity was called *Escuela de Cristo,* and its purpose was the sanctification of its members. The members used to meet once a week to carry out its exercises in its special chapel, and the public was never admitted during the days when flagellation was practiced. The director was a priest, called Obedience. He did the spiritual readings, the meditations, etc., and was stationed near a table on which were placed a crucifix, a human skull, and two candles. The *disciplinas* (whips) were distributed by a brother. There were all kinds of them and each one selected the one best suited to his fervor and strength. Since the chapel of our order was too small we used to go out to the nave of the cathedral for flagellation. This exercise took place when the church was dark and closed and when one of the brothers slowly chanted the Miserere.[56]

Both the practice of flagellation and the presence of a human skull recall similar traits among the New Mexico Brothers. In fact, in his 1817 inventory of the Santa Fe parish church, Don Juan Bautista Ladrón del Niño de Guevara commanded that the seven human skulls on the altar in the chapel of the Third Order of St. Francis be reburied forthwith. He claimed the skulls had been placed there in imitation of the Schools of Christ, which actually used wooden ones.[57] Contemplation of a human skull was of course not peculiar to such societies, and saints, scholars, and various ascetics are often pictured gazing upon this symbol of mortality. Nonetheless, it is

33

clear that the Visitor from Durango was familiar with the *Escuelas* which had been so popular in the Old World.

New World Confraternities and Penitential Practices

Confraternities were immediately established in the New World, where they often supported and managed hospitals. The oldest, "the Hospital of the Immaculate Conception in Mexico City, since the seventeenth century generally known as *Jesús Nazareno* because of a much-venerated image in the church, was founded by the Confraternity of Our Lady, of which Cortés was a leading member."[58] Many other sacramental confraternities were instituted to convert, educate, and secure ecclesiastical support from the Indians.

Penitential discipline was encouraged among both natives and colonists, and many confraternities also sponsored occasional processions of flagellants. As early as April 16, 1612, a Mexico City ordinance prohibited such processions during Holy Week, but they persisted into the twentieth century, in Mexico and elsewhere.[59]

Early New Mexicans were accustomed to express their penitential spirit with practices which were common throughout Spain and the Spanish colonies. On March 20, 1598, somewhere south of present-day El Paso, the colonizing expedition led by Don Juan de Oñate stopped to observe Holy Thursday rites of the Blessed Sacrament. According to the group's historian, Captain Gaspar Pérez de Villagrá, whose report to King Philip III of Spain was presented as an epic in thirty-four rhymed cantos, everyone spent the night in prayer and penances ranging from barefoot pilgrimages to self-scourging.[60] Woodward notes these rites resemble "the custom of the penitents of the *Cofradía de Jesús Nazareno en Jerusalem,* who in their private chapel throughout Holy Thursday night devoted themselves to pious exercises."[61]

Evidence for seventeenth-century penitential practices in New Mexico comes from Fray Alonso de Benavides, whose *Memorial,* the report of his 1626–29 term as Custos and Commissary of the Inquisition, was written for Philip IV of Spain in 1630. A revised version of this popular account was addressed to Pope Urban VIII in 1634. Benavides casually mentions preaching on April 4, 1627, at a pueblo southeast of present-day Albuquerque, where a cacique upbraided him for advocating "crazy" flagellation like other Christians.[62] Elsewhere in the 1634 *Memorial,* Benavides ridicules certain Indian initiation rites involving flagellation, yet describes how the Indians "Observe Our Holy Catholic Faith Well":

> During Lent they all come with much humility to the processions, which are held on Monday, Wednesday, and Friday. On these days of meeting with the friars, they perform penances in the churches. During Holy Week they flagellate themselves in most solemn processions.[63]

The early missionaries and colonists were clearly familiar with and adherents of longstanding penitential traditions.

After Captain General Diego de Vargas's 1692–96 reconquest of New Mexico, certain confraternities were established or reestablished. In his 1776 report, Domínguez only lists six: Confraternity of St. Michael at Santa Cruz; Confraternity of Our Lady of the Rosary (La Conquistadora), founded at Santa Fe before the reconquest; Confraternity of the Blessed Sacrament at Santa Fe and Santa Cruz; Confraternity of Carmel, licensed in 1710; Confraternity of the Poor Souls, founded in Albuquerque in 1718; Confraternity of Our Lady of Light, founded at Santa Fe by Governor Francisco Marín del Valle and approved by Bishop Tamarón in 1760.[64] Neither these societies nor the Third Order groups discussed later were vital, let alone "in order."

On November 18, 1794, Governor Fernando Chacón forwarded a *razón* ("statement") describing existing confraternities to Don Pedro de Nava, Commandant General of the Western Provinces. It had been prepared, as ordered, by the Reverend Custos, Fray Cayetano José Bernal, who lists the Confraternities of Our Lady of Carmen and of the Blessed Sacrament at Santa Cruz; and the Confraternities of the Blessed Sacrament, of Our Lady of the Rosary, of Our Lady of Light, and of the Poor Souls at Santa Fe.[65] Again, none of these societies seems to be either vigorous or solvent. Indeed, a letter from Governor Real Alencaster to the Intendant at Durango, dated April 1, 1806, reports no real estate owned by benevolent organizations.[66] Cofradías persisted, then, but did not flourish.

Although she did not have access to many of the documents now available, Woodward found sufficient evidence for eighteenth-century New Mexican confraternities similar to those of Spain and Mexico to propose an unbroken tradition through the Penitentes of the nineteenth and twentieth centuries:

> Confraternities of penance brought in by the early Spanish colonists, the society has persisted as a religious organization down to the present day. Practicing what they had learned in the home land, believing in bodily expiation for their sins, the New Mexicans continued during the difficult days of Indian wars, lack of adequate ecclesiastic guidance, and active opposition of the Church what was to them an intimate, personal expression of their devotion.[67]

That penitential activities as such or specific names referring to penance are not recorded she considers consonant with the tendency to take Spanish colonial customs and rituals for granted, in favor of detailed reports on Indian mission affairs.

Woodward's thesis has been revised by Fray Angelico Chavez in light of documentary evidence from the Archives of the Archdiocese of Santa Fe and the Domínguez report of 1776. Since this report makes no mention of the Penitentes in name or practice, whereas Bishop Zubiría's of 1833 does, Chavez believes that the Brotherhood began sometime between 1790 and 1810 or so. He stresses that it is *not* mere coincidence that the Penitentes "appear full-blown," and that their "terminology and its accompanying practices are exactly the ones pertaining to the penitential societies of Seville that date from the early part of the Sixteenth Century."[68] Since none of the documented confraternities in New Mexico exhibit comparable traits, he concludes that the society came from outside as a late transplant, in one of two ways:

(1) . . . some individual, or more than one, came to New Mexico from New Spain . . . or from some other Spanish colony in the south, where such penitential societies had long existed. Such individuals had belonged to such a society, to be able to impart its organization and ritual to their new neighbors here in New Mexico.

(2) An alternate supposition is that some book, which described the old Spanish penitential societies and their rites, had found its way to New Mexico at this time . . . to inspire the first *Hermandad.*[69]

Chavez further bolsters this theory by noting the resurgence of severe penitential activities in Mexico during the early 1800s, "evidently the source of the movement in New Mexico brought up by some migrant at the turn of the century."[70] The transplant found fertile ground; local variations accrued; and the organization quickly diffused, replacing moribund Church societies, including the Third Order. This process might well have been similar to the one by which the cult of Our Lord of Esquípulas in southeastern Guatemala came to be established at what is now the Sanctuary of Chimayo, also in the early 1800s.[71]

At the present time it is impossible to document a continuing tradition of penitential confraternities in New Mexico. Neither is it possible to point to the decline of a particular cofradía and the emergence of the Penitente Brotherhood from its "ruins," especially since, for example, the widespread and comparatively vital Confraternity of Our Lady of Carmel continued at Santa Cruz at least until Lamy checked its "abuses in gathering dues" in October 1860.[72] Certainly the notion of the late transplant of a cofradía similar to the early Sevillian penitential ones is plausible and attractive. However, an investigation of ideas and practices associated with Franciscanism in New Mexico, particularly the long-established Third Order of St. Francis, suggests a more immediate and equally likely source for the developing Brotherhood.

Lay Franciscanism in New Mexico

Even after surrendering their Custody, the Franciscans continued to command the spiritual feelings and affections of the provincials. In 1812, Pino was adamant that the long-desired first bishop be a Franciscan:

> Since the order of Saint Francis has been, so to speak, the spiritual conqueror—and it has actually been unique in New Mexico—the settlers have become so accustomed to seeing the Franciscan gown that it is likely that any other order would not be so welcome. In view of this fact, therefore, it would be advisable for the twelve ecclesiastics and even the first bishop to belong to the Franciscan order.[73]

Pino was an established citizen of Santa Fe, but his sentiments
were presumably shared by the poor and those in outlying areas.
Barreiro's 1832 sketch includes this assessment of the religious
temper during his stay:

> Most of these parish districts are visited only a few days
> during the year. How resentful must be the poor people who
> suffer such neglect! They realize that their harvests and their
> herds are paying for the maintenance of a priest who does not
> live among them and who does not provide them with the
> comforts of religion even in that last hour, when they most
> need such comfort![74]

Neither man mentions the Penitentes, but it is likely that the
"resentful," neglected "poor" referred to had reworked and revived
elements of the familiar, beloved Franciscan approach to ritual
and the exemplary Christian life.

St. Francis of Assisi (ca. 1181–1226; canonized, 1228) founded
three religious orders. The First Order, the Friars Minor or Lesser
Brothers, was verbally approved by Pope Innocent III in 1210. The
fast-growing group, which practiced absolute poverty and humility
and preached repentance and faith, received a confirmed Rule
from Pope Honorius III on November 29, 1223. The Second
Order, or Poor Ladies of St. Damian, had been established by
Francis during Lent of 1212. St. Clare of Assisi (ca. 1194–1253;
canonized, 1255) obtained a "privilege of poverty" for these early
sisters, now known as Poor Clares, from Pope Innocent III about
1216.

According to tradition, Francis conceived the idea of a Third
Order Secular while preaching in Cannara or Poggibonzi, when
too many people wished to abandon their homes and follow him.[75]
The earliest Rule for these Tertiaries was drawn up by Cardinal
Hugolino (later Pope Gregory IX) in consultation with Francis in
1221:

> It provides that brethren and sisters of penitence living in
> their own houses should dress plainly, eat and drink with
> moderation, avoid dances and plays, keep certain fasts,
> observe the canonical hours at home or in church, confess
> thrice a year, pay their debts and restore any goods which

belonged to others, live peaceably, not bear arms, abstain from oaths, contribute to the support of poor or sick members and other people, and attend the funerals of deceased members. . . . New members were admitted by the ministers, with the approval of some discreet brethren, after promising to observe the conditions and after a year's probation; once admitted, no one might withdraw from the fraternity except to join a religious Order. . . . The fraternity met once a month in a church selected by the ministers, and should on these occasions, if it was convenient, be instructed by a religious.[76]

Neither this lost Rule nor the Capistran Rule of 1228, discovered by Paul Sabatier during the early 1900s at the Franciscan Convent of Capistrano in the Abruzzi, specifies regulation of local fraternities by the Franciscans, referring only to guiding visitors and ministers.[77] Thus, for many years, these Brethren of Penitence were governed locally by secular clergy or friars.

The more familiar Rule of the Third Order, the revision issued by Pope Nicholas IV in 1289, explicitly states that "whereas the present form of living was instituted by St. Francis, we advise that visitors and instructors be chosen from the Order of Friars Minor."[78] The Rule also prescribes: "simplicity of dress; considerable fasting and abstinence; the Divine Office or other prayers to take its place daily; confession and communion three times a year; monthly assembly in Church for religious instructions; upon the death of a member the whole confraternity must be present at the funeral; forbids carrying arms or taking solemn oaths without necessity; after admission every member must make his last will within three months; dissension among members must be settled peaceably; in case of trouble with local authorities the ministers should act under advice of the Bishop; no heretic or anyone suspected of heresy may be received into the Order; women may be received only with consent of their husbands; the ministers must denounce shortcomings to the visitor (inspector) who shall punish the transgressor; each year new ministers and a treasurer shall be elected; no point of rule obliges under pain of sin."[79] This general structure was diffused by the Franciscans throughout Europe, including Spain. The friars also carried the idea to their distant missions, and Spanish colonists in the New World affiliated themselves with the simple Christian life.

Before Domínguez's report, there are few extant references to the Third Order of St. Francis in New Mexico. On December 23, 1694, Fray Antonio Moreno, Commissary of the Third Order, witnessed a document in Santa Fe.[80] In 1716, Bartolomé Lobato, a native of Sombrerete, Zacatecas, then residing in Santa Cruz, declared himself a Franciscan Tertiary "de Avito descubierto" ("of exposed habit").[81] Juan Antonio Pérez Velarde, a native of Asturias living at Guadalupe del Paso in 1725, was Hermano Mayor of the Third Order of St. Francis.[82] A document dated April 11, 1755, at Galisteo, indicates that the Vice-Custos Tomás Murciano de la Cruz accepted the resignation of Fray Juan José Hernández as Commissary of the Third Order in Santa Fe and appointed Fray Manuel Rojo to replace him.[83] In 1765, Bernardino de Sena was buried in the San Miguel Chapel at Santa Fe "vested in the Franciscan habit."[84]

Little about Third Order organization is contained in Domínguez's 1776 account. At Santa Fe, where the canonical visitor received "a certification by the present Chief Brother, Don Miguel de Alini, signed by the members of the board," no accounts were kept, even after orders to do so, perhaps because "the body of this Order is composed of members so dry that all its juice consists chiefly of misfortunes."[85] Domínguez personally presented the treasurer of the Albuquerque Third Order with a new account book "consisting of thirty-four leaves (not counting the first and last)" to record monthly dues and penalties for their nonpayment. He also commanded that "because, according to their rule, the tertiary brethren must be punctilious in their attendance at the devotional exercises, they are exorted to fulfil their obligations and charged to abandon the lethargy and laziness in which they had lived up to now, to the loss of many graces and indulgences."[86] Apparently, Santa Cruz supported the most vigorous congregation, with the 127 men and women members each contributing three pesos annually, except that "for the past six years twelve brothers have not contributed because of their extreme poverty."[87] The dues, mostly collected in crops or goods, were handled by a chief brother.

A nearly illegible Santa Cruz document of 1781 shows the Third

Order there to be in a "decadent state."[88] Nevertheless, it still existed at the time of Bernal's 1794 report, as did a group at Santa Fe and a barely existent one in Albuquerque.[89] An abbreviated version of this report is transcribed in Archbishop Salpointe's 1898 history of the Church in the Southwest, and the title given the Tertiaries therein—"La Venerable Orden Tercera de Penitencia de N. S. P. San Francisco"—appears to have influenced the French clergy's official stand on the Penitente Brotherhood.[90]

Documents in the Archives of the Archdiocese of Santa Fe detail further similarities between Third Order affairs and later Penitente procedures. Formal petitions to join the Third Order were presented to the mission father, the hermano mayor, and several brothers. The petitioner appeared before this *mesa* ("board") and attested to devotion for St. Francis, desire for the protection of the Order, a blameless life, and a wish to become a brother. Apparently, another brother was questioned regarding the petitioner's qualifications—whether he was of Christian parents, whether he knew the Christian doctrine, whether he was peaceful, and so on. The petition was then approved by the various officials. For example, Francisca Rodrigues's petition was approved in Santa Cruz on May 26, 1778, after testimony by Hermano Juan Bautista Vexil. It was signed by Fray Manuel José Rojo; Antonio de Mestas, Hermano mayor; and Francisco Baldes y Bustos, *Secretario.* An appendix marked "diligencias" and signed by Hermano Ignacio Mestas proclaims that there was no public or secret impediment to membership discovered in the affairs of *Hermana* Francisca Rodrigues.[91] Another petition was presented to General Comissario [*sic*] Visitador Fray José Mariano Rosete on May 20, 1801. Testimony regarding Tolentino Domínguez of Rio Arriba was given by Hermano Miguel Sanches.[92] Both these documents are difficult to decipher, but they do show important common elements in Third Order and Penitente membership procedures.

A letter from Fray José Benito Pereyro, Custodio, to his superior, written at the Mission of Santa Clara on March or May 15, 1810, is especially illuminating about organizational matters.[93] The Custos has been ordered to review the case of Josef Ignacio Vegil, who claims to have been relieved of his habit (a modified Franciscan garb signifying membership in the Third Order) without due cause, and who has maligned "La Venerable Mesa" in Santa Cruz. He has cast aspersions on the Hermano mayor and the *Maestro de novicios*. Pereyro lists the rules which guided his decision to expunge Vegil's name from the list of brothers after the ex-member refused to be reconciled with the Board which he had through pride denounced. Pereyro made the Board members swear out declarations that Vegil's allegations were calumnious.

Even after the beginning of secularization, then, Fray Pereyro considered himself a guardian of the Third Order whose duty it was to root out harmful plants, replacing them with ones which would bear fruit. He claimed the authority of the See of Durango for his task, and it is probable that the letter itself was written to the Bishop and not to a Franciscan superior. He petitioned the superior to decide in his favor lest the door be opened for revolution and insubordination. If such cases became increasingly common, it is very possible that discontented outcasts could have begun a rebel organization, or even that mesas without suitable guidance could have developed into autonomous bodies.

Both Woodward and Chavez reject this theory, concluding that Penitente rules do not resemble the Rule of the Third Order of St. Francis, which governs the total Christian life to be lived by all members at all times.[94] The Brotherhood's rules are similar to those of confraternities—organized corporate structures with specific, stated purposes to promote various kinds of public worship.[95] According to Chavez, Lamy "watered down" original rules of the *hermandades* Zubiría had condemned and attempted to impose a nominal Franciscan Third Order Rule which he hoped would prove congenial to the troublesome Hispanic groups. Chavez has examined many copies of Penitente rules, both in the Archives and in the possession of various Hermanos:

> While bearing the title of the Third Order and the fact of their Lamy derivation, the copies I have seen in no way resemble the Rule of the Third Order. Nor have I found evidence that the good archbishop ever had authority, or knew how, to establish the Third Order, or that the Penitentes ever wore the strictly required scapular and cord of St. Francis.[96]

This presupposes, of course, that there were actually Penitente rules formulated and written early in the nineteenth century. On the other hand, it is entirely possible that Tertiary Hermanos were no better equipped than the "good archbishop" when it came to maintaining and evolving their own regulations.

Catholic churchmen have undeniably perpetuated the notion of a Third Order origin for the Brotherhood.[97] Early secular sources for this theory, which was later popularized by Charles Fletcher Lummis and Rev. Alexander M. Darley, are indicated in the William G. Ritch papers. A group marked RI-1866 contains the draft of an article which begins "Penitentes de la Preciosa Sangre de Nuestro Señor Jesucristo or the 3rd order of the Seraphic Father Saint Francis Assisium—(*Padre San Francisco de Asisi*)" and includes the following text:

> All three [Franciscan Orders] flagellate themselves especially on the Fridays of Lent. . . . The Penitentes of New Mexico were originally founded by the Franciscan Missionaries, and have made this flagellation more severe than the rules of the order require.[98]

It is possible that this article is the one referred to in Ritch's notebook, although it does not appear in the *Tribune* issue indicated:

> The third order of the seraphic Father Saint Francis Asisium 1878 "Holy Brotherhood".[x]—Traced by Denver *Tribune* correspondent Mch 2 5/78 writing from Santa Fe to the Franciscan monks of the 13th century.[99]

In any case, the idea was clearly current in both ecclesiastic and secular circles.

If the evidence for Franciscan influence on rituals and the meager inventory of Tertiaries' material culture is added to available data on the organization of the Third Order during the eighteenth and early nineteenth centuries, the case for Tertiary origins is considerably strengthened. Lenten and Holy Week observances at Santa Fe, Santa Cruz, and Albuquerque mentioned by Domínguez involve Via Crucis, Tenebrae, doctrinal sermons, and, at Santa Cruz, "Mondays, Wednesdays, and Fridays of Lent and Advent, exercises of the Third Order with their homilies."[100]

Voluntary discipline at Abiquiu was the only instance of public flagellation as a penance noted at the time. Domínguez reports that thirty-four-year-old Fray Sebastián Fernández, a native of Asturias, Spain, had been missioner at Abiquiu for two and a half years. Under his administration there was: "Fridays of Lent, *Via Crucis* with the father, and later, after dark, discipline attended by those who come voluntarily, because the father merely proposes it to them, and, following his good example, there is a crowd of Indians and citizens."[101] Ahlborn quotes another Domínguez paper of 1777, in which he again praises Fernández for his Via Crucis devotions and "scourging by the resident missionary and some of the faithful."[102]

Whenever possible, all three Third Order congregations supported monthly Sunday masses with a procession and responsory or sermon. All three also observed an anniversary for deceased brethren with the office of the dead, mass, and responsory. Whether or not their exercises included self-flagellation, it is clear that the Third Orders primarily sponsored Lenten and Holy Week observances, as well as death benefits for deceased members, both of which are characteristic of later Penitente concerns. In sum, in 1776 at least, the Franciscans and the Tertiaries, *not* the confraternities, were involved in activities relating to Lent, Passion, and Holy Week.

Finally, in 1776, the Third Orders maintained altars in the parish churches. No specific one is mentioned at Albuquerque, although altars in the nave are dedicated to St. Francis, St. Anthony of Padua, and *Jesús Nazareno*. The Third Order altar at Santa Fe was dedicated to St. Francis. The transcept altar at Santa Cruz, dedicated to Our Father St. Francis, was the most elaborate. Domínguez inventories an image of St. Francis on a litter, a *bulto* (carved figure in the round) of Jesús Nazareno, another of the Mater Dolorosa, a wooden table, "a wooden cross of the kind used by the Third Order, a very old frontal of blue ribbed silk, and a bench."[103] In short, he could be describing the main furnishings of a Penitente morada.

By 1814, there was a separate chapel for the Third Order at the Santa Fe parish church.[104] Church records indicate burials "en la Capilla de Tercera orden" as late as September 1816.[105] When de

Guevara began his visitation in 1817, this chapel was the object of stern rebuke:

> It is clear that de Guevara's inspection of the chapel of the Third Order was the occasion for his diatribe against 'this intolerable abuse' of exposed human skulls. It is also to be inferred that de Guevara saw to it that the entire chapel in front of the parroquia was demolished; no more burials in it are recorded, nor has further mention of the building been found. As a rule, the later extension of the Third Order, the New Mexican brotherhoods of Penitentes, kept one or more yellowed human skulls in a wall niche in the morada, at least as late as the decade of the 1930s (personal observation).[106]

The demolition of this structure may well have caused members faithful at least to the memory of their Franciscan fathers to build or appropriate separate places of worship.

The new chapel built onto the south transcept of the Santa Cruz church by 1787 fared no better. When de Guevara visited that parish in 1818, he emphatically stated that the adjoining room was in no way recognizable as of the Third Order or anything which pertained to it.[107] The original character of such chapels as centers for devotions to St. Francis and other saints popular among Franciscans and Tertiaries, for the occasional celebration of mass and anniversaries for the dead, and for spiritual instruction, had apparently been completely lost by this time.

Santa Cruz seems consistently to have supported the strongest Third Order group. Thus, when Zubiría mentions a *"Piesa"* for storing instruments of mortification in 1833, he could have meant either the chapel of the Third Order or a separate room, where Tertiaries might have moved following de Guevara's 1818 visitation. In any case, the likelihood of the Third Order Hermanos being those termed an *hermandad* by Zubiría is strengthened by an 1831 act of Visitor General and Vicar Don Juan Rafael Rascón.[108]

An April 6 request by Dionicio Vigil and Policarpo Cordova, citizens of Santa Cruz de la Cañada, was referred to the Vicar in Santa Fe. Sixty brothers of the Third Order of St. Francis in the Santa Cruz area sought permission to hold instructional exercises in Taos. On April 12, 1831, Rascón found no impediment to such a merger to observe their religious acts. He instructed them that according to their constitutions as Tertiaries they were not obliged to follow practices which placed them under pain of sin in order to gain indulgences and graces, and that they must not commit any abuses which would require correction during the bishop's coming visitation. This would indicate that Santa Fe officials were aware of Third Order practices which tended to exceed any condoned by the Church. Presumably, these had something to do with Lenten or Holy Week rituals, very likely the flagellation and cross-bearing condemned by Zubiría, since the request was made and granted in early April. In any case, this is another example of the strength of the northern Tertiaries. Santa Cruz was furthermore the central parish for Abiquiu, Taos, and Las Trampas, areas which had exhibited active signs of discontent with religious ministrations, as well as staunch independence.[109]

One final piece of evidence for Franciscan and very probably Tertiary origins of the Brotherhood comes from Arroyo Hondo, a village founded about 1815, some twelve miles northwest of Taos. According to Rael, this is the only community in northern New Mexico and southern Colorado which observes the feast of La Porciúncula (in New Mexico, La Percíngula or La Precíngula), directly related to St. Francis's chapel near Assisi and to the plenary indulgence which could be obtained by visiting this sanctuary on August 2:

> The act of devotion that was to be performed consisted of confession, the receiving of Holy Communion, and the visitation of one of the churches designated. Later . . . the privilege was extended not only to all the churches of the Third Order, but also to all churches with which the Franciscans were connected in any way, including non-Franciscan churches in which the Third Order held its meetings.[110]

Both Rael and Cleofas M. Jaramillo have described the August 2 procession and wake, sponsored by the Penitentes and joined by flagellant Brothers.[111] Such observances may once have been more common; nevertheless, even this single instance appears significant in the context of other data on the Third Order.

The Franciscan regime in New Mexico thus seems to have

46

fostered a number of worship patterns similar to later Penitente expressions, such as public self-discipline, Way of the Cross, Holy Week sermons on the Blood of Christ, the Three Falls, the Descent from the Cross, Tenebrae services, and, in one place at least, La Porciúncula. Documentation indicates that the friars set up and took responsibility for lay orders which maintained their own altars or chapels; which were governed by a board (including an Hermano Mayor, Maestro de novicios, Tesorero, and Secretario—all official titles later used by Penitente moradas) and had procedures for inducting and expelling members; which sponsored anniversaries for dead brothers; and which held some Lenten and Holy Week exercises. It seems quite likely that these loose congregations, found in all three villa centers, formed the basis for the hermandades Zubiría denounced. If indeed the idea for some confraternity devoted to penance and public Holy Week observances was imported during this period, it fell on fertile ground prepared by the Franciscan missionaries.

The Enigmatic Role of Don Antonio José Martínez

Don Antonio José Martínez emerges as a near-heroic figure in New Mexico history. Born in Abiquiu on January 16, 1793, he moved to Taos in 1804, but married in Abiquiu on May 20, 1812. His wife died a year later, and his daughter in 1825, by which time Martínez had entered the Durango Seminary (in 1817) and been ordained on February 10, 1822. Back in New Mexico, he spent time in Taos (1823), assisted at Tome (December 1823–March 1824), briefly served as pastor at Abiquiu (1826), and then returned to Taos, where he served officially and unofficially until his death on July 27, 1867.[112] His association with these separate Penitente strongholds and his education in Durango during the time of the wars of independence in Mexico strongly suggest a definite relationship between the dynamic priest and the developing Brotherhood.[113]

In the Ritch papers, Martínez is twice cited as the "Superior" of the Penitentes.[114] This evidence is by no means substantial, but Ritch does include another interesting reference:

Holy Brotherhood—Padre Martinez in his lifetime, wrote a pamphlet in defense of the Penitentes using the title of "Order of the Holy Brotherhood" as synonymous with Penitentes.[115]

The document is not extant, but perhaps it was printed on the first New Mexico printing press, brought in by Josiah Gregg and eventually purchased by Cura Martínez from Ramón Abréu's widow in 1837.[116]

In 1831, members of the Santa Cruz Third Order had asked permission to hold their exercises in Taos, where Martínez was cura and, by his admission, "delegate minister of the Third Penitential Order of St. Francis, among the devout of this parish of Taos, as attested by document 24 [not extant] of the Father Custodian."[117] In a letter to Bishop Lamy dated October 1, 1856, some twenty-seven days before his suspension, Martínez explained that he held a subdelegation to receive novitiates of both sexes into *"la EnCorporacion de Terceros de S. Francisco de Asis en el orden de penitencia"* and to sing mass at the Church of St. Francis in Ranchos de Taos on the fourth Sunday of each month. Since this power was delegated to him personally, he had not surrendered it to Cura Dámaso Taladrid, the former Spanish army chaplain Lamy had sent to Taos in 1856.[118]

If it is true that Martínez had something to do with Third Order affairs, and if he indeed wrote a defense of the Brotherhood, it seems plausible to suggest that the priest had some definite influence on the Penitentes' evolution. Perhaps he himself provided the Tertiaries with an organizational structure derived from penitential confraternities he had known firsthand or from books while a student in Mexico. He could thus have formed *cofradías de penitencia* out of Third Order congregations which he may have felt tended in that direction anyway. In other words, Martínez, an astute, practical ecclesiastic and politician, could have given already-existent groups their Sevillian "trappings," as well as something of their overall organization.

Whatever Martínez's actual relationship to the Penitentes, persistent family tradition in Taos linked him to the Brotherhood. In the early twentieth century, Lorenzo de Córdova recalls every Holy Week hearing his grandmother's account of the wake for

Martínez, which was attended by flagellant Brothers from "all over northern New Mexico." He wonders whether the ex-priest had attempted to consolidate the moradas: "this is mere conjecture on my part, but one word sticks with me, a word which grandmother used in referring to *Padre* Martínez, namely: *El Conciliador,* one who seeks to unite."[119] In any case, Martínez's official obituary, by Pedro Sánchez, who has also written his biography, states that the wake (from 9:10 p.m., July 27, until 9 a.m., July 29) was also attended by over three hundred members of *"la fraternidad piadosa de Taos."* The *"hermanos"* also walked in the funeral procession.[120] Apparently, Martínez was a strong spiritual influence, if not an active supporter and leader of the Brotherhood.

At present, then, scant evidence suggests Martínez may have exerted some influence on the Penitentes and their development. His self-proclaimed Third Order association and the 1831 Santa Cruz Tertiary Hermanos' petition to conduct exercises in Taos point to a possible movement which the priest could have catalyzed or crystallized. In any case, it is doubtful that, during his brief tenure (1845–48), the ill-fated Fray Mariano de Jesús López of Isleta, Laguna, Acoma, and Zuni, who carried among his titles that of "Comisario Visitador del Ven. e Orden Tercero," presented any challenge to Don Antonio José's role as "delegate minister of the Third Penitential Order of St. Francis" in the parish of Taos.[121]

Conclusion

In all likelihood, the problem of Penitente origins will never be decisively resolved. Extant documentation supports no positive conclusion, either for a Third Order-Franciscan origin or for a confraternity introduced from outside New Mexico. Indeed, the only possible solution may be to accept Reginald Fisher's compromise notion of "tertiary-Franciscan-penitential-brotherhoods."[122]

Chavez has suggested that the idea for a cofradía of penance was imported to and quickly developed in the Santa Cruz-Chimayo area of the Rio Arriba. Perhaps the same unknown traveler or merchant who "must have had first hand knowledge of the original Image and cult [of Our Lord of Esquípulas] in

Guatemala" also possessed an intimate knowledge of Sevillian-like confraternities.[123] Maybe even the donor-builder of the Sanctuary, Bernardo Abeyta, knew of such cofradías himself. Abeyta children were christened Esquípulas as early as 1805, and "when Bernardo Abeitia received permission to build the chapel from Durango in 1814, it is said that he made a trip to New Spain to purchase ornaments for it."[124] One local legend even claims Abeyta (variously spelled in the records) was practicing customary Penitente penances when he discovered the miraculous crucifix of Our Lord of Esquípulas.[125]

Unfortunately, a crucial document is missing from the present Microfilm Edition of the Archives of the Archdiocese of Santa Fe. According to Chavez's calendar, this is a Penitente book approved by Lamy on February 17, 1853.[126] Entitled *Arreglo de la Santa Hermandad de la Sangre de Nuestro Señor Jesucristo, etc.,* it contains, among other entries, 1853 and 1861 "counsels" from the Hermano Mayor of Santuario de Esquípulas to the Hermano Mayor at Cochiti. In view of the following excerpt from the constitution of a Brotherhood in Cenicero, Colorado, it may be that Bernardo Abeyta wrote the first counsel:

> Done this 17th day of February, 1860. This copy is taken from the Rule given by the Hermano Mayor Principal of all the Brotherhoods, the deceased Bernardo Abeyta, at present in use as the accepted Rule of the Brotherhood of San Buenaventura de Cochiti. . . .[127]

Abeyta died on November 21, 1856, and, by special permission from Bishop Lamy, was buried in his chapel at El Potrero. An influential, traveled man, he too could have been instrumental in establishing a penitential confraternity, the idea for which might easily have diffused from the pilgrimage center he helped found.

However, it is also impossible to ignore the chain of evidence delineated above showing the comparative strength of the Third Order of St. Francis at nearby Santa Cruz de la Canada. There is *no* documentary evidence for Penitente rules preceding Lamy's administration, so they cannot be compared with the Rule of the Third Order. Extant documents do indicate that Tertiaries had formalized membership procedures to induct Hermanos and governing Mesas composed at least of an Hermano Mayor,

Maestro de novicios, Tesorero, and Secretario. In the absence of guiding friars or even secular clergy, these could easily have become the hermandades Zubiría denounced in very general terms. Any formal confraternal organization involving Brothers of Light and Blood and significant terminology, such as references to Nuestro Padre Jesús Nazareno, could have been introduced later, possibly by some more sophisticated and educated individual such as Don Antonio José Martínez, who was at Taos during the time of the Third Order exercises in 1831, and who is alleged to have written a defense of the Penitentes, or even Bernardo Abeyta.

Certainly the larger tradition of worship as perpetuated by the Brotherhood seems to be basically Franciscan.

> In the minds of members of the cult, their adherence to traditional practices and to any additional routines devised by themselves, their forms of devotional penance were legitimate extensions of the old Franciscan Lenten observances. Graphic and verbal references to "Our Father St. Francis" were constantly preserved, although this fact has been overlooked in many surveys of Penitente ceremonies which have focused rather upon gory images of Our Father Jesus and the acts of members of the brotherhood.[128]

A century or more of improvisation in religious expressions, necessitated by the lack of ecclesiastics to minister in times of sickness and death and to celebrate the important events of the Christian year, especially Lent and Holy Week, may well have resulted in a varied conglomeration of lay practices, prayers, penances, and processions. Unsurprisingly, these localized, even makeshift observances preserve much of the worship fostered by the friars who were for years the sole religious on the frontier. It seems unlikely that pioneers from independent communities highly involved in mutual aid and defense would have been immediately responsive to or even in need of a new, imported formal organization and form of worship. In all probability, by the early 1800s, they had already evolved both in order to survive physically and spiritually.

Ecclesiastical Aspects
of the Territorial Period

When Bishop Zubiría visited Santa Fe in October of 1850, he was unaware that the Diocese of Durango no longer exercised official jurisdiction over the region. By a decree dated July 19, 1850, Pope Pius IX had established the Vicariate Apostolic of New Mexico as a suffragan to the Archdiocese of St. Louis. Father Jean Baptiste Lamy was appointed bishop and consecrated in Cincinnati, Ohio, on November 4. Accompanied by a close friend and fellow Frenchman, Father Joseph Projectus Machebeuf, the new bishop arrived in Santa Fe during the summer of 1851, almost a year after the Compromise Bill of September 9, 1850. This statute incorporated the Organic Act of the Territory of New Mexico, thus ending the military government which had been established by Brigadier-General Stephen Watts Kearny after the Army of the West occupied Santa Fe on August 18, 1846.

During the second half of the nineteenth century, the Catholic Church in the southwest was faced with a tremendous task of renovation and reconstruction. Lamy devoted his considerable energies to this rebuilding. He recruited religious, a majority of them from his native France; he established schools; and he ordered churches built. Over a decade after the Vicariate Apostolic had been elevated to a see (the Diocese of Santa Fe, by papal decree of July 28, 1853), the Bishop assessed his work:

In a report to the Holy See, March 12, 1865, he stated that he had found ten priests only, and these neglectful, their churches in ruins, and no schools. Now he had 37 priests and six theologians in minor orders soon to be ordained. He had built 45 churches and chapels, and repaired 18 or 20 old ones. There were four houses of the Sisters of Loretto in the Diocese, and three of the Christian Brothers, all in a flourishing condition.[1]

New Mexico had been affected by the Civil War, but its influence on the Church was negligible.

In 1868, the Vicariates Apostolic of Arizona and of Colorado (including Utah) were established. Father Jean Baptiste Salpointe was appointed Bishop of the former, and Machebeuf of the latter. Meanwhile, Lamy continued to augment his workers by bringing in the Sisters of Charity from Cincinnati, in 1865, and Jesuits from the Province of Naples, in 1867. The cornerstone for the new church to replace the adobe *parroquia* was laid on July 14, 1869. Work on this French Midi-Romanesque stone structure as originally conceived was never completed, but the unfinished Cathedral was blessed on March 7, 1886.[2]

By a decree of February 12, 1875, Pope Pius IX had elevated Santa Fe to a metropolitan see with the Vicariates Apostolic of Arizona and Colorado as suffragans. Lamy was consecrated archbishop on June 16, 1875, amid much ceremony and celebration. He continued his work until failing health necessitated the appointment of a coadjutor in 1884. The Right Reverend Jean Baptiste Salpointe arrived in Santa Fe on February 19, 1885, and Lamy resigned on July 18. The old archbishop retired to his Tesuque Valley ranch outside Santa Fe, but he returned to the city before his death on February 14, 1888.[3] Lamy was buried in the Cathedral on February 16.

Lamy's Rules for the Penitentes

Bishop Lamy apparently approved rules for the Penitentes as early as February 17, 1853. Although this document is not now available, it very probably resembles the "Constitution" reprinted in translation by Darley and Woodward.[4] The ten articles describe the duties of the various officers, with certain prayers and meditations, as well as indications of proper penitential exercises.

Lamy issued at least two further sets of rules for the Brotherhood. The first group, entitled "Reglas que deven obserbarse por hermanos de la cofraternidad catolica de penitencia," is dated October 27, 1856.[5] These rules have three main thrusts: regulation of the Confraternity by the priests and prelate, specification of the responsibilities of the Hermano Mayor and other officers of the Brotherhood, and definition of membership procedures, including the rights and duties of full-fledged Brothers. The final paragraph states that Lamy minutely examined the prayers (*"las oraciones"*) used by the Brotherhood of Penance (*"la hermandad de la penitencia"*) and found in them nothing contrary to the Catholic faith. These twelve regulations may well be a version of the ones Don Dámaso Taladrid, then of Taos, mentions in a letter to Lamy dated October 23, 1856.[6] He claims that the two Hermanos Mayores were shortly to bring the bishop rules which Taladrid himself formulated for the Brotherhood.

Since there is no record of these rules having been copied before 1858, it may be that Don Jose Eulogio Ortiz, who replaced Taladrid at Taos in 1857, was finally instrumental in getting them accepted and instituted. In a letter addressed to Lamy on November 27, 1856, Don Antonio Jose Martinez accused Taladrid of joining the Penitentes in secret nocturnal meetings (*"ciertas juntas secretas de parte de noche"*) and of authorizing their public exercises in Lamy's name (*"que V. S. Illmõs los autorise para que hagan en la luz del publico sus ejercicios"*).[7] In the same letter, Martinez also mentions that, during his visit of homage to Lamy, the bishop had told him of an order from the Holy Father to eliminate such fraternities (*"que del Santo Padre traia orden para extinguir estas fraternidades"*). There is no further record of this papal command.

Nevertheless, on March 9, 1857, at San Juan de los Caballeros, Bishop Lamy issued five more rules governing the Penitentes. These were copied by Don Jose E. Ortiz and presumably taken by him to Taos.[8] The first two of these concern the proper form of Brothers' penances, which they have long been accustomed to perform (*"segun han tenido de costumbre desde mucho tiempo"*). The second two involve membership procedures, while the last states that all other rules are still in effect. A tax of two candles for the altar is also imposed on each Brother.

None of these rules indicates that Lamy was concerned with "returning" the Penitentes to a Third Order regime, or, indeed, that he was overtly as outraged as Bishop Zubiría had been in 1833. However, certain documents still preserved by the Brothers do contain references to Franciscan guidance. Whether Lamy actually approved or even knew of these sections cannot be ascertained.

Beshoar, who is familiar with various Colorado moradas, claims that the earliest rules "were formally approved at the first general council of Penitentes, held March 25, 1810, in the village of Santa Cruz de la Cañada in New Mexico" and reaffirmed at a second Santa Cruz meeting in 1835.[9] It may be that his information comes from a document reportedly "presented to a Salida [Colorado] priest by the former leader (or mayor) of the Penitente group there, Louis Trujillo, before he died 15 years ago." A notation on this document allegedly reads: "These rules go back to the time of our predecessors, the Franciscan Brothers, and were revised from time to time by Franciscan Fathers as appears in the rules of the bishop. (Signed) Antonio Subiria of Durango, Mexico, 1810."[10] A recently published *Reglamento de la Hermandad de Nuestro P. Jesus de Nazareno* begins with the notation that the Rule was enacted and consecrated at Santa Cruz de la Canada in 1835 by the Franciscan fathers.[11] Documents such as these may have prompted the late Hermano Supremo Arzobispal Miguel Archibeque's statement that "the Penitentes in New Mexico were founded by the Franciscan Fathers at Santa Cruz in 1835."[12]

The idea of a Third Order background for the Penitentes seems to have been popularized by the Jesuits, although this does not necessarily mean that it originated with them. "The Society of Jesus date their labors in the interior of New Mexico from the Feast of the Assumption, August 15, 1867," when three priests and two lay-brothers from the Province of Naples arrived in Santa Fe at Lamy's request.[13] One of the Santa Fe group, the Belgian Father De Blieck, went to Denver in 1868, to serve the new Vicar Apostolic Joseph Projectus Machebeuf there.[14] After a year in Bernalillo, the New Mexico Jesuits set up their motherhouse at

Albuquerque's San Felipe. Besides preaching at various missions, for which they were soon renowned and beloved, they established a school at Las Vegas in 1874, and, on January 2, 1875, began publishing a Spanish-language religious weekly, *La Revista Católica,* which was soon moved from Albuquerque to Las Vegas.[15] In 1877, this paper printed the first extant statements of Franciscan origins for the Brotherhood.

Earlier, Jesuits had begun mission work in southern Colorado at Conejos (1871), Pueblo (1872), and Trinidad (1875).[16] They encountered Penitentes in all these areas. At the Conejos mission in 1874, Father Personé reported that "the priest, however, can go in when he wishes, and can even assist at the meetings and know everthing that is said or done."[17] He characterizes the Brothers as "poor simple people" who "count on buying heaven with such indiscretions, and maybe they do, because they do it in good faith," but goes on to say that "we are working, little by little, to destroy these abuses."[18]

The Sisters of Charity who served at Trinidad before the Jesuits took over that parish from Father Munnecom were clearly aware of the Franciscan influence on the Penitentes:

> The Way of the Cross, of course, was taught the natives by the good Franciscans; so also penance was preached to them. When the Franciscans were obliged to leave the Southwest, it naturally fell to the stronger-minded and piously inclined to perpetuate what had been taught them, but in this teaching each leader followed his own idea; hence, we find that whilst the members of some lodges are perfectly docile to the teachings of the Church, other lodges have not the least conception of the correct spirit of Catholicity, though they consider themselves good Catholics. . . . The *Penitentes* interpret the teachings of the Franciscans in their own way.[19]

This is a milder form of the *Revista Católica*'s 1877 diatribe against the Penitentes who had disfigured, adulterated, and corrupted the idea and fundamental rules of their founders, *"probablemente los piadosos hijos del gran Patriarca de Asís"* ("probably the pious sons of the great Patriarch of Assisi").[20] The occasion of this denunciation was the rumored atrocious and violent death, as a result of insane penances, of one of those men who had the "audacity" to call themselves Brothers of Our Father Jesus.[21] The paper's editors termed this *"un cruel suicidio"* ("a cruel suicide"), not a penance. Although the editors later retracted their report, noting that the Brother had only fainted, they still warned the Penitentes that death under such circumstances would not lead to glory but directly to the inferno below.[22]

Although he did not mention the possibility of a Franciscan origin for the Brotherhood in his Lenten Pastoral Letter of 1879, Archbishop Lamy overtly condemned "los Penitentes" in much the same terms the Jesuits had used in 1877.[23] Brotherhoods in remote places had disregarded the rules he had approved earlier and had continued practices which resulted in sickness and even death to penitents. They had also sworn in very young men as members. According to Lamy, obedience to the Church was paramount, not undirected and rigorous penance, which he deemed "blasphemous and unexemplary" behavior.

The 1885 Lenten pastoral Letter at the end of Lamy's administration contains a paragraph prompted by a papal encyclical of the previous year.[24] It cautions against secret societies, warning that the understandable desire for membership benefits must not blind parishioners to the evils of unrecognized and unapproved associations. Although the Penitentes are not specifically named, some chapters were probably among those groups Lamy mentions as being dangerous and disobedient.

On the whole, however, little tangible evidence of Lamy's relationship with the Brotherhood remains. He seems to have been most alarmed by any threat to Church authority in organizational and doctrinal matters. Very likely, practical concerns in establishing the new diocese and archdiocese dictated this attitude. Lamy was interested in assuring internal ecclesiastical order and parishioners' financial support, as well as in projecting a good image for civil authorities and the increasing number of non-Catholics. His condemnation of the Penitentes was therefore never vehement, and he seems to have left the more direct attacks to his successor.

Archbishop Salpointe's Stand

Ordained in France on December 21, 1851, Jean Baptiste Salpointe met Lamy's vicar general, Father Pierre Eguillon, at the

Clermont Ferrand Diocese Seminary in 1859. He agreed to work in the southwestern United States and arrived in New Mexico during October of the same year. He first worked at Santa Fe, but Lamy soon assigned him to Mora. On November 23, 1860, he took over jurisdiction of that parish from Don Damaso Taladrid, formerly of Taos.[25]

It was most likely at Mora that the new missioner became acquainted with the Penitentes. He states that "from 1859 until 1866 when we lived in New Mexico, we never heard of such criminal extravagances" as deaths resulting from simulated crucifixions. He also describes what he knows of Brotherhood organization and rituals, including the observation that "we have seen and heard it a couple of times, and the most astonishing feature of the ceremony was to see it followed by numerous good old women devoutly saying their beads."[26] This early experience probably influenced Salpointe's later dealings with councils from Mora and San Miguel Counties.

In 1865, Lamy asked for volunteers to man the missions of Arizona. Salpointe accepted, and arrived in Tucson on February 7, 1866. He spent the next eighteen years there, becoming bishop when it was made a Vicariate Apostolic on September 25, 1868. Back in Santa Fe as Lamy's coadjutor and then his successor, the new archbishop continued his predecessor's work in education, particularly of Indians, and administration. Besides engaging in controversy with the Jesuits, Salpointe also quarreled with the Penitentes, who "were never countenanced by the Church; on the contrary, since there have been bishops in New Mexico, they have denounced the practice and made of it the subject of some very strong circulars."[27] The strongest of these were by the second Archbishop of Santa Fe himself.

On September 12, 1885, Salpointe signed rules for any Catholic association already established or to be established in the Archdiocese of Santa Fe. Apparently, these rules had been published in 1872 by the bishops of California and approved by the Holy See. The title of the official document in the Archives of the Archdiocese of Santa Fe is "Reglas de la Sociedad de la Santisima Cruz ó de la Hermandad de Nuestro Padre Jesus."[28] The text clearly states that Catholic associations were recognized by the late Pope Pius IX and the present Pope Leo XIII and that they were always protected by the ecclesiastical hierarchy as *"auxiliarios de Nuestra Santa religion"* ("auxiliaries of our Holy Religion"), particularly at that time, in order to counteract the *"influjo deletereo de las Sociedades secretas, irrelegiosas inmorales"* ("deleterious influence of secret, unreligious, and immoral Societies").[29]

The 1885 rules were apparently part of Santa Fe's response to Pope Leo XIII's attempt to revive various lay associations of the faithful. Among these was the Third Order of St. Francis, for which the Pope published amended rules on May 19, 1883. These regulations seem to have been the real impetus for an official stand regarding the origin and nature of the Penitentes.

Salpointe's Lenten Pastoral of January 28, 1886, announced that one of the ways the Pope had proclaimed for the faithful to better their lives was through penance. In order that this penance not be merely transitory, the Holy Father had decreed that the people preserve their penitential spirit through some pious association which practiced mortification, such as the Tertiaries of St. Francis.[30]

In March, the archbishop distributed copies of the Pope's *Regla de los socios de la Tercera Orden de San Francisco* to the priests. The accompanying Circular stated that the Penitentes definitely came from the Third Order of St. Francis, and that they must return to this Order to obtain the indulgences promised by Pope Leo XIII. All forms of mortification not mentioned in the Rules, specifically, *public* flagellations and cross-bearing, were prohibited. Obedience to God and to the will of God's earthly vicar, rather than sacrifice, was stressed. All parishioners, including the Brothers, were to be given an opportunity to join the Third Order. Salpointe delegated the authority he himself held from the Minister General of the Franciscans to the parish priests, who could then enlist members, give them their habit, receive their profession, and so on.[31]

The First Synod of the Archdiocese was held in 1888. Some forty clergymen, among them seven Jesuits, participated in the retreat (from June 26) and the business of the Synod (from June 29 to July 1) at the Christian Brothers' College in Santa Fe.[32] Laurence F. Lee claims that decisions about the Penitentes were issued in a circular letter in 1888. In his 1910 thesis, he quotes this as follows:

With regard to the Society called Los Penitentes we firmly

believe, that it fully deserves all blame. Consequently, it must not be fostered. This society, though perhaps legitimate and religious in its beginning, has so greatly degenerated many years ago that it has no longer fixed rules but is governed in everything according to the pleasure of the director of every locality, and in many cases it is nothing else but a political society. We therefore desire:

That our Priests, as far as possible, speak opportunely with the leaders of the said society, and induce them to embrace the rule of the Tertiaries of St. Francis.

That mass must not be celebrated in the chapels, where the Penitentes observe their rites and abuses. Moreover, we command that the following rule be observed by our Priests toward the Penitentes who celebrate the wake over the dead bodies, with scourgings, not excluding eating and drinking and despised our ordinances and penalties, published to that effect in the year 1886. They are to be deprived of the Sacrament until they amend.[33]

This text agrees with Chavez's summation of the published proceedings and with Smith, but there is no present record of its having been circularized before the 1893 publication, and, in 1892, Salpointe himself mentions only his 1886 and 1889 Circulars.[34]

Because the Penitentes were returning little by little to the old abuses, and out of regard for the good of their souls as well as for public decency, Salpointe issued another Circular on March 31, 1889.[35] He outlines the development and demise of the fourteenth century flagellants and mentions the 1776 (i.e., 1777) ruling against *"disciplinantes"* in Spain. By practicing public flagellation, the Penitentes must incur the same censures as these earlier groups. Salpointe again stresses his opinion about the Brotherhood's degeneration from the Third Order of St. Francis and reiterates the terms of his 1886 Circular.

The *Mora Democrat* apparently objected to the 1889 Circular, because the editors of the *Revista Católica* call the paper to task in their issue of April 28.[36] They accuse the *Democrat's* editors of political intrigue, like those Brothers who remain recalcitrant and disobedient. This alleged political involvement was part of the Church's growing concern about Penitente activities.

The political question came to the fore during the Archbishop's negotiations with members of the Brotherhood from San Miguel County in late 1891. The confusion surrounding these transactions resulted in Salpointe's final Circular on the Penitentes dated February 7, 1892. Unfortunately, however, complete details of the communications between the archbishop and the various Penitente officials are not available in the Archives of the Archdiocese of Santa Fe.

A General Council of the Brotherhood for San Miguel, Mora, and Taos Counties was apparently convened in Mora on June 7, 1890, perhaps in response to Salpointe's 1889 Circular.[37] It seems likely that an undated *Peticion* to the archbishop was sent by this Council, since one of its four signers is from San Miguel and one is from Mora County.[38] This elaborate document contains the signers' proclamation of loyalty to the Catholic Church and pleas for official approval of the *"Fraternidad Piadosa."* Their penitential acts are explained as an imitation of the flagellation of Christ which honor His Passion and which are practiced by members who believe in their beneficial effects. The signers conclude with the hope that the continuation of their penitential exercises, the benediction of the archbishop, and their frequenting the Sacraments of the Church will bring them at last to heaven.

Sometime in October 1891, Salpointe received a petition from five members of the *"Concilio General del Condado de San Miguel."*[39] They request the archbishop to recognize them as a Catholic society protected by the Church and subject to whatever just restrictions Salpointe deems beneficial for the Brotherhood and for the Catholic Church. The signers wish to end certain differences which have existed between the Fraternity and the priests in the area. They also request that Salpointe give permission to Rev. J. M. Coudert to bless an expensive, beautiful *"Estandarte"* ("Standard") for their Brotherhood. This Standard, which represents the Passion and Death of Our Lord, has been brought from the East.

Salpointe's official answer to this latter request is not among the available documents, but the ceremony was celebrated in Las Vegas on November 1, 1891. According to *La Voz del Pueblo,* Lorenzo Lopez had presented the banner to *"la Sociedad de Jesús."*[40] Almost four thousand people attended the rites and procession, some fifteen hundred of them Penitentes, as well as many members of the Catholic societies of San Jose and San Juan de la Salle. Father Coudert and an assistant conducted the services. The *Hermano del Centro,* Don Serafin Baca y Armijo, vice-presidents Alexander Branch and Lorenzo Lopez, and marshall N. Segura, assisted by ten others, led the procession through town to a meeting hall where official speeches were exchanged. Interestingly, Salpointe was in the East at the time, so there may have been some kind of tacit agreement about the timing of such an unabashed display of strength. Perhaps the General Council's petitions were merely a ploy to get permission for this blessing of the standard, and that is why Salpointe heard no more of the Brothers' "reforming zeal," as he says in his final Circular.

The five original petitioners from San Miguel County—Serafin Baca y Armijo, N. Segura, Lorenzo Lopez, Rafael Baca, and Julian Trujillo—had declared their approval of Salpointe's rules on October 9, 1891.[41] These regulations include ten standard ones for all Catholic associations, and eleven specific ones for the Society of the Holy Cross or the Brotherhood of Our Father Jesus. However, according to the archbishop's final Circular on the Brotherhood, dated February 7, 1892, the signers had actually validated another set of rules at the General Council in Mora on June 7, 1890.[42] They were said to be traveling through other areas claiming that Salpointe had approved these regulations. The archbishop concludes that the two-faced leaders are only interested in personal political gain, and he labels them and their followers *"rebeldes"* ("rebels"), who are to be deprived of the Sacraments until they submit to Church jurisdiction.

The 1890 rules are undoubtedly those translated and published by Charles Aranda in 1974.[43] These eight *reglas* fit Salpointe's description and contain the quoted material. Of course, the archbishop sees the oath of perpetual obligation to the fraternity as an example of Masonry, a secret society condemned by the Church. He considers the oath of a fourteen-year-old immoral, although rule seven sets this as the minimum age for members. He is also alarmed by the political ramifications of the second rule, which claims for the Brotherhood all the rights granted by the Constitution and laws of the United States. This he reads as indicative of an obligation to vote according to the dictates of others, rather than with "conscientious convictions." Nonetheless, it is clear that these earlier rules, and few of the official ones approved in 1891, have been preserved by at least one district in San Miguel County.

The actual implementation of the official Circulars was left to the local priest. As far as the press was concerned, the archbishop was engaged in a vigorous fight to damn the Brotherhood.[44] This is consistent with the ecclesiastical hierarchy's attempts to maintain a good Church image in the eyes of civil authorities and non-Catholic citizens. In reality, local enforcement was highly variable.

Salpointe's Lenten Pastoral of February 10, 1892, indicates a possible reason for the ambivalent condemnation of the Brotherhood. The Archbishop writes that: *"no solamente no progresamos, sino que visiblemente vamos retrocediendo año por año con el decurso del tiempo"* ("not only do we not progress, but we are perceptibly retrogressing year by year, with the passing of time").[45] He maintains that when he first came to the area, although things were by no means perfect, men and women were interested in learning and performing their religious duties. Sundays and holy days were carefully observed, churches and chapels built, and priests supported as well as possible. He depicts the present state of the archdiocese as a deterioration from this pious tradition, particularly on the part of the men, who even frequent *"cantinas"* ("bars") during mass. The remainder of this long letter is devoted to the five Commandments of the Church, primarily the last—that the faithful must contribute to church maintenance. It is clear, then, that the Catholic Church was enjoying neither the ritual nor the financial support ecclesiastical authorities deemed proper.

Rather than jeopardize their standing with the bulk of the parishioners, who were Spanish-American, the Church hierarchy, a majority of whom were French, seems to have left action on the Penitentes to the discretion of the local pastors. If nothing else, financial realities necessitated the archbishop's somewhat ambiguous stand. The priests then had to face the individual consequences of the interpretations of Salpointe's declarations.

The Local Clergy's Attitudes

Few sources reliably report the attitudes and practices of the local clergy in their dealings with the Brotherhood. At least three priests are known to have copied rules for moradas under their care, as did Father Clement Peyron for the Cochiti union in 1870.[46] Some priests apparently took decisive actions against the Brothers. According to Lummis, "when Father Brun assumed the parish of Taos, nearly thirty years ago, the whitewashed walls inside the church of Fernandez de Taos were splattered shoulder-high with blood, from the Penitente whippings; and when he refused to let the Brethren profane the building again, they tried several times to kill him."[47] At Tome, on the other hand, Father Jean Baptiste Railliere, parish priest from June 13, 1858, until 1911, seems to have substituted other observances, so that public flagellation began to disappear.[48] Hurt states that at Manzano, "in the 1880's, the Penitente order was dissolved by Padre Sembrano [Tafoya?], a priest of the local Roman Catholic Church."[49]

In Mora, a legend persists in local tradition that Father Etienne Avel was murdered by local Brothers angry over his opposition to their rituals. They are supposed to have poisoned the altar wine, which Avel drank anyway because it had been consecrated. The priest supposedly expired soon afterward.[50] More recently, local residents recount stories of Father C. Balland's attempts to disperse Brothers gathered at Buena Vista for Good Friday observances.[51] The priest was allegedly reassigned after being accused of threatening his parishioners.

In 1891, Father J. M. Coudert evidently participated in the blessing of the new standard for the San Miguel County Brotherhood. In 1895, the *Las Vegas Daily Optic* published two sensationalized articles on the Penitentes by Warren M'Veigh.[52] McVeigh, who identified Cura Martinez as a Franciscan monk who had founded the Penitentes some two hundred years previous, also claimed Father Defouri had told him of Apaches who broke up a simulated crucifixion west of Santa Fe. The Cristo, who was left tied on the cross, was shot full of arrows. Defouri hastened to deny everything in a letter to the editors, declaring: "All I have to say is that I never gave histories of penitentes to any one, because I know absolutely nothing about the penitentes, only from hearsay, and never was I in a position to see their performances."[53] In view of the large ceremony in 1891, Defouri's urgency and emphasis are perhaps understandable.

Two cases from the early twentieth century indicate continued secrecy on the part of the Brothers and possibly of those priests who openly sympathized with them. Mary Austin reports:

> At Taos, the Priest located there during the early part of this century, told me that on one occasion he was asked by the Chapter of Llano, to depose the Hermano Mayor who had incurred the displeasure of the members. This he refused to do until charges had been preferred, but so dearly did they prize the secrecy of their order that it was finally decided to be preferable to endure the unpopular Mayor, than to expose the inner workings of the order to the Priest.[54]

The most interesting case is recorded by Laurence F. Lee, allegedly at San Rafael, New Mexico, about 1908. In a letter to Dorothy Woodward, he describes the photographs which appeared in *El Palacio,* entitled "Scenes in a Penitente Plaza during Lent."[55] His description of the top picture on page two follows:

> The upper picture shows the Veronica wiping the face of Christ and the miracle of the print appearing upon the cloth, but the principal significance of the picture is that it shows Father Berry, the then presiding priest at Gallup, New Mexico, taking part in these rites when, of course, as you know, the Catholic Church is supposed to condemn the practice and prohibit its members from taking part. Father Berry was incensed at these pictures being taken and ordered that they be destroyed.[56]

Since Archives are not available after 1900, there is no record of any action taken by or against Father Berry after the publication of the incriminating photograph.

None of these fragments points to a consistent picture of local priest-Penitente relations. Presumably, these were almost a personal matter, despite official Church stands. Austin suggests:

> Possibly the opposition of the Church was always more for the public than for the Penitentes. Certainly as one gets

further and further from centers of White influence, the relation between the Church and the Order is seen to be very much closer.[57]

Barker concurs, claiming that more isolated settlements maintained more cordial or relaxed relationships with the priests who visited them so seldom.[58] Rev. George Wharton James avers that "the priests do not seem able clearly to separate the sheep from the goats," while his earlier counterpart, Rev. Darley, cites the unlikely story of a priest who, after the 1886 and 1889 Circulars, "permitted the processions at $1.00 a head for the privilege."[59] Nevertheless, implementation of official policy was clearly an individual matter.

Local pastors certainly received the various archdiocesan statements. Some did refuse Sacraments to known Penitentes and legitimacy to their children.[60] However, many seem to have adopted a *laissez-faire* attitude, preferring to recognize the exemplary piety of many Brothers, whom they probably knew personally, and to forestall internal division which might facilitate Protestant encroachment. In any case, no widespread, concerted attempt at dissolution of the Brotherhood and wholesale excommunication of Brothers was ever mounted at a local level.

Archbishops Chapelle, Bourgade, and Pitaval

Rev. Placide Louis Chapelle, then rector of St. Matthew's Church in Washington, D.C., was appointed coadjutor to Archbishop Salpointe and arrived in Santa Fe on December 7, 1891. Salpointe resigned on January 7, 1894, but Chapelle was not consecrated until October 17, 1895. His predecessor claims that his work was brief but remarkable, that "he visited all parts of the diocese and administered Confirmation to 28,000 candidates, besides bringing from Europe twenty-two missionaries who are now working as parish priests or assistants in the missions of the diocese."[61] However, the archbishop was unaccustomed to living in the Southwest, and, in December 1897, he was reassigned to the Archdiocese of New Orleans.

The Most Rev. Pierre Bourgade, brought from France by Lamy

and successor to Salpointe in Arizona, was officially transferred to the Metropolitan See of Santa Fe by Papal Rescript dated January 7, 1899. He was consecrated on October 4, 1899, the Feast of St. Francis, in the Cathedral. The most significant aspect of this occasion was that "conspicuous among the clergy were three Franciscan Fathers, with cowl and brown habit, whose presence, pleasing to all, meant the return of the sons of St. Francis into the land assigned to them of old, by Ferdinand and Ysabel."[62] These friars had been called by Bourgade to establish Navajo missions in Arizona. They were then asked to take over at Pena Blanca in 1900, at Jemez in 1902, and at Roswell in 1903. It had been some fifty years since the death of the last Franciscan in New Mexico, and almost a century since the friars lost their spiritual control of the territory.

In 1907, L. Bradford Prince wrote to one of the first new Franciscans, Father Albert T. Daeger, O.F.M. (later archbishop), about his views on the Penitentes and the Third Order. Daeger's reply, from Pena Blanca, reads in part:

> The Third Order of St. Francis, I suppose, was discontinued when the Franciscan Fathers left New Mexico. We have not as yet re-established it and will not for a while—either here in Peña Blanca or Jemez, Roswell or Carlsbad.
>
> The Penitentes *might* be a relic or an offshoot of the Third Order. Some say so. But they are surely not *the* Third Order.[63]

The friar was early aware of the official controversy and the Brotherhood itself.

Apparently, preliminary steps to regulate the Brotherhood further were taken during Bourgade's administration, but these do not seem to have been incorporated into an official document. When more of the Archives of the Archdiocese of Santa Fe are made available, perhaps further Circulars will be uncovered. For the present, however, only a signed *Comisión* report, presumably submitted to Bourgade, and a number of *puntos* to add to the rules of the Penitentes, definitely submitted to Bourgade, remain.[64]

According to these two documents, the Church did not change its stand appreciably throughout the second half of the nineteenth century or, presumably, during the early twentieth century. Again, there is concern that the Brothers observe their duties as Catholics and not engage in public demonstrations of any sort. All rules, decisions, and new members must be approved by Church officials. Politics are to be strictly excluded from the religious society. Disobedience is rebellion, and it results in exclusion from sponsorship at a baptism or confirmation, deprivation of the Sacraments of penance and Holy Eucharist, and final denial of assistance and Church burial. These penalties are more explicit than Salpointe's, and they are indicative of continuing Penitente strength and an unrelentingly firm Church stand against many core aspects of the Brotherhood.

Jean Baptiste Pitaval, brought from France to work in the Diocese of Denver, was appointed auxiliary bishop for Bourgade in 1902. The archbishop died on May 17, 1908, and Pitaval succeeded him on January 3, 1909. According to Chavez, "by 1908 there were 45 parishes with 340 mission chapels in the archdiocese, denoting a marked increase in the population as well as a definite economic progress."[65] Pitaval resigned in 1918, the last of five successive French archbishops of Santa Fe.

The Protestant Denominations in New Mexico and Southern Colorado

From the beginning of American occupation, there were attempts by Baptists, Methodists, Presbyterians, Congregationalists, and others to evangelize the natives of the new Territory. At first more concerned with Anglo settlers, these missionaries soon became involved with the Hispanic and, to a lesser extent, the Indian populations.

As the Catholic Church foresaw, the public rituals of the Penitentes both delighted and outraged the incoming Protestants. They translated their indignation at the excesses of Romanism into eloquent pleas for funds and support from the "civilized" parts of the country. These flights of rhetoric sometimes brought rebuke not only from the ever-vigilant *Revista Católica* but from the secular press as well.[66] After all, New Mexico's image suffered as well as the Catholic Church's.

According to a later Church assessment, the main threat lay in the sixty or more schools Protestants set up in towns and rural areas between 1879 and 1891:

> Many of them were frankly educational institutions for the betterment of the people. . . . But others, those called "Spanish Mission Schools," went all out under the guise of education to take away the Faith of the poor and ignorant by offering them an education which the Church at the time could not afford. Their procedure was to blacken Catholicism in the eyes of simple folk. The old canards about the evil secret lives of priests and nuns, the adorations of images, and other such lies were broadcast in print and by word of mouth in rural settlements. . . . What these sects did effect too well was to confuse souls; they took away the Faith of many and left them, not Protestants, but infidels and scoffers.[67]

It is usual to read that the Protestant ministers "went so far as to organize *Penitente* groups that had been reprimanded by the Catholic clergy into Protestant sects, thus making life that much more uncomfortable for the already harassed Catholic pastors."[68] However, it is not yet clear to what extent Protestantism actually influenced the Hispanic population, especially in the more isolated settlements, during the late nineteenth century. The actual situation cannot be reconstructed without a close study of all the denominations in the Territory, as well as the Catholic parishes.[69]

There has been good research into the early work of the northern branch of the Methodist Episcopal Church in New Mexico and southern Colorado,[70] but most documentation about the religious difficulties of the period involves the Presbyterians and the Jesuits. These mutual recriminations were prompted in large part by the vociferous Rev. Alexander M. Darley, self-styled "Apostle of the Colorado Mexicans." The Presbyterians' relationship to the Penitentes, because it is better reported than that of other denominations, will thus exemplify local Protestant pressures and effects in the Hispanic communities.

According to the 1882 *New Mexico Blue Book*, Rev. W. J. Kephardt was the first Presbyterian missionary in the area, reaching Santa Fe in 1851.[71] "On 22 November 1866 the Reverend David F. McFarland, commissioned by the Board of Domestic Missions of the Presbyterian Church (Old School), arrived in

Santa Fe and began 'laboring as a Domestic Missionary,' "
organizing the first church in January 1867.[72] Soon, Rev. J. A.
Annin began work at Las Vegas, New Mexico, Rev. James M.
Roberts at Taos, and Rev. Sheldon Jackson in the Colorado
region. These three, and later Darley of Pueblo and southern
Colorado, came under attack from the Catholic press.

The Synod of Colorado, established on May 18, 1871, originally
included New Mexico and Wyoming as well. On May 27, 1889,
the Synod of New Mexico, comprising the three Presbyteries of
Arizona, Rio Grande, and Santa Fe, was erected. An early history
describing this new Synod is instructive:

> In 1895 there were in the Mexican field twenty-six schools,
> fifty-three teachers, and one thousand seven hundred and
> seventy-four scholars. In the Synod of New Mexico there were
> thirty-six churches, thirty-two missionaries and helpers, and
> eight hundred and seventy-seven church members. At the
> present time (1902) we have three presbyteries . . . with
> sixty-two organized congregations, of which twenty-seven are
> American, twenty-nine Mexican and six Indian, with a total
> membership of over three thousand five hundred. We have
> thirty-eight ordained ministers, twenty-two evangelists and
> helpers, sixty commissioned teachers, and one thousand five
> hundred pupils in our schools.[73]

Clearly, the denomination had not made major inroads into the
Catholic Hispanic population.

Other important developments were in the press and higher
education. Rev. Sheldon Jackson started the *Rocky Mountain
Presbyterian* as a monthly on March 1, 1872. It was published
weekly in 1874, then monthly until its last issue in December 1881,
when it was renamed the *Presbyterian Home Missionary* and taken
over by the Board of Missions.[74] In 1883, the College of the
South-West was established at Del Norte, Colorado. Before it was
closed, by 1906, it had trained some forty-four "Mexican evangel-
ists, missionaries, and ministers," many of whom worked within
Hispanic communities in the region.[75]

However, the Presbyterians considered their day and boarding
schools the "opening wedge" in their mission fields:

The schools are influencing the Penitentes, the home life of the people, and the lives of the children and young people. . . . The Penitentes are often anxious to have their children educated, but the great masses of the people are under the dominating influence of the Catholic Church and it will require both patience and time to win them away from this allegiance and to make it possible for them to appreciate and to participate in the advantages of Protestant Christianity. But from our schools will soon come a generation that will throw off this yoke of bondage, and the harvest time of souls will be here.[76]

The elaborate system of mission schools developed during the late nineteenth century continues in certain areas today.[77]

Evangelistic work among the Hispanic communities was much slower and less readily accepted. The history of notable converts and early Bibles in the area—the "Madrid Bible," the "Gómez Bible," and the "Chimayó Bible"—is sparse and not well documented as yet.[78] Still, observations of the change in Jemez, New Mexico, between 1875 and 1903, indicate some Presbyterian influence. When Englishman R. B. Townshend visited the village in 1875, he witnessed a Penitente flagellant procession.[79] A Presbyterian mission was established in 1878, and the astonished Townshend exclaimed about the changes when he revisited the community in 1903:

It used to be the Dark Ages. Flagellants, witches, and murderers! It would take a Hardy to give the curious irony of it . . . as for me, who thought this "rincon," this most out-of-the-way part of the world, would remain as it was, I can only say it makes me feel topsy-turvy. And that Presbyterian service this morning has put the finishing touch on it. My dear, fancy Sankey hymns villainously translated into Spanish, how they go! In Spanish nothing not Catholic can seem other than grotesque.[80]

Of course, Townshend may have had no way of knowing the real extent of Protestant influence; nevertheless, his subjective impressions indicate it was not unremarkable.

Like other denominations, the Presbyterians were not immune

to boasts about their converts, especially those supposedly ex-Penitentes, and to the exaggeration of their missionary hardships. Highly colored "reports" of the Penitentes appeared in various sources.[81] The *Revista Católica* subjected the ministers to scathing sarcasm in 1877, after receiving an account of the Presbyterian Assembly in Chicago, at which it was reported that New Mexicans obtained the right to do whatever they pleased throughout the year by inflicting terrible penances on themselves during Lent. This, according to the Presbyterians, made the Territory very dangerous for the Protestant missionaries. The Jesuit editors replied with a *"Comedia de Los Ministros mártires en Nuevo Méjico,"* exhorting their readers to imagine the poor Presbyterian clerics dragged by enraged Penitentes over thistles, thorns, and sharp rocks, naked but for a trouser, or burdened with a heavy cross, and violently whipped by some Hermano Mayor.[82] They also included stern warnings to the Brothers.

In 1893, Lummis noted a "cynical commentary on our mission work," reporting that the Hispanic wife of the Presbyterian missionary walked in the San Mateo Penitente procession.[83] According to a later article, this invoked "the wrath of a Rev. Superintendent of Missions over my allusion to the fact that the most noticeable figure (because the tallest) in the procession of 1888 was the Mexican wife of the Presbyterian missionary [Montgomery] then stationed at San Mateo."[84] However, this seems to be the only Anglo reference to such discrepancies.

According to available records, some Penitentes did join the new Presbyterian groups. The editors of the *Revista Católica* found this a mixed blessing, since it rid the Catholic Church of the vain, domineering, and rebellious Hermanos Mayores. They concluded that no great dent would be made in the Catholic population and that ringleaders might become Protestants and even ministers as long as they spared others the shame and disgust of seeing them in their churches.[85] Earlier, they had voiced similar sentiments about a November 1 meeting in the Presbyterian church at Las Vegas, New Mexico. Two Hermanos Mayores from Mora County were present with the three ministers—Annin of Las Vegas, Smith of Santa Fe, and Roberts of Taos.[86] Some of these defections may have been due to Church pressure against the Brotherhoods, but it is not clear how many morada members followed their leaders in this regard, or even whether many of the "converts" were not simply nominal Protestants.

Four alleged Penitentes are specifically mentioned as Presbyterian converts:

(1) *J. D. Mondragon.* "In 1856 he was the chief Brother or Captain of the Penitentes in Taos Valley and a member of the Legislature of New Mexico."[87] After obtaining a Bible in Santa Fe, he read it and gave up Penitente membership, later meeting Rev. Roberts and converting in 1872.

(2) *Pedro Sanchez.* The story of how Sanchez obtained a Bible is not clear. One account indicates that, in 1868, he got it in exchange for a spelling book; another that he and not Gomez traded an ox for it, near Ojo Caliente, New Mexico, in the 1860s.[88] In any case, the Penitente constitution which Darley published was copied at the request of the Hermano Mayor of Cenicero, Colorado, Pedro Sanchez. Darley notes that Sanchez, "evidently a seeker after the best to be found in Romanism, and according to his light, eventually found Christ, the all-sufficient penitent, and died in the true Christian faith."[89] Sanchez's brothers-in-law, Jose P. and Pedro Ortega, also joined him in the new religion.

(3) *Jose Pablo Ortega.* The Ortega family lived in Cenicero, Colorado, where Rev. Roberts of Taos occasionally stopped. In 1877, Roberts organized a church at their home.[90] The *Revista Católica* scornfully reprinted a letter describing the proceedings of this September meeting with the comment that the Presbyterians were welcome to an ex-Hermano Mayor such as Ortega.[91] In any case, Darley also baptized persons there, and at least one other convert, Antonio Jose Rodriguez, of Penitente parents, is attributed to the influence of Sanchez and the Ortegas.[92]

(4) *Nestor Pacheco.* In the winter of 1898–99, Rendon was traveling between Del Norte and Saguache, Colorado. He met Pacheco, discovered he had been reading the Bible to his family, preached, and converted the household and three other families. According to Rendon, Pacheco had been a strong Penitente.[93]

The "famous" conversions seem generally to have come before Salpointe's strong stand against the Penitentes, although the second archbishop may have precipitated more converts among the Brothers.

The Rev. Alexander M. Darley was the most actively boastful of his "conquest" of the Penitentes. His Pueblo, Colorado, newspapers—*La Hermandad* and *The Individual*—and his controversial 1893 book, *The Passionists of the Southwest,* incorporating material on the Brotherhood into a vitriolic attack on the Roman Catholic Church, provoked much public outcry. According to MacLeod, in early 1875, Darley was called by Rev. Jackson to undertake work in the San Luis Valley and beyond the Continental Divide in the San Juan country, where gold had reputedly been discovered.[94] Darley's work included the establishment of churches at Del Norte on April 11, 1875, and to the west at Lake City on July 19, 1876. He traveled a great deal and was helped by his brother George M. Darley in the San Juan region.[95] While stationed at Del Norte (1875–77), Darley undertook an evangelistic itinerary through the Hispanic communities of southern Colorado. Until the fall of 1881, he had charge of the Hispanic churches in the San Luis and Arkansas Valleys. Afterward, he worked in the Arkansas Valley only, including Trinidad, Huerfano Canyon, Pueblo, Walsenburg, and Las Animas. He is listed on the church rolls as a resident of Pueblo, with dates of service from 1880 to 1883, and from 1891 to 1896. Much of his time must have been occupied in editing his newspapers, writing articles, and preparing his book, which seems to have been based largely on his experiences in Conejos County, presumably, from 1875 to 1880.

Lee claims that Darley's April 1890 issue of *La Hermandad* "was the cause of much excitement; in fact, there was a threatened uprising among the Mexican population of Southern Colorado."[96] Besides reprinting a constitution and by-laws supposedly given him by Pedro Sanchez, Darley included innumerable bits of information and diatribe. This prompted vehement reactions from the *Revista Católica,* which then denied charges from *La Hermandad* and *El Anciano,* another Protestant paper, that it derived its only inspiration from the Protestant press.[97] In any case, no uprising is reported, and in his book Darley remarks casually that "the Jesuits of Las Vegas, N.M., once denounced the Penitentes Cenicero, of Conejos Co., Colorado, as the cause of the Presbyterians there, because under our ministry nearly all of them were converted, and

74

their Rule, etc., learned by us."[98] Elsewhere, he claims of the "Holy Brotherhood" that a "thousand Bibles broke its back in the San Luis Valley; but it will take nigh five thousand to do it in this 'Texas of Colorado,' east of the Range [Sangre de Cristo], and many thousand more in still priest-ridden New Mexico."[99] Presumably, such declarations sold papers and books.

Available information, then, points to definite cracks in the Catholic monopoly. However, there seems to have been no massive exodus of Brothers from Catholicism. Anglo ministers avidly observed Penitente rites, but, like the earlier Mexican and later French priests, they were too few and too foreign to make a substantial impression. Much of the hysteria seems to have been generated by the press in endless verbal battles. The people largely remained true to their Brotherhood and their religion.

Conclusion

Neither priest nor preacher seems to have recognized the important mutual aid and community functions of the Brotherhood. To the Protestant, these social aspects masked a dark fanaticism which threatened to subvert decency and extinguish the true Gospel. For the Catholic clergy, secret societies were anathema —disobedient organizations involved in political intrigue. Imitating Christ through acts of charity kept secret to preserve humility was overlooked; the more visible rites of worship received the brunt of the lopsided attack.

The amount of rebuke and repudiation suffered by the moradas varied with the local priest and to a much lesser extent the (usually itinerant) preacher. A man interviewed by Montano claims that at the beginning of the twentieth century there were very strict Penitente initiation rites to weed out any spies the Church might have sent.[100] This is only in one area (San Miguel County), however. Elsewhere, a village might not have received a priest at all during Holy Week. It is thus difficult to judge the extent to which the Penitentes felt beleaguered by the Church.

Whatever their experiences, it appears reasonable to conclude that at first comparatively few Brothers actually left Catholicism for Protestantism. They seem to have protected themselves by increased secrecy and more stringent internal controls. They may have resolved whatever dissonance they felt by scapegoating the French Church hierarchy, the Italian Jesuits, or the local priest himself. They probably distinguished between "true" Catholicism, i.e., traditional Hispanic practices, and "administrative" interpretations. While this fierce integrity may seem almost Protestant in itself, it should be noted that the Brothers did *not* usurp priestly functions or even abandon the traditional prayers and rituals. Their patterns of worship and probably their deepest self-conceptions were strictly Roman Catholic and definitely Hispanic.

The sociocultural situation of the Penitentes, their families, and their communities, was simply not such that easy reconciliation to the new Church regime or wholesale conversion to Protestantism could have been effected. Various Anglo pressures were slowly undermining traditional village and town life. It was clear that the Hispanos needed whatever political leverage they could muster, to say nothing of an effective community organization to combat the consequences that loss of land and livelihood gradually made manifest. By ignoring the important local functions of the individual moradas and concentrating on questions of doctrine and ritual, the established churches demanded too high a price. To portray this as a "purge," however, is perhaps less accurate than to view it as a sustained indifference which one side or the other may have subjectively experienced as aggressive intrusion or resistance.

CHAPTER 3

Secular Aspects
of the Territorial Period

On August 19, 1846, Brigadier-General Stephen Watts Kearny read a proclamation in the plaza at Santa Fe announcing that New Mexicans were thereby citizens of a Territory of the United States. He appointed civil officials and, on September 22, "promulgated the 'Organic Law of the Territory,' a codification of Spanish-Mexican and U.S. Law popularly known as the Kearny Code."[1] This usurpation of Congressional powers was the subject of a rebuke by President Polk in December. Nonetheless, military governors continued to administrate the territory even after the Treaty of Guadalupe Hidalgo, formally transferring New Mexico and other areas to the United States, was ratified on March 10, 1848.[2]

A compromise bill affecting all new western lands was finally approved by both Houses of Congress on September 9, 1850. New Mexico was officially established as a Territory, with popular sovereignty on the slavery question.[3] The executive branch was headed by a governor with extensive powers and a secretary, both of whom were appointed by the President for four-year terms. The Territorial Legislature consisted of a Council with thirteen (later twelve) members and a House of Representatives with twenty-six (later twenty-four) members elected by the suffrage of males over twenty-one. James S. Calhoun was inaugurated governor on March 3, 1851. The first census, in April, showed the population to be 56,984. "Among the most pressing problems faced by Calhoun and the legislature were education, the problem of Indian attacks, and New Mexico's isolation."[4]

George I. Sanchez calls Hispanic New Mexicans under the new regime the "stepchildren of a nation," irresponsibly and uncomprehendingly administered by a government which viewed them as aliens.

> What has been said of education can be said with equal or greater force about other public services intended to raise the cultural level of a society. Health programs, the administration of justice, economic competition and development, the exercise of suffrage, land use and management—the vital aspects of the social and economic incorporation of a people were left up to the doubtful ministrations of improvised leadership. The New Mexican was placed at the mercy of those political and economic forces, of those vested interests, that could control the machinery of local government. In an area of cultural unsophistication and of economic inadequacy, he was expected to lift himself up by his own bootstraps.[5]

This indifference eventually resulted in extensive cultural and socioeconomic disenfranchisement in predominately Hispanic areas, a process which accelerated following the Civil War and the construction of a railroad system linking New Mexico with markets and urban centers to the east, north, and west.

The first train entered New Mexico on December 7, 1878, with lines to Las Vegas completed by 1879, a branch to Santa Fe on February 9, 1880, and the main tracks to Albuquerque on April 10 of that year. Economic slumps curtailed building at various times, but "about 80% of the common carrier mileage was built in two periods: 1878–1882 and 1898–1910."[6] This rail network brought a steadily growing influx of settlers and speculators.

> New towns were created and old ones stimulated by the maintenance of the railroad itself, as well as the needs of its personnel. Furthermore, the locomotives required coal, and the mines at places such as Dawson and Madrid became important local sources of this fuel and employers of men. With the new means of transportation to eastern markets,

mining of other minerals and lumbering was further stimulated, as was the livestock industry. . . .[7]

Unfortunately, an increasingly poverty-stricken Hispanic populace did not on the whole share in the new wealth.

Problems of attaining statehood and establishing public education were exacerbated by mounting prejudice against Hispanos and Roman Catholicism.

Factional strife and political discord do not fully account for the fact that New Mexico was never considered in the same light as other territories. The unique population of New Mexico profoundly separated the territory from most of the remainder of the West where Anglo pioneers had slowly filled the frontiers with a fairly homogeneous population of Western European stock. . . . The actions of the territory's Catholic hierarchy, especially its determined opposition to the constitution of 1889 because of a secular school provision, only aggravated the prejudice and dislike of a predominantly Protestant nation.[8]

Colorado, the thirty-eighth state, was admitted to the union on August 1, 1876, but New Mexico was proclaimed the forty-seventh state only on February 12, 1912.

As early as 1877, the editors of *La Revista Católica* had melodramatically voiced apprehensions about the approaching railroad and its effect on Catholicism and on Territorial government:

Especially now that the trains come as far as the frontiers of New Mexico, there will be great dishonor to the religion which they [Penitentes] profess if they are seen naked and bloody on plains and mountains. Men who only seek pretexts for mobilizing public opinion against the Catholic Church come here in order to observe these places and then to report to newspapers in the States—attributing to the entire Catholic population in this land that which is only the effect of the aberrations of a few Mexicans who make their whole religion consist of these practices.[9]

Such warnings were ineffective because the Brothers served important new functions during the adjustment to rapid socioeconomic changes in the region. Lummis's rejoicing that the railroad tolled the death knell of the Brotherhood was premature.[10] Encroachment cemented solidarity and intensified the need for mutual aid, thus accentuating burgeoning rural-urban, *pobre-rico,* and Hispano-Anglo differences.

Popular Misconceptions of Penitente Political Involvement

From the earliest days of American occupation, exaggerated allegations of Brotherhood involvement in politics circulated throughout the Territory. Both Anglos and politically ambitious Hispanos were rumored to have undergone token initiation in order to secure a morada's vote as a solid bloc.[11] For example, two entries in W. G. Ritch's "Memo Book," marked 1850–78, suggest:

> Reputed members of the Penitenties—*The.° D. Wheaton* a lawyer, several times a member of the Legislature, lived variously at Santa Fe, Taos & Mora since the American occupation, & died in Mora Co about 1875. *LaFayette Head* at one time a member of the Legislature from Taos Co. and in 1877–78 Lt. Governor of the State of Colorado. Residence at or near Conejos. Rep. in politics. "Americans are accused of joining them for power & politics" Albuq. Rev. Apr 6/78.[12]

Most such speculations have yet to be substantiated.

The majority of the Brotherhood in New Mexico was traditionally supposed to have been Republican.[13] Rev. Darley claimed that Colorado was more heterogeneous, most of the Brothers east of the Sangre de Cristo Range being Democrats, and those to the west, Republicans.[14] However, no careful study has ever proved or disproved such popular notions.

The Presbyterian Darley is also largely responsible for publicizing an old anti-Catholic stereotype. The longstanding Protestant mistrust of priestly influence over parishioners in political matters was easily transferred to officials of the Brotherhood, and, according to Darley, " 'pull Padre pull Penitente' is a very simple political penance to get office."[15] Even Church officials often suspected the Brothers, and retired Archbishop Salpointe wrote that "their leaders encourage them, despite the admonitions of the Church, in the practice of their unbecoming so-called devotions, in order to secure their votes for the times of political elections."[16]

A 1901 incident in southern Colorado is typical of the confusion about the Brotherhood and its secular (as well as religious) concerns. The *Denver Post* printed an article in which J. R. Killian, a Walsenburg attorney, accused Juan Dios Montez, who lived nearby at Crestone, of keeping a harem "like the Sultan of Turkey" and heading a "strange religious sect" with male and female flagellants. Killian further charged that "several hundred votes are cast every year just as Montez directs, which is generally for the Republican candidate."[17] The *Denver Times* answered by labeling the charges "base libel" and exposing Killian's own machinations in Huerfano County politics, where he supposedly "sold out the Democratic party to the Republicans, for which he received many favors." The *Times* noted that Montez was a "governor" of "the order of Penitentes" but attributed his political influence to "personality and generalship," *not* Brotherhood membership.[18] A second article three days later denounced the *Post* report as "another cruel fake" and printed Killian's formal denial.[19]

The Brotherhood was of course only a part of the complicated Territorial political picture in New Mexico and an even smaller part of Colorado state politics. Popular misconceptions have nonetheless persisted well into this century, and they are unlikely to abate without serious and sensible case studies. Brothers' rights were and are those of any citizen of voting age. Candidates and party workers very likely sometimes used moradas as convenient meeting places to communicate (using the usual rhetorical methods) with an otherwise dispersed, remote, and often illiterate populace, *not* as centers for coercion and bribery of a "captive" bloc. Most rumors of Brotherhood political involvement were probably politically expedient ploys. The circumspect nature of the Brotherhood and its staunch refusal to publicize chapters or their charitable and religious aims unfortunately helped to intensify wild speculation and allegation.

The New Judiciary and the Brotherhood

Local justice was traditionally the province of the *alcaldes mayores* and their subordinates, the *teniente alcaldes.* During the late Spanish period, "by and large, judgment of the alcaldes, when it was not corrupted by personal interest or sheer malicious obstinacy, conformed to the prevailing customs of the country."[20] This system prevailed throughout the Mexican period.

Under the Kearny Code, the *alcaldes* became local justices of the peace. The Organic Act of 1850 set up a supreme court whose members, appointed by the President of the United States, also served as district court judges. At first, the governor appointed and/or confirmed county probate judges (prefects), county sheriffs, and local justices of the peace, who were later elected. Probate courts and informal proceedings presided over by justices of the peace were supposed to review and rule on minor cases, wills, and the like. Often, men who had served as Mexican alcaldes became Territorial justices of the peace.

During the Territorial period and before, judicial administration was not always adequate and effective. Local moradas often supplemented the official system with procedures to try and if necessary punish Brothers guilty of various offenses. Such proceedings have been described in both nineteenth- and early twentieth-century sources.[21] Sentences might include financial restitution, assigned self-inflicted penance, or punishments administered by other Brothers.

Outsiders seem rarely to have understood the important additional judicial functions the Brotherhood had traditionally filled. Misconceptions like those alleging untoward political involvement were rife. Most centered around the jury system. As early as 1878, an anonymous *Albuquerque Review* article claimed that "a jury empanelled to try a *Penitente,* if they also be of the order, will never convict, no matter how overwhelming the evidence."[22] In 1885, journalist Birge Harrison wrote that "there are twenty thousand Penitentes, and as they are mutually sworn to assist and protect one another, even to the extent of perjury, it will readily be seen what a formidable hydra the New Mexican judges have to deal with."[23] These were typical contemporary attitudes.

Such popular beliefs persisted into the twentieth century. In 1924, S. Omar Barker even cited a preposterous "case of a petit jury [which] so threatened, harassed, and intimidated the one juror who was not one of them [the Penitentes], that he became insane and remained so for several years as a result of it."[24] The story is

82

the sort of legend sometimes associated with the jury system anywhere; it is easily attached to any possible alliance of jurors. Because of their seemingly secretive association, the Brothers were an easy target in the Hispanic Southwest.

In some past cases apparently, a Brother tried in the courts had already been judged within the morada. Dorothy Woodward, who had personal contacts with prominent members of the state's legal profession, concluded in 1935 that "it is unquestionably true that Penitentes upon the jury of a case concerning a Brother abide by the action of the Brotherhood."[25] This was not a matter of conspiracy or subversion of justice but insurance that the miscreant not be placed in double jeopardy.[26] Malefactors were definitely called to account, but additional retribution was not always necessary in such cases as came before both Brotherhood and official judiciary proceedings.

Another misconception about the Brotherhood's code of conduct seems to have been common among both nonmember Hispanos and non-Catholics. This notion of "confess today, sin tomorrow" has long been a Protestant belief about Catholicism. It is illustrated by an entry among Ritch's early notes:

> Thieving and lawlessness, according to the statement of a Sheriff and translator, both Mexicans of a court held at Taos, during the time of Col. T. H. Hopkins (before Ch. J. Benedict) as acting Dist Atty and to him stated, Immediately following passion week among the penitenties and immediately following confession among other Mexicans, is the time more frequently than any other in which thieving, murder and crime generally may be expected.[27]

Local folklore to a certain extent perpetuated such attitudes about the Brothers in a frequently recited verse. Unsympathetic Congregational minister Rev. William E. Barton published a nineteenth-century version:

> The general testimony was that the average member is one who is pleased to do up his religion for the year in forty days. The Mexican people sing a mocking little couplet as to the self-inflicted penance:
>
> "Here's for the cow I stole,
> And this for the cow I intend to steal."[28]

Charles Fletcher Lummis also recorded a variant in 1888, and Fray Angelico Chavez uses a remembered version as the starting point for *My Penitente Land,* his spiritual autobiography and interpretation of Spanish New Mexico.[29] Traditional Hispanic as well as immigrant Anglo sentiment thus dealt with certain apprehensions about the Brotherhood and its affairs.

Notes on Judicial Matters

As in political matters, intensive specialized research would be required to ascertain the Brotherhood's actual relationship with the new Territorial laws and judicial process. Available fragments, assembled below as a chronological and heuristic series of notes, are merely indicative of local sentiment during the Territorial period and are by no means conclusive as to general patterns.

1850s: An unidentified item in Ritch reads simply: "1854 convicted of murder in Socorro Co."[30]

1860s: After the Civil War, the U.S. Army is supposed to have intervened in a San Luis Valley Good Friday observance to prevent the "murder" of a Cristo.[31] Bourke claims that most Army officers who served in the Southwest can remember incidents involving the Penitentes, but he does not say whether any were ordered to interfere.[32]

1875: On September 14, Rev. F. J. Tolby, a Methodist-Episcopal minister from Cimarron, New Mexico, was murdered some distance south of that town on the Elizabethtown road. Popular sentiment in Colfax County blamed the Santa Fe Ring, which was attempting to gain control of Maxwell Company land.[33] Somewhat later, Rev. Thomas Harwood, demonstrating Anglo readiness to attribute many criminal offenses to Penitente instigation, suggested another "motive" for the murder: that Tolby had testified aganst an Hermano Mayor, who in turn ordered a nephew and accomplice to assassinate the minister.[34]

1877: Frank Springer, a lawyer for the anti-Santa Fe Ring faction in Colfax County, filed an affidavit on August 30, charging that the 1876 annexation of Colfax to Taos County meant that Colfax cases would be tried by Taos juries largely composed of Penitentes "unfit" for such service.[35]

1880: Ritch notes: "1880 Ap A leader indicted for murder in Rio Arriba Merced Sanches . . . and subsequently acquitted."[36]

1881: A series of documents among the Adjutant General Papers in the New Mexico State Records Center and Archives record 1881 measures to impose order on lawless elements in the Farmington and Bloomfield areas of Rio Arriba County (San Juan County was not established until 1889). A militia headed by Captain William Bullock Haines was organized to implement indictments against various members of the Stockton gang of outlaws. Adjutant General Max Frost also appointed Haines to be jury commissioner, and the latter became irritated at the problems he encountered in Tierra Amarilla, the county seat. On September 27, he wrote Frost that "it is a decided fact here that no more prisoners will go to Tierra Amarilla, to be tried by Mexican penetentes (don't know if spelt right) & get off."[37]

1884: On March 27, Juan Romero of Cabezon, New Mexico, was killed by a gang of cattle rustlers from Cebolleta, led by Candido and Manuel Castillo. A posse tracked the Castillo brothers to Espanola on the night of Good Friday, April 11. Candido was mortally wounded. His body was secretly buried by the Penitentes, who also allegedly helped his brother Manuel escape apprehension.[38]

1898: On December 12, during a Taos fiesta honoring Our Lady of Guadalupe, two Anglos were arrested for not removing their hats as they watched the procession. They were jailed and later freed by the reportedly intoxicated sheriff, Luciano Trujillo. The sheriff then entered a predominately Anglo saloon, apparently threatened the crowd, and was shot. Trujillo died later, and a young man named Albert Gifford was blamed for the mortal wound. A marshal and deputies dispatched from Santa Fe returned on December 17, announcing that "race war" rumors had been unfounded, and that "the real state of affairs is that it was a conflict between whisky infuriated penitentes and the rest of the people in Taos." According to the authorities, "the procession was not one held by the church, but one by the penitentes, and the facts are that the strangers did take their hats off while the procession was passing, but because they saw fit to leave the street and replace their headgear before the rag-tag and bob-tail of the penitentes were out of sight, they were assaulted, insulted and thrown into jail by a drunken sheriff and his intoxicated deputies, all of whom are members of the penitente organization."[39]

The Penitentes were certainly not unique in their attempts to cope with the new administration. However, because they were secretive, organized, and Catholic, they became ready symbols for projected failures in the implementation of the new laws and jural procedures. Only an accurate picture of all the forces with which the American judicial system had to contend will reveal a more refined perspective on the Brotherhood's position.

Penitentes, Politics, and Protest in San Miguel County

At least two leaders of the Brotherhood in San Miguel County have attracted notice for their political involvements. Lorenzo Lopez is by far the better known of the two. Born in 1837, at San Jose, San Miguel County, Lopez was a well-to-do grazier who had married into the Eugenio Romero family, Republicans powerful in county politics. When he left the Republican Party in 1890, because of a bitter personal feud with Romero, Lopez "was one of the top two Republican *jefes* in the county, controlling, in [Thomas B.] Catron's estimation, four hundred votes directly, able to command a large following among the lesser *jefes* and *patrones,* and alternating with his in-laws in the most lucrative and influential offices in the county."[40] In an attempt to usurp Eugenio Romero's power, Lopez served as organizer and member of the County Executive Committee of El Partido del Pueblo Unido, and was elected sheriff, a position he earlier held as a Republican, on the new party's ticket in 1892.

Officially established in 1888, the San Miguel "People's party" quickly gained popularity and power due to reputed and actual affiliation with Las Gorras Blancas ("The White Caps"), secret groups organized to cut fences, burn haystacks, scatter stock, and generally to harass and intimidate outsiders encroaching on Hispanic communal landholdings.[41] When Lorenzo Lopez joined the People's party in 1890, Eugenio Romero and his followers accused Lopez and his group of an alliance with the White Caps.

> The Romero faction had even charged that Lopez and his new-found political friends were allied with the notorious Society of Bandits of New Mexico. Such a charge was unfair, since the Society of Bandits of New Mexico—or the Forty Thieves as it was often called—was nothing more than a group of desperados. . . . It represented neither third party nor pressure group, but rather was an instrument of the infamous Las Vegas Tavern owner Vicente Silva, who later killed his wife and brother-in-law and was himself slain by his associates. Murder was almost commonplace with the society.[42]

Although the charge of banditry was farfetched, the accusation of White Cap involvement was so commonplace that by 1891, *La Voz del Pueblo* editors complained that even two lovers quarreling were called White Caps![43]

Inevitably, the Penitentes were accused of threatening merger with the White Caps or themselves forming the backbone of the secret groups.[44] A letter dated April 19, 1890, from Severino Trujillo of Guadalupita, Mora County, to Governor L. Bradford Prince eloquently expresses the plight and confusion of even Hispanic victims of Las Gorras Blancas:

> There are some people around me, who belong to that sort of fellows who pass their life in idleness most of the time, but always on mischief, and they belong to the society of Penitentes. These took me in ill will, and put in their head to run me off the place. They have repeatedly tried to insult me in several ways. The parties who burned the hay me and my wife identified them very well, as we saw them that night around the stack, and I shot three times at them. I had the case investigated before the Justice of the Peace, and they were put under bond for their appearance before the District Court. They in the meantime claimed the help of the

politicians, who volunteered them their influence, evidently for the sake of their *votes*. I was informed by some of the respectable members of the Grand Jury, that an endictment was found against the parties, on the last term of the court in Mora County, but it would seem not because they have not yet been put under arrest.[45]

La Revista Católica, a staunch opponent of the Brotherhood, also directed a strong attack against the White Caps in 1891, and, on March 14, 1892, the *Albuquerque Citizen* was quoted in the *Santa Fe Daily New Mexican* as attributing Salpointe's February circular to a threatened merger of Penitentes and White Caps.[46]

Archbishop Salpointe's firm stand against the Brotherhood had much more to do with Lorenzo Lopez than with the by then declining White Caps. Lopez's obvious political success and his public display of apparent control over the Penitentes during the November 1 blessing of the Standard represented involvements incompatible with a purely religious society. Earlier that year, *La Voz del Pueblo* had belittled a rival paper's concern about Lopez's connections with the Brotherhood, maintaining that outsiders simply did not know the reasons for acceptance or rejection of potential members.[47] The archbishop, however, could not afford such blatant evidence of political and societal power. By 1894, it was apparent that at least some 433 Brothers could no longer tolerate the vicissitudes of San Miguel County politics either, and they announced their "self-vindication" in *La Voz del Pueblo* and the *Las Vegas Daily Optic.*[48]

Only coincidentally, 1894 was also the year of Brotherhood County Concilario Serafin Baca y Armijo's first imprisonment in the New Mexico Penitentiary. Sentenced to a one year term by Judge Thomas Smith of the Fourth District Court for "permitting prisoner to escape," the thirty-nine-year-old Baca, who had pleaded not guilty to the charges, served eleven months, with "good time allowed and *Out* Nov. 27, 1895."[49] At the time of his second incarceration, Baca was still or again served as president of the Council. The fifty-two-year-old Baca pleaded guilty to "larceny of horses," and Judge William J. Mills of the Fourth District Court sentenced him to three years in the penitentiary, a term commencing on December 23, 1907.[50]

On January 4, 1909, Governor George Curry received a letter

from Secundino Romero, Clerk of the Fourth District Court at Las Vegas. It reads:

> Friend Curry:-
>
> You will remember that I spoke to you about the pardon of Serafin Baca while you were here with Delegate Andrews during the campaign and we agreed that the matter should be left until after the election. Mr. Baca is very strong with the Penitente Element they agreed to stand by us and they fulfilled their promise. Mr. Baca's family have been supported during his absence by his son in law Mr. Frank M. King who died on the second of this month, and his friends are now asking me to come to the fulfillment of my promise. I hate to trouble you but under the circumstances I must appeal to you; Mr. Bacas family and that of Mr. King have been left in a state of misery and would ask you to see your way for Mr. Bacas pardon.
>
> With best wishes I remain,
>
> Yours very truly.[51]

Romero here refers to the general election of 1908, in which Republican William H. Andrews defeated Democrat Octaviano A. Larrazolo by 388 votes, to become New Mexico's delegate to Congress. Andrews, who had been elected Delegate in 1906 by a margin of 264 votes, carried San Miguel County by 704 votes in 1908. He had lost there to Larrazolo by 783 votes in 1906, so the promised pardon for Baca may well have proved crucial.[52]

In a letter to Captain John W. Green, Warden of the New Mexico Penitentiary, Curry states that "I did not promise Mr. Romero that I would pardon [Baca], but I did promise him that I would take the matter up and make a thorough investigation after the election. " He asks "my dear Captain" to "kindly let me know what Mr. Baca was sentenced for and what his conduct has been while a prisoner."[53] A letter of January 11, 1909, brought "My Dear Governor" the following reply:

> Regarding Serafin Baca, Convict No. 2235, he was sentenced from San Miguel County on Dec. 11th. 1907 to three years imprisonment for horse stealing, with good time allowence his time will expire June 10th. 1910.
>
> Old man Baca (as he is called here among the prisoners)

has been a convict of excellent conduct and has been a trusty, going to the Depots for freight and hauling lime and etc to the Capitol without any guard, he is an old man fifty-five years old and has very poor eyesight, if any leniency can be shown him I can cheerfully recommend him.[54]

Baca was pardoned on April 17, 1909. In December of that year, *The Santa Fe Eagle* somehow secured and reproduced a copy of a letter Baca had written from prison soliciting his Brothers' support for Andrews.[55] The newspaper's criticism of the governor seems rather futile, however, since Curry had already submitted his resignation to President Taft on October 25, 1909, and was serving only until February 28, 1910, after which time William J. Mills, the judge who had sentenced Baca, became governor.

San Miguel County was decidedly important in the Church's stand with regard to the Brotherhood, and it has certainly proved a vigorous center of political activity, whether connected with the Penitentes or not. Other strong Penitente counties were perhaps equally involved in Territorial politics and judicial process,[56] but public concern about Brotherhood power seems to have shifted from Taos to Mora and San Miguel Counties by the beginning of the twentieth century.

Adaptive Measures During the Territorial Period

Increased secrecy was a major protective reaction of the Brotherhood, especially after the Civil War. Although Brothers in Taos County were publicly incorporated in a Legislative Assembly act of 1861, by 1892, Archbishop Salpointe accused Penitentes from San Miguel, Mora, and Taos Counties of holding secret meetings and approving rules which embodied "the principles of Masonry a society which is condemned by the Church."[57] This is a very serious charge because, by virtue of various papal decrees, "no Catholic may join a Masonic lodge or affiliated organization without incurring excommunication reserved *simpliciter* to the Holy See . . . [depriving] him of the Sacraments, the spiritual treasures of the Church, Christian burial, and such rights as acting as a godfather in Baptism."[58] Since extant documents do not record an official statement branding the Penitentes as a secret society of the same order as Freemasonry, it is perhaps more accurate to refer to the Brotherhood as an increasingly secretive association.[59]

The custom of covering the penitent's head with a black hood to conceal his identity was often interpreted by outside observers as hiding from Church and civil officials, or even from employers. This practice has been traditional in almost all Spanish penitential confraternities, however, and stems from a conviction that public penance must be carried out anonymously and with humility. Even during the Mexican period, the Penitentes observed by Gregg in Tome "were completely muffled," although still recognizable to members of the community.[60]

Another custom is more difficult to trace. The nineteenth-century practice of tattooing a cross on the Brother's face is occasionally reported. Woodward mentions that this insignia of membership appeared on the chin or forehead, but most sources indicate the latter.[61] Unlike the incisions inflicted as a seal of obligation, which could be covered by a shirt, the facial tattoo would have been impossible to conceal. Such markings obviously had to be discontinued in the interests of privacy and continued affiliation with the beleaguered Brotherhood.

Anglo encroachment may have been more feared than clerical disapproval. By the end of the nineteenth century, rituals were more and more held in remote, inaccessible places. According to Ritch:

> The Penitentie *avoids close observation* especially, and orders away those who approach too close. This is true more especially in neighborhoods where there are many Americans. The thoughtless, idle or irreverent curiosity of the American makes the penitentie shy.[62]

This is clearly a religiously inspired reaction. To allow outsiders to observe was to risk disruption of the sacred bond generated by community participation in the public penitential rituals. Unfortunately, observers and would-be observers have too often attributed Brotherhood guards and irregularly scheduled processions to secular motivations, claiming that the Brothers were criminals and political subversives. This common misconception helped titillate scores of "Penitente hunters" over a number of years.

The Brotherhood's major adaptive measure during the Territorial Period was the organization of local moradas into larger, more effective networks. Although an 1853 booklet not now on the Microfilm Edition of the Archives of the Archdiocese of Santa Fe is supposed to record a "Union" of the Brotherhoods of Santuario de Esquipulas and of Cochiti,[63] the first definite proof of an early organizational structure comes from La Fraternidad Piadosa del Condado de Taos. The incorporation of this group was approved by the Legislative Assembly of the Territory of New Mexico on January 30, 1861, and constituted the first establishment of the Brothers "into a body politic and corporate, in law and in fact."[64] Darley had published a fragment of the constitution of this association, dated February 23, 1861, Don Fernando de Taos, and listing six *"secciones"* at Don Fernando de Taos, Ranchito, Rancho, La Placita, La Agua Negra, and El Arroyo Hondo.[65] Copies of the constitution and rules were to be communicated to moradas in the various plazas and Mora, in hopes of persuading others to join the union. The General Council which met at Mora on June 7, 1890, and later aroused Salpointe's ire may have grown from this early Taos incorporation.

Other networks in the nineteenth century were probably less formal. For example, three unions (*"tres unidades"*) in the Cochiti area were apparently united under Manuel de Jesus Hurtado, who refers to himself as *"hermano principal y concilario de hermandades"* in documents dated March 19, 1869, March 24, 1870, and April 8, 1871.[66] Details of this group are lacking, but it is likely a development of the 1853 union mentioned above, with the *"rezador"* now the *"hermano principal."* In any case, it doubtless typifies the sort of local association operant among moradas in the same vicinity, possibly even at the instigation of a priest. The Cochiti booklet contains references to Father Clemente Peyron and two pages written by him, so he may have encouraged the formalization.[67]

On February 11, 1880, the Legislative Assembly passed an act to provide for the incorporation of religious, benevolent, scientific, and literary bodies. The certificate stating name, objects, location, and term of existence had to be signed by five persons who were to appear publicly before a commissioner of deeds or notary public to file the document with the Secretary of the Territory. Other sections of the act specified the rights of and regulations for such "a body politic and corporate."[68] Dorothy Woodward lists several Taos benevolent societies which incorporated under the new law. Only the Catholic Brotherhood of Taos County, which filed its certificate December 14, 1881, had a board of trustees bearing titles similar to Penitente officers. The elective officials were "to-wit: Eldest Brother, Second Eldest Brother, Mayor Master of Novices, Mandatory, Treasurer, Infirmary and Arbitrator, trustees who are elected at the Regular election of said Society and their successors in office and Guillermo Trujillo, Antonio J. Vigil, Pedro Tenorio, Donaciano Gallegos, Tomas Trujillo, Jose Vicente Martinez, Abraham Sandoval and Prudencio Curse [Cruse?] all citizens of the United States and of the Territory of New Mexico are the names of the persons who shall be the trustees of said Association for the time from the date of this instrument to the last Monday of March, 1882 when their successors shall be elected."[69] Except for the provision for meeting halls, the stated purposes are identical with those in the 1861 act incorporating the Pious Fraternity, so this may be another Penitente group. More such incorporations as a result of the 1880 law may come to light when records from other counties become more readily available.

In any case, however secretive they became, and however strong their developing council structure, the Brothers were primarily concerned with charitable and religious activities. Nevertheless, they still provided ready targets for frustrated officials and eager journalists, as in the following newspaper article:

> It is well known that the practices of the Penitentes are cruel in the extreme; they are criminal, often ending in self-destruction and murder. They are subversive of all good government as the Penitentes usually stand together, regardless of all else, when one of their members runs for public office or is upon trial for violations of the law of the land.[70]

Such statements imply that it was somehow wrong for the Brotherhood, in many respects a "lobby" or "interest group" no more or less "subversive" than any other, to enjoy equal rights and means to the same constitutionally guaranteed ends. These attitudes are in clear contradiction to the Treaty of Guadalupe

Hidalgo and to basic American political ideals, as well as the principles of religious freedom. Such misconceptions persisted even after New Mexico had been granted statehood, and Hispanos had served the United States in World War I.

CHAPTER 4

The Brotherhood
in the Twentieth Century

Soon after statehood in 1912, New Mexico became decisively involved in the international and domestic fortunes of the United States. New Mexicans, a majority of them Hispanos and Indians, served in both World Wars, for many a first opportunity to leave their native areas. The first atomic bomb, produced by the secret Manhattan Project at Los Alamos in the Jemez Mountains northwest of Santa Fe, was exploded at Trinity Site, White Sands, New Mexico, on July 16, 1945.[1] Since that time, research into peaceful and military uses of nuclear energy has continued in the state, providing some new economic opportunities.

Although New Mexico's economy prospered during World War I, it declined sharply in 1919 and 1920, and still further during the drought of 1920–21.[2] The picture brightened somewhat until the nationwide devastation of the Depression was compounded in the state by another severe drought in 1931–34. By the mid-1930s, it was no longer possible to ignore the deplorable conditions which forced a substantial portion of the region's populace into state and federal relief programs. Wage labor elsewhere was curtailed, and traditional agricultural and pastoral subsistence patterns could not support the increased population on lands diminished both naturally and legally. As a result, "the various New Deal policies for recovery were vigorously pushed in the state, especially during the 1935–1938 administrations of Governor Clyde Tingley."[3]

Nevertheless, it was not until the Second World War that New Mexico's agricultural and industrial fortunes changed appreciably.

When Archbishop Edwin V. Byrne officially recognized the Brotherhood of Our Father Jesus of Nazareth on January 28, 1947, he sanctioned an organization which had undergone substantial changes during the first half of the twentieth century. Membership had declined markedly, but many chapters had incorporated and established effective councils to regulate and perpetuate the affairs of the Brotherhood. Although rituals were modified, the commitment to year-round acts of charity remained. Unfortunately, increasingly acute socioeconomic conditions, especially in rural areas, overtaxed the meager resources for such mutual and community aid. Fewer men joined or stayed in the Brotherhood after serving in the armed forces or migrating to urban areas, and remaining Brothers found it difficult to maintain their chapters as effective religious centers and social agencies.

Penitente Membership and the Changing Hispanic Populace

During the second half of the nineteenth century, it is probable that a large percentage of Hispanic males in New Mexico and southern Colorado retained Penitente ties. In 1910, Lee made the somewhat exaggerated claim that "only a few years ago, nearly every native in the Territory belonged to the order including the highest or controlling political class."[4] Mary Austin reports that in the 1920s, "a member of the Republican Committee estimated that practically ninety-five percent of the Spanish-speaking population of New Mexico had been *at sometime in their lives* members of the Penitentes."[5] An exact membership figure will never be known, but a sizable majority of Hispanic males definitely maintained moradas in most villages, at least until the early 1900s. From World War I on, mounting social and economic pressures caused members to withdraw, deterred others from joining, and generally undermined the chapters' effectiveness within the beleaguered communities.

Between 1900 and 1960, the population of the five southwestern states of California, Arizona, New Mexico, Colorado, and Texas increased 443 percent, as compared with 111 percent in the remainder of the nation. In 1900, Colorado ranked thirty-second in population, with 5.2 persons per square mile; New Mexico ranked forty-fourth, with 1.6 persons per square mile. By 1960, Colorado's population had increased 225 percent, ranking twenty-second in the nation, with 16.9 persons per square mile; while New Mexico had grown 338 percent, ranking thirty-seventh, with 7.8 persons per square mile.[6] During this period, New Mexico experienced its greatest gain in population, 67.9 percent, in the first decade of the twentieth century, and the second highest increase, 39.4 percent, from 1950 to 1960.[7]

One of the most significant factors in these dramatic population gains was the influx of non-Hispanos, most of whom had little regard either for traditional Hispanic customs or for the indigenous Indian cultures of the region. At the turn of the century, most of New Mexico's approximately 195,000 residents were native-born Hispanos. Immigration accelerated, and Holmes estimates that "as late as 1915, Spanish Americans numbered 57 percent of the state's total population and constituted 75 percent or more of the population of eleven counties—between 50 and 75 percent in three, and from 25 to 50 percent in four others of the state's twenty-six counties."[8] In 1940, not quite half of New Mexico's population was Hispanic, and "Winnie estimates that between 1940 and 1950, the population was increased by 50,780 Anglos and decreased by 31,680 Hispanos."[9] Later census figures indicate that Spanish-surname persons constituted 36.5 percent of New Mexico's population in 1950, and only 28.3 percent in 1960, having grown but 8.1 percent during the preceding decade. Spanish-surname individuals in Colorado made up 8.9 percent of the state's population in 1950, and 9.0 percent in 1960, growing 33 percent in ten years, largely in the urban counties of Denver and Pueblo.[10]

During the decades following World War I, the Hispanic population in the Southwest became increasingly urban, mobile, and poverty-stricken. New Mexico, for example, which had been only 15 percent urban in 1900, was 65.9 percent urban in 1960.[11] Drastic outmigration from rural areas, particularly after the start of World War II, is vividly illustrated by the fact that "while the United States and the State of New Mexico experienced a rate of growth of 84.0 and 190.6 percent between 1910 and 1960, respectively, the northern New Mexico counties showed a 3.5 percent gain (4,269 individuals)."[12] A diminishing percentage of those remaining in rural areas (of less than twenty-five hundred people) were Hispanic. According to the 1960 census, 31.2 percent of Colorado's Spanish-surname population was rural, and 42.4 percent of New Mexico's.[13]

Families with an income of less than three thousand dollars in 1959 were classified as poverty-stricken or "low-income" in the 1960 census. Spanish-surname families accounted for 13.8 percent of the poor in Colorado, and for a high 41.6 percent of all New Mexico's poor.[14] Much of this poverty strained rural communities. "Accounting for only 34.1 percent of the State's total population, rural areas included 49.3 percent of New Mexico's low income families in 1960."[15] Often traditionally supported by strong Penitente chapters, these areas had already been forced to turn to government relief programs during the Depression and drought of the 1930s and were decimated by postwar migration to population centers within the state and outside it. The Brotherhood could not continue to provide spiritual support or material security in the face of such overwhelming change.

In 1951, Rev. J. M. McKeon, editor of the official Archdiocesan newspaper, the *Santa Fe Register,* estimated, perhaps conservatively, that there were some eight hundred Penitentes in New Mexico.[16] After interviews with the late Hermano Supremo Arzobispal Miguel Archibeque, Holmes concluded that "estimates of the size of membership are far from precise, but the 1960 rosters probably included some two to three thousand members." He also noted that "in an interview in 1960, Don Miguel estimated that there were 400 members in the Walsenburg area of Colorado, and nearly 200 in Colorado's San Luis Valley."[17] Whatever the accurate figures, it is clear that even a 1960 membership of three thousand represents a small percentage of the 157,173 Hispanos in Colorado and the 269,122 in New Mexico, not all of them males, of course. While the Brotherhood was by no means extinct then, it had clearly declined dramatically from the nineteenth-century estimates of 85–95 percent of the entire Hispanic male populace.

Because local membership rosters remain secret, no reliable figures are available. However, Walter reports that the Sandoval,

New Mexico, group diminished from over a hundred Brothers in 1900 to about twelve in the early 1930s. The Penitentes' traditional August feast of La Porciúncula at Arroyo Hondo, New Mexico, attended by hundreds at the turn of the century, attracted less than thirty older people when Rael witnessed it in 1940. Montano describes a chapter in the Las Vegas area which had had about a hundred members, according to a roster dating from 1890. A new morada was built in 1910, and after World War I there were about sixty-five Brothers. In 1967, there were fifteen members, and in 1968, twelve—the oldest eighty-eight and the youngest twenty-one years old. Montano attributes the decline to political strife, a more mobile populace, the credulity of would-be Brothers who believe "tall tales" about Penitente practices, and the negative status Brotherhood membership has come to hold in the eyes of many who consider it "backward" and anachronistic.[18]

Protestant missionary groups also contributed to the decline in Penitente membership, as well as to some defection from Catholicism among various Hispanos in the region.[19] The Fundamentalists seem to have been most influential in the rural areas of northern New Mexico and southern Colorado. "The semiliterate Pentecostal missionary supporting himself by his own labor, preaching in Spanish, visiting and exhorting the village population, is in closer harmony with basic village values than either the English-speaking Catholic priest or the middle class Anglo Protestant missionary."[20] Converts to such sects came to be known as "Aleluyas."

Johnson identifies the Allelujahs proper as a part-Holy Roller movement which had its impetus in the conversion of a middle-aged shepherd, Isaaco Morfin, at Monticello, Utah, in 1930. "The fact seems to be that Morfin unknowingly touched a fundamental complex in his people, and his own identity has been completely overwhelmed in the spontaneous movement which resulted."[21] He describes the "drama of sin, repentance, and forgiveness," with its intense emotional expressions, including shaking and glossolalia, as basically attractive to the Catholic villagers, whether Penitente or not. By 1935, an appreciable number had joined the new churches. According to Swadesh's findings in the Chama River Valley and San Juan Basin:

In more recent periods of pressure and dissension, [the Brothers] have lost many more members to a variety of Protestant Evangelical sects lumped under the popular nickname, "Aleluyas," of which the Asamblea de Dios (Assembly of God, or Pentacostal [*sic*]) sect probably has the largest membership of former Penitentes. Some have also joined the Jehovah witness [*sic*], United Brethren and Baptist Churches, which have established pre-fabricated worship centers in a series of villages of northern New Mexico.[22]

However, the extent of such defections, whether among Brothers or nonmember Catholics, is not yet accurately documented.

The Brotherhood seems to have enjoyed limited renewals at various times in the early twentieth century. Austin "was told that the prevalence of the Influenza epidemic during last winter [early 1920s] increased the membership this spring and gave new life to the observances of Holy Week."[23] In a letter to his father written from Espanola, New Mexico, on March 21, 1920, W. B. Prince reports:

There have never been so many Penitentes. Most of the Mexican returned soldiers have joined. It seems that they made some sort of a vow after entering the army that if they were spared and not killed and returned they would do certain things.[24]

Similar vows or *promesas* could account for other wartime and postwar resurgences, even to this day. However, E. Boyd maintains that "at the end of World War II, many veterans who had enlisted as youths refused to join the Penitentes on their return home."[25]

Observers gathering data for the 1935 Tewa Basin Study discovered an unexplained increase in the Dixon, New Mexico, membership. "In recent years the Penitente Society has increased in size from 30 to 50 members, and they have divided into a sort of 'Old Guard' group and the younger progressive group."[26] If such "progressive" groups, presumably though not necessarily with less rigorous rites, emerged elsewhere, they too may have attracted new members.

On the whole, however, most extant moradas admit few novices. Remaining Brothers practice modified Lenten devotions approved by the Church and render such mutual and community aid as is within their very limited means. "Folksay insists that a few renegade groups persist in their old ways, but these will end with the death of their present members."[27] Most groups are reconciled with the Church and the approved Council structure after a long period of negotiation and modification.

Archbishop Daeger's Administration

Fr. Albert Thomas Daeger, O.F.M., was consecrated as the sixth archbishop of Santa Fe in the Cathedral on May 7, 1919. His appointment was hailed as the return of the Franciscans to the parroquia they founded and long sustained. Daeger faced a serious problem in the postwar lack of clergy. He recruited religious for parishes, schools, and hospitals from various orders. Further, "after many years of no native clerical ordinations, Archbishop Daeger ordained three New Mexicans from 1929 on: Fathers Jose A. Garcia of Santa Fe, Juan T. Sanchez of Tomé and Philip J. Cassidy of Mora."[28] The Archbishop died as a result of an accident on December 2, 1932.

Before his consecration, Daeger had worked in missions at Pena Blanca, in the San Juan Basin, and the Indian Mission of Jemez. He was familiar with and sympathetic toward the Penitentes at Pena Blanca and in the San Juan Basin, asking only that they conduct their exercises privately.[29] His attitudes seem to have remained consistent, judging from a newspaper account dated March 31, 1923:

> The church, he says, has looked upon the Society of Penitentes as a political organization. As far as doing penance is concerned, the church has no objection, he pointed out, to Penitentes or anyone else, flagellating themselves in private—in their homes or in their "moradoes." But the church forbids her children to make a public demonstration by such acts as carrying a cross, beating the flesh and crucifying. . . . Penitentes, or any other sect or organizations or persons who carry out these forms of public penance are denied the sacraments, the archbishop declared; they are violating the rules of the Catholic church and if they wish to remain practical Catholics they must give up these customs.

"The Roman Catholic church today advocates fasting as one of the excellent forms of penance," added the archbishop.[30]

In any case, Daeger did not take any decisive public actions regarding the Brotherhood. Church policy seems to have relaxed somewhat, leaving local priests fairly free to work out their own compromises. According to Woodward, after the end of Archbishop Daeger's term, "the present policy of the Church is to recognize any practicing Catholic, overlook Penitente connection, and through the influence of local priests to lessen penance practices and emphasize the purely pageant aspect of the devotion."[31]

An apparently successful compromise by a parish priest was reported by Rev. Emile Barrat of Costilla, New Mexico. In a letter to Mary Austin dated March 7, 1920, Father Barrat described a group of some three hundred seemingly "ideal" Penitentes at Pina, Cerro, Questa, and Costilla:

> The people belonging to the "moradas" . . . are here all practical Catholics. Nobody is allowed to join that is not a practical Catholic. The members pledge themselves to go to church every Sunday, when possible; no man divorced or married outside the church can belong to them. Every Lent every member has to go to his Easter duties. They are the best men in the community. During Lent they have special private practices of penance, consisting mostly of hymns in the honor of the passion of Christ, a most proper exercise for Lent, and some other "private exercises" in their own "meeting halls" directed by a serious sense of sincere faith and, by a long shot, less ridiculous than anything practiced in secret by our American "Masons" and other secret societies forbidden by the church.

Elsewhere in the letter, he indicates that his nonintervention is a sanctioned forebearance:

> Now we have orders from the authority not to bother them in their private practices in their "moradas" as no priest would bother you about what you do in your own private room, a free country you know. We all wish they would drop a few

Serafin Baca y Armijo, early Concilio leader in San Miguel County. *New Mexico State Records Center and Archives.*

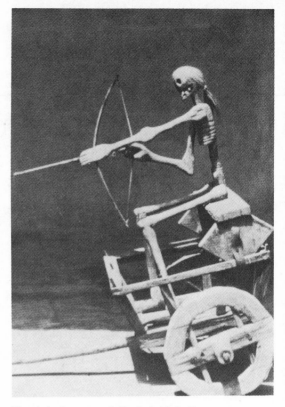

Death in her cart. *Collection of John B. McManus, Jr.*

Procession of cross bearers and Brothers of Light, ca. 1920s. *Collection of John B. McManus, Jr.*

Abandoned morada with rooms of adobe, wood, and stone. *Photo by Thomas R. Lyons.*

Morada with bell tower and storage loft. *Photo by Thomas R. Lyons.*

Morada with separate chapel (right) and meeting-house. *Photo by Thomas R. Lyons.*

Stone morada chapel. *Photo by Thomas R. Lyons.*

Brothers are joined by faithful from the community in a feast day observance, 1973. Note the Stations of the Cross (above) and the standard (below). *Photos by Thomas R. Lyons.*

Handmade Brotherhood standards, in a private chapel (left), and beside a morada altar (right). The initials stand for Fraternidad Piadosa de Nuestro Padre Jesús de Nazareno. *Photos by Thomas R. Lyons.*

Morada chapel. *Photo by Thomas R. Lyons.*

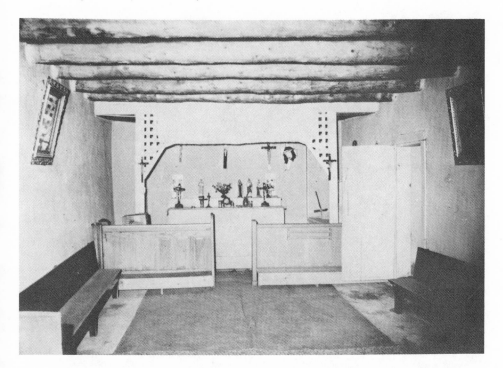

Maderos stored beside a morada. *Photo by Thomas R. Lyons.*

Calvario. *Photo by Thomas R. Lyons.*

Maderos stored beside a log storage room. *Photo by Thomas R. Lyons.*

Morada with Our Lady of Guadalupe on front wall, set in cemetery. *Photo by Thomas R. Lyons.*

Morada and Calvario. *Photo by Thomas R. Lyons.*

Morada in town. *Photo by Thomas R. Lyons.*

Brotherhood leaders stand before the standard of the Archbishop's Supreme Council at the organization's annual meeting in Santa Fe. The first Hermano Supremo Arzobispal, the late Miguel Archibeque (then a Director) is on the right, the third (and present) Hermano Supremo Arzobispal, M. Santos Melendez, on the left. *The New Mexico Register,* June 18, 1965.

antiquated customs, but we cannot change the world in one day. We have patience with sincere men, and we know with the 20 centuries experience of the church that all men of good will shall be some day facing the truth they have been looking for and be saved.[32]

Father Barrat also publicly defended his parishioner Brothers in an article for *The Southwestern Catholic*. Here, he is quite candid about the "few antiquated customs":

> The "moradas" are now under the benign influence of the Church and are on their way to more perfection. Modern crucifixes, banners and statues are replacing the old, ugly, antiquated, wooden scarecrows. The singing still is to be "brought down" to the modern rules of music.
>
> The only abuse that still exists is that in the missions: the Penitentes take charge of all the funerals and bury the dead according to their own ritual, even in the presence of the pastor, who sits "boiling mad" in the sacristy. But why get mad? "Argue, insist, scold in all science and doctrine," until the custom disappears little by little. . . . These men are serious, profoundly religious, sincere in their humble faith. Indeed, if anybody would try to touch the faith of their families, I believe they would eat him up. In the missions, in spite of a few abuses and antiquated customs, they are the defenders of our faith, and for that reason alone a good deal should be tolerated and we can afford to close our eyes on a few things that look queer to Christians of the East.[33]

These sentiments exemplify many longstanding attitudes of the French clergy toward the Hispanic Catholicism they found in the Southwest.

Rev. Peter Kuppers of Chaperito, New Mexico, likewise contributed a defense of the Penitentes to the same issue of *The Southwestern Catholic*. In his refutation of a sensationalized article in the *Literary Digest* entitled "Uncle Sam's Medieval Citizens and Their Passion Play," Kuppers rails against the notion that the Brothers are not good citizens and good Catholics. He claims them to be no more secret than the Knights of Columbus, who allow a priest to know their activities but resist other attempts to pry.

According to Kuppers, most of the information first given him about the Brotherhood was erroneous, so he set out to discover the truth. He concludes that the Penitentes rightly avoid publicity, which is usually prejudicial and slanderous. "And we, for our part, as Catholics and Americans, are proud of these splendid people that regard the Passion of Christ not as an object of theatrical diversion or buffoonery, but to be held in sacred remembrance of our Lord Savior, who was crucified and died on the cross for the sons of humanity."[34]

Other churchmen were more reluctant to defend or tolerate the Brothers. Austin notes one instance:

> The following songs were copied from a book loaned me by an Hermano Mayor of Truchas, who said that he had been obliged to leave the Order because the priests had two counts against him: 1. That he belonged to the Penitente Order. 2. That he sent his children to the Presbyterian Mission School. To please the priest he gave up being a Penitente, as he thought it more important to keep his children in a good school.[35]

A second example comes from Fr. Zephyrin Engelhardt, O.F.M., a Franciscan scholar from Santa Barbara, California. He objected strenuously to the publication of Lee's thesis, maintaining that all Hermanos Mayores should be incarcerated and themselves whipped.[36] In an article for the *Franciscan Herald* entitled "Franciscans in New Mexico," he hastened to explain the fervent penitential spirit of Brother Pedro de Vergara, a lay brother who accompanied Oñate's party into New Mexico in 1598, in much the same terms the Jesuit Inigo Deane and the Sister of Charity Blandina Segale had used in the nineteenth century:

> Catholics know that such extraordinary mortifications as were practiced by Brother Pedro, are not prescribed; that they are not even permitted, neither in private nor much less in public, without the approval of the ecclesiastical authorities, whose duty it is to decide whether the Holy Spirit or some bad spirit prompts such singular penances; and that *of themselves* such penitential works of this nature forgive no sin, and are without value for eternity. Here is the essential

difference between the mortifications practiced by the saints of God or those who aspire to Christian perfection, and the tortures inflicted upon themselves by the fakirs of East India, the fanatical Mussulmen, or the scarcely less fanatical and ignorant Penitentes or degenerate Tertiaries of New Mexico. These misguided people imagine themselves sanctified after undergoing various unapproved, self-imposed corporal castigations.[37]

Although not a local resident, Engelhardt's opinion as a scholar and a Franciscan was likely of some influence in the Archdiocese of Santa Fe while Daeger was archbishop.

The Brotherhood seems on the whole to have enjoyed both a limited resurgence of membership and a reasonable official Church tolerance in the years following World War I. In this respect, an uncorroborated item is notable. Grant claims that "during the summer of 1924 there was sent out a command from the yearly council that there should be no scourging in public, unless it be done in the small hours of the night when no one is about."[38] This official Brotherhood action, presumably from the Taos Council, may have resulted from generally amicable relations with the Franciscan archbishop.

Archbishop Gerken's Decade and the Carl Taylor Murder

The apparent good will between Church and Brotherhood under the Franciscan regime was severely tested early in Archbishop Gerken's administration by the sensational nationwide publicity following the murder of journalist Carl Taylor on February 5, 1936. Although the Penitentes were wrongly implicated, the archbishop's reluctance to recognize the embryonic Supreme Council probably stemmed in large part from this unfortunate incident.

Rudolph Aloysius Gerken was named the first bishop of Amarillo in 1927. In 1933, he was promoted to the Archdiocese of Santa Fe and consecrated as its seventh archbishop on August 23 of that year. During his ten-year term, the archdiocese was reorganized geographically and administratively. "With him began the 'American way' of church administration in the Archdiocese, the Daeger administration having been but a transition period from the old 'French way.' "[39] Earlier, in 1914, the Diocese of El Paso, which includes part of western Texas and the southernmost New Mexico counties, had been erected and made a suffragan see of the metropolitan see at Santa Fe. In 1939, the Diocese of Tucson, a suffragan see since 1897, was reassigned to Los Angeles, California, and the Diocese of Gallup, including northern Arizona and northwestern New Mexico, erected as a suffragan see of Santa Fe. The province was further restricted in 1941, when the Archdiocese of Denver was erected, with the Diocese of Pueblo as one of its suffragan sees. This meant that the Province of Santa Fe came to embrace New Mexico, northern Arizona, and a small part of western Texas before Archbishop Gerken's death on March 2, 1943.

Indications of Archbishop Gerken's stand with regard to the Brotherhood are scant in presently available sources. A note in *El Palacio* announcing that Col. Jose D. Sena was cataloguing the Archives of the Archdiocese of Santa Fe at Gerken's request contains the following item:

> An example is the rules promulgated by Archbishop Gerken. In some cases, notably in Socorro, the [y are] translated into English. It states officially the church's attitude toward the practices of Los Hermanos.[40]

It is possible that the editor mistakenly identified Lamy's or Salpointe's rules as Gerken's, but the archbishop certainly had reason to consider action regarding the Brotherhood, since he had already been approached by Brothers anxious to effect a reconciliation with the Church.

Published sources disagree regarding the details of this early Supreme Council, headed by Don Miguel Archibeque. Holmes, who interviewed Archibeque in 1958 and 1960, claims that "the office of *hermano supremo* was established in 1936 when, with the assent of Archbishop Gerken, several members seeking to bring the organization under the sanction of the church designated Don Miguel Archibeque of Santa Fe to assume such a post."[41] According to Hogue, Archibeque told her in early 1970 that "when

Archbishop Gerkin came to Santa Fe, Miguel asked that the Brotherhood be recognized by the church [and] Gerkin ordered him to leave his presence immediately."[42] The 1970 interviews, when Archibeque was eighty-six years old, probably exaggerated Gerken's reaction, which may well have been adversely influenced by news of Taylor's killing.

Free-lance journalist Carl N. Taylor had been living in a mountain cabin near Cedar Crest in the Sandia Mountains while completing an article about the Penitentes. Earlier, he had traveled in the Philippines, where he witnessed flagellant rites and described them in *Odyssey of the Islands*.[43] His New Mexican venture was prompted by this experience.

Taylor was assaulted and then shot twice on Wednesday night, February 5, 1936. Friends immediately attributed the slaying to the Penitentes because of a letter mailed to his literary agent, Roy De S. Horn:

> Last night I made 3 flashlight exposures within a Morada —something I don't think has ever been done before. I'm praying over those, for there will never be a chance to repeat the performance.[44]

According to the *Albuquerque Journal* report of February 7, "Taylor's publisher and literary agent in New York, told the Associated Press Thursday that they were not entirely convinced that robbery was the sole motive in the crime and that Taylor may have been the victim of some strange Penitente plot." Raymond Morley, editor of *Today Magazine,* for which Taylor had completed his Penitente story, quoted the portion in which Taylor mentions that his houseboy had aspirations to become the annual Cristo.[45] Someone even suggested a Filipino penitente had committed the crime!

Investigation and questioning of Taylor's houseboy, Modesto Trujillo, elicited a confession from the fifteen-year-old youth. Robbery was the apparent motive. On Monday, February 17, Trujillo was sentenced by Judge Fred E. Wilson to ninety-nine years in the state penitentiary. District Attorney Thomas J. Mabry announced that his investigation showed conclusively that the Penitentes "had nothing to do with the murder."[46]

Despite Mabry's announcement, the story was never retracted nationally. Newspapers across the country had already transformed the crime into the ghoulish act of bloodthirsty blood brothers. Sample headlines read:

"Youth Confesses Killing, Absolving 'Torture' Cult" (*New Haven Evening Register,* February 6)

"Boy Scout Says He Killed Writer" (*New York Times,* February 7)

"Brutal Murder of Wandering Writer Unveils Weird New Mexico Torture Cult Rites He Was About to Expose" (*The Cleveland News,* February 8)

"Boy's Confession in Killing of Writer Fails to Calm Cult Vengeance" (*New York American,* March 1)

Magazine writers also capitalized on the sensation, one speculating "how a backward people could be so happy and harmless and indolent, on the surface, and yet have religious emotions capable of being whipped up to the frenzy of a mad dog."[47] The murder was a windfall for the pulps and the papers.

A so-called documentary movie was also made from the case. The full text of Governor Clyde Tingley's letter of protest to Mr. Will Hays, chairman of the National Board of Censorship in Hollywood, California, reads as follows:

> As Governor of New Mexico, I desire to protest the approval (if it has been approved) of your Board of the motion picture "The Penitente Murder Case", which had its premiere in San Francisco last week.
>
> I have been told that it is being advertised as a factual presentation of the Carl Taylor murder case. As a matter of record, Taylor's murder had nothing to do with Penitentes, and the motive was robbery, not religion.
>
> I have been told also that advertisements show nude women being lashed by flagellants and are shown standing at a cross in the attitude of crucifixion. If the advertisements are an indication of what the picture itself is like it is a libel on the State of New Mexico and on the penitenties and is an appeal to cheap sensationalism.
>
> The picture will be banned in New Mexico if I have to make use of my police powers to prevent it.[48]

There is no further correspondence relating to this travesty, nor has the exploitation of the case ceased. In 1969, a journalist, claiming to be a friend of Taylor, presented his own version of the "story" and asserted that "it has been rightly said that even Klaus Fuchs, the Rosenbergs and others who betrayed the atomic secrets of Los Alamos would have been afraid to tamper with the soul-shattering secrets of the black-hooded, naked flagellants who enact a sacrament of torture, agony and death each Easter and then soak the New Mexico soil with the blood of their 'Christ.' "[49]

After such an avalanche of unfavorable publicity, it is no wonder that Archbishop Gerken refused to sanction the Brotherhood. Toward the end of his administration, however, he had begun to modify his views:

> Fr. Clarence Schoeppner, chancellor of the archdiocese of Santa Fe, said the late Archbishop Rudolph A. Gerken had come to "think quite a good deal of the Penitentes," pointing out that the prelate had blessed one of their moradas in a village near Las Vegas about a year ago.
>
> "There used to be abuses," Fr. Schoeppner said, "but they have all been corrected. The Penitentes are a strictly fraternal-religious organization, not in conflict with the church, but on the contrary, staunch supporters of the church."[50]

This modified stance was likely the result of Archibeque and other Brothers' ongoing work.

There are few indications of the Colorado clergy's relationship to the Brotherhood. Beshoar records the 1921 incorporation of Council No. 1, Long's Canon, Las Animas County, Colorado. "This group then elected the Rt. Rev. J. Henry Tihen, the late Bishop of Denver, as instructor of the Council, and asked him to designate Father Stefano Bueno (Stephen Good) 'whom we consider well posted in the history and affairs of the fraternity,' as his assistant, to give the actual instructions." Tihen's letter to Father Bueno contained but one caution:

> The constitution or by-laws you send have no objectionable features that I perceive and upon your suggestion and in view of approval given by former bishops I am ready to give my placet. If the original rules contain no reference to parish priest and the deference due him it might be well to safeguard his authority to an extent at least, but not to the extent of suppression and disbanding the order.[51]

The Colorado ecclesiastical authority was seemingly more ready to accept the Brothers, perhaps because they were fewer in number and less well known in the state at large. Charles W. Hurd notes the same leeway in local interpretations of the formal Church stand as occur throughout New Mexico:

> Most of the Penitentes continue with their membership in the Catholic church and regularly attend its services. They are privileged to do so, but they are exorted by the priests to not carry their Penitente activities to excess, to not exceed the bounds of reason and to not suffer bodily injury. When an individual fails to heed these warnings, and persists in doing body injury to himself, or others, as recently occurred at Walsenburg, the Priest puts the bans upon him and he is cut off from certain of the church privileges until he reforms.[52]

Apparently, then, the same formal stand, adamant in its distrust of traditional penitential practices and inadequate priestly supervision, continued to be informally interpreted and applied at local levels in both New Mexico and southern Colorado.

Archbishop Byrne and the Sanctioned Supreme Council

Edwin Vincent Byrne, a native of Philadelphia who had served in the Philippines and Puerto Rico, was consecrated as the eighth archbishop of Santa Fe in June 1943. Approached almost immediately by the indefatigable Don Miguel Archibeque and several others, the new prelate was amenable to rapprochement with the Brothers, provided a suitable organization could be established and agreement reached about modification of penitential rites. At their own expense, the leaders renewed efforts to obtain the consent of chapters in New Mexico and southern Colorado.[53]

On February 19, 1946, Archbishop Byrne wrote Archibeque approving an official book of rules.[54] However, not all groups were agreeable to the Church requirements, and some still maintain their autonomy. In an interview with Holmes, Archibeque claimed he had the consent of about two-thirds of the Brotherhood, some 125 moradas, but the Archbishop demanded unanimity.[55] Nevertheless, Byrne was finally persuaded to grant Church recognition to the Brothers.

The official statement recognizing the Brothers of Jesus of Nazareth was signed on January 28, 1947. Fray Angelico Chavez, historian and poet, helped draft the document.[56] The text, which was published in the official newspaper of the archdiocese, the *Santa Fe Register,* was prefaced with the following tribute and statement:

> Through the admirable zeal and edifying sacrifices of Miguel Archibeque and other members of the association its affairs have been so arranged that the Archbishop feels confident in being able to use the good offices of its members for the progress and welfare of the Catholic Church in New Mexico. Certain elements which have caused disedification and trouble will be removed from the society. And all its members will give proof of being docile and respectful parishioners of their respective pastors.[57]

The main points of the statement involve correction of the long-standing areas of dissension: political involvement, public and injurious penances, and the lack of priestly supervision. An official Archbishop's Supreme Council had been formed in 1946, to direct the several district councils, and Don Miguel Archibeque was appointed the first Hermano Supremo Arzobispal.

In a 1952 interview with John Curtis of the Associated Press, Archibeque stated that there were forty-five Church-recognized moradas in Rio Arriba County, thirty-two in Taos, thirty in Mora, nine in Santa Fe, five in San Miguel, and scattered ones in Sandoval, Colfax, Harding, and Guadalupe Counties. Those outside the Supreme Council's jurisdiction included five in Rio Arriba County. Archibeque is quoted as follows: "I believe that the Penitentes should limit their activities to penance and prayer. I thank the Lord that I have been very successful in bringing that about. I fought to get the Penitentes completely out of politics and make them a purely religious organization. In that also I believe we have been successful." Curtis reports Archibeque "said members are told to exercise their rights as citizens by participating in politics as individuals; but they are not asked to take political action as a group under any political leader."[58]

111

In 1958, a limited edition of *The Way of the Cross: A New Mexico Version,* edited by Reginald Fisher, was published in Santa Fe. It contained the Via Crucis service and four traditional Penitente *alabados.* Archbishop Byrne and Dr. Fisher presented an inscribed copy of this portfolio to Archibeque, who had assisted in its preparation. A translation of the inscription reads: "For Don Miguel Archibeque . . . in appreciation of the important role his Brotherhood has had in the development and preservation of this beautiful expression of the true vocation of New Mexico Spanish people."[59]

Archbishop Byrne died on July 25, 1963. Saddened Brothers came to Santa Fe to join the many who paid him tribute.[60] Archbishop James Peter Davis, transferred from Puerto Rico, was consecrated as the ninth archbishop of Santa Fe on February 25, 1964, a position he held until his resignation a decade later.

Political Involvement

Archbishop Byrne's 1947 statement expressed concern that certain moradas had made themselves a "political football." It is possible that he was referring to events in San Miguel County during the preceding year. In publicity surrounding the lawsuit between a newly incorporated and an established council, the former was alleged to be Democratic and anxious to acquire power within the Brotherhood and the county. These allegations were never publicly substantiated, but the split between groups of Democrats and the traditionally Republican moradas apparently had precedent within the county:

> Several chapels were called the "Cherry moradas" for sharing with Cherryvale a strong Democratic attachment. Other chapels were fostered by adherents of the Cutting Progressive faction and ultimately came to favor the Democratic cause. In consequence, many villages had two moradas.[61]

Whatever the case, the archbishop's admonition emphasized the possibilities for abuse of pious associations which continued to threaten the ecclesiastical hierarchy of the chronically impoverished and understaffed archdiocese.

112

Such concerns prompted an important theme in Rev. Emile Barrat's defense of the reformed Penitentes in his Costilla parish and missions:

> They used to belong to the political center of Taos. These last years, all the Penitentes of the Parish united together in one great Catholic organization, from which is excluded all political influence. Politics may not be mentioned in their meetings. The members must be practical Catholics exclusively. . . . Any member mentioning politics is expelled without pity. . . . If a politician would try to get around these people nowadays he would be fooled.[62]

Implicit in Father Barrat's disclaimer are at least three popular notions: (1) that a morada's vote was easily manipulated and "deliverable"; (2) that the Penitente vote was invariably Republican; and (3) that the Brotherhood's vote was overwhelmingly powerful. In a salutary study of Penitente political activity in San Miguel County, Holmes concluded that "much more likely is the proposition that the Penitente precincts comprised a vote large enough, and variable enough, to make them a marginal factor critical in the election strategies of both parties."[63]

Political leaders and aspirants had to work for the Penitente vote, perhaps using the morada as a convenient meeting hall for bargaining, discussion, and rhetoric. The negotiations involved were by no means as simple as outsiders fancied. Three gashes on a candidate's back did not assure him a bloc vote, despite numerous anecdotes such as the one Austin recounts:

> Speaking of a man very high in public office, highly educated and a radical in politics, I said to a member of the State Legislature, "Surely he isn't a Penitente!" "So he pretends," said the Legislator, "but I have been in swimming with him!" meaning that he had seen on the politician's bare back the three scars of initiation.[64]

Similar tactics were attributed to Bronson Cutting, New Mexico's United States Senator from 1927 to 1935. "Senator Cutting, as late as the 1930's, helped to obtain the support of the Spanish-Americans by condoning Penitente practices and attending their rites as one of the group."[65] Nonetheless, Holmes's provocative research in his chapter on the "Political Acculturation of Hispanic New Mexico" demonstrates a sophisticated, competitive political system at all levels, including the local, where "it appears that the typical precinct was probably one in which the precinct chairman of each party worked hard at his business."[66]

Woodward suggests that a statewide organization existed by 1935:

> From a reputable source the information was secured that a definite political organization now exists among the lodges of the state. They send representatives to meet together, usually in early August, and there determine their political course. This is all done without show, since secrecy overshadows the entire society in their politics as well as their religion.[67]

A widespread network seems unlikely at that time, but county council meetings were probably a matter of course, with political discussions perhaps a regular part of the proceedings. While this may have violated the strict ecclesiastical definition of pious associations, it was certainly a legitimate involvement for concerned citizens of the United States. The ambiguities between religious and secular rights and duties have never been easily resolved. Until there is more decisive evidence available, the Brotherhood's attempts to solve this longtime problem cannot be assessed.

Secular Protection for the Penitentes

By the end of World War I, the Penitentes had become a regular stop on tourist itineraries and an inevitable highlight in regional travelogues. For example, a Couriercar publication distributed to passengers on the Santa Fe Chief train prepared the traveler for the Southwest's marvels. Entitled *Hitting the High Spots,* it notes that "If Your Time's Your Own," in March, you can see "Good Friday. . . . The Flagellation of Los Penitentes (N.M. only)." This page faces one headed "And What to Wear." On at least one occasion, at Chamita in 1933, about a hundred persons who solved the problem of what to wear to a flagellation paid about a dollar to witness a fake Penitente procession. "This was done by non-

Penitentes, usually younger men and boys and was considered a great lark."[68] The Brothers attempted to protect themselves from such travesties, which were relatively infrequent. However, it became increasingly difficult to protect honest rituals from irreverent intruders.

In 1924, Mary Austin wrote that "a year or two ago, on the day of the Assumption of the Virgin when I had gone into the little chapel at Fernandez de Taos to pray, with full courtesy of the brotherhood, a party of curiosity-mongers undertook rudely to force their way in after me, with the result that there were pistol-shots exchanged and a narrow escape from a tragedy."[69] A similar incident in 1931 prompted action by Judge M. A. Otero, Jr., Justice of the First Judicial District Court in Santa Fe. The *Santa Fe New Mexican* applauded the Judge's warning:

> It is reliably reported that several carloads of callow youths parked their autos close up against a morada or Penitente chapel at the settlement of Hernandez the other night, commenced making merry and that when a group of natives appeared and asked them what they were doing, one bright boy drew a revolver and discharged the same in the general direction of the residents. "Penitente chasers" are forming the habit of making a Roman holiday out of the Easter week observances of this religious sect and it is growing worse year by year.
>
> The action of the district court here in warning that a law will be invoked which protects religious rites from disturbance is commendable in the interest of peace and order, because the molestation of or interference with these people by jeering or merely curious sightseers is bound to lead to serious trouble, if not tragedy.[70]

Judge Otero wrote Dorothy Woodward explaining his decision:

> There is nothing much to say except that it is a matter of general knowledge that for a long time these people have been subjected to a great deal of annoyance and interference by curious persons anxious to see them engaged in their religious practices. The Penitentes complained to me that they did not object to having people come around to watch

115

them if they did so in a respectful way, but what they did object to was having people come around their morada and flashing automobile search lights on them and laughing at them and in other ways making themselves obnoxious. Their complaint seemed to me to be very just indeed, and consequently I requested the Sheriff of Rio Arriba County to deputize a number of people whom the Penitentes themselves recommended to see to it that Section 35-4606 of the Code was complied with. This was done, and the Penitentes themselves seemed quite satisfied with it.[71]

Beshoar notes that sheriffs in Colorado also frequently deputized Penitente guards so they could keep unwelcome onlookers at a distance.[72]

Although Brothers were able to police their rituals with some success, their chapels eventually became vulnerable to vandals and burglars. As Hispanic folk art came to be appreciated and to increase steadily in monetary value, moradas, especially those in secluded locations, became the target of art thieves. Such robbers were very active in the early 1970s. A dramatic announcement on November 28, 1972, reported the recovery of seventy-six religious artifacts stolen by "persons who burglarized more than 23 moradas and chapels in the area" over a two-year period.[73] Measures are being taken to safeguard all religious structures from such desecration in the future.

Conclusion

The history of the Penitentes in the twentieth century is characterized by persistent adaptation in the face of profound socioeconomic change, and a cautious but increasing candidness. Still, certain elements seem unchanged. Public releases from Church and state are superficially similar to those from the Territorial period on. During Holy Week of 1970, in an Associated Press release explaining the "new mass" then being introduced, Archbishop James Peter Davis is quoted as saying: "Some of them in this area have gone overboard in being penitential during Holy Week. . . . For instance, the Penitentes (a cult in northern New

Mexico) are an example of this."[74] Century-old political insin-
uations are suggested by an announcement from the governor's
office, also released by the Associated Press:

> Gov. David Cargo and movie-television star Burl Ives at-
> tended Good Friday Penitente ceremonies in northern New
> Mexico and were allowed to enter a morada, the religious
> lodge of the group.
>
> The religious group of rural northern New Mexico, often
> surrounded by mystery and the subject of legends going back
> several centuries, rarely allow a nonmember or an anglo into
> a morada.
>
> Cargo said he and Ives attended a ceremony and procession
> Friday morning in the village of Cordova, where they were
> allowed into the morada.[75]

The governor also reported he had been to Penitente services in
Las Trampas and Truchas.

The 1970 census figures showed that in a total New Mexico
population of approximately 1,016,000, some 407,286 persons,
about two-thirds of them in urban areas, were of Hispanic
heritage. At the time of Don Miguel Archibeque's death on June
16, 1970, the Hermano Supremo Arzobispal, Mr. M. Santos
Melendez, of Mora and Albuquerque, estimated that there were
approximately 1700 Brothers in New Mexico and southern Colorado.[76] While this figure indicates a continued decline in membership, the tributes to Archibeque and the dignified public solemnity
of his funeral belie the apparent numerical insignificance of the
Brotherhood. Its spiritual significance remains considerable.

On July 25, 1974, Robert Fortune Sanchez was ordained in
Albuquerque as the tenth archbishop of Santa Fe, the first prelate
of Hispanic descent. Perhaps during his administration more
religious men will come to feel a spiritual need for affiliation with
the continuing but changing Brotherhood of Our Father Jesus.
Perhaps, too, all people will realize again the faith and community
which are the enduring and important legacy of the Penitente
Brothers.

PART III
Brothers of Our Father Jesus

Recuerda si estás dormido,
Deja de vivir atroz
porque el vivir divertido,
Hombre, has olvidado a Dios.

Recuerda del año y mes
y el día de tu promesa
Engañaste a Jesucristo
Juraste con ligeréza.

Como fuistes engañado
Hombre dispierta y advierta
Entre las horas del dia
Te asercas mas a la muerte.

Si de esa suerte comienzas
Sin llegarte a comulgar,
Como puedes alcanzar
El don que el Señor te ofrece.

Vuelve, vuelve pecador,
Vuelve, vuelve arrepentido;
Vuelve a la casa de Dios
En pos de Cristo tu Amigo.

Allí recibirás la gracia
Y el Sacramento divino,
Mira a Cristo en esa mesa
Hombre ingrato, entretenido.
        Fin Amen

—Transcribed from a Rio Arriba County
Penitente's notebook by Lorin W.
Brown for the New Mexico W.P.A.
Writers' Project, ca. 1938.

CHAPTER 5

The Council Organizations

The formal structure of the Brotherhood of Our Father Jesus has generally been ignored or misconstrued. Moradas are described as independent, unsophisticated, localized groups. Although officials and rituals definitely vary from chapter to chapter, various associations of chapters have been formed at least since the early days of the Territory and possibly before. The Brotherhood could not have survived otherwise. Inter-morada councils facilitated considered corporate decisions on matters involving the aims of the Brotherhood and infringements on its religious freedom. Governing council officials administered internal affairs and executed Brotherhood policies. When the Concilio Supremo Arzobispal was established in 1946, most of these existing bodies were organized into a network of district councils headed by an Hermano Supremo directly responsible to the archbishop.

Twentieth-Century Councils

Legislation affecting Brotherhood corporations, considered fraternal and not fraternal benefit societies, was passed in 1901, 1921, and 1923.[1] Like the 1880 regulations, later acts stipulated filing procedures and "the powers, rights, and duties of such corporations." As a result of these laws, some Brotherhood councils were registered with the Office of the Secretary of the Territory of New Mexico and later with the State Corporation Commission of New Mexico.

A partial list of such twentieth-century corporations follows:

The Brotherhood of Our Father Jesus of Nazareth, of the County of San Miguel, Territory of New Mexico

Certificate of Incorporation sworn to on November 25, 1901, and filed as no. 2985 (vol. 5, p. 179) on January 13, 1902, for fifty years.

Principal place of business: Sheridan; with directors listed as residing in Las Vegas, Sheridan, Penasco Blanco, Las Torres, Gallinas, Chaperito, and Tecolote. Seventy members attended the organizational meeting and voted in the election.

Purpose: ". . . for the mutual aid and protection of its members according to the rules of the Catholic church; to foster a spirit of brotherly love among them, and, by means of pious practices, to preserve a high standard of christian morality among the members and their families."

The Fraternal Brotherhood of Our Father Jesus of Nazareth of the Counties of Taos, Mora, Colfax and Union, Territory of New Mexico, and Conejos, State of Colorado

Certificate of Incorporation sworn to on August 15, 1908, and filed as no. 5689 (vol. 5, p. 575) on November 28, 1908, for fifty years.

Principal place of business: Taos; with directors listed as residing in Ranchos de Taos, Taos, Arroyo Hondo, Rosiada, Chico, Sapello, New Mexico, and Conejos, Colorado.

Purpose: ". . . to help, and the mutual protection of its members according to the rules of the catholic Church, and to cultivate a spirit of fraternal love among the members, and by means of pious practices to maintain in a high degree the christian morality among the members and their families."

Fraternidad Piadosa de Nuestro Padre Jesus de Nazareno, Condado de Rio Arriba

Certificate of Incorporation sworn to on May 7, 1928, and filed as no. 13992 (vol. 7, p. 523) on the same day, for one hundred years.

Principal place of business: Tablas, although this was amended on

November 1, 1930, to read: "wherever the Supreme Brother, and his successors reside." This Certificate of Amendment was notarized on December 12, and filed as no. 16745 (vol. 8, p. 64) on December 15, 1930. According to the *"Preambule"* of the appended constitution (a copy of Lamy's 1856 *"Reglas"*), moradas from Alcalde, Velarde, Las Tablas, Canon de Vallecitos, Vallecitos, El Rito, Dixon, and Rendones were united by the incorporation. This may be the fourteen-morada district Weaver mentions in 1959–61.[2]

Purpose: ". . . to teach morality, to practice charity and to provide benefits, mutual and otherwise, for its members and their dependents, to increase its membership in the manner provided by its by-laws, and to aid our members."

La Fraternidad de Nuestro Padre Jesus del Condado de Taos

Certificate of Incorporation sworn to on March 27, 1931, and filed as no. 16980 (vol. 8, p. 101) on April 27, 1931, for fifty years.

Principal place of business: Arroyo Seco. According to Beshoar, "this particular group has jurisdiction over a number of *Moradas* in Fernando de Taos, Ranchos de Taos, Arroyo Hondo, Pilar, Cimarron, Valdez, and Ranchitos."[3]

Purpose: ". . . to teach morality, to practice charity, and to provide benefits, mutual and otherwise, for its members and their dependents, to increase its membership in the manner provided by its by-laws, and to aid its members." A constitution was appended.

Concilio Original de Nuestro Padre Jesus Nazareno, de Sheridan, Condado de San Miguel, Nuevo Mexico

Certificate of Incorporation sworn to on February 2, 1946, and filed as no. 24028 (vol. 6, p. 4) on February 4, 1946, for fifty years.

Principal place of business: Sheridan; with directors listed as residing in Las Vegas, Sapello, and Gabaldon. Seventeen members, from Las Vegas, Sapello, Gabaldon, Serafina, and Sena, attended the organizational meeting, voted in the election, and signed the appended by-laws.

Purpose: ". . . for the mutual aid and protection of its members according to the rules and rites of the Catholic Church; to foster the spirit of brotherly love among them, and by means of pious practices, to preserve a high standard of christian morality among the members and their families."

It was this more recent San Miguel County corporation which immediately came into conflict with the one incorporated in 1902.

On April 23, 1921, there was an organizational meeting at the Long's Canyon morada near Trinidad, in Las Animas County, Colorado. "A month after that meeting, which was attended by delegates from Southern Colorado *moradas,* the group incorporated under the laws of Colorado as Council No. 1, Long's Canon, Colorado."[4] Another San Miguel County organization, the Original Council of the Center of Our Lady of Santa Ana, is the same one that published the "resolutions of self-vindication" after a May 1894, meeting at Agua Zarca.[5] On August 10, 1915, again at Agua Zarca, Prospero S. Baca, "Hermano del Centro," Jose Felipe Maes, "Concilario General," Serafin Baca, "Consejero Organizador," Adelaido Tafoya, "Secretario General," and five "miembros del Concilio" approved the rules for the "Morada Original del Centro de N. S. de Santa Ana."[6]

According to a later document, the Council of Our Lady of Santa Ana met with Council No. 1, Long's Canyon, on October 21, 1934, forming a "Fraternal Alliance."[7] The Concilio Ministerial de la Alianza Fraternidad de Nuestro Padre Jesus de Colorado y Nuevo Mexico ("Ministerial Council of the Alliance Fraternity of Our Father Jesus of Colorado and New Mexico") was officially begun in 1938. Several men, including Don Miguel Archibeque, were important in this organization, which became the Archbishop's Supreme Council after 1947.[8]

Less formalized associations may have been instigated by parish priests like Rev. Emile Barrat of Costilla, New Mexico. In a postscript to his letter of March 7, 1920, Barrat noted:

> I must add also that the "worst" moradas are near Santa Fe where the corrupt politicians still play havoc with them. But those of the Northern part of Taos Co., that is 2 at Questa, one at Cerro, one at Pina, one at Costilla, that is nearly 300 men are altogether separated from the political center of Taos, and are now being transformed into a thoroughly

catholic organization, the best, the most honest men of the country.[9]

However, most council groups apparently utilized the legal means at their disposal to secure their formal associations. While councils seem primarily to have been concerned with regulating internal and external affairs, internecine difficulties did erupt in 1946, generating much unwelcome publicity for the Brotherhood.

1946 Litigation in San Miguel County

On February 20, 1946, "La Fraternidad de Nuestro Padre Jesus de Nazareno del Condado de San Miguel, Territorio de Nuevo Mexico" filed a complaint in the Fourth Judicial District Court of the State of New Mexico against the newly incorporated "Concilio Original de Nuestro Padre Jesus Nazareno, de Sheridan, Condado de San Miguel, Nuevo Mexico." Because no statutory agent had been designated in the incorporation documents, the summons listed all seventeen members of the Concilio's organizational meeting as defendants.

The seventeen-point complaint charged that seven moradas with less than one hundred members, most of them suspended or expelled from the Fraternidad, had outlawed themselves from the longstanding corporate body. Hermano del Centro Severo Lucero, who swore the complaint, claimed that La Fraternidad had been in continuous existence since 1902, and comprised twenty-one moradas with over six hundred members in San Miguel, Mora, and Guadalupe Counties. Because the names, objectives, place of business, rules, and regulations of the defendant and plaintiff corporations were "so nearly identical and similar," the Fraternidad charged that the Concilio would mislead and confuse the public, as well as "cause confusion and discord amongst the membership of the fraternity to the end that the domestic tranquility, the high purposes of the society, is threatened by the fraudulent action of the defendant corporation and its members." They requested that the defendant corporation "be enjoined and restrained from using the name Concilio Original de Nuestro Padre Jesus Nazareno de Sheridan, Condado de San Miguel, Nuevo Mexico, and from transacting any business under said

125

name," as well as "such other and further relief in the premises as to the Court may seem meet and proper."[10]

District Judge Luis E. Armijo, who had witnessed the February 21 summons, disqualified himself, and the case was to be heard by Judge James B. McGee of Roswell.[11] A stipulation signed by representatives of both parties indicated that "His Highness, the Archbishop of Santa Fe" suggested the eventual compromise settlement "in order to promote the general welfare of both organizations and the cordial relations between the members of the said organizations and the Catholic Church." According to Roberts, this agreement came after a Church representative approved the defendant corporation. The plaintiff finally consented to Church restrictions in order to secure Church approval for its own council. Besides ordering a change of name for both parties, the Church demanded final word in cases of expulsion and of recognition for new moradas, and indicated approval of the by-laws and rules of the defendant corporation.[12]

The judgment by stipulation, signed on June 10, 1946, enjoined both groups from using their original names. "La Fraternidad de Nuestro Padre Jesus de Nazareno del Condado de San Miguel, Territorio de Nuevo Mexico" was "within a reasonable time" to become "El Concilio del Centro de Nuestra Senora de Los Dolores." The "Concilio Original de Nuestro Padre Jesus Nazareno de Sheridan, Condado de San Miguel, Nuevo Mexico" was to change its name to "El Concilio del Centro de Sangre de Cristo" and on July 14, 1946, filed a resolution to that effect with the State Corporation Commission of New Mexico. Both parties were ordered to pay court costs.

In addition to the ecclesiastical ramifications, there were strong political overtones to the case. The older group was reputed to be solidly Republican, the newer Democratic. Severo Lucero was a Republican party leader. Interestingly, Judge Armijo was also a Republican. All but two of the seventeen named defendants were registered Democrats on February 1, 1946, and one of those two changed his registration from Republican to Democrat on September 16, 1948.[13] The Hermano del Centro of the defendant corporation, Manuel Jose Baca, publicly denied charges of political motives, stating that "insofar as our group is concerned, we are organized for religious purposes . . . we do not discriminate against anyone because he is a Republican."[14] Whatever the actual state of affairs, Roberts claims that in 1957 Severo Lucero maintained leadership of the older group, while the newer organization had increased to twelve moradas with some three hundred members.[15]

Council Structures

Most councils seem to have been organized like local moradas, but with less ritual and more administrative emphasis. Council officials bear titles similar to local counterparts. Their duties resemble those of local leaders, but they are more likely to interact with representatives of the established judicial, political, ecclesiastical, and communications hierarchies. Their power to represent the Brotherhood is usually legally rather than traditionally constituted.

The 1869–71 Cochiti association of *"tres unidades"* is the earliest informal council for which structural information is available.[16] According to several documents, it was governed by an elected *hermano principal y concilario* who guided the confraternity *"en nuestros Ejercicios de virtud."* A *celador general,* responsible for the morals and good conduct of the Brothers, took over in the absence of the *hermano concilario* and supervised the treasurer. The *vegislador general* checked on all the *hermandades* under the *hermano principal,* making sure that all members, including the various *hermanos mallores,* fulfilled their duties and caused no scandal or disorder.[17] Father Clemente Peyron apparently fostered this association, and it is likely that the council officials served as mediators between him and the Brothers.

Taos County has the oldest legally incorporated group of moradas. In 1899, Darley published a portion of its 1861 "Constitución" and "Reglas para el govierno interior de la Fraternidad Piadosa del Condado de Taos." The organization was divided into *secciones* with the Hermanos mayores and other officials responsible to an *Hermano Mayor Principal* and his aide, *"un segundo Hermano."* The Hermano Mayor Principal was to reside in Don Fernando de Taos, to be an intelligent and competent person, and to keep all the official papers of the Society. Like the various sectional

Hermanos Mayores, he had power to use the name of the Society to acquire property for the use of members and to bring persons who disturbed or impeded the Fraternity before civil authorities. He also presided over county-wide meetings. Other rules were concerned with the acceptance of new members and matters of local internal government. This structure apparently served for at least seventy years because the constitution filed with the 1931 incorporation papers for La Fraternidad de Nuestro Padre Jesus del Condado de Taos contains an identical text with the more recent date of acceptance.[18]

A 1928 document filed with incorporation papers for the Fraternidad Piadosa de Nuestro Padre Jesus de Nazareno, Condado de Rio Arriba, indicates a simple organizational structure similar to the nineteenth-century one at Cochiti.[19] The *concilio supremo* was to consist of three men—an *"Hermano mayor de centro supremo,"* an *"Hermano consiliario de centro supremo,"* and an *"Hermano selador de centro supremo"*—with full powers to act on behalf of the Fraternity. These elected officials could call general meetings of all moradas and could assess each group five dollars for council expenses. As in most councils, primary stated concerns were for matters involving public relations and the maintenance of internal order.

The Preamble and Rules of the Concilio Original de Nuestro Padre Jesus Nazareno de Sheridan, Condado de San Miguel, Nuevo Mexico, dated February 2 and filed February 4, 1946, give explicit organizational details.[20] The Council was composed of nine elected officials plus three or more additional members:

1. *Hermano del Centro,* who is in general charge, with rights to discipline and expel Brothers.
2. *Conciliario General,* who sees to the general order of the Center and visits the various moradas.
3. *Consejero Organizador General,* who advises the Brotherhood on various matters, in accord with the ritual.
4. *Celador General Primero,* who supervises the ritual and other discipline, including that of Council members, and who is in charge of the local *celadores.*
5. *Celador General Segundo,* who serves in the absence of the first.
6. *Secretario General,* who keeps the papers and votes in the transactions of the Brotherhood.

128

7. *Tesorero Colector General,* who collects and keeps records of the money.
8. *Mandatorio General,* who advises members on the will of the Council.
9. *Guardia de Concilio,* who guards the door during Council meetings and carries out wishes of the Council members.

Meetings were to be held at least once annually, on August 10. Executive power resided with the Hermano del Centro, backed by the Conciliario General; legislative and judicial power was exercised by the first seven officials. The Council could defend the rights of the various moradas and could expel, suspend, or receive members or moradas.

This group of officials was presumably identical to that of the earlier San Miguel County Council. The complaint filed by La Fraternidad de Nuestro Padre Jesus de Nazareno del Condado de San Miguel, Territorio de Nuevo Mexico stated "that the number of directors of plaintiff corporation and its general officials and/or officers are nine and that said Board of Directors constitutes the general officials of said fraternity and have for some time become known amongst the membership of said association as the central council, or Concilio Del Centro."[21] The August 10, 1915, rules for the Morada Original del Centro de N. S. de Santa Ana, signed by an Hermano del Centro, Concilario General, Consejero Organizador, Secretario General, and five *"miembros del Concilio,"* would also support such a coincidence.[22] The newer Council apparently adopted the older group's organization intact.

Councils clearly provided a relatively simple organization to govern inter-morada affairs and to mediate between the Brotherhood and the society at large. An effective centralized association was needed in order to instigate formal action against outside intrusions and to insure that the local groups' charitable and ritual aims could be carried out unobtrusively and piously.

Corporate Actions

By the early twentieth century, Brothers had acquired considerable expertise in defending themselves using the legal means at their disposal. While some evidence of Penitente involvement in judicial proceedings seems to repeat nineteenth-century stereotypes, most recorded instances of corporate actions are directed toward outsiders whose sensationalized accounts of Penitente beliefs and practices threatened the Brotherhood's freedom of worship.

Taos was the scene of a widely reported case involving the Brotherhood in 1914.[23] Jose Dalio Cordova, a known Penitente leader from Arroyo Hondo, was charged with selling liquor to the Taos Indians, a federal offense. He and others were not convicted because witnesses provided satisfactory alibis for them. However, new information resulted in charges of perjury being filed in February 1914 against Cordova and four others who had testified on his behalf. Arrests were made and the trial was set for March 11, 1914.

According to Acting Judge of the United States Commissioner's Court Francis T. Cheetham, he was "told by *El Capitan* of one group of Penitentes that the Society to the number of 3,700 would come to the court to defend their brethern."[24] Fred Lambert, United States Deputy Special Officer in the Indian Service, who served the warrants on Cordova, claims he was threatened twice before the proceedings opened—once with a presentation of ten .30-.30 Winchester cartridges and once with a statement signed by "hundreds" of Brothers. The last page of this document supposedly contained a threat lettered in blood: "EL ESTRELLAS CAER DE CIELO PRIMERO USTED MANDAR DALIO CORDOVA EL PENITENTCIARRO. 'The stars shall fall from heaven before you send Dalio Cordova to the penitentiary,' is the English translation."[25] An Assistant United States Attorney was deputized and sent to Taos to survey the unstable situation.

When the cases finally came before the Grand Jury in April, the charges were dismissed, and Judge Pope sternly censured the attempts to tamper with the legal process. This confrontation with federal authority "had a salutary effect, according to one Taos lawyer, in considerably lessening any attempt on the part of the society to influence the procedure of the courts, and elicited great respect for Federal power."[26] Nevertheless, a 1922 murder trial in Taos was allegedly influenced by the Brotherhood.[27]

Most council activities concerned unsympathetic outsiders.

Until 1915, such actions were informal and sometimes volatile. Armed guards accompanied public processions and stood watch at morada doors. Lee claims there was "a threatened uprising" against Darley after the publication of his April 1890 issue of *La Hermandad.*[28] Lee himself was pressured by unnamed parties to alter his 1910 student paper at the University of New Mexico:

> The thesis as first filed contained considerably more definite information than the one that is now on file but it caused some feeling among certain people in the State and I was advised by older men to withdraw it as it might have a serious "kick back" in later years if I intended to go on in the State. I, therefore, withdrew it and filed an expurgated edition.[29]

The Santa Fé Daily New Mexican reported a Taos incident involving Charles E. Griffith, editor of the *Taos Valley Herald.* Griffith published an article on the Penitentes by D. J. Flynn, which had earlier appeared in *Harper's Weekly.* The *New Mexican's* editors were skeptical of Griffith's story, which they quoted from the *Denver Times-Sun:*

> The day after the article appeared Griffith was set upon by a mob of Mexicans and beaten and bruised. He was also warned to leave town and, though a courageous man, was finally driven to desperation and, shouldering his rifle, he started to walk to the railroad station here [Tres Piedras], a distance of 3–5 miles.

According to the disdainful Santa Fe editors, "Griffith is a wild-eyed, long haired rooster who hails from the sand dunes of southern Colorado, and knows as much about running a news paper as a guajalote does of heaven." They labeled the affair "a tempest in a teapot."[30]

A "law by limitation" was passed during the Second State Legislature of New Mexico on February 20, 1915. Apparently the result of concerted Brotherhood pressure, it was entitled "An Act to Further Define the Offense of Libel and Providing the Punishment Therefor." Charges of criminal libel could be brought against "any person who, with intent to injure, publishes or circulates any malicious statement in writing, with reference to or concerning any fraternal or religious order or society." To be libelous, such "written or printed or published" statements had to "convey the idea either: (a) That said fraternal or religious order or society has been guilty as an order or society of some penal offense or has conspired to commit some penal offense. (b) That said fraternal or religious order or society has, as an order or society, been guilty of some act or omission which, though not a penal offense, is disgraceful and the natural consequences of which act or omission are to bring such order or society into contempt among honorable persons."[31] Almost immediately, proceedings were instituted against Rev. F. F. Thomas of Taos County.

Thomas, a Protestant missionary, had written a letter to a friend in Garden City, Kansas, in the spring of 1914. A portion of this correspondence appeared in the *Garden City Telegram* on April 3, 1914, and was reprinted in *The Aurora, Missouri Menace* on May 2, 1914. According to a typescript among the Dorothy Woodward Penitente Papers, the newspaper quotation read as follows:

> I like the work here first rate. There is no denominational rivalry except the Catholics and now during Lent the "Penitentes" are making the nights hideous. They howl and whip themselves with cactus whips on the bare back until the blood flies. Also carry heavy crosses for miles until they come to the calvary designated by a standing cross. But they will lay that cross down while on the way and steal a fat sheep or calf if the opportunity is afforded them. One of their jargon songs is "I stole a good fat cow" etc. They stole my best hat and a quirt and I would like to handle that cactus whip awhile. One of the mission teachers Miss Lizzie Craig has lost a sheep every Lent fiesta. . . . I was at Questa, thirty miles north of this place, during a funeral last fall, and the Penitentes were on one side of me and the coyotes on the other, and it made my hair stand straight up. I don't know to which party I would give the prize for making the night hideous, but rather think the penitentes would take it.

In Case No. 1107 of the Eighth District Court of the County of Taos, the Brotherhood alleged that Thomas, "in so composing, writing and publishing the said scandalous and malicious libel of and concerning the plaintiff, as hereinbefore alleged, acted maliciously, and meant thereby to accuse the plaintiff and did accuse the plaintiff of being habitually guilty of the crime of larceny by and through the members composing said plaintiff corporation, and meant to accuse and did accuse the plaintiff corporation, by and through its members, of being guilty of unseemly, disreputable and opprobrious practices and conduct."[32] They demanded five thousand dollars in damages and five hundred dollars for court costs.

The complaint was filed in June 1915. The plaintiff corporation, the Fraternal Brotherhood of Our Father Jesus of Nazareth, was officially represented by J. Dalio Cordova and defended by attorneys J. H. Crist and M. P. Davies. On June 10, Thomas was served with a summons. Judge Thomas D. Leib presided over the hearings. Thomas's attorneys, William McKean and Francis T. Cheetham, submitted a demurrer which Leib sustained on June 21, 1916. The case was dismissed.

A more flagrant slander received national publicity two years later, but no legal action resulted. In August 1918, the *North American Review* published a letter to the editor from one Henry Wray, a pseudonym for H. R. Walmsley of Kansas City, Missouri. Under the title "America's Unguarded Gateway," it accused Hispanic New Mexicans of sympathetic loyalties to Mexico. If a few German officers and sufficient German gold were used to muster a Mexican army, Wray insinuated, they could march northward up the Rio Grande to Colorado and into the heart of the nation, aided and abetted by Spanish-Americans. According to Wray, "a state of treason exists in this part of our country [and] New Mexico confidently expects to arise and join the mother country, taking its place in the sun, among the children of the sun."[33]

Almost a third of the letter concerns the Brotherhood, whose main object, Wray claims, is to "keep the State loyally Mexican."

> The Penitentes are a strange sect, practising weird religious rites, self-tortures, political oppressions and the elimination of enemies. The deserts are dotted with their calvary crosses at which human crucifixions are annually carried out, despite the efforts of the Government to prevent them. The Penitentes are secretive, and will stone any unfortunate

American passer-by who chances to witness one of their devotional marches. Americans who learn too much and become talkative are found on the highways, their hearts decorated with neat perforations. It is whispered that no one can talk against the conditions of New Mexico and live.

Wray repeats the old canards that no Penitente is ever convicted because "the juries are composed mostly of Spanish speaking Penitentes, and if any juror votes for a verdict contrary to the instructions of this organization, he moves quickly—or forever after ceases to move." On the other hand, "Americans tried by a Penitente jury for an offense against the Penitentes are likely to be held indefinitely in a filthy jail kept by a Penitente sheriff; some have been so held, without trial or attention, until they died." Wray further refers to the 1915 libel statute, which he so blatantly violates, as "a law passed expressly to keep Americans from voicing any protest against the Penitente control."[34]

These vicious allegations provoked widespread indignation and resulted in a public retraction and apology by the editors of the *Review*. They admitted negligence in not checking the facts and stated that the law protecting the Penitentes was similar to many libel statutes. A list of the letters of outrage was published, as well as transcripts of an August 7 telegram from United States Senator Albert B. Fall and Congressional remarks by Representative W. B. Walton. The New Mexico Congressman explained that the state's Spanish-Americans, "noble descendants of the Conquistadores," had absolutely no sympathy with the "peons" of Mexico. He termed all accusations against the Penitentes "old women's tales."[35]

Correspondence to and from Charles Springer, Chairman of the Executive Committee, Council of Defense of the State of New Mexico, indicates that most demands for Wray's prosecution came from the southern part of the state.[36] Some attempts at investigation are documented, but United States Attorney Burkhart scotched the suggestion to prosecute under the Espionage Act. Interestingly, however, Representative Walton's remarks are the only presently available testimony which exonerates the Penitentes. Other letters ignore the wild charges against the Brothers and the possibilities of prosecution under the 1915 statute.

In 1938, Monsignor Philip F. Mahoney began a series of articles on Penitente history for the *New Mexico Sentinel*. Although these were based on documents in the Archives of the Archdiocese of Santa Fe, the series was discontinued after the fifth article appeared, apparently because of action taken by Miguel Archibeque. Writing to the *Sentinel* editors from Palma, New Mexico, Archibeque, who signs himself the "Monitor of the Supreme Council for Colorado and New Mexico," protests that "we consider these articles as being slanderous, offensive and defamatory inasmuch as they besmirch the character and good name of our fraternal organization." He disclaims all contemporary knowledge of the Lamy and Salpointe regulations and cites the Brotherhood's corporate right "to institute any suits for damage should it be deemed necessary." This public admonition to a Church official seems to be unprecedented. Although Mahoney's public reply was conciliatory, the remaining translations and proposed laudatory impressions were never printed.[37]

A less significant letter in the same vein appeared in *The Horsefly*, a Taos publication billed as the "smallest and most inadequate newspaper ever published," edited and printed by Spud Johnson. The issue of April 1, 1939, reproduced a woodblock by Manville Chapman, depicting a Penitente crucifixion, with the caption: "Once Upon a Time Good Friday was Celebrated Like This in Good Old Taos." The subsequent issue of April 8 reprinted a letter received on April 5. A Commission of three—Juan J. Tenorio, Levi Martinez, and Alfonso T. Martinez—"of the organization of Jesus Christ of Nazareth" objected to the picture and its caption. Their remarks read in part:

> Coming down to brass tacks, Mr. Johnson, we know that there are a few world unknown writers in Taos and what would be friends of the native people or the penitentes that have made great efforts to enrich their bins with gold, writing great falsifications and exaggerations about the penitentes. We believe that our doings are in accord with the Christian religion of which we are members and we resent criticism on the part of would be friends like yourself, Chapman, and others now living in Taos. We would cite, many religions and their practices, but feel it uncalled for. Let us keep in mind the greatest charter ever written by civilized man in this

continent, The Constitution of America. Do also unto others as you would have them do unto you. Let us work together in the right way which is the only way.

Johnson apologized for having offended the Brotherhood.[38]

More recently, public defense of the Brotherhood has been in the name of the Hermano Supremo Arzobispal, head of the Supreme Council of the Brotherhood. On May 6, 1969, the National Broadcasting Corporation aired one of its "First Tuesday" programs, which included a documentary on Reies Lopez Tijerina and the land grant problems, entitled "The Most Hated Man in New Mexico." The Penitentes were also cited. According to a bitter attack on the program's content, the Brotherhood was "considering a suit against NBC for its 'First Tuesday' program's use of photos and other material about them 'without permission and without sincerity.' "[39] However, a cautionary letter from M. S. Melendez, dated May 26, from Albuquerque, appeared in the next issue of *El Grito del Norte:*

> As the Hermano Supremo Arzobispal of the "Hermanos de Nuestro Padre Jesus Nazareno," commonly known as the "Penitentes," I am the only one authorized to give any information as to any legal matters being considered by the Hermandad. As of now, nothing has been decided as to what will be done about the falsehoods televised (on the NBC program). I am sure that something will be done in the near future to stop such criticism.[40]

No further reports were published.

The Archbishop's Supreme Council

After Archbishop Byrne's declaration in 1947, the Concilio Supremo Arzobispal became the official administrative body of the Brotherhood of Our Father Jesus. Largely due to the labors of Don Miguel Archibeque and several others, local moradas and councils were organized into districts eventually subservient to the Archbishop's Supreme Council. According to Holmes:

Districts were first created in 1937 in southern San Miguel

and in Rio Arriba counties, and by 1955 the Brotherhood was organized in nine districts or *concilios*. The more isolated chapels are directly under the supervision of the *hermano supremo*, the others comprise three districts in San Miguel, one in Mora, three in Taos, and two in Rio Arriba counties. By 1960 there remained perhaps 135 chapter houses in New Mexico and southern Colorado.[41]

Recently published translations document Districts No. 1 (Santa Ana), No. 2A (Rio Arriba), No. 2B (Rio Arriba), No. 3A (Taos), No. 3B (Taos), No. 3C (Taos), No. 5 (San Miguel), and No. 6 (Mora).[42] In other papers, District 5, Council of the Blood of Christ, is referred to as No. 5A, so it is possible that there was a ninth San Miguel district in the Council of Our Lady of Sorrows. Brothers at Long's Canyon, Colorado, are mentioned as a separate group which, in 1953, requested that the Book of Regulations be translated into English for them and that there be a Supreme Council created in Colorado.[43]

A Supreme Elder Brother, a Supreme Counselor, a Supreme Advisor, a Supreme Secretary, a Supreme Treasurer, and a Supreme Curator were elected annually to head the Archbishop's Council. Yearly meetings were convened at Santa Fe, where, for example, some two hundred Brothers were reported in attendance at the St. Francis School on June 4, 1955.[44] Besides Elder Brothers and elected councilmen from each district, interested visiting Brothers were permitted to attend. All Brothers originally paid annual dues of twenty-five cents to support the Supreme Council, which, in 1952, received $117.50, expended $105.85, and stated a balance of $179.80 (including $165.00 from the preceding year) on February 8, 1953.[45] Most expenditures went to provide food for Brothers attending the Council meetings.

The main item of annual Supreme Council business seems to be the approval of a Book of Regulations to govern Lenten observances. Officers of the Supreme Council discuss and arbitrate district matters and discipline council officials. The Supreme Council meetings also serve as a forum to air problems with local priests and unsympathetic outsiders.[46]

Pastoral letters from the archbishop and occasional letters from the Hermano Supremo Arzobispal provide spiritual and ritual guidance for districts and local congregations. The constant emphasis in these missives is on private and very moderate penances. Brothers are urged to cooperate with parish priests, to attend Church Sacraments, to obey Church commandments, particularly with regard to marriage, and to avoid drunkenness. Strict attendance at local moradas on the Fridays of Lent and during Holy Week is required, and special permission is necessary for absences or for members wishing to visit other congregations.[47]

The office of Hermano Supremo Arzobispal is thus the highest and most important in the Brotherhood of Our Father Jesus. Besides convening and chairing annual and special meetings, he oversees all the Brotherhood's affairs, officially represents the Brothers, and acts as the liaison between the archbishop and the recognized district councils and local chapters. Archbishop Byrne appointed Don Miguel Archibeque of Santa Fe to serve as the first Hermano Supremo Arzobispal. Archibeque was later elected to that position, serving from June 1946 until June 1953, when he was replaced by Roman Aranda of Las Vegas. Aranda served for one year only, and Archibeque was reelected from June 1954 until 1960, when his health began to fail.[48] The third Hermano Supremo Arzobispal, M. Santos Melendez of Mora and Albuquerque, was elected in June 1960, and continues to serve in this capacity.

CHAPTER 6

The Local Moradas

The Brothers of Our Father Jesus require that all members practice fraternity, community, and piety. Too often, their Lenten and Holy Week rituals have been emphasized and their year-round commitments overlooked. Although they annually commemorate the Passion of Jesus, Brothers also attempt to emulate His life by living simply and morally and by performing unobtrusive good deeds. This rule is vividly expressed by former Penitente Cleofes Vigil of San Cristobal, New Mexico:

> In those days when a man's harvest was ready he did not say to his neighbor, "Come, help me." His neighbor watched the field of his neighbor, and he knew when it was time to go and help. He did not have to be asked. . . . That is the way it should be. A man should help his neighbor without being asked.[1]

In general, the stated corporate purposes of the councils—charity, mutual aid, pious practices, and the fostering of brotherly love and Christian morality—apply to the local chapters. Moradas conduct rituals at times of death, during Lent and Holy Week, and sometimes on appropriate feast days. They are organized to render mutual aid and to help their communities throughout the year. Collective as well as individual life is thus enhanced and has at times been sustained by the Brotherhood's objectives and observances.

Brothers and Their Nonmember Neighbors

Even during the nineteenth century, villages were not necessarily solidly Penitente.[2] Men from wealthier families seem rarely to have joined the Brotherhood. Those who became Brothers were generally ranchers with small holdings, tenant sheep herders, and laborers.[3]

According to Mary Austin, "the better class Spanish families never belonged to the order, especially after it came under the displeasure of the church, and make a point of speaking of it disparagingly."[4] The traditional satirical verse cited by Lummis and others—"Penitente sinner,/Why do you go whipping yourself?/For a cow that I stole,/And here I go paying for her"[5]—was a widespread part of this derision. Cleofas Jaramillo, whose family was of the upper class in Arroyo Hondo, New Mexico, recalls watching the Brothers through field glasses and also cites a more common practice:

> A few days after the close of Holy Week, some of the young men would appear at the store looking pale and haggard. My brother, curious to find out if a certain young man were a *penitente,* gave him a friendly slap on the back. Taken unawares, the man betrayed his secret by a painful shrug and expression of agony on his face.[6]

On the whole, however, mutual respect prevailed between Brothers and nonmember villagers, whether rich or poor.

Brothers honored Holy Week visits to their moradas, requests for prayers, and gifts of food or money from nonmembers. Lorenzo de Cordova recounts a moving tribute to his schoolteacher mother following their Holy Wednesday visit to the Cordova morada in the early 1900s:

> After the prayer service, we received thanks for our offerings of candles and money. We returned thanks to them for their intercessions for our departed ones. Courteously escorted through the door, we stepped out into the dusk. There, close to our path, three figures, masked and scourging themselves, paid a remarkable tribute to a woman they revered and respected, and for whom they chose this supreme recognition of her worth as neighbor, mentor, and friend.[7]

In a study of sample baptismal records in the San Juan Basin, Swadesh found that non-Penitente parents sometimes chose Penitente couples as sponsors "on the basis of personal character," a sign of respect and confidence.[8] These and other practices probably prevailed throughout northern New Mexico and southern Colorado.

Some outsiders have attributed the general respect accorded the Brotherhood to fear of Penitente retribution.

> Those not affiliated with the organization regard it with fear, probably an attitude remaining from the days two generations ago when it was the dominating force in the village. For fear of offending the penitent brothers, the residents of the village [in Sandoval County, New Mexico] will deny that there is such an organization in the village, or profess total ignorance of it.[9]

While such apprehensions may be exaggerated, the Brothers did inculcate a certain respect for their public processions and services by consciously elaborating beliefs and legends about ghostly flagellants.

> Then there was the fixed belief, fostered by the Penitentes themselves, that the dead members returned bodily to mingle with the living ones at the Lenten orgies. This superstition, you may be sure, kept the non-members in a very wholesome awe of the society.

Jaramillo terms these "mystic stories which the penitentes' families were made to believe in order to keep their flagellant practices secret."[10] The perpetuation of such legends to insure Brotherhood privacy and integrity with family and neighbors does not of course preclude members' sincere belief in such revenants; it does, however, account for some of the fear associated with the Penitentes locally. Thus, although discretion resolved many inter- and intra-ethnic conflicts, this solution also created much fascination for the rather mysterious Brothers.[11]

Ideally, then, nonmember villagers seem to have expected Brothers to be morally upright and to abide by a deep but simple faith. More cynical outsiders believed exemplary behavior applied only to relationships with other members and their families.

Because of the deliberately cultivated secrecy surrounding Penitente observances and code of conduct, both the Brothers' anti-social lapses and their private rituals were viewed with some awe and exaggeration. Nonetheless, the vow of secrecy remained an important one for members.

Brotherhood Membership

There was much variability regarding candidacy for Brotherhood membership. On the whole, novices came from Penitente families. Recruitment was never indiscriminate; ideally, only those of known background and conviction were chosen to undergo the novitiate.[12]

Since initiation was in part a rite of passage into adult male status, the age of acceptance has varied according to community concepts of maturity. Despite isolated reports to the contrary, fourteen appears to have been the generally accepted minimal age for novices.[13] Most were probably in their late teens. Of course, men could decide to join at any time later in life, as was apparently the case with Don Miguel Archibeque, the first Hermano Supremo Arzobispal.

Aspirants might apply for admission to the Brotherhood after mature thought, as a matter of course, or because of a vow or *promesa*. Lorenzo de Cordova records the play morada set up by young boys in Valdez, New Mexico, to emulate their elders and former playmates who had been initiated. Aranda claims that the eldest son of a Penitente father "atuomatically" joined the Brotherhood at the age of eighteen to honor and obey his parent.[14] *Promesas* were made by a boy's relatives or by the individual himself. In Cordova, New Mexico, for example:

> . . . a certain mother . . . promised to deliver her son *a la sangre de Jesús* if he were permitted to recover from a seemingly fatal illness. The boy recovered, and from that time was considered a member of the local *morada*, receiving, through his mother, his share of whatever monies the Order accumulated through gifts or otherwise. When the lad was ten years of age, he appeared at the head of a penitential procession, carrying one of the sacred images. Everyone knew

that he was now a recognized member of the lodge, that he had been fully initiated. . . .[15]

Individuals might vow to seek admission as a condition to any number of requests for divine assistance to themselves or their families. The most common of these involved recovery from an illness, the safe return from a journey or from war, and material relief of various kinds.

New candidates expressed their desire for novitiate status by application to the Hermano Mayor, the secretary, or some other morada official. After a thorough investigation of the petitioner's life and motives, he received elaborate instruction in the Brotherhood's regulations and rituals. If he passed an examination on this material, he was allowed to present himself, together with a sponsor, at the morada door for the actual rite of initiation.[16]

Technically, the novitiate was not final until the end of a *novio* or *novicio*'s tenure as a Brother of Blood. This period varied—three to five years of active penance during Lent and Holy Week being the usual length of time. After that, the new Brother accompanied public processions wearing ordinary clothes and became eligible to hold an office in the morada.

There were thus three main ranks in the local chapter: (1) *Hermanos de Sangre*, Brothers of Blood, sometimes referred to as *Hermanos de las Tinieblas*, Brothers of Darkness; (2) *Hermanos salidos a luz*, Brothers who have returned to the light, or emerged from their novitiate and penances, the members-at-large; and (3) *Hermanos de Luz*, Brothers of Light, the usual term for officials of the morada. Novices and others engaged in active penances, whether voluntarily or as a punishment, were known as Brothers of Blood or *Hermanos disciplinantes*, Brothers in Discipline.

It is possible that there was another informal category for certain morada affiliates:

A still larger number are called, in the nomenclature of the sect, *hermanos de obscuras*, or, as it may be rendered, "unknown or hidden brothers." These are those who have joined the sect for purposes of political advancement, or the hope of gain, and who, while they make use of the sect, laugh at it in their sleeves.[17]

Similar terminology is suggested by Trujillo, who divides full-fledged members into *acompañadores* or *civiles,* those who accompany or police public processions, and *ocultos* or *secretos,* the clandestine or secret members.[18] Whether for political or personal reasons, some Brothers may indeed have wished to avoid public acknowledgment of Penitente affiliation. Still, the existence of such circumspect members is rarely mentioned.

Members usually prefer to be known as Hermanos rather than Penitentes, a designation with pejorative connotations. According to Swadesh, "in the San Juan hamlets today, the term of address used toward and between people of Penitente or formerly Penitente families is 'mano' (short for *hermano,* brother) and 'mana' (short for *hermana,* sister)."[19] These fraternal terms connoted the mutual respect and reciprocity associated with the best aspects of Brotherhood membership, *not* the annual penitential exercises.

The Relationship of Women to the Brotherhood

In the nineteenth century, women are reported to have maintained their own meeting places and to have practiced various forms of penance. Ritch noted that "the women also are among the Penitenties in N.M. and meet at separate times. Their self inflictions takes place in the church with the doors closed."[20] An undated New Mexico W.P.A. Writers' Project entry from J. B. Cisneros of Taos, based on his personal knowledge, reads:

> About 40 years ago (1895) there were Women Penitentes in and around Questa. This Fraternal Society was composed of women who were the wives of the men Penitentes. What the members of this organization did was much like the men Penitentes do. They did not have any Moradas but they would meet in the houses of some member. The members used to go up to the mountains or to any other secret place and whip themselves. They did not cut their backs but they whipped their bare backs with cords. The cords used were much like the cords that are used today on Kimonas. It is hard to say if such an organization exists today [late 1930s], if there is such society they must be very secret.

A woman informant told Hurt that there had been female Penitentes in Manzano before she was born:

They had a small single-roomed chapel furnished with a large table. In their processions, held at night, they carried no cross, but only tortured themselves. There is also a recollection that women had joined with the men in their ceremonies.[21]

If the Brotherhood did grow out of the Third Order of St. Francis, which accepted devout persons of either sex, women may well have been more actively involved as Penitentes during the last century.

Penance during Lent is of course important in Roman Catholicism, and various public and private penitential expressions are especially marked in Hispanic tradition. Women's participation may thus have been customary religious behavior and not indicative of official Brotherhood status. Women following public processions or carrying *santos* could do inconspicuous penance by walking with rice in their shoes or a *cilicio*, penitential "bracelet," of cactus underneath their clothes. During a 1964 interview with a resident of Mora, New Mexico, Craig was told that rigorous female penances were stopped "when it was felt that men would suffer for the women."[22] This attitude is not mentioned elsewhere, and it is difficult to separate expected expressions of penitential resolve from organizations designed to facilitate such expressions among women.

Women generally served as informal auxiliaries to the local morada. These groups of *Auxiliadoras,* female auxiliaries, were loosely organized, usually from wives and relatives of the Brothers. More formal associations have been reported in Costilla, New Mexico, and San Luis, Colorado, where groups held regular meetings presided over by older women who did not carry particular titles. They cleaned the interior of the morada, cared for the sick, prepared meals for Brothers during the Holy Week retreat, and assisted at wakes. Auxiliadoras could petition to do penance late at night or early in the the morning during Holy Week. Accompanied by at least three Brothers, a woman would crawl on her knees to the *Calvario,* a distance of some two hundred feet at Costilla, and about one hundred at San Luis. The funeral of an auxiliadora was apparently much like that of a Brother, with the body laid out in the altar room of the morada and the midnight supper served in the common, outer room.[23]

Several cases of specific women definitely associated with moradas have been reported. According to Abreu, in the 1920s,

"Magdalena was the widow of a former *Hermano Mayor* . . . and was a highly respected citizen of the little village [of San Ysabel] as well as ex officio member of the Confraternity." Wallrich heard of an Auxiliadora named Scholastica Chacon, who "actually became the *Hermano Mayor* of the *Morada* in San Rafael in Southern Colorado in the 1920's." This may be legendary. Far more likely would be the affiliation Swadesh suggests:

> Guadalupe Trujillo, wife of the Navajo, Juan Mateo Casías, was an honored person among the Brothers of La Posta [Colorado]. During Holy Week, she wore the badge of a religious confraternity and spent a great deal of time in the morada when no other women were present. She may have served as *rezadora* (prayer leader) for the Brothers, a function which was not restricted to initiates of the Brotherhood and which actually was carried out (in one other instance) by a woman in the San Juan Basin.

La Farge recounts a similar instance in Rociada, New Mexico, where an ex-Baptist convert, a blind woman called La Tulisa, easily able to master the long ritual corpus, was appointed *rezadora*.[24]

Physical penance during Lent and Holy Week was customary for women in Hispanic tradition. This would not necessarily mean such practitioners were female Penitentes, except in the broad sense of the term. Separate groups of women Penitentes seem to have existed in the nineteenth century, but, more recently, loosely organized auxiliary groups were associated with each local morada. Women almost invariably played subordinate, supportive roles with respect to the male cadre of the Brotherhood. Close formal ties and equal membership status were exceptional.

Officials of the Morada

Officers with specialized roles in the ritual, judicial, and charitable activities of the morada were elected annually, often at the end of Holy Week. The Hermano Mayor ("Elder Brother") was the superior in charge of the chapter and all its concerns. He served as administrator, arbiter, and overseer of all rituals. He was also the morada's chief representative in council affairs and in dealings with priests and various outsiders. Competent, respected men were elected to fill this position, and responsible, effective individuals were frequently reelected year after year.

Besides the Hermano Mayor, there were perhaps ten or twelve official positions filled by eligible Brothers. In general, these *Hermanos de Luz* included all or some of the following:

1. *Celador* (Warden), or *Corregidor* (Corrections Officer or Magistrate), or *Disciplinario* (Disciplinarian): maintains order within and outside the morada; administers punishments; sergeant-at-arms.

2. *Mandatorio* (Agent): notifies members of meetings, observances, and duties; collects alms or dues; instructs novices.

3. *Maestro de Novios,* or *de Novicios* (Teacher of the Novices): examines all novices petitioning for admission and supervises their instruction.

4. *Tesorero* (Treasurer): in charge of chapter funds.

5. *Secretario* (Clerk): custodian of records and rule book, from which he may read upon request.

6. *Enfermero* (Nurse), or *Hermano Caritativo* (Charitable Brother): cares for sick members and their families; performs various charitable acts in the community throughout the year.

7. *Coadjutor* (Assistant): washes the whips; attends to the wounds of Brothers performing penances; generally helps other officials.

8. *Sangrador* ("Blood-letter"), or *Picador* ("Pricker"), or *Rallador* ("Grater"): skillfully inflicts the *obligación* or *sello* (seal of the Brotherhood) on the back of a novice or a Brother preparing to do penitential exercises; whips the novices.

9. *Rezador* (Reader), or *Rogador* (Petitioner): reads prayers and rituals from a copybook; takes an important role in most observances.

10. *Pitero* (Piper or Flutist): plays the *pito,* homemade flute, as musical accompaniment for various services, never for pleasure.

The last three positions required special skills. Some sources also mention a *Cantador* (Singer), who led the hymns, and a *Matraquero,* who whirled the *matraca,* or wooden clacker, at the appropriate times during the rituals. Persons who filled such posts often held the position because of their talents rather than by majority vote.

The 1860 rules published by Darley list ten officials: Hermano Mayor, Coadjutor, Mandatorio, Celador, Enfermero, Maestro de Novios, Secretario, Picador, Rezador, and Pitero.[25] After the 1871 elections, the Cochiti Brotherhood was governed by an Hermano Mayor, Celador, Maestro de Novicios, Picador, Enfermero, Resador, Tesorero, two Coadjutores, and two Mandatorios.[26] Reliable sources from this century cite a slightly different set of officers. Trujillo gives eleven: Hermano Mayor, Secretario, Maestro de Novicios, Coadjutor, Celador, Sargento de Armas (Sergeant-at-arms, or guard), Mandatorio, Enfermero, Pitero, Matraquero, and Rezador. Beshoar lists nine: Hermano Mayor, Hermano Segundo (Second Brother, lieutenant of the Elder Brother), Hermano Celador, Hermano Consegero (Adviser), Hermano Tesorero, Hermano Sangrador, Hermano Secretario, Hermano Rezador, and Hermano Maestro de Novicios. According to Holmes, the tendency now is to elect officials with religious duties plus several councilmen to aid the Hermano Mayor and to represent the local chapter at council meetings.[27]

During Holy Week, *Ayudantes* or *Ayudans* (Helpers), or *Acompañadores* (Attendants) representing Simon the Cyrenian, were appointed to accompany, and if necessary aid, each flagellant and cross-bearer. Food for the Brothers was supervised by Auxiliadoras or *Mayordomos* (Stewards) selected from among the members. Darley refers to this supervisory post as the *Mayordomo de la Muerte* (Steward of Death), but his is the only such reference. Chacon reports an *Hermano Mendicante,* who went from door to door on Holy Thursday, begging alms for the morada.[28] However, unsolicited gifts of food, candles, and money, given out of respect for the Brotherhood, seem to have been more usual. These were reciprocated by special prayers for the donors.

In a morada of some fifty to a hundred members, then, there were probably positions of status for at least a third of the membership eligible to hold office. There was enough turnover to give most Brothers a chance to serve in some recognized official capacity. This recognition doubtless provided an added incentive toward Penitente membership.

Rule and Regulations of the Morada

Brotherhood membership required adherence to a rule in the sense of a guide to conduct and a pervasive religious orientation. Expectations of fraternal integrity and Christian ethics extended to a Brother's life in the community throughout the year. The first chapter of the 1861 "Rules for the Internal Government of the Fraternidad Piadosa del Condado de Taos" states the principal objects of this rule as: service to God through Christ's teachings; observance of the Ten Commandments; leading a humble life like Jesus; avoidance of discord; shunning worldly temptations such as saloons; and charity and mutual love toward Brothers by setting a good example, aiding in times of illness or anguish, pardoning, tolerating, and respecting one another.

The model given for the oath required of members expressed these concerns. The two-part declaration suggested as a guide for local chapters may be summarized as: (a) dedication to the Fraternity; compliance with its constitution, rules, and object (charity and good works); devotion to the blood of Christ; imitation of Christ's example; and observance of the Ten Commandments; (b) willing adherence to the corporation; regulation of conduct and repentance of misconduct; love of God; profession of the fraternal life and hope for God's mercy through Christ. The new member was then counseled to maintain a strict silence about his affiliation and his merits, humbly keeping both hidden from the world.[29]

Available by-laws and regulations stress secrecy, obedience, fulfillment of religious duties, and certain customary procedures within the morada. The seven rules from a southern Colorado chapter, translated by Beshoar, may be summarized as follows:

1. A Brother proved guilty of revealing secrets, breaking his oath, failing in his duties, or disobeying an official will be expelled.
2. A crime against the Ten Commandments will be punished by assigning penance.
3. Suspended or retired members may be readmitted and must go through a year's probationary period.
4. Consent of all is required for readmission or withdrawal, but

149

the same responsibilities pertain and the same penalties are required in the case of withdrawal.

5. The officers decide all claims, but they must consult with the General Council on difficult cases.
6. Confession and communion during Lent are compulsory before a Brother may be admitted into the morada.
7. Benefactors must be given proof of gratitude and prayers offered for them.[30]

Similar regulations are followed in every morada.

Penalties for transgressions and infractions of the rules and regulations vary. Heresy or revealing the secrets of the organization are supposed to have been punished by burial alive, but these rumors have never been authenticated.[31] The usual sentence for serious transgressions was expulsion, probably followed by ostracism. Punishments for lesser wrongdoing took the form of imposed penances or floggings administered by the Celador. Lorenzo de Cordova describes the case of two young Brothers who had fought each other during the last dance before Lent. On Ash Wednesday, they appeared as flagellants in the first public procession of the Brotherhood. Denied entrance to the church, they knelt by the sacristy door and disciplined themselves for some two hours.[32] Every morada had the right to impose such sentences after deliberation and according to written regulations or informal precedent.

The morada clearly governed both the group and the private life of its members. Morality as defined by community consensus and gossip influenced the interpretation of the broader rule of life which a Brother was pledged to observe. Internal customs and procedures developed both formally and informally. Misdemeanors, misconduct in the community, and acts of treason against the Brotherhood, as well as heresies, were judged by the Hermano Mayor and other officials. These Brothers of Light coordinated and maintained the cooperation that Brothers expected from other Brothers, and the community expected from the local chapters.

Practical Social Functions of the Morada

The Brothers often organized the various important religious observances involving the whole village. Their management of Holy Week rituals, Corpus Christi processions, feast days for patron saints, and other ceremonies traditional to the locale assured villagers of an opportunity for worship and fellowship, important spiritual dimensions to their community life.

One of the Penitentes' most important social contributions was to render material and spiritual assistance to the bereaved family of a deceased individual, whether member or nonmember. The corpse had to be prepared, the *velorio,* or wake (including the singing, praying, and midnight supper) managed, the grave dug, the procession to the *camposanto* ("cemetery") supervised, and the body finally buried. Until priests were more readily available and mortuaries more common, these funeral procedures were handled by the Brotherhood in many villages. Since the turn of the century, however, other lay societies have been formed to provide burial funds and mutual aid for their members.[33]

Sick persons and their families would also be cared for by the Brothers. The Enfermero or an Auxiliadora would usually make the necessary arrangements. Sometimes, each Brother would take a night and donate food and aid. Most moradas also maintained a *fondo* ("fund") of supplies and money to distribute in times of individual or communal need. George Lopez, noted woodcarver in Cordova, New Mexico, recalls the spiritually supportive measures, no less important than the material benefits:

> All my life . . . I've seen Penitente processions pass my house. In the old days they'd have a procession when somebody died or even to say prayers at a sick person's home. Nowadays they just have processions in Holy Week.[34]

Both members and nonmembers enjoyed such support.

Officials of the morada judged, sentenced, and punished misconduct within and outside the morada, usually only involving members. In fact, however, any community problem could be discussed within the chapter, and the morada provided a good forum for airing mundane and unusual problems of communal and individual concern.

There are no studies comparing Penitente communities with those which had no chapter. Many researchers have emphasized the social integrational functions of the Brotherhood, functions

151

which may in some places have been filled by powerful *patrones*
("patrons"), or other active Church societies and the resident
priest. Wesley Robert Hurt, Jr., for example, claims that when the
Brothers were active at Manzano, New Mexico, during the
nineteenth century, they were a strong force for integration,
perpetuation of tradition, and village self-sufficiency.[35] In a recent
survey of the San Miguel County area, Knowlton is more strongly
pessimistic:

> The yearly calendar of religious ceremonies no longer in-
> volves most of the male population, and village social life has
> become more monotonous and drab. The Elder Brother of
> the Penitente lodge cannot maintain control of the behavior
> of those who violate village mores. No other mechanism has
> yet developed . . . to fulfill the social or the religious
> functions of "Los Hermanos Penitentes." Village life, as a
> result, is marked by vandalism, factionalism, and conflicts
> between families and individuals.[36]

Thomas Weaver, working in Rio Arriba County, does not support
this view, claiming that "in remote villages, today, Penitentes pray
for the sick, help the needy, conduct burial services, and constitute
a vital force in public opinion formation."[37] Whatever the actual
relationship between declining Brotherhood influence and increasing village distress, it is clear that moradas did once serve to unite
people across kin lines and over distances, demanding cooperation
and unity on specific occasions, during crises, and throughout the
year, to the best of members' abilities and resources.

Ideally, then, the Brotherhood fostered an ethic of cooperation
and mutual respect, while also bolstering male dominance. Local
chapters were organized to govern Brothers and their families and
to help needy members and nonmembers, generally in the form of
tangible aid and spiritual support. The division between Brothers
and nonmembers generated some tensions, but, on the whole,
community life seems to have been enhanced by the presence of an
active morada.

The important practical social functions of the Brotherhood
should not eclipse the faith upon which their society was based.
The Brothers were organized to serve community needs *and* to
enact spiritually beneficial rituals. They were to imitate the life *and*

the suffering and death of Jesus. Their highest good was an ethical *and* a mystical complex. "Faith, exalted by its very simplicity, Hope of Salvation, through the imitation of Christ's suffering, and Charity unlimited toward their fellowman—these form the Trinity governing the 'Penitente' cult."[38]

CHAPTER 7

The Rituals

The Brotherhood of Our Father Jesus is devoted to the Passion, and Holy Week observances are the most important in their annual cycle of worship. The Penitentes' devotion is shaped and expressed through prayer, discipline, music, and ritual. They worship in retreat and in both public and private rites and processions. In addition, initiation into the Brotherhood provides a significant individual rite of passage, while funerals conducted by the Brothers for members or nonmembers enrich and sustain community life.

Brotherhood rituals are orthodox and Roman Catholic. Although observances vary from place to place, the basic patterns are derived from traditional Church rites. The Hermano Mayor, guided by local precedent and conditions, oversees all worship, deciding which services, processions, and penances are collectively appropriate for any particular year. Brothers also have individual vows and needs to fulfill. The resultant variability in the actual conduct of worship thus depends on a complex of personality, situation, and tradition, both local and cultural.[1] Ritual patterns outlined below are therefore modal and fundamental, *not* specific and idiographic.

The Entrada and the Initiation

Although not necessarily blessed by the Church, the morada was considered a sacred place. As such, it was demarcated from the profane world outside by rituals of entrance and expectations for appropriate behavior inside. At certain times, it was also customary to exclude people whose presence might desecrate the ritual setting.

Moradas contain at least two rooms—an *oratorio* or *capilla* ("chapel"), and a common room where the Brothers can congregate and eat. There is generally a loft or storage room besides. Nonmembers are allowed to visit the chapel to pray and meditate before the holy images kept there. Early accounts emphasize the "dark" aspects of the altar and the *mementa mori,* but more recent descriptions and photographs give an impression of warmth and sanctuary. "The immaculateness of the interior of the *morada* always is remarkable, and with spotless whitewashed walls, packed earth floors clean enough to eat from, and white lace curtains, suggests more domestic feeling than violence."[2]

Persons making a *visita* recite an *oración,* or prayer, as they approach the morada door, sometimes continuing inside the chapel. These prayers include some version of the six lines given below, which also serve as a formulaic query and response for Brothers entering the morada to be initiated, to do active penance, or to attend various gatherings there:

—*¿Quién en esta casa da luz?* [from the outside]
—*Jesús.* [from the inside]
—*¿Quién la llena de alegría?*
—*María.*
—*¿Quién la conserva en la fe?*
—*José.*[3]

This invocation of Jesus, Mary, and Joseph further emphasizes the building's familial character as a dwelling place or domestic abode rather than a tomb or coffin as has so often been suggested.

Even more elaborate entrance rituals were required of Brothers desiring to do corporal penance and new members ready for their initiation, the latter accompanied by a sponsor. Most sources concur that these *entradas* ("entrances") took place on the night of *Martes Santo,* Holy Tuesday, although Shrove Tuesday before Lent and the first Friday in Lent have also been reported as the time of initiation. Accounts of this entrada vary, but two basic patterns are discernible, the first apparently more characteristic of the initiation rites, the second probably used when any Brother was to perform active penances.

After the ritualized interchange at the door, the new initiate was admitted and removed his clothes to don the white *calzones* ("trousers"), of the penitent. He recited a creed and swore an oath of allegiance. The seal of obligation was cut in his back. He then asked for lashes equal to the three meditations on the Passion of Jesus, the five wounds of Christ, the seven last words, and the forty days in the wilderness, prefacing his requests with the words "for the love of God." The full fifty-five (or more) strokes were not administered if the initiate fainted before the end. Although the infliction of the seal signaled membership, full status was not granted until a certain number of years' participation in corporal penances was completed.[4]

The second pattern emphasizes the penitent's supplication both to the crucifix as symbolic of the Lord Jesus Christ and to his assembled Brothers. After the ritual entrance, the novice or Brother declared his devotion to and adoration of the crucified Christ. He then crawled from Brother to Brother, begging forgiveness from each. Those who did not respond with a set formula could instead choose to administer lashes to the offender. After these obeisances and assurances, the penitent would fast, pray, meditate, and subject himself to various disciplines.[5]

The *sello* ("seal") or *obligación* ("obligation") served a useful as well as a symbolic function. Cut with *pedernales*—sharp flints, pieces of obsidian, or broken glass—these wounds assured a free flow of blood so the scourgings would not cause welts and bruises. Martinez describes the skill of the Sangrador (also called the "Picador" or "Rallador"), who must not harm the musculature of the back:

> They are stripped to their waists and by a special process of massage applied with the palm of the hands, the Rallador benumbs the muscles on both sides of the spine. Using a razor-edged piece of flint for the purpose, he makes from three to six surface cuts into the flesh, lengthwise on each side, then hands the brother a whip made of hemp or sizal with which he at once starts to whip himself with vigor.[6]

The cuts did leave a lasting scar, however.

A more recent account of the entrada contains a modified version of the entrance formula:

> Penitentes who participate in the ceremony [on Holy Tuesday] go to the morada at an appointed hour and knock on the door. From the inside the officers ask, "Quien toca en las puertas de esta morada?"—Who knocketh upon the doors of this morada? From the outside the other brothers answer, "No son las puertas de la morada, solo las puertas de su conciencia."—They are not the doors of the Morada, only the doors of your conscience.[7]

Although the seal of three gashes is maintained, penitential sacrifices now usually involve prayers, fasting, abstinence, kneeling, prostration, and the like. Nonetheless, it is clear that admission into the morada, whether as a member or a visitor, means self-dedication to penitential devotion in whatever expressive form. Entrance entails not just sanctuary but a direct confrontation with oneself and one's deity.

Annual Observances

According to George M. Foster, religion in Spain may be viewed as comprising the basic cult of the seven Church Sacraments (Baptism, Confirmation, Matrimony, Holy Orders, Holy Eucharist, Penance, and Extreme Unction) and the specialized cults of Christ, Mary, and the saints, with their associated feast days, pilgrimages, dramas, legends, and sundry popular beliefs.[8] In the New World, the fundamental cult pattern was officially transplanted, and the specialized cult complexes more informally transmitted and established.

> If we look at the basic pattern of fiestas in Hispanic America, as manifest in all countries, the picture is surprisingly similar: Epiphany, Candlemas, Lent, Holy Week, Corpus Christi, All Saints' and All Souls' days, and Christmas, plus a fiesta, usually for the patron saint of the community. Presumably these are the feast days the Church considered central to dogma, and the activities of each were thought best calcu-

lated to educate the Indians in the new faith, as well as to maintain the faith of Iberian settlers.[9]

This overall pattern also prevailed in the Hispanic Southwest, where, in many places, the above observances were often sponsored by the Brotherhood in the absence of ecclesiastics.

The Brothers did not usurp the priestly functions of administering the Sacraments. They did not baptize (except in emergencies, as is permissible), confirm, marry, grant absolution, give communion, or admit into Holy Orders. Theirs were special devotions which laymen could practice—rosaries, prayers, hymns, penances, the Way of the Cross, processions, and so on. On special days, their *morada oratorio* would be open to worshippers. It might also serve as the *depósito* ("repository") for the village *santos*, from which they would be carried on feast days and at times of illness or mourning, or where they might be honored by all-night vigils.

The days traditionally celebrated varied from village to village. In Arroyo Hondo, New Mexico, for example, Cleofas Jaramillo describes observances for the village *función* ("feast day"); *El Día de la Santa Cruz,* Feast of the Holy Cross (May 4); *El Día de San Juan,* St. John's Day (June 24); *El Día de Santiago,* St. James's Day (July 25); *El Día de Santa Ána,* St. Anne's Day (July 26); *La Porsiúncula,* sponsored by the Penitentes (August 1); and various times during the Twelve Days of Christmas.[10] Ash Wednesday, Lenten, and Holy Week rites were everywhere the most important in the Church year.

Sources differ as to which holy days Brothers particularly observed, besides the all-important ones during Lent and Holy Week. The times most frequently cited are: *Corpus Christi* (the Thursday after Trinity Sunday, the eighth Sunday after Easter, usually in June); *La Asunción,* the Assumption of Our Lady (August 15); *Todos los Santos,* Feast of All Saints (November 1); and *Aniversario de los difuntos,* All Souls' Day, Day of the Dead (November 2). The day of the *morada's* patron saint was also celebrated.[11]

The season of Lent begins forty-six days before Easter, on Ash Wednesday. Except for the six Sundays, various fasts and abstinences are observed throughout in commemoration of Jesus's forty days in the desert. The last two weeks of Lent, known as Passion

Week and Holy Week, closely follow the final days of Jesus's mortal life.

In the Catholic Church, Lent is considered a preparation for Easter and a time of spiritual renewal. Originally, it was a kind of baptismal retreat, the last stage of the Catechumate, with Catechumens initiated on the night before Easter. Later, physical penances began to assume more importance. Older masses contain themes of "penance, conversion, return to God, sorrow for sin, redemption, the Passion, and especially Baptism." Now, Lent involves individual and collective observances and "is thus a collective retreat of 40 days, a time when one tries to live in the spirit of his Baptism, a time of penance in the ancient sense of repentance, *metanoia,* change of heart and mind, conversion."[12]

The Penitentes observed *La Cuaresma* (Lent) as a time of preparation for Holy Week. The season was one of general moderation and sobriety for all, and the Brothers were no exception. Each morada had its traditional Lenten customs. In Cordova, New Mexico, Brothers appeared in procession on *Miércoles de Ceniza* (Ash Wednesday) to take the statue of *Nuestro Padre Jesús* from the church to the morada, where it remained throughout Lent, and to receive the church keys from the *mayordomo* (sexton). They met in the morada every Wednesday and Friday evening of Lent until Holy Week "for the purpose of prayer and adoration, with acts of penance performed in accordance with vows made . . . [and to] prepare for Holy Week and decide on the extent and scope of their activities during those days which are customarily observed: Holy Wednesday, Holy Thursday, and Good Friday."[13] Some years, Brothers from Cuba, New Mexico, would undertake a long pilgrimage as far as St. John's, Arizona. This practice, called *La Procesión del Estandarte* (Procession of the Standard) was discontinued around 1912.[14] Such a tradition was unusual, public recitations of the Stations of the Cross on Fridays, with private meetings and/or flagellant processions on Friday nights being customary Lenten practice.

Penitential Exercises

The first Lenten observances rarely involved physical penances.

However, "as the season progresses, the penitential passion rising with it, one is likely to meet anywhere in the deep lands between the fields, or in the foot-trails of the wild-sharp gorges, the solitary penitent, dragging his bloody cross, or two or three making their way from morada to morada on their knees, accompanied by the resador reciting the prayers that make the office effective."[15] These were the exercises that inculcated spiritual discipline and expressed religious devotion.

Ejercicios ("exercises") were supervised by the Hermano Mayor, who granted permission to petitioners, assigned roles to participants, and governed the nature and duration of the penances. Some exercises were necessarily public; most were conducted inside the morada. Eventually, most public penitential processions came to be held at night or in remote places to preserve their sanctity.

Brothers doing active penance wore only white trousers, sometimes called *en paños menores* ("in undergarments"). If they emerged in procession, they wore black *vendas* ("hoods") over their heads to insure humility. At the end of the exercise, the *Coadjutores* "wash their lacerated back with *romerillo* [silver sage] tea which acts as an astringent."[16] Whips were also dipped in this tea during the discipline, making them heavier and slightly antiseptic. Alcoholic or herbal stimulants may also have been used.[17]

Modes of physical penance varied. Self-flagellation with whips called *disciplinas* was the most common form.

> These were loosely plaited yucca fibre whips which served as substitutes in New Mexico for the barbed link, iron whips of Spain and the iron-rich colonies. There was another form of small whip of finely knotted wool called *la cuerda,* the cord. Anciently used for personal discipline in Medieval Europe, the cuerda in New Mexico was reserved for lashes given by one member to another upon request, as an added form of devotion.[18]

The other common form of penance was to drag the heavy wooden *maderos,* or crosses, which were taller than a man.

> Some idea of the weight of the maderos . . . may be gained by the fact that processions had to be halted at short

intervals, to allow for the acompanadores to lift the maderos from the shoulders of the penitentes, to allow them to recuperate their strength. . . . And not all penitentes would be allowed to pull the maderos, as only those of sturdy physical development would be equal to the task.[19]

Other penitents might wrap themselves in ropes, cacti, or chains, or bind their arms to small crosses. Tradition and imagination apparently influenced the choice. "The use of obsidian knives and spiny cactus, of yucca scourges, for drawing blood and causing pain, the penance of kneeling on *arroz* (rice) composed of tiny sharp stones from our Southwest anthills, all these were features and modifications suggested and provided by the local landscape."[20]

Some penances were performed to fulfill personal vows, others traditional to the morada might be done by volunteers or appointed representatives. The upper morada at Arroyo Hondo had a special madero called *El Doncello:*

This madero was much heavier than the rest. . . . [It] was seldom used, but on some rare occasions a strapping young penitente would ask to be permitted to carry it. The distance from the morada to the church is at least two hundred yards, altho it is down hill all the way, the road is rough, and the bumping of the rear end of the madero along the ground would cause severe injury to the bare shoulder of the penitente who dragged it. And then the return trip . . . would be uphill, requiring much more exertion . . . the scars resulting on the shoulder of the penitente, would bear mute evidence, throughout his life, of the sacrifice entailed.[21]

A morada near Las Trampas, New Mexico, each year required a lone man, scourging himself at intervals, to cover the distance between that morada and a church some seven miles distant—a feat which took three or four hours.[22] Groups of Brothers from neighboring moradas would also make *visitas* to worship and do penance together.[23]

Whatever their form, the most important aspect of these penitential exercises is their "embeddedness." They were not random or uncontrolled. Brothers of Light who permitted and supervised them attempted to balance what could be expected of a man physically, what the season traditionally demanded, and what the man personally wished to do and why. Penitents were almost always accompanied, not only by helpers but also by persons singing, praying, playing the pito, and carrying sacred images as guides.[24] Their exercises were thus a strict discipline within a total worship complex, *not* masochistic self-indulgences or sadistic tortures. These guarded and guided practices were considered appropriate devotional expressions beneficial for the individual and the community.

Holy Week Observances

Brothers spend most of *Semana Santa* (Holy Week) in retreat at their morada. As a rule, they do not return home until officers for the coming year have been elected. In some communities, the men were absent from *Domingo de Ramos* (Palm Sunday) through *Sábado de Gloria* (Holy Saturday). A retreat from the evening of *Mártes Santo* through *Viernes Santo* (Good Friday) night is more usual, however. In keeping with Hispanic tradition, both the Brothers and their nonmember Catholic neighbors emphasize "not the resurrection message of Easter Sunday [*Pascua*] . . . but rather the mournful imagery of Good Friday: the crucifixion and the sorrowing Virgin."[25]

During the retreat, Brothers slept little, maintaining constant vigils, welcoming and worshipping with many groups of visitors, and undertaking various public processions and services. Their meatless meals were brought in by mayordomos or auxiliadoras. The most popular and nutritious dish was *panocha,* a sweet, porridge-like substance made from the meal of sprouted wheat flour with boiling water and baked in an outdoor oven. This exchange of *charolitas* (Lenten dishes) was part of a community-wide network during Holy Week.[26] The Brothers reciprocated by opening their chapel to visitors and by conducting public religious services.

The Penitentes' Holy Week observances are best considered a devotion to the Passion of Jesus.

In the strict sense devotion is an act of the will giving oneself with fervor to the service of God or divine cult. The Passion is the suffering both interior and exterior endured by Jesus Christ from the Last Supper until His death on the cross.[27]

St. Francis of Assisi, the first known person to receive the stigmata as a result of devotion to the Passion, furthered the popularity of this fervor among the people. "All of this devotion was strengthened among the laity by practices the Crusaders brought back from the Holy Land and by the instructive devices that mendicant preachers had developed, such as the Way of the Cross, miracle plays, Passion tropes, hymns, prayers, and Books of Hours, replete with Passion references."[28] The Franciscans carried many of these devices and expressions to the New World, and such forms provided the basis for over four centuries of Hispanic worship there.

The Passion of Jesus includes the following events, according to New Testament accounts:

a. Agony in the Garden of Gethsemani, in which Jesus sweated blood: Matthew 26:36–46; Mark 14:32–42; Luke 22:39–46; John 18:1.
b. Arrest of Jesus, who was betrayed by Judas: Matthew 26:47–56; Mark 14:43–52; Luke 22:47–53; John 18:2–12.
c. The religious trial before the chief priests: Matthew 26:57–27:1; Mark 14:53–15:1a; Luke 22:54–71; John 18:13–27.
d. Peter's denials: Matthew 26:69–75; Mark 14:66–72; Luke 22:55–62; John 18:15–18, 25–27.
e. The civil trial before Pontius Pilate: Matthew 27:2–26; Mark 15:1b–15; Luke 23:1–25; John 18:28–19:16a.
f. The Way of the Cross: Matthew 27:31–33; Mark 15:20–22; Luke 23:26–32; John 19:16b–17.
g. Crucifixion and death: Matthew 27:34–56; Mark 15:23–41; Luke 23:33–49; John 19:18–30.

The chief sufferings of Christ were His spiritual agony, bloody sweat, scourging, crowning with thorns, crucifixion, and death. The "seven last words" spoken by Jesus during his three hours on the cross are the following:

1. "Father, forgive them; for they know not what they do." Luke 23:34.

2. "Truly, I say to you, today you will be with me in Paradise." Luke 23:43.
3. "Woman, behold, your son! . . . Behold, your mother!" John 19:26–27.
4. "My God, my God, why hast thou forsaken me?" Matthew 27:46.
5. "I thirst." John 19:30.
6. "It is finished." John 19:30.
7. "Father, into thy hands I commit my spirit!" Luke 23:46.[29]

These incidents, sufferings, and last words are selectively emphasized and symbolized in Penitente devotions. Although the Brothers literally followed many of Jesus's sufferings in their penances, they did not always precisely and explicitly recreate the exact sequence of events leading to His death. Passion plays as such were unusual, and the Passion was more frequently evoked through *alabados* (hymns), the Way of the Cross, penitential processions, and certain stylized, dramatic tableaux.

The most famous Penitente-sponsored passion play at Talpa, New Mexico, "is in reality a service" in which a Brother dressed as a centurion strikes the wooden Cristo "in the side at the proper time in the reading."[30] Among the many alabados describing and recounting the Passion is the long cycle usually referred to as *La Pasión del Señor.* Another, *Lloren, pecadores,* includes most events of the Passion and was supposed to have been sung after dramatizations of Jesus's seizure by Roman soldiers.[31]

The *Via Crucis,* a devotion disseminated throughout the world by the Franciscans, played an important part in Penitente worship. Moradas had interior stations of the cross. In addition, during Holy Week, small wooden crosses were set up outside to mark these *estaciones,* generally from the morada to the large cross several hundred yards distant designated the Calvario. The large cross immediately in front of the morada served as the first station, and the Calvario the fourteenth. People knelt at each station while the Rezador led the chants and songs. Nonmembers could participate, and they followed the Brothers, some of whom might be active penitents.

Originally, "devotion to the Passion of Christ, which became widespread in the 12th and 13th centuries, was promoted by many veterans of the Crusades who erected tableaux at home representing various places they had visited in the Holy Land."[32] Franciscans brought the custom to Spain, and it was also carried to the New World colonies.[33] The number of stations varied historically between five and thirty or more, but was stabilized at fourteen by Pope Clement XII in 1731.

> The accepted stations today are: (1) Christ is condemned to death by Pilate; (2) Jesus is made to carry the cross; (3) Jesus falls the first time; (4) Jesus meets His blessed Mother; (5) the cross is laid on Simon of Cyrene; (6) Veronica wipes the face of Jesus; (7) Jesus falls the second time; (8) Jesus speaks to the women of Jerusalem; (9) Jesus falls the third time; (10) Jesus is stripped of His garments and receives gall to drink; (11) Jesus is nailed to the cross; (12) Jesus dies on the cross; (13) Jesus is taken down from the cross; (14) Jesus is laid in the sepulcher.[34]

The devout move from station to station, meditating on each, and customarily reciting an Our Father, Hail Mary, and Gloria in order to gain the indulgence.

An early version of the Way of the Cross is found in the 1870 *cuaderno* (copybook), of the Cochiti Brotherhood.[35] A more recent one has been transcribed, translated, musically annotated, and artfully published in a limited edition portfolio prepared by Dr. Reginald Fisher and formally presented to Don Miguel Archibeque by Archbishop Edwin V. Byrne in 1958. The fourteen-verse alabado, *Considera alma perdida,* provides a verse for each station, along with prayers, meditations, and the Our Father, Hail Mary, and Gloria.[36] Another version, recorded from a woman in Arroyo Hondo, New Mexico, by Reyes N. Martinez, includes a short prayer (*"Adoremos a este Cristo y bendicenos, que por tu santa cruz y pasion y muerte redimiste al mundo y a mi pecador. Amen"*), "said at the end of the recital at each station, people kissing the ground as they rise to walk to the next station," and a short hymn response (*"Lloren los corazones de todos los cristianos, por la pasion y muerte de nuestro Senor"*), "sung as people walk from one station to the other."[37]

Major processions with or without active penitents and with or without a formal observance of the stations of the cross generally took place on Wednesday, Thursday, and Friday of Holy Week.

Sources differ as to the identity and times for these. According to Woodward, *La Procesión de los Dolores* (the Procession of Sorrows) was formed on Holy Wednesday, *La Procesión de la Santa Cruz* (the Procession of the Holy Cross) on Holy Thursday, and *La Procesión de la Sangre de Cristo* (the Procession of the Blood of Christ) on Good Friday. Juan B. Rael cites a procession on Holy Wednesday, two on Holy Thursday, together with a dramatization of the seizure of Jesus, the Good Friday dramatization of the fourth station of the cross, and an afternoon recitation of the stations of the cross. Lorenzo de Cordova describes a Holy Wednesday procession to venerate former Calvarios of the morada and "the bloodiest procession of all," *La Procesión de Sangre,* on Good Friday afternoon.[38]

Dramatic Tableaux

Most enactments of final events in Jesus's earthly life were highly stylized and symbolic, centering on a single moment and involving santos carried in procession. These tableaux took place on Holy Thursday and Good Friday. In the Catholic Church, Holy Thursday is primarily a commemoration of the institution of the Holy Eucharist.

> In some places in the past it was called *dies traditionis,* referring to the many *traditiones* (betrayal or handing over) that occurred on that day: the betrayal of Jesus by Judas, our Savior's handing over of Himself for the salvation of mankind, and lastly, the giving of His Body and Blood in the Eucharist. English-speaking lands often call it Maundy Thursday, a corruption of the Latin word Mandatum, used to describe the rite of the Washing of the Feet associated with Holy Thursday for centuries.[39]

Good Friday is a day of mourning; no bells are rung, *matracas* (wooden ratchets or clackers) being used instead.[49]

Sometime on Holy Thursday, there may be a dramatization of the seizure and religious trial of Jesus. At Arroyo Hondo, New Mexico, this *Emprendimiento* took place at two o'clock in the afternoon. Men carried the life-sized statue of Nuestro Padre Jesus from the church, followed by the Rezador, who read the appropriate lines, and the women.

> From *la morada* . . . two files of brethren of light, representing the Jews, started out. These men had red handkerchiefs tied over their heads with a knot on top representing a helmet. They were preceded by a man dressed like a centurion. The Jews carried long iron chains and *matracas*. . . . On meeting the procession coming from the church, they stopped before the statue and asked, "Who art Thou?" The men carrying the statue answered, *"Jesus El Nacareno* (Jesus of Nazareth)." The Jews then seized the statue, tied the statue's hands with a white cord, while their leader read the arrest sentence. The other Jews stood loudly clanging the chains and rattling the *matracas.* They led the procession back to the *morada,* carrying with them the statue.[41]

El Despedimiento de Jesús a María, a Holy Thursday afternoon rite commemorating Jesus's taking leave of His mother before the Last Supper, is mentioned only once, as a current Brotherhood observance.[42]

El Encuentro (the "Encounter") is a dramatization of the meeting between Jesus and His mother on the way to Calvary, the fourth station of the cross. It is usually enacted during the late morning of Good Friday. Most of the villagers, whether with Brotherhood ties or not, participated in and shared the intense emotions of this encounter, particularly the women.

The women process from the church or chapel, carrying an image of the Virgin Mary, usually *Nuestra Señora de los Dolores* (Our Lady of Sorrows). The Penitentes come from the morada bearing an image of the Cristo, usually *Padre Jesús Nazareno.* When the two groups meet, there is a recitation or an alabado commemorating the Passion. At the appropriate time, the figures are tipped and brought close together in a symbolic last embrace of Mother and Son.[43]

In some places, elements of the sixth station of the cross—Veronica wiping Jesus's face—were incorporated into the Encuentro. At Arroyo Hondo, when the two groups met, "one of the women took a white cloth from her head, and approaching on her knees wiped the face of the statue, while the grieving Marys wept real tears aloud."[44] At Arroyo Seco, New Mexico, five girls from nine to thirteen years old were chosen to be *Las Veronicas*. Four carried the statue of the Virgin and the fifth the *rostro,* a cloth with three embroidered imprints of Jesus's face. The Encuentro took place in the afternoon; after wiping the Cristo's face three times and a recitation describing His meeting with His mother, both groups returned to the morada.[45]

In 1925, seven girls took part in the procession on Good Friday afternoon at San Mateo, New Mexico.

> Three young girls, in white confirmation robes, led the march going forward on their knees. Each one carried a platter on which there were a crown of thorns, a hammer, and a reed. . . . Following them were St. Veronica and the three Marys.[46]

This procession also included the Brother who was to be the Christ figure in the simulated crucifixion, which took place later. The whole passion-play-like proceedings appear to be unusually elaborate, however—the morning *Encuentro* and perhaps *Las Veronicas* being more common enactments.

The Death Cart

Carved figures of *La Muerte* (Death) were a part of the paraphernalia of most moradas. Exhumed human skulls were originally used as *mementa mori* and symbols of intense contemplation, both in the Old and the New Worlds. Sometime during the nineteenth century in New Mexico, these began to be replaced by wooden death angels.

According to tradition, Nazario Lopez of Cordova made the first death figure in northern New Mexico. This statue, from Las Trampas, was described by Army lieutenant John Gregory Bourke in his diary for July 20, 1881:

> In a room, to the right of the door [of the church], which corresponded to our church vestry, there was a hideous statue, dressed in black, with pallid face and monkish cowl, which held in its hands a bow and arrow drawn in position . . . [and] was seated upon a wooden wagon, something similar to

an artillery limber, but made in the crudest way of wood, fastened with pins of the same material. The wheels were sections of a pine trunk; ungreased axles, and ungreased pole made unearthly music and to add to the difficulty of hauling such a vehicle, the box seat upon which Death sat as grim charioteer was filled with smooth-worn and heavy boulders.[47]

Such images, so reminiscent of the elaborate royal triumphal processions of the Renaissance and later Spanish and Mexican *pasos* (religious floats) depicting Christ's triumph over Death, were very likely patterned after the thirteenth card of the Tarot trumps, which depict a skeleton or mummified corpse with a scythe or bow. These cards had in turn been inspired by Petrarch's fourteenth-century poem *I Trionfi*, in which the Death Angel was female, like *Nuestra Comadre Sebastiana* or *Doña Sebastiana,* as the New Mexican figures came to be called.[48]

Early death figures were completely carved, so they might appear exposed or dressed in black. They carried a bow and arrow, and generally had large hands and small heads. Later Muertes from outlying areas, especially the San Luis Valley, have larger heads, sometimes without the lower jaw, and were usually finished only at the extremities because they were invariably clothed in black. More recent statues often brandish a wooden ax rather than the bow and arrow. Some of these "doll-sized" figures, without the cart, were intended "to be carried by women and children who made a penitential pilgrimage, barefooted, to the local Calvary."[49]

In certain moradas, pulling the death cart was a traditional penance, especially during Good Friday processions. Henderson notes the Brother followed the cross-bearers in the Abiquiu procession and pulled the *carreta* ("cart") "by a horsehair rope passed over his shoulders and under his armpits, the painful weight of the dragging cart cutting into his naked flesh." At Trampas, according to Leyba:

> Just two penitents are chosen by the *Mayordomo* [Hermano Mayor] to pull this cart. The penitents are required to wear only their drawers and a red rag to cover their faces. Even should it be snowing these exercises have to be performed in this way, bare-footed, etc. The persons performing this task

were said to live longer, and if there were any who did not relish it, they were never chosen.

In describing a Muerte from Garcia, Colorado, E. Boyd claims that "it is said to have required two brothers to help the penitent who dragged the box in Holy Week processions, in order to hold the figure as it passed over rocky slopes and ravines."[50] Stones were placed in the cart for stability and to increase the difficulty of the penance.

Various beliefs are reported in connection with the death cart and its use. The most common is cited by Henderson:

> Tradition has it that the arrow once left the bow to strike the heart of a mocking bystander, killing him instantly. Variations of this tradition exist through all the mountain villages and are occasionally applied to some specific person, long since dead.

Reyes N. Martinez claims that such an incident happened at Arroyo Hondo, New Mexico, in 1867, but the penitent Brother himself was the victim. At the Calvario, when the Brother dropped to his knees, he jolted the cart and released the arrow, which pierced his kidney and killed him. Some believed that the released arrow indicated the next Cristo. "By another account, it is considered good fortune to be bumped by the cart while it is being wheeled in the procession to Calvary," according to Wilder.[51]

The Brotherhood did *not* worship death. The death figures and *calaveras* ("skulls") served as a reminder of mortality and the necessity for preparing and praying for a *"buena muerte,* one in the state of grace leading to entrance into heaven."[52] In addition, the use of Muertes for penitential exercises was less an allegorical float depicting the "Triumph of Christ over Death" than a literal struggle against death, or rather against the death which suddenly claims the unprepared soul. Thus, George Mills has suggested that Penitente processions involving death carts vividly juxtapose the two types of death—Christian death, symbolized by the crosses, and "unprepared-for" death, symbolized by *La Muerte* in her crude New Mexican ox-cart.[53]

170

The Simulated Crucifixion

The term "crucifixion" strictly refers to a particular "method of capital punishment commonly used among the ancient peoples surrounding the Mediterranean basin from approximately the 6th century B.C. to the 4th Christian century."[54] Although they imitated the suffering of Jesus, the Brothers did not intentionally and literally recreate His death. Theirs were simulated or symbolic crucifixions only.

Among men determined to follow Jesus's example in their daily lives, there were also those for whom the imitation of His final suffering, even at the risk of possible death, was an honor. According to the New Testament and official Catholic tradition:

> To take up one's cross means to turn away from the service of the world and the flesh (Gal 5.24), and thus to be a true disciple (Lk 14.27), a follower of Christ (Mk 8.34; Mt 16.24). . . . Anyone who refuses to take up the cross is unworthy of Jesus (Mt 10.38); the true disciple takes up his cross daily to follow the Master (Lk 9.23). As a follower of Jesus he is willing to deny himself many things (Mt 10.34-39) and even to make the supreme sacrifice of his life for the sake of Christ and the gospel (Mk 8.35).[55]

The man who played the cherished role of the Cristo was designated by miracle or inspiration, by lot, by appointment, or by selection from among petitioners. Brothers of Light, or sometimes the Hermano Mayor alone, supervised the method used or made the choice. Since actual crucifixion was not intended, the man was usually young and sturdy, and his sacrifice very closely supervised.

There is absolutely no substantiated evidence for nails ever having been used in the simulated crucifixion. William G. Ritch has noted the earliest extant references to such simulations, and in both places—Mora (in 1859 or 1860) and Pena Blanca (in 1867 and 1868)—Samuel Ellison saw individuals "lashed" to the cross. As early as 1878, the Catholic "Viator," although anxious to discredit the Brotherhood, stated that no nails were ever used. These references occur a good ten or twenty years before Charles F. Lummis's fanciful account of 1888, when the chosen Cristo supposedly sobbed for the nails rather than the "dishonor" of the rope. As recently as 1960, the editors of the *Denver Post* appended a disclaimer to an article on the Brotherhood stating that: "Catholic authorities in Denver who have read this . . . say that 'little credence is to be put in the Lummis story that Penitentes were actually nailed to the Cross. Careful Catholic observers never record this.' "[56]

All photographs and reasonably reliable accounts of simulated crucifixions indicate the chosen Brother was bound to the cross for a short period of time. Available photographic evidence consists of three pictures:

1. *San Mateo, New Mexico, March 30, 1888,* taken by Charles F. Lummis with the help of Ireneo Chaves, who wore a pistol and told the Celadores "that if anyone attempted to hurt [Lummis] or the instruments, he would blow his head off." The photograph shows a man bound to a wooden cross with a white sheet around his trunk and legs and a black hood covering his face. Two Brothers hold guy-ropes. In all, eight Brothers of Light, each wearing a circlet of thorns like a crown, are visible. A black blob below the Cristo was a Penitente who "lay down with his feet against the cross and his head pillowed upon the stone, while the mass of *entraña* [cactus] kept his back sixteen or eighteen inches above the ground." Lummis claims the Cristo remained on the upright cross for thirty-one minutes, but a letter written by Amado Chaves indicates that "when they arrived there was a man tied on the cross . . . [who] was fainting, so they [the Brothers] brought him down and soon revived him."[57]

2. *Near Trinidad, Colorado, 1909,* taken by O. L. Orton at a small, apparently isolated cross. One man is lashed to the cross, while the other two penitents flagellate themselves. A Rezador kneels in front, and the two remaining acompañadores stand near the penitents.[58]

3. *San Mateo, New Mexico, 1925,* taken by Harriet Mayfield. Three men, hooded and apparently draped, are lashed to crosses in front of the morada. They are standing on wooden platforms. In a letter to Dorothy Woodward, Mayfield wrote that "the only point where it became hysterical was while the Christ was on the cross (one film of this) when there was sobbing and wailing from the crowd."[59]

During the 1920s, any number of people witnessed the simulated crucifixion at Abiquiu, New Mexico, including various noted artists such as B. J. O. Nordfeldt. Nordfeldt's wife, Dr. Margaret Nordfeldt, writes that they saw in 1921: "A man previously chosen to portray the *Cristo,* a great honor, was bound to the cross with thick ropes; cross and man were erected and surrounded by worshippers until the man lost consciousness, which took from twenty minutes to half an hour."[60]

On March 30, 1923, Will Shuster saw a Cristo lashed to a cross steadied by several Brothers who sang while several others flagellated themselves. After about twenty minutes, "as the *Cristo*'s head dropped forward, the *Hermano Mayor,* who was wearing dark glasses, blew a whistle which was the signal for terminating the ceremony, whereupon the cross and man was carried back into the *morada* followed by the flagellants."[61]

William Penhallow Henderson sketched and painted many of the Abiquiu scenes he and his wife, Alice Corbin Henderson, witnessed. Some of these works illustrate her sensitive, excellent written account.[62] There are also photographs of two undated "paintings from life" by Gerald Cassidy, which show a flagellant procession and a simulated crucifixion at Abiquiu, among the W.P.A. Files in Santa Fe.

Other notable artistic evidence comes from a set of thirteen paintings entitled "Los Hermanos Penitentes." These were painted by I. L. Udell after his experiences in the Taos area during the 1930s.[63] Judging from such evidence and reliable verbal accounts, the simulated crucifixion appears to have been a time of intense emotion focused on the stark symbolism of the muffled human on the cross or the life-sized wooden crucifix.[64]

The human Cristo was not expected to die, although there are any number of traditions about such a death, which allegedly assured the Brother's soul salvation in Heaven. Relatives were said to have been notified by shoes or clothes placed on the doorstep. The grave supposedly remained secret for a year or forever, or it was marked with a large cross. Some believed such a Brother was buried upright. However, most of these traditions seem to be part of the mystique outsiders projected onto the Brotherhood, or Brothers themselves fostered to reinforce respect for and awe of their most important services.

Tenebrae Services

During the Middle Ages, Tenebrae (from the Latin: darkness, lower world, death) services were recited in total darkness, giving the ritual its name. In the official Roman Catholic service:

> At the end of each psalm, one of the 15 candles is extinguished on the triangular candlestick placed before the altar. At the conclusion of Psalm 146, only one candle, at the top of the triangle, remains lighted. When the *Benedictus* is sung, the six altar candles are extinguished one by one after every second verse; and when the antiphon *Traditor autem* is repeated after the canticle, the one lighted candle is taken from the triangle and hidden behind the altar, where it remains until the end of the service. . . . The gradual extinguishing of all but the last candle was meant to point to the Apostles' desertion of Christ, and the last candle was supposed to depict Christ's burial (in its disappearance . . .) and resurrection (in its reappearance).[65]

The din at the end was originally the sound of chant books being closed, but it came to be interpreted as the chaos following Jesus's death at the "sixth hour," when "there was darkness over the whole land until the ninth hour, while the sun's light failed" (Luke 23:44-45), and "the curtain of the temple was torn in two, from top to bottom; and the earth shook, and the rocks were split; the tombs also were opened, and many bodies of the saints who had fallen asleep were raised, and coming out of the tombs after his resurrection they went into the holy city and appeared to many" (Matthew 27:51-53).[66] Before Pope Pius XII's reforms of Holy Week in 1955, Tenebrae services were held in the Catholic Church on Holy Thursday, Good Friday, and Holy Saturday.

Las Tinieblas of the Brotherhood is very similar to the official Church observances. Usually held on Holy Thursday and Good Friday nights and preceded by a rosary service, it is open to both members and nonmembers. Outsiders to the village often attend too. In the past, active penitents might prostrate themselves in front of the door so worshippers would step on them going into the church or morada. The Brothers of Blood would gather in the back or in a side room for the services.[67]

After the doors are closed, the only light comes from thirteen to seventeen candles in the triangular white candelabrum, black *tenebrario* (a special candle holder), or on the altar. Each candle or pair of candles is extinguished following the singing of an alabado verse, which replaces the psalms of the official Church ritual. When the last light, which represents the dead Lord, has been removed or covered, a signal is given, and a period of loud, raucous noise ensues. Chains, matracas, drums, flutes, clapping, and stamping simulate the time of chaos while, formerly, the Brothers of Blood flagellated themselves. This tumult alternates with periods of silence during which *sudarios,* prayers for the dead, are offered for deceased relatives after requests from members of the audience. The single candle is finally brought back, and the rest relit from it. If held in a church, the Brothers leave first, walking backward through the door to keep facing the altar. If at a morada, the visitors depart immediately.

Las Tinieblas is perhaps the least variable and certainly the most public of Penitente rites. The basic pattern of progressive darkness and then alternate cacaphony and prayer, with a final return to light, is widely reported.[68] Afterward, most moradas elect officers for the coming year, and the Brothers then return to their homes and their secular lives.

Funeral Rites

Roman Catholic rites at death involve Confession, Holy Communion, called *Viaticum* if given before death, and Extreme Unction, or Holy Annointing, to give health and strength to the departing soul. These Last Sacraments must be administered by a priest. In communities without resident priests, the Rezador would likely be called in to recite prayers at the end and then "gritarle Jesus, call out the name of Jesus three times as the person was expiring." This custom is rarely reported, but certain alabados such as *La encomendación del alma* ("The Commending of the Soul") were sometimes sung when a person expired.[69]

In Hispanic Catholic tradition, a *velorio de difuntos* ("wake for the dead") followed. The corpse was washed, dressed, and laid out in the largest room of the house, surrounded by lighted candles. It was never left alone until burial. Sympathetic neighbors arrived and went first to pray over the body and then to another room where *los dolientes* ("the mourners") waited to receive *pésames* ("condolences"). Throughout the night, alabados were sung and prayers recited, with a rosary service around midnight.

Outside, small bonfires were lit, and the men gathered around them to talk and joke while the women prepared *la cena,* the supper that was to be served shortly after midnight. These were warm and friendly occasions which lent "communal support to the immediate survivors in their time of crisis while at the same time providing them with a ritualized (and therefore safe) outlet for personal grief."[70] Praying and singing continued until dawn, when an appropriate, final alabado was sung.

If the deceased is a Penitente or a member of such a family, Brothers and Auxiliadoras take charge of all proceedings. The body may be laid out in the morada's chapel, while mourners congregate in the common room. In other communities, the body may be taken to the morada for special services there sometime during the night. Formerly, processions of flagellants would be formed to visit the body and aid the dead Brother's soul on its journey by their penitential expressions. These public processions were the subject of Church rebukes during the nineteenth century, but they were considered important and efficacious observances in Brotherhood funerals.[71]

Official Church rituals on the morning after the wake involve a Requiem mass, a procession to the cemetery, and the burial. The body could be interred without a priest in attendance, the Requiem mass and the blessing of the plot being reserved for the cleric's next visit. The funeral procession sometimes stopped to rest on the way to the cemetery. These *paradas* ("stops") were "determined by the distance covered and the route traversed," as well as the wealth of the bereaved family, for "in the towns where there is a resident priest and where he himself accompanies the funeral cortege, there is a charge for each *parada* since the *difunto* [deceased] is blessed at each stop." Paradas were designated by small wooden crosses and a pile of stones "to remind all passersby to say a *sudario* (prayer for the dead) each time they go by." These *descansos* ("resting places") "have nothing whatever to do with Penitente rites, as ordinarily believed."[72] Neither descansos, which were commonly found around villages, nor old Calvarios, then, are related to the burial of Brothers who died naturally or while doing penances, including the simulated crucifixion.

The dead were not always buried in coffins; sometimes they were interred wrapped in a *mortaja* ("shroud"). This practice has often been associated with the Brotherhood, but it was not exclusive with them. Persons might be buried without a coffin because of a promise made or because of membership in a particular lay religious organization.

> Members of the Sodality of Our Lady of Carmel almost always ask to be buried in the habit of their intercessor and protector. No shoes are worn with this habit and it is the custom to lay the corpse on the floor with an adobe brick placed upon its head, for an hour. This is done in order to receive *las gracias del suelo* (the blessings of the floor). . . .[73]

Other groups also earned the privilege of burial in an *hábito* ("habit") and sometimes children were promised by their parents, in which case the habit might be that of the Holy Child. Shrouded adult corpses were carred upon a *taur* (homemade platform) and children on an *andita,* such as the one used to carry santos in procession.[74]

After burial, members of the immediate family traditionally went into mourning for a full year. A *misa de ocho dias* a full week after the death and a memorial novena or mass at the end of the first year were observed. Rosaries at these and other times were conducted by the Brotherhood for those who could not afford such memorials. *Las Tinieblas* services with prayers for the dead might also be included here.

> Among the Hispanos, to pass away is to go on to a better life, to fulfill one's destiny. There is a strong communion between the departed and the living. Masses, novenas and prayers are constantly being said for those who have gone on. Like other Latins, New Mexico Hispanos and those of the Southwest are philosophical about death. They do not invite it but neither are they afraid of it. ¡*Sea por Dios!* (God's will be done) is the expression used to comment upon the passing of a loved one.[75]

This characteristic "fatalism" stems in part from the conviction that the soul exists and that life is in an important way a preparation for death and salvation or damnation.[76] Among Brothers, this communion and conviction was further expressed by their belief in ghostly penitents and similar phenomena.

Conclusion

Reliable eyewitness accounts of Brotherhood rituals are not numerous, and Brothers themselves seldom divulge their beliefs and practices. In assembling materials for a 1955 exhibition on the Penitentes at the Taylor Museum of The Colorado Springs Fine Arts Center, George Mills and Richard Grove classified sixty-five sources "in terms of their credibility." Later work by this author brought together in chronological order some 110 sources claiming eyewitness status.[77] Approximately forty of these date from the nineteenth century. Unfortunately, the bias of most early observers, although in most cases obvious, makes their accounts unreliable for historical study. With the exception of a few photographs, manuscripts by Laurence F. Lee, Mary Austin, Dorothy Woodward, and certain documents in the Santa Fe files of the New Mexico Writers' Project of the Work Projects Administration, most twentieth-century reports tend to be more influenced by the earlier literature than by actual experience. Few can claim Alice Corbin Henderson's talent for synthesizing personal feeling, observation of onlookers' and participants' reactions, and a description of events exactly as they happened. Combined with her husband's illustrations, *Brothers of Light* remains one of the most vivid, accurate and reliable sources.[78]

Such evidence as is properly available confirms the simplicity, sincerity, and spiritual expressiveness of Brotherhood observances, as well as their localized variability. Although the more public and severe penitential practices have disappeared, two historically crucial aspects of Penitente rituals endure—the commemoration of the Passion of Jesus during Holy Week and the celebration of community both then and in times of need and bereavement. By maintaining traditional forms of devotion through prayer, hymn, discipline, and rite, the Brotherhood succeeded in sustaining that sense of the sacred which is vital to community life and individual faith.

The Legends and the Sacred

Penitentes' Day
The Penitentes will hold their orgies at Los Griegos, a village three
miles north of Albuquerque, to-day. Their rites consist of flagellations,
carrying crosses, and other horrid rites which should be suppressed. W.
L. Trimble & Co. will run hacks to Los Griegos this afternoon, leaving
the San Felipe hotel at noon. Those who have not seen the penitentes
ought to go. The sight is similar to drawing back the curtain from the
14th century.
—*Albuquerque Morning Journal,* Friday, April 23, 1886, p. 4.

There were also daytime processions. Córdova was dominated by an
old *Calvario* on the crest of the grade leading to Truchas. Although not
in current use, it was visited faithfully at least once a year by fulfillers
of vows. When this happened, we were afforded a rare sight of
sombrely garbed *Acompañadores* and white-drawered flagellants with
their black hoods limned against the sky and the imposing background
of the Sangre de Cristo Mountains. Distance rendered the whole a
pantomime, and the fitful wind brought snatches of singing and the
wail of the flute.
If I chanced to meet such a daylight procession at firsthand, I would
step aside and join the onlooking villagers with bared head. As some
familiar figure passed by, I too would wince, echoing with them the
silent prayers uttered by lips which barely moved.
—Lorenzo de Córdova, *Echoes of the Flute,* 1972, p. 11.

By preserving longstanding Hispanic Catholic traditions, the
Brothers of Our Father Jesus contributed substantially to spiritual
security and physical survival in the isolated villages. They
appropriated orthodox forms of worship and adapted them into
vital, significant religious and social expressions, however
shortlived. These rites provided the setting for individual religious

179

experiences and served to consecrate and confirm basic communal ties.

The outsider, however reverent, is still very much an onlooker without this deep sense of place. The nonmember villager can become a participant observer, moved by the worship to recall and renew his or her own faith. The Brothers themselves, suffering a period of darkness before returning to the light, or guiding others through this ritual of transformation, are participating in an important sacred dimension of experience which has roots in ancient religious forms.

Penance

Penance generally indicates some kind of voluntary suffering or punishment undergone to express sorrow for recognized sin or shortcoming. Sorrow and regret, usually called repentance, are motivated not only by acknowledged guilt but also by the desire to change, to undo a past which cannot be reversed or recovered, and to reform the future course of life, which leads to demonstration of atonement and amendment. The Greek term is *metanoia*, transformation of mind, similar to the conversion experience. Penance is thus both a physical and a spiritual exercise to relieve painful feelings and to restructure thoughts, values, and deeds.

The process of restoring spiritual and social relationships involves confession, expiation, and release. These steps are simply illustrated in Hebrew ritual on the Day of Atonement:

> First, public confession of sin was made over the heads of two goats. Then one of the goats was slain in atonement and was burnt upon the altar as a sacrifice; and finally the other goat was led into the wilderness to show that the guilt had been removed, never to be found again.[1]

Similar steps are formalized in the Roman Catholic Sacrament of Penance, which requires of the penitent contrition, confession, and satisfaction in order to gain absolution from a priest, the only person authorized to absolve in the name of the Father, Son, and Holy Ghost.

Satisfaction in general is compensation for injury inflicted; as a part of the Sacrament it is compensation for temporal punishment due to sin, since eternal punishment is compensated for by the merits of Christ in virtue of the Redemption and is remitted by absolution. Sacramental satisfaction has its foundation in the doctrine that, after sin itself is forgiven, further reparation is required for the removal of certain of the effects of sin that may remain. This is effected by penitential works freely performed in a spirit of genuine contrition.[2]

The nature of the satisfaction imposed is variable. Indeed, the history of formalized satisfactions, such as in penitentials or manuals for confessors, provides a rich social commentary.

The Sacrament of Penance is unequivocally reserved to the Apostles and their successors, the priests of the Church. Nevertheless, "perfect contrition, which means sorrow perfected by love, can justify a person even outside the sacramental forum,"[3] and manifestations of true penitential feeling have usually been encouraged by the ecclesiastical hierarchy. Historically, of course, the permissible expressive forms have varied from prayer and fasting to physical mortifications. On the whole, they have been rationalized by the following texts (from The Revised Standard Version Common Bible):

a. The demonstration of devotion to Christ by imitation:

"And he said to all, 'If any man would come after me, let him deny himself and take up his cross daily and follow me. For whoever would save his life will lose it; and whoever loses his life for my sake, he will save it.' " (Luke 9:23-24)

"For to this you have been called, because Christ also suffered for you, leaving you an example, that you should follow in his steps." (I Peter 2:21)

b. The mastery of human passions through self-discipline:

". . . but I pommel my body and subdue it, lest after preaching to others I myself should be disqualified." (I Corinthians 9:27)

These mandates have been interpreted both literally and figuratively by all Christians.

Asceticism (derived from the Greek *askesis*, meaning training, practice, or discipline) in Christianity came to be associated more with those who had vowed to serve God in various formalized roles.

> In the early Middle Ages . . . there was an increasing difference between the minimum standard expected of the layman and the ascetic practice of the monk . . . [and] the layman often sank into the position of a spectator in the life of the Church, while the clergy performed its sacred rites and monastics accepted more intense obligations. . . . The coming of the friars began to bridge the gap between secular and ascetic Christians. . . . The "Third Orders" of lay associates . . . combined a semimonastic discipline with life in the world . . . thus beginning to bring asceticism out of the cloister into the home and market place.[4]

This renewed commitment to lay ascetic practices was transplanted to the New World and preserved there by devout settlers such as those on the northern Hispanic frontier who eventually evolved the Brotherhood of Our Father Jesus.

Brotherhood rituals might best be viewed *not* as makeshift (and illegal) substitutes for the official Sacrament of Penance but as attempts to guide the expression of and even to induce contrition or true repentance in Brothers and their Catholic neighbors. Ideally, this was accomplished through a disciplined concentration on the Passion of Jesus, made vivid by prayers, alabados, santos, personal mimesis, various deprivations, and a set of traditional rites which had to be appropriately enacted. For the Brothers, atonement involved rigorous physical expiation. Although forgiveness was undoubtedly hoped for and sought, like all practicing Catholics, Brothers were officially required to attend confession and communion at least once a year. Thus, while Brotherhood rituals technically did not usurp the clergy's power to absolve,[5] they did supplement the Church rites and substitute for them when the official hierarchy could not fulfill its ministry.

Ghostly Penitents

Various local traditions attest to the deep symbolic importance of physical penance. In 1882, Bandelier noted that Pena Blanca "Mexicans" maintained the "superstition" that flagellation "makes the clouds form and thus brings rain," a belief also reportedly held by Manzano residents in the late nineteenth century.[6] In an 1874 letter from Conejos, Colorado, the Jesuit Father Personé wrote that despite the great physical hardships endured by the Penitentes, "on the contrary, only a few take sick; this they ascribe to a special help from heaven."[7] One of the local legends associated with the miraculous crucifix of Our Lord of Esquipulas in El Santuario at Potrero (Chimayo), New Mexico, recounts how the figure was found by Bernardo Abeyta while he was performing his customary penances near the Santa Cruz River.[8] Such beliefs were not necessarily widespread, but other, similar ones were probably maintained throughout the region, possibly well into the twentieth century. Without further corroboration, their importance is less in their specific content than in their indication of the powerful symbolic meanings attached to physical penances.

One set of widely reported beliefs and legends is thematically coherent—the association of Brothers of Blood with revenants. According to Reyes N. Martinez, "in those days [late nineteenth century], a strong belief existed among the people of the small villages that the souls of departed penitentes used to assume human form and come to this world to accompany processions, taking their places in the rows of penitentes." An Arroyo Hondo woman around sixty years old told him about fulfilling a vow made when she was sixteen (ca. 1890s). She was to carry the Muerte from the morada to the church on Holy Thursday during the dark period of the Tinieblas. Two rows of nine Brothers accompanied her. However, she counted twenty in all, with the last in each row seeming "to possess a translucency of the flesh that showed the outline of his skeleton, the ribs especially seemed to show more prominently." These "unearthly figures" accompanied her into the church and then disappeared. As late as 1967, Branning too was told that people at Truchas, New Mexico, used to refer to the Penitentes as people of the dead.[9]

Some versions stress the more comical and cautionary aspects of ghostly penitents. Chacon notes the village idiot caught spying on the morada. He was pursued and overtaken by two Brothers, one

183

of whom lifted his hood to reveal a grinning skull. Cordova recounts the Abiquiu story of Chispitas, who despite warnings followed a lone Brother some distance before he realized that "all that remained smiling at [him] was a shiny ivory-colored skull [and] he saw a thin, fragile skeleton tightly grasping a bloody *disciplina*, and floating within the skeleton's chest cavity, its flame flickering with the wind, was a three inch candle." The figure left blood but no footprints, and "the fright received by Chispitas was quite enough to warn other village youths against trailing after stray Penitentes during Holy Week." Reyes Martinez's father, Julian A. Martinez, told him about an amusing incident before a Tinieblas at Arroyo Hondo about 1890:

> The lashing of backs continued unceasingly, while their leader went inside to make room for the members. . . . Presently, the veil of one of the penitentes loosened and fell off his face, down to the ground. The antics of the "brother," as this happened, were amusing indeed. He ceased whipping himself and stood straight and stiff, looking straight down, his "discipline" . . . held in one hand, down by his side, his chin jerked back on his chest, all much like a bronco horse that balks at being led by a rope. Conscious that he was being observed by those on the side lines, he engaged in making all kinds of faces, evidently in an effort to make himself unrecognizable.

No one noticed his plight until Don Julian drew it to the Acompañador's attention. Later, when Martinez confronted the man, he "expressed utter ignorance of it, saying 'Don't you know that those (the penitentes) are the dead, come down from the other world to perform these sacrifices?' "[10]

Other versions were maintained by the Brothers themselves and involve unfulfilled vows. Lummis was told by a Penitente who had seen "two skeletons, whipping themselves upon the naked bones of their backs" that these were Brothers who had broken their promises. Aurelio M. Espinosa, Sr., heard a story current in Taos, New Mexico, from his father. A mysterious flagellant in the church loft led the Brothers into the mountains and disappeared. "The Penitentes later explained that this was doubtless the soul of a dead Penitente who had not done his duty in life,—a false

Penitente,—and God had sent him back to earth to scourge himself properly, before allowing him to enter heaven." The most elaborate ghostly processions supposedly took place for three years on Holy Thursday at Arroyo Hondo, New Mexico—in 1886, *El Año de Nevada* (the year of the great snowfall), when many shepherds from the area perished, in 1887, and in 1888. There were so many Penitentes that a house in La Atalaya at the lower end of the valley was used as an auxiliary morada. The procession back to the village oratorio passed through a gulch called La Canada Mamona, where they were joined by men with white linen hoods, semi-transparent bodies, and bloodless backs. These dead Brothers disappeared when the village was reached. On the return, the ones *del otro mundo* ("from the other world") rejoined those *de carne y hueso* ("of flesh and bone"), disappearing again in the gulch.[11]

The mysterious appearance of Brothers apparently did not always coincide with Lenten and Holy Week activities. Martinez reports the story of Hermano Manuel Avila, who was walking the old road from San Cristobal to Arroyo Hondo when he heard two voices but saw no people and then encountered two lighted candles which he could not extinguish. Upon reaching Arroyo Hondo, he learned that two of his Brothers had that morning been killed by lightning on that very spot! In 1940, a seventy-year-old informant from Antonito, Colorado, told Juan Rael about seeing seven flagellants while herding sheep. The next day, there was blood on the rocks where they had passed by and disappeared. More recently, Montano interviewed a Brother who remained in the morada for several days after Easter. About midnight, an unknown visitor knocked, motioned toward the chapel, prayed inside for a while and left.[12]

In part, such stories had practical value—both in insuring privacy by frightening nonmembers and, very likely, in stimulating Brothers' obedience by suggesting that broken vows had to be fulfilled before the soul could hope for salvation. In part, these beliefs, which were associated with a general fear of ghosts, might simply be expected in the traditional Hispanic culture.

> People are afraid to go out alone in the dark, young and old, through fear of ghosts (*los difuntos* or *dijuntos,* also the word for "dead people," "the body of a dead person"). When a person

dies, every one fears his return. . . . People conjecture as to whether his soul has gone to heaven, hell, or purgatory; and long arguments and explanations follow. . . .[13]

The appearance of ghostly penitents would thus add an emotional dimension to nighttime exercises and processions especially.

The belief in revenant Brothers also validates the basic importance of physical suffering. Brothers from Cordova, New Mexico, making visits to moradas at Alcalde and Ranchitos, near Santa Cruz, would be joined by departed Brothers around Canada Ancha.

The lights from our lanterns seemed to shine thru them and we could see their ribs and the bones of their arms as they walked along with us. They were all hooded, some were flagellating and others dragged crosses. How strange to see those "disciplinas" fall on those ghostly, scarred backs and to see those heavy crosses being dragged along without a sound. And when we stopped to pray our brethren from the other world stopped with us, crossing themselves at the proper times, but never making a sound. You may be sure we were very glad when they would leave us and we waited until daylight to make the return trip.[14]

To at least one Brother this encounter was "of great significance to him, a sort of personal revelation that his quest for redemption was fruitful":

Manuel says he was not particularly afraid when he noted that the rest of his original company were unaware of these ghostly apparitions. He averred that these souls in torment had been revealed to him alone. This confirmed to him that his salvation was certain, that his life of self-denial had assured him of heaven. In this belief, he died.[15]

Whether or not such a conviction was generally so meaningful, it was clearly both reassuring and disquieting to encounter revenant Brothers. Still, "to the Penitente the symbolic sharing of suffering with Jesus brings him closer to God," thus serving "a very real psychological purpose" and meeting "what is for him an important felt need."[16] The potential for this experience of the sacred is preserved symbolically in legends about ghostly penitents.

Brothers of Blood, Brothers of Light:
The Liminal Period in Rites of Passage

In a sense, the Brothers of Blood are themselves involved in a liminal or transitional period similar to that attributed to the returned souls who must fulfill vows before finding their place in the other world. Brothers in discipline are engaged in a confrontation of their shortcomings in order finally to return to the light, in effect, to be reborn. The entire retreat is thus a "transformative" ritual.[17] As such, its pattern exemplifies the general one Arnold van Gennep delineates for all rites of passage. The individual is separated from his society, "marginalized" in the liminal or transitional period, and later reincorporated in his or her new status, in this case, returned to the light.[18] The Brother of Blood eventually becomes a Brother of Light and enters a new existential and social status.

The applicant, the novice, and the penitent are separated from the outside world upon entering the morada. They are stripped of their clothes and of whatever status they may have had outside. By donning the uniform calzones and (in public) hood of the anonymous, humble penitent, such Brothers become what Victor Turner calls "transitional beings" or "liminal *personae*" who are felt to be imbued with extraordinary and "dangerous" powers, often symbolized in terms of death, decay, or various revenants.[19] This common symbolism is seen in the widespread regional tradition of ghostly penitents, as well as in the terminology of Brothers of Blood or Darkness and the like.

The infliction of the seal of obligation indicates submission to the superior authority of those who are enlightened and signals the beginning of the rigors of the marginal period. However, the violation of physical integrity, either imposed or self-inflicted, should not under such circumstances be viewed as an aberration:

> These again were not basically self-tortures inflicted by a masochistic temperament but due to obedience to the authority of tradition in the liminal situation—a type of situation in which there is no room for secular compromise, evasion, manipulation, casuistry, and maneuver in the field of custom, rule, and norm. Here again a cultural explanation is prefer-

able to a psychological one. A normal man acts abnormally because he is obedient to . . . tradition. . . . He does not evade but fulfills his duties as citizen.[20]

The mortification of the Brother of Blood is thus not a self-indulgence but a total surrender, a self-sacrifice which yields important psychological and religious gains.

A related experience during liminality is what Turner calls "communitas," a sense of comradeship and brotherhood "which emerges recognizably in the liminal period as an unstructured or rudimentarily structured and relatively undifferentiated *comitatus,* community, or even communion of equal individuals who submit together to the general authority of the ritual elders."[21] After examining the history of various attempts to institutionalize such spontaneous feeling, Turner concludes that "in these sources, both religious and secular, a fairly regular connection is maintained between liminality, structural inferiority, lowermost status, and structural outsiderhood on the one hand, and, on the other, such universal human values as peace and harmony between all men, fertility, health of mind and body, universal justice, comradeship and brotherhood between all men, the equality before God, the law or the life force of men and women, young and old, and persons of all races and ethnic groups."[22] One of the most important of these efforts to establish "permanent liminality" was by St. Francis, and the history of the Franciscan Order is in part that of the organization and routinization of the original spontaneity.[23]

The Brotherhood, which in many ways continued the early Franciscan tradition in New Mexico, may also be viewed from a similar broad historical perspective. The council organizations of chapters with internal controls and executive and ritual roles were attempts to insure both the periodic (during Lent and Holy Week) and the permanent benefits of liminality. The first chapter of the 1861 Taos Rules dictates that Brothers are, in effect, to remain marginal—to serve God and obey His Ten Commandments, and to follow Christ's example throughout the year—living modestly and humbly, shunning worldly temptations, and practicing brotherhood through charity, good example, mutual pardon, and tolerance. Besides taking up the cross literally and figuratively, they are to become as little children:

At that time Jesus declared, "I thank thee, Father, Lord of heaven and earth, that thou hast hidden these things from the wise and understanding and revealed them to babes; yes, Father, for such was thy gracious will." (Matthew 11:25-26)[24]

This genuine wisdom is another of the benefits of liminality, "which may be partly described as a stage of reflection."[25] By being outside the established social order and value system, the liminal *persona* or "child" can reconsider his world and even "play" with its components. Rituals of initiation may thus stimulate meditation, creativity, and growth and not simply enforce rigid indoctrination.

The experience of initiation cannot be reduced. It is not just a passive and highly affective state but a mobilizing and vivifying process through which men may become aware of their own potentials and their gods. "The notion that there is a generic bond between men, and its related sentiment of 'humankindness,' are not epiphenomena of some kind of herd instinct but are products of 'men in their wholeness wholly attending.' "[26] For the Brothers, this meant awakening to the divine—turning from sin to grace, as in the alabado quoted at the beginning of Part III, *Recuerda si estás dormido.* It meant wholly attending on the Passion of Jesus and always living by His example, in the spirit of comradeship and community. It also meant participating in the sacred renewal of the wider community of which the Brotherhood was a part.

The Sacred Dimensions

Mircea Eliade, elaborating the insights in Rudolf Otto's analysis of the religious experience as involving an overwhelming encounter with the *ganz andere* ("wholly other"), claims religious man finds power and enduring reality only in the sacred dimensions. In order to participate in this timeless, unbounded "being," religious persons periodically renew individual faith and collective bonds by demarcating special times and setting apart special places for worship. These sacred dimensions symbolically recreate the cosmogony, the beginning of all things, when the world was new and full of power.[27] For the Christian, this *illud tempus,* the beginning of things, is the period of Christ's suffering, death, and resurrection. The cross is its supreme symbol.[28]

The Catholic is renewed through the commemoration of Christ's sacrifice, the celebration of the Mass, a function reserved for the ordained priests. In a broad sense, however, the Brothers undertook annually to recreate this sacred time and space for themselves and their isolated communities. Although technically without ecclesiastical authorization, their Holy Week observances may be "understood as a folk equivalent of the Catholic Mass," according to Father Thomas J. Steele, S.J. He concludes: "that the New Mexican Spanish of the last century developed a quasi-sacramental system of their own which ranged from the santos themselves through Corpus Christi processions with a bulto of Christ and velorios for the dead, Christmas and Passion plays, and enactment of the passion of Christ using a statue of Jesús Nazareno, all the way to the Penitente crucifixion by tying one of the members of the brotherhood to a cross. In other words, what the sacraments and the Mass were to a village with a priest, the communal Penitente initiations, penances, wakes and enactments of the death of Jesus were to a village without one."[29] Viewing Brotherhood rituals in this way does not condemn the Brothers but illustrates how, as Archbishop Byrne stated, "groups among the faithful tried to keep up Catholic practices without priestly guidance, and though certain excesses crept in, it is to these groups of penitential brethren that we owe, in a manner, the preservation of the faith in those hard and trying times" during the last century.[30]

In effect, Brotherhood observances periodically sacralized an entire settlement. The morada, the "home," became the center from which processions to calvarios, camposantos, oratorios, and churches wove a kind of sacred network around the community. For a time, everyone lived within the sanctuary. Food was shared; worshippers joined the Way of the Cross and El Encuentro processions. During the Tinieblas too, neighbors quite literally huddled together in the midst of the souls and chaos from the other world.

The climax of this sacralization was the simulated crucifixion, a time of intense religious feeling. The raising of the cross recalled the redemption of the world and reconsecrated the territory of the local community, symbolically reaffirming and re-establishing it.[31] The sacred drama involved all the faithful in an important

expression of communion and community. Brotherhood observances were thus not only rituals of transformation for religious
individuals, they were also a reconfirmation of the original
interpersonal ties which made continued existence possible and
meaningful. Ideally and actually, the Brothers of Our Father Jesus
were truly significant, and they have much to teach today.

Adios acompañamiento,
Pues ya todo esta cumplido;
Ponganmen en la sepultura
En la tierra del olvido.

De la nada fui formado
Por obra de mi criador,
Y en el juicio universal
El será mi defendor.

A Dios me póstro humillado
De mi culpa arrepentido,
El que me a de perdonar
Por lo mal que le a servido.

En Dios espero repóso,
En Dios espero consuelo,
De que en el juicio tremendo
Me ábra las puertas del cielo.

Soy de mi Jesús cofrado,
Soy de Jesús y sere,
Porque con mi voluntad
A Jesús yo me entregaré.

Adios por ultima vez
Que me ven sobre la tierra,
Me echan a la sepultura
Que es la casa verdadera.

Adios todos los presentes
Que me van a acompañar,

Rezen algun sudario
Para poder alcanzar.

Adios todos mis proximos,
Toditos en general,
Encomienden mi alma a Dios,
No me vayan a olvidar.

                    Fin—Fin—Amén[32]

Afterword

Of all the writers on the history of the "Penitentes" in New Mexico, Dr. Marta Weigle is the only one to have had the courtesy of letting the Hermano Supremo review her manuscript before going to press. Several items have been deleted and others amended at my suggestion. For this I am grateful to the present writer.

However, this comment does not constitute an official Brotherhood authorization for the publication of this book.

Albuquerque, New Mexico
June 20, 1975

M. Santos Melendez
Hermano Supremo Arzobispal
Concilio Supremo Arzobispal
   de la Fraternidad Piadosa de
   Nuestro Padre Jesús Nazareno

Appendixes

APPENDIX I
Bishop Zubiría's Special Letter condemning the Penitentes, July 21, 1833

Sta. Cruz dela Cañada Julio 21, de 1833.

Impuestos áno poder dudarlo de qu^e en esta Villa hay una Hermandad de Penitentes, ya de bastantes años atras, pero sin autorisacion ninguna ni aun conocim^{to} de los ordinarios, que ciertam^{te} no habrian purtado su consentim^{to} para semejante Hermandad, aun quando hubiera sido solicitado, p^r ser tan contrario al espiritu dela Religion, y á las determinaciones dela Santa Iglesia, el exeso de penitencias corporales muy indiscretas que suelen practicar en algunos dias del año, aun con publicidad, que entre otras cosas ó incombenientes de mucha gravedad que puede traher, no es nada conforme con la humildad cristiana; porlo que no debieran haber dejado sin reducir [?] tales practicas y mucho menos permitirse p^r ningun Cura la construccion de Pŝa. [piesa] destinada a la custodia de instrumento de mortificacion, y de reuniones de Penitentes, que se han que [blot] oran, y mortificarse algunas veces con moderacion justa, tenian Templo en que poderse congregan; deviendo cerrar la Puerta á abusos de esta clase, que en algun tiempo hicieran derramar lagrimas a la Santa Iglesia: mandamos estrecham^{te} encargando la conciencia de nuestros Curas Parrocos de esta Villa el actual y venideros, que no se permitan en lo succesivo tales reuniones de Penitentes por ningun pretexto: que la Pŝa. en que han guardado sus cruzes & [etc.] sino es de alguna persona determinada, quede p^a el servicio de la Santa Iglesia Parroquial, y que dĥos. instrumentos se saquean y pueda cada uno llevar el suyo a su casa sin constarse mas en lo de adelante por congregante ó Herm? de tal hermandad de Peniten- cia, que anulamos y deve quedar istinguida, prestando todos en el particular la mas puntual obediencia a la determinacion del Prelado, que es uno de los sacrificios mas aceptos que deve hacerse a los divinos ojos: é igualm.te mandamos: que si el Señor Cura que lo fuere de esta Parroquia, llega á entender que en algun otro curato del Territorio hay tales reuniones ó hermandades de Penitentes, á fin de que no se permitan, oficie al Cura respectivo insertandole este Decreto, que queremos valga otra semejante abuso en cualquiera lugar del Territorio. El Illmõ Sr. Don José Antonio de Zubiria Dignisimo obispo de esta Diocesis mi Señor así lo Decreto mandó y firmó. Doy fé.

Transcribed by Marta Weigle from the Microfilm Edition of the Archives of the Archdiocese of Santa Fe, New Mexico State Records Center and Archives, Roll 50, Frames 0147–0149. Books of Patentes, No. 73, Box 7, described by Chavez, *Archives of the Archdiocese,* p. 156.

APPENDIX II
Paragraph from Bishop Zubiría's Pastoral Letter of October 19, 1833

En conclucion de este art? para atajar otro grande mal que puede ser mallor en adelante proibo esas hermandades de penitencia ó mas bien de carniceria, que há ido tomando cresimiento ál abrigo de una tolerancia indebida. Cada Parroco ó Ministro en todo el distrito de su administracion cuidará de que no quede ninguna de estas hermandades, y que no halla en parte ninguna Recogida ó guarda de estos grandes maderos, y otros instrumentos de morti- ficasion conque algunos medio matan los cuerpos, tal béz al tpõ. mismo q? no hasen caso de sus almas, dejandolas estar años enteros en la culpa. No se proibe la penitencia moderada que es tan saludable al espiritu, pero agase sus reuniones malamente llamada hermandades que no han tenido autoricasion ninguna legal en fin tenga cada uno á quien anime buen espiritu, los instrumentos usuales que guste de mortificasion, no de distrucion; pero tengalos en lo pribado=

(The paragraph concludes a section on the sacrament of penance.) Transcribed by J. Richard Salazar from the Microfilm Edition of the Archives of the Archdiocese of Santa Fe, New Mexico State Records Center and Archives, Roll 49, Frame 0266. Books of Patentes, described by Chavez, *Archives of the Archdiocese,* p. 182.

APPENDIX III
Report of Rev. Custos Fray Cayetano José Bernal to Governor Fernando Chacón, October 1794

3.ª Orn. de Penitencia de N. Stô. P. S. Frâñ.ᶜᵒ

En las dos expresadas Villas esta tambien fundada en cada una de ellas [Santa Fe and Santa Cruz de la Cañada] La Vᵉ 3ª Orñ. de Penitencia de N. Stô. Pᵉ S. Frañ.ᶜᵒ casi desde los principios de la Reconquista de esta Prova (aunqᵉ no se sabe el año fixo) con la previa Lisencia de los Prelados de N. Sagrada Religion como superiores legitimos, é imediatos de ella, y áquienes sola pertenese su conozim̃to y govierno como consta de muchas bulas Appᶜᵃˢ Confirmatorias y Declaratorias demanadas de Varios Romanos Pontificos, por lo qual lapongopᵣ separada de las Cofradias por no perteneser en nada á anas [?], y ser verdadera Orñ. como la 1ª qᵉ professan los Relig̃ aunqᵉ con distintas Constituciones y Regla. Estas Venerabᵉˢ Orñs 3ˢ solo han existido y existen á esmoro de la Devocion de los hermanos 3ˢ y asi sus Fondos es aqⁱ qᵉ se junta cada año entre los d̃hos. hermanˢ de la quota conqᵉ cada uno contribuye conlo que se paga en la Cañada la Fiesta de S. Luis, y de la Purísima Concepcion y como á sus Patrones, y una misa cantada con Procession el segundo Domingo de cada mes, pero siempre esta empeñada ó es nãrio, que el m̃ntro haga las mas [?] de pura devocion, por no alcansar las Limosnas para su satisfacion, por ser muy pocos los hermˢ 3ˢ

La de la Villa de Sã Fe imbierte sus limosnas en pagar la Fiesta de S Luis missas con Procession de los Domingos Segundos de todos los meses, y el Sermon de 3. Caidas el Viernes Stã. qᵉ lo paga por costumbre y en ? para d̃has. Funciones, y aunqᵉ ? 3ª Orñ y bastantes hermˢ siempre esta empeñada como puede verse.

La Vᵉ Orden Tercera de Penitencia de la villa de Sⁿ Phᵉ de Alburquerqᵉ se ignora el principio de su fundacion, y solamᵗᵉ

continua se existencia con las pocas y escassas limosnas con q^e
contribuyen los herm^s de ella, y por esta causa suelen ser pocas las
funciones q^e celebran annualm^{te} midiendose los Miños á donde
llegan, por lo q^e se diera entender, no tener fondos, y la
distrivucion de Limosnas, como consta por la Certificacion original
del actual Miñõ.

Transcribed by J. Richard Salazar from photostat copies in the Dorothy Woodward
Penitente Papers. These copies are identified as being from the Archivo General de la
Nación, México, D.F. (AGN) Ramo de Historia, vol. 313, f. 350. A version of this appears in
Salpointe, *Soldiers of the Cross*, p. 294, but it does not contain the Albuquerque reference,
which is written in a different hand.

APPENDIX IV
Letter of Fray José Benito Pereyro, Custos, to his Superior, 1810

Illmo Señor.

Con la devida veneracion recibi el oficio de S.S.Illmã de fecha 3,
de Febrero de 1810, en elque me previene sele devuelva el havito al
exhermano Josef Ignacio Vegil, por haversele quitado sin formarle
cause en devida forma, resultando de esta comprovado lo que sele
imputa, y no ser sentenciado por los que componen la Ve Mesa y
que por mi solo no devia quitarle el havito.

Me causa admiracion al ver, que el citado Josef Ignacio Vegil
[torn] la audacia de representar en el Justificado Tribunal de
S.S.Illmã unas calumnias tan denigratibas al honor dela Ve Mesa y
al mio. Estoy persuadido como devo, que si S.S.Illmã oyera las dos
partes, conoceria su caracter altivo y falaz, y no sentenciaria a su
favor, en perjuicio delo alegado, y provado en la causa inclusa.
Siendo de mi obligacion el mirar por el lustre dela Tercera Orden,
y la de arrancar las plantas viciadas, plantando en su lugar las que
puedan dar fruto, que para este [torn] leable, tengo autoridad dela
Silla Apostolica, pasé ala Cañada en donde estaba la Ve Mesa,
ante la qual le mande verbalm^e que provara los delitos imputados
al Hermano Mayor Adanto Fresquis, y al Maestro de Novicios
Luis Archuleta: y no dando prueba alguna, corregi con amor sus
falsedades como lo ordena la Bula de Martino S^o que comienza,

Licet inter cetera, y [torn] a que pidiera perdon a la Ve Mesa, y supliqué a esta, estando inocente, [torn] pidiera perdon a Josef Ignacio, atruegue de que Reynata en todos la paz [torn] Ve Mesa estaba pronta a este auto de humilidad; pero el prescitado [torn] el Calumniador, lleno de altivez nose avino ála mutua reconci [torn] mandé al R. P. Comisario dela tercera Orden, que como miembro poda [torn] este cuerpo mistico, lo borrara dela Lista delos hermanos, a causa de haverle perdido el havito y no haverlo querido entregar. Arreglandome a la Bula de Innocencio 4° que principia *vote devotarum,* y ala de Sixto 4° que empieza; *Romani Pontificis providentia,* dado en Roma a 15, de Diciembre del año de mil quatrocientos setenta y uno. Este mi procedimiento, ni fué injusto, ni precipitado, sino arreglado a lo que ordena mi Gran Padre Serafico Sⁿ Fran^{co} en el Capitulo diez y seis dela Regla delos Terceros en donde dice: Y alos Incorregibles seles hagan primero tres amonestaciones, y sinose emendaron, con consejo delos Discretos, sean hechados del todo de este santo orden. Y en el Capitulo diez y nuebe de dicha Regla previene lo mismo, pues manda que los Incorregibles sean hechados dela Compañia de esta Fraternidad de consejo de algunos hermanos discretos. Y podiendo proceder arreglado a este Capitulo, me sugeté alo que ordena en el Capitulo diez y seis. Solo con remitir a S.S.Illm̃a la causa inclusa, falsificaba lo que [obscure] Josef Ignacio de haversele quitado el havito sin formarsele causa, e indenizaba mi honor y el dela Ve Mesa. Pero para corrobarar mas la verdad y la justicia que nos asiste, tome declaraciones a todos los Miembros dela Mesa ante el Juez Real, las que comparaban ser calumnias las expuestas por Josef Ignacio Vegil. Si a este sele aplicara el condigno castigo, temerian representar falsedades en un Tribunal tan respetable como el de S.S.Illm̃a.

Suplico a S.S.Illm̃a. con el mayor respeto y sumision, que se digne ante [torn] las dos partes; pues delo contrario es abrir puerta franca los revoluccionarios, y mal subordinados. Pongo [torn] S.S.Illm̃a; qual seria mi rubios [?] y sentimiento al ver sobre mi, una sentencia [torn] cada por una falsa seducion, el verme reprendido no siendo delinquente, y aman [obscure] do nada menos que por un principe dela Iglesia? Bastantes trabajos padecemos en estos retiros, sinque no los aumenten con calumnias, algunos espiritus inquietos de esta Prov^a

Amas de esto: antes de entregarme la superior resolucion de S.S.Illm̃a ya era publica por haverla dicho Josef Ignacio vociferando. Esta promulgasion la hizo con vastante desdoro de mi caracter; y me será muy facil el provarlo sifuere del agrado de S.S.Illm̃a.

Sin embargo dela altaneria de Josef Ignacio Vegil, y dela provada prudencia con que me manege en compañia dela V.ᵉ Mesa, estoy pronto a obedecer la superiores dictamenes de S.S.Illm̃a.

Dios que a S.S.Illm̃a m.ˢ a.ˢ Mission de Sᵗ̃a Clara 15 de M [torn] de 1810.

Fr. Josef Benito Pereyro
custodio.

Transcribed by J. Richard Salazar from the Microfilm Edition of the Archives of the Archdiocese of Santa Fe, New Mexico State Records Center and Archives, Roll 53, Frames 0719–0720. Loose Documents, 1810, No. 2, described by Chavez, *Archives of the Archdiocese*, p. 73.

APPENDIX V
Act of Vicar Don Juan Rafael Rascón, April 12, 1831

Auna representacion dha 6 de Abril de esta año 831 gratos ciudadanos Dionicio Vigil y Policarpo Cordova por dicir [?] a nombre de los 60 hermanos de la 3ªOrn de S.ⁿ Fran.º hicieron p.ª q.ᵉ en lugar de la cañada observen sus exercicios de instrucion en Taos, se proreyó = S.ᵗᵃ Fee Abril 12 de 1831 = Por presentado. No ocurre obice en este Gob.ⁿº ec̃co p.ª q.ᵉ los devotos presentantes soliciten del Sup.ʳ de la Orñ de Sⁿ Fran.cº ó sus subdelegados q.ᵉ hayga en este Territorio, o la Republica, el reducirse a practicar en el curato de Taos ádonde viven los actos religiosos q.ᵉ dicen obserbaban en la cañada; advirtiendoles q.ᵉ a sus constituciones de Terceros, o devotos aunq.ᵉ no les obligan bajo pecado las observaran p.ª ganar las indulgencias, y gracias; yno cometeran abusos q.ᵉ merescan correcion en la visita del ordinario q.ᵉ haga en tpo oportuno = Rascon

Transcribed by J. Richard Salazar from the Microfilm Edition of the Archives of the Archdiocese of Santa Fe, New Mexico State Records Center and Archives, Roll 48, Frame 0285. Books of Patentes, No. 70, Box 4, described by Chavez in *Archives of the Archdiocese,* p. 154.

APPENDIX VI
Bishop Lamy's Twelve Rules for the Brotherhood of Penance, October 27, 1856

FOR THE GREATER GLORY OF GOD

Rules that must be observed by the Brothers of the
Catholic Confraternity of Penance.

Rule 1st

No individual, can be admitted to this brotherhood who does not profess the religion of the Catholic, Apostolic and Roman Church.

Rule 2nd

Every person, who desires to enter into the confraternity shall present his application to the President (Hermano Mayor) for his consideration and who after mature examination will determine the acceptance or non-acceptance of the candidate. In case of his acceptance he shall deputize certain brothers to confidentially collect information regarding the conduct of the pretender and if nothing infamous results against such a postulant, he may be admitted and delivered to the master of novices who during the year within which he is under his charge shall attentively and conscientiously watch his inclinations and in case he should discover some grave faults, which might be incorrigible he shall be obliged to inform the President (Hermano Mayor) the councellors and other officers of the brotherhood, so that they themselves may observe the conduct of the novice, and if being satisfied that all is according to the report of the master of novices, he shall now be allowed to form a part of the brotherhood.

Rule 3rd

All brothers must keep secret all matters that may be transacted at the meetings to be had and the President (Hermano Mayor) shall himself or through another notify the parish Priest in order that he may attend and be present at all meetings, if he so desires. If any one of the brothers should break the secrets he shall be severely reprimanded according to the disposition of the President (Hermano Mayor) and councellors and if he after being admonished should insist, he shall be expelled from the brotherhood.

Rule 4th

The individuals composing the brotherhood have to be moral and virtuous men in order that by their good example and virtues and obedience may induce others to a good life. But if some brother gives scandal, regarding the sixth, seventh and second commandments, he shall be severely punished by the President (Hermano Mayor) and Councellors and should he insist he shall be expelled from the brotherhood.

Rule 5th

All brothers, who formerly formed a part of this brotherhood and who were not, due to some crime, excluded from it, or who are not actually in compliance with the foregoing rules may if they desire return to form a part of the brotherhood.

Rule 6th

If any of those who shall in the future be expelled ask to again become duly incorporated into the brotherhood, and when it has been proven after prudent investigation that they have mended their ways, these may be re-admitted into the brotherhood. But if they again should happen to offend, they shall be forever excluded from the brotherhood.

Rule 7th

The President (Hermano Mayor), Councellors and Aids are empowered to take part and know all matters and questions that may come up between the brothers concerning the good order and compliance by the brothers with their obligations. The First Assistant shall be the marshal, and in all matters which may seem difficult to him or where it is necessary to pronounce some sentence the Parish Priest must be notified and given a concise, clear, faithful and conscientious statement of the facts and circumstances available.

Rule 8th

All and every one of the components of the confraternity must frequent the Holy Sacraments of Penance and Holy Eucharist particularly during the holy season of Lent, and if any one shall fail in this sacred obligation he shall be expelled from the confraternity forever and without being entitled to being again admitted.

Rule 9th

All and every one of the individuals of the Brotherhood shall obey and respect the legitimate Supreme Pastor of this territory, His Grace, the Most Reverend Catholic Bishop, Don Juan Lamy, and his successors in all matters which he may be pleased to ordain, whether it be this or any other matter and likewise in the same manner the parish priest, whom he may be pleased to place in this or any other point of his diocese without complaining or grumbling regarding the dispositions of these matters which the prelate may be pleased to ordain and anyone who having been duly advised should insist in so doing he shall be expelled from the brotherhood as unworthy of being a member of a Catholic congregation, the fundamental basis of which is obedience and charity.

Rule 10th

As in the foregoing rule, obedience and respect to the parish priest is prescribed and as the pastor is directly responsible to his prelate for anything which might occur within the brotherhood regarding such abuses which might be committed by some of the components of the brotherhood. It shall be the duty of the president (Hermano Mayor) to deliver to the parish priest a list of all the persons who may belong to the brotherhood so that he may be at all times able to answer as to the conduct of each of the individuals and thus foresee the slander that may be committed by some ill intentioned members in the name of the brotherhood.

[Rule 11th]

Each president (Hermano Mayor) shall keep an original copy of these rules duly signed by the parish priest under the strict responsibility not to permit any copies thereof to be made so as to avoid in this manner the changing of the originals either through malice or due to a bad scribe. In the same manner they shall also receive their corresponding titles duly signed by the parish priest.

203

Rule 12th

All these rules must be shown to all the individuals for their knowledge and in order that they may not be forgotten they must be read from time to time, it not being possible for anyone to interpret them at his will but they must be understood literally. In case of doubt they must be referred to the parish priest that he may determine the controversy after due consultation with his prelate. The same method must be taken in case that any rule may have to be added or eliminated according to circumstances.

Msgr. Mahoney chose to translate only portions of the subsequent *"Parte administrativa"*:

The greatest and best method of preserving a brotherhood consists in the good selection of its superiors. The angelic St. Thomas of Acquin used to say: 'Give me a superior who to his sanctity has added the virtue of prudence and such a community will be well conducted.' We must bear in mind also that all nature tends to unity. The Divine Nature itself is admirable and undivided in three persons. The Superior (Hermano Mayor) must always have before him the example of Our Lord Jesus Christ who humbled Himself even unto death giving His life for the salvation of souls.

For the management of the brotherhood there shall be named as has been customary all the officers with their same faculties and privileges endeavoring at all times that said individuals be men of good behaviour, probity and above all of good morals.

All the prayers which the Brotherhood of Penance has used having been examined with all due care and attention and nothing having been found contrary to the Catholic faith the president and the others may continue the use of same for their services and pious practicts; but they shall not have a power to add to or to subtract from any of them under the pretext of zeal, devotion or for any other reason without first consulting the parish priest and submitting them for his revision.

As translated by Monsignor Philip F. Mahoney in *The Santa Fe New Mexico Sentinel,* February 2, 1938, p. 12, and February 9, 1938, p. 16. (See note 5, chapter 2.)

APPENDIX VII
Bishop Lamy's Five Rules for the Penitentes, March 9, 1857

In this the year 1857, there has been granted by His Grace Don Juan Lamy, the permission to continue the devotion of the Passion and death of Our Lord, Jesus Christ, as a penance, by all its devotees. The rules, granted on petition of the President or Elder Brother (Hermano Mayor) and Councilman, Jose Francisco Zamora and given by His Grace, that no person may doubt it, are as follows:

Rule First

All men, that desire to do penance, as it has been their custom for many years back, may do so, after first having made their confession.

Rule Second

The Penance must be done, as hidden as possible, without giving scandal, to the rest of the faithful according to the spirit of the Church and without doing it with vain-glory; for such penance is disapproved of by Holy Mother, the Church, and the brothers, subjected to censure for abuses in matters of religion.

Rule Third

It will be the bounden duty of the President (Hermano Mayor) not to admit into this confraternity any person who has lately lived in vice or crime, and he shall behave in like manner towards murderers, adulterers and thieves and other men, who on account of their former habits, it would not be proper, that they enter into a community of brotherhood, and an institution, which shall be for the sanctification of souls and the edification of the faithful.

Rule Fourth

This investigation to be made by the President (Hermano Mayor) or his subordinates, regarding the life, being led by men who desire to be admitted into the brotherhood, must be done without giving scandal and in accordance with the charity of Our Lord, Jesus Christ.

Rule Fifth and Last

All other rules not included herein, and which had been before approved by the Ecclesiastical authority of the Diocese shall remain in force.

> Given at San Juan de los Caballeros on
> the 9th of March, 1857.
> Rev. Jose E. Ortiz, Sec.

P.S. There is hereby imposed on all brothers for the benefit of the Altar a tax of two reales for wax. All brothers who may desire to abandon the devotion, and all persons, who on account of their wrong deeds, may be dismissed from the brotherhood, will not be obliged to this assignment.

As translated by Monsignor Philip F. Mahoney in *The Santa Fe New Mexico Sentinel,* January 26, 1938, p. 2. (See note 8, chapter 2.)

APPENDIX VIII
A Portion of Archbishop Lamy's *Carta Pastoral por la Cuaresma de 1879*, Santa Fe, February 9, 1879

En fin faltaríamos á nuestro deber si no hiciésemos alusion á otro abuso que por desgracia es demasiado comun en algunas plazas. Queremos hablar de los Penitentes. En tiempos pasados habíamos aprobado las reglas de estas cofradías con la condicion expresa de que no se haria ninguna penitencia sin contar con el párroco respectivo, y bajo su direccion. Pero desafortunadamente los jefes de estas sociedades no han hecho caso de nuestras órdenes; antes bien ellos han seguido sus prácticas y costumbres crueles en partes retiradas, y de noche, dándose azotes tan terribles que muchos no solamente se han enfermado á consecuencia de estas penitencias, sino que tambien algunos se han muerto. Por otra parte en estas cofradías se hace prestar juramento á unos tiernos jóvenes con que ellos se obligan á seguir sus reglas. Todos estos son abusos grandes que la Iglesia reprueba en lugar de aprobarlos. Os exhortamos encarecidamente á no dejaros alucinar por una falsa especie de devocion, que lejos de agradar á Dios mas bien le ofende porque no se hace segun la obediencia que se debe á la Iglesia y la hacen despreciar. En las parroquias mas arregladas que pudiéramos mencionar no existen estos abusos ni tampoco estas cofradías. Imitad sus ejemplos y comportaos como hijos obedientes de la Iglesia. Y tened bien presente esta máxima del Espíritu Santo: "La obediencia vale mas que los sacrificios." Sí, la obediencia á la autoridad de la Iglesia en todo lo que ella manda y prohibe de parte de Dios, os valdrá mas que todas aquellas penitencias que practican algunos fuera del órden y con rigor excesivo, de las cuales Dios no les tendrá cuenta, porque no se hacen segun la obediencia; á mas de que han dado y dan lugar á hacer blasfemar de nuestra religion. Pudiéramos añadir que muchos de los mas celosos de estas cofradías no se comportan como cristianos ejemplares.

Published in *La Revista Católica*, vol. 5, no. 6 (February 8, 1879), p. 66. (Also on the Microfilm Edition of the Archives of the Archdiocese of Santa Fe, New Mexico State Records Center and Archives, Roll 57, Frame 0997. Loose Documents, 1879, No. 1, described by Chavez, *Archives of the Archdiocese*, p. 138.)

APPENDIX IX
Archbishop Salpointe's 1886 Circular on the Third Order of St. Francis

Al Reverendo Clero de Su Diócesis.

Rev. muy Señor mio:

Las Reglas que con esta carta le acompaño, son las de la Tercera Orden de San Francisco, llamada tambien la Orden de la Penitencia. Estas, he tomada palabra por palabra, en cuanto me ha sido posible, de la Constitucion de Su Santidad el Papa Leon XIII, publicada el dia 19 de Mayo de 1883, suprimiendo por ahora solamente lo que en ellas se refiere á los sacerdotes que quieran entrar en la Orden.

Tendrá Vd. la bondad de dar una copia de estas reglas á cada uno de los Hermanos Mayores de las Hermandades que puedan existir en su jurisdiccion, haciéndoles ver que la devocion de los Penitentes viene ciertamente de la Tercera Orden de los Franciscanos, y debe volver á ella si se quieren ganar las Indulgencias con que ha sido enriquecida esta Orden por los Sumos Pontífices.

Lo mismo le encargo, en conformidad con el deseo del Santo Padre, que dé á conocer estas mismas Reglas á sus feligreses para que puedan los que quieran, gozar de los privilegios de la Orden Tercera con hacerse miembros de ella. Y para que pueda Vd. alistar miembros, darles el hábito, recibir su profesion, etc., le delego la facultad que al efecto tengo del Ministro General de los Franciscanos.

Cuando vea más ó menos cuál es el número de miembros de la Orden que pueden juntarse en la diócesis, procuraré para todos el libro de las Reglas con todas las instrucciones que les puedan ayudar á cumplir con las prescripciones. Se ve por la letra de las Reglas que toda clase de personas, hombres ó mujeres, pueden, hallándose en las debidas condiciones, pertenecer á la Orden. Por lo presente deseo que ambos sexos tengan sus listas y reuniones separadamente.

Por esta carta dispensamos á los Hermanos de la Penitencia de toda mortificacion que no esté mencionada en las Reglas y aun les prohibimos la flagelacion y el arrastre de los maderos practicados públicamente como lo hacian antes. Poco se les pide, pero eso basta para que puedan ganar Indulgencias grandes y para que hagan la voluntad de Dios con conformarse á la de su Vicario sobre la tierra. Se acordarán de lo que está escrito en el libro de los Reyes que mejor es, en la presencia de Dios, la obediencia que el sacrificio de víctimas.

Su atento Servidor en Xto.

✠ J. B. Salpointe,
Arzobispo de Santa Fe.

Published in *La Revista Católica,* vol. 12, no. 12 (March 21, 1886), pp. 138–39. (See note 31, chapter 2.)

APPENDIX X
Undated Petition to Archbishop Salpointe from Four Conciliarios de la Fraternidad Piadosa

Peticion
Los hermanos de la Fraternidad Piadosa. A su Señoría Ilustrisi-

ma de la Diosesis de Nuebo Mejico; el muy Piadoso Representante de Jesucristo J. B. Salpointe por la Gracia de Dios.

Ilustrisimo Señor los abajo firmados Conciliarios de la Fraternidad Piadosa con el mas alto respeto y veneracion; muy humildemente en el nombre de Dios y de todas la sociedades Cristianas, Apostolicas Romanas; que existen en el orbe Terraqueo: pidemos que su Santidad bendiga con Paternal afeto las formas de nuestra asociacion, bajo las cuales se rebela la accion armonizada de Cristo para fines nobles y Santos. Todos los miembros de nuestra Fraternidad sin excepcion estamas firmemente adheridos al espiritu de Nuestra Santa *Madre Iglesia Catolica Apostolica Romana;* y para que sea mas perfecta Nuestra Union en caridad Fraternal; y mas amplio y firme el *Reino* de *Cristo sobre* la *Tierra,* que es lo que de todo corazon deciamos extablecer; pidemos en toda forma del derecho que nuestra Religion nos concede; que su *Señoría Ilustricima* en el nombre de Cristo bendiga nuestra union Fraternal; para mantenernos siempre en el Gremio de la *Iglesia de Cristo* y ser participantes *de sus Sacramentos* y *bendiciones.* Declaramos que nuestros actos Penitenciales no tienen otro objeto que emitar la Flagelacion de Cristo Nuestro Redentor "y cremos que Nuestra Santa Madre Iglecia Catolica, Apostolica, Romana jamas á obrado con precipitacion prudencia, ni error; para abolir ó desaprobar las hermandades, ó cofradías de sus berdaderos crellentes; por ese principio esperamos que su Señoría Ilustrisima apruebe y bendiga las Formas de nuestra asociacion Fraternal; para el fomento de la *Religion Catolica"* para honrra de la Pacion de Cristo, y finalmente para el beneficio que esperan de sus ejercicios Piadosos todos los miembros de la Fraternidad.

En conclucion Ilustricimo Señor; con la perceverancia en nuestros ejercicios Penitenciales con la bendicion de su Señoría y frecuentando los Sacramentos de Nuestra Santa Madre Iglesia; esperamos la Suerte de los Bienabenturados que Reinan en el Cielo en Unidad del Padre del hijo y del Espiritu Santo Dios por todos los ciglos y de los ciglos Santos Amen

Esperando una respuesta consoladora de su Señoría Ilustricima nos suscrivemos con mucho respectos.

Miguel Martinez

J. Rafael Arellano

Serafin Baca y Armijo

Martin Rael
Conciliarios de la Fraternidad Piadosa.
Su contesta la mandara á
Miguel Martinez
Mora
Nuebo Mejico

Transcribed by Marta Weigle from the Microfilm Edition of the Archives of the Archdiocese of Santa Fe, New Mexico State Records Center and Archives, Roll 58, Frames 0763–0764. Loose Documents, 1891, No. 6, described by Chavez, *Archives of the Archdiocese,* p. 144.

APPENDIX XI
San Miguel County Brothers' Petition to Archbishop Salpointe, October 1891

A su Señoría Ilustrisima Don Juan Bautista Salpointe Arzobisbo de Santa Fé.

Vuestros humildes peticionarios, los abajo firmados, muy respetuamente representan ante vuestra Señoría Ilustrisma que somos miembros de la Santa Iglesia Católica, Apostolica Romana de la cual vuestra Señoria es jefe en esta Archi-diosesis; que como sumisos miembros de la antedicha Santa Iglesia exponemos á voz esta nuestra peticion, á saber: Los que nos suscribemos somos miembros y Jefes de una cierta Hermandad por nosotros titulada y reconocida como de "Nuestro Padre Jesus de Nazareno" y de otro modo llamada de "Los Penitentes" cuya Hermandad de buena fé creemos se halla adentro del gremio de nuestra Santa Madre la Iglesia: Que sabedores que somos de que ciertas diferencias existen entre varios de nuestros Sacerdotes y nuestra dicha Fraternidad y deseando ahora y en todo tiempo evitar toda cosa que pueda ponernos en desavenencia con nuestra Madre La Santa Iglesia por lo tanto con toda humildad demostramos á vuestra Señoría Ilustrisima que deseamos ser considerados bajo el gremio y proteccion de nuestra Madre Iglesia y reconocidos por *voz* como una sociedad Católica que dando todos los miembros que residen en el Condado de San Miguel y quienes están bajo nuestra autoridad como jefes; sujetos á las justas restricciones que por vuestra Señoría Ilustrísima sean impuestas sobre nuestra órden; para benficio de nosotros mismos y de nuestra Santa Religion si en algo podemos cooperar benificiarla.

Impetramos además, que habiendo hecho venir del Oriente á gran costo un hermoso Estandarte para nuestra Hermandad, el cual representa la Pasion y muerte de Nuestro Señor, etc., rogamos á vuestra Señoría de digne permitir ó licenciar al Parroco principal de nuestro condado, al Rev. J. M. Caudert, de bendecir el mismo con propia solemnidad, para tener y guardar el dicho estandarte en memoria de aquel que representa.

Esperando que vuestra Señoría Ilustrisima se digner ver con consideracion esta nuestra humilde peticion la sometemos á nombre de toda la Hermandad del Condado de San Miguel y Vuestros Peticionarios, siempre humildemente impetraran.

Serafin Baca y Armijo

N. Segura

Lorenzo Lopez

Firmados por autoridad   Rafael Baca

Julian Trujillo

Atesta: José Valdez, Secretario.   Miembros del Concilio General del Condado.

Transcribed by Marta Weigle from the Microfilm Edition of the Archives of the Archdiocese of Santa Fe, New Mexico State Records Center and Archives, Roll 58, Frames 0765–0766. (See Appendix X for particulars.)

APPENDIX XII
Archbishop Salpointe's Circular on the Penitentes, English Version, February 7, 1892

LETTER OF THE MOST REVEREND DON JUAN BAUTISTA SALPOINTE, ARCHBISHOP OF SANTA FE.

By the Grace of God and the Authority of the Holy Apostolic See, Archbishop of Santa Fe, to the Clergy and Faithful of our Archdiocese, Health and Benediction in our Lord.

Reverend Brother Priests, Beloved Christian Faithful:

It having come to our knowledge, that some men are making use of our name, to give credit to their political views before the members of the Sodality which we here call "Los Penitentes", telling them that we have approved, or are about to approve all their rules, it seems to us convenient and very much to the purpose to publish what follows, for the correct information not only of the Penitentes, but as well of all the faithful, under our care.

About the beginning of October of the year past of 1891, we received a letter through special messenger, which was not dated, and which letter we here quote, in its full text, suppressing only a petition therein, which does not concern the matter, and the names of those who signed it.

"TO HIS GRACE, DON J.B. SALPOINTE, ARCHBISHOP OF SANTA FE:

Your humble petitioners, the undersigned, respectfully represent to your Grace, that we are members of the Catholic, Roman Apostolic Church, of which Your Grace is the head in this Archdiocese and as submissive members of the Holy Church, we present to you this our humble petition, to-wit:

The undersigned are members and chiefs of a certain brotherhood, by us entitled and recognized as "De Nuestro Padre Jesus Nazareno" otherwise called "Los Penitentes" which brotherhood, we believe, in good faith, to be within the fold of our Holy Mother the Church, and with the knowledge that we have that certain difficulties exist between several of our Priests and our said fraternity, and wishing at this time and for the future to avoid everything that may place us in disagreement with our Holy Mother the Church, therefore, with all humility, we put before the consideration of Your Grace that we wish to be considered by you as a Catholic Sodality and under the fold and guidance of our Holy Mother the Church, thereby, all the members who reside in the County of San Miguel, and who are under our authority, subject to the just restrictions which Your Grace might impose unto our order, for our own benefit and that of Our Holy Mother the Church and our Religion, in case we can co-operate in any way to its benefit.

Hoping that Your Grace will deign to give our humble petition its due consideration, we submit to you the names of all the brothers from San Miguel County, and your petitioners, shall always humbly pray" . . .

Here follow the signatures of the five members of the General Council of the county and of the secretary".

In view of the way that the petitioners expressed themselves, we believed naturally in their good faith and although we did not lack work we were about to take a trip to the East. We made it our duty to formulate the principal points of certain rules for the reformation, which we are left at liberty to place in practice by the Moradas de los Penitentes. We offered at the same time to approve with the rules any necessary details that might be added by the parties interested, provided they did not oppose in any manner those that we had formulated.

During the Month of November, when we were in Washington, we heard through private letter, that the Hermanos Penitentes of the County of San Miguel, very joyfully accepted the rules which we had proposed for them, and that they did not desire anything more than our final approval of the same for the public. What has happened since that time? We are unable to state; certainly since the seventh of December, when we returned from our trip, no one, up to the present time, has ever spoken to us again regarding the matter.

Neither as we have heard have those who signed the petition remained idle. Two of them, not many days ago, traveled through Chimayo, Rio Arriba and Taos, looking for Penitentes from that part of the territory, to show them not the rules that we had given them, but others that were drawn, (so the title head states) at Mora, June 7, 1890 by the General Council of the counties of San Miguel, Mora and Taos.

These last rules were the ones presented to the Penitentes here as already approved, there and as very soon to be approved by us since they say that they had been drawn in our presence at the aforesaid General Council of the Counties of San Miguel, Mora and Taos.

That seems to be the way the gentlemen who signed the letter which we have reproduced, conducted themselves, as true and submissive sons of the Church. They desire to receive the favor of the Penitentes, and in order to arrive at this point, they have two different banners, in order to show one or the other according to the required circumstances. That of the Church and the one opposed to it, to their advantage. This appears a very good way to become friends at all hazards, but surely it cannot be called honest.

This said: We formally declare, 1st, that we have never assisted at any General Council of the Penitentes, where rules have been drawn for the Society. 2nd, that we have never approved, nor are we about to approve at any time a set of rules as those stated, which are mere and simple, a bombastic appeal to all males from the age of fourteen up to join with them. "Under their oath and honesty to defend, persistently and unitedly, the honor, privileges and immunities of the members of the Fraternity, againt any person or persons, who due to their conduct may show themselves enemies of the Fraternity, or any of its members.

They joined and always bound themselves, under their honor and oath, "to protect themselves, mutually and unitedly in all and for all, and to all that which might be just and beneficial . . . and to this each one is compromised from now to the future and forever, according to the principles of the ancient rules of the Fraternity".

Thus therefore, we have an example of the principles and Rules of the ancient Fraternity of the Penitenties. It is very much more than what we know at present, although we have read many pamphlets of said ancient rules; but, who can doubt that the matter is so, when a whole council of three counties, has so declared it? Now let them not say that the Church reproves them unjustly: they condemn themselves, by professing the principles of Masonry a society which is condemned by the Church. They ask from their members the oath of perpetual obligation, and this under penalty of punishment. From what we know, even the Masons do not require so much from their members, although we know of some of these who have withdrawn from the society without suffering punishment in any form.

The oath that is asked of the Penitente Members, is unmoral and unjust for it deprives man from obeying God according to the dictates of his conscience, and subjects him to the will of men. And for what reason do they require this oath? In order that the members obligate themselves to protect each other against imaginary enemies and above all against the Church which does not want to admit and approve the disorderly, indecorous and indecent practices of the Fraternity. And the Oath of the youth of fourteen years of age, will it be a moral oath? It is so declared by the supreme chiefs of the Fraternity of the Counties of San Miguel, Mora and Taos, in their memorable council of the 7th of June, 1890. Not withstanding all this, they consider themselves humble and submissive sons of the Church and want to defend themselves against who or whom may be opposed to any of their practices.

With what has been said we have sufficient to confirm the idea which we have had for more than thirty years, that those who take so much interest in making themselves the protectors of the Penitentes, are doing so more for political reasons than any other thing. For them the religion which they introduced is only a pretention, what they are looking for is the vote of the members of the Fraternity, for their political ends. This is what we wish the Penitentes would understand well, and that they should know that as citizens, they can and should vote according to their conscientious convictions without obliging themselves in any other way by an oath to vote as others should tell them to do. We also wish to declare once and for all, that having agreed to formulate some Rules for the Reformation of the Penitentes, we have not understood to become protectors of political pretenders, no matter who they might be.

As to the Penitentes, we will add in conclusion, that if we have reproved them on account of some of their practices, we have done it, as a duty, and not in order to place them away from the church. A good number of them have correctly interpreted our intention, and have shown their obedience to our authority, by subjecting themselves to what we had prescribed in our circular of 1886 and 1889. To these we extend our congratulations. In regard to those who up to now have resisted our orders, we will again say to them, that we consider them as rebels to their mother the Church, and that until such time that they submit, they will be deprived of the reception of the Sacraments. We do not put them out of the Church. They themselves go out by persisting in their disobedience.

This circular shall be read in all the Churches on the Sunday after its reception, and in the chapels at the first visit of their respective Priests.

Santa Fe, Febrero 7, 1892.

✝ J. B. Salpointe
Archbishop of Santa Fe

From the Microfilm Edition of the Archives of the Archdiocese of Santa Fe, New Mexico State Records Center and Archives, Roll 58, Frames 0788–0790. The printed Spanish version is on Roll 58, Frames 0785–0787. The first part of the above appeared in Msgr. Mahoney's article in *The Santa Fe New Mexico Sentinel,* February 16, 1938, p. 16. Loose Documents, 1892, Nos. 1 and 2, described by Chavez, *Archives of the Archdiocese,* p. 144.

APPENDIX XIII
Commission Report on the Penitentes
(probably submitted to Archbishop Bourgade ca. 1900)

Informe de la Comision tocante á los Penitentes.

1º. Todos y cada uno, concordamos en lo que la Autoridad Eclesiastica ha ordenado, segun Circular en 1886, de Monseñor Salpointe, sostenido fielmente hasta ahora por sus muy dignos sucesores.

2º. Sugiere esta comision que se obliguen á los penitentes á que no se flagelen, ni arrastren sus maderos públicamente, ni de dia ni de noche, afuera de sus respectivas moradas.

3º. Item, que se les prohiba extrictamente toda demostracion pública, en calidad como tales, con sus imagenes y sus procesiones. Puesto que así se llevan á la gente tras sí, é impiden el concurso de esta en los oficios divinos de la Iglesia ya sea en la cabecera de las Parroquias ó en las capillas.

4º. Item, que se les suprima entera y completamente é incondicionalmente aquel juramento que ellos toman para ser admitido como miembros lo [?] mismo que no se les permita admitir á ningun menor de edad, en termino de la ley civil.

5º. Seriamente se pide de que toda materia politica sea estrictamente prohibida en todas sus juntas generales ó particulares de ellos.

Son estas las sugestiones, que la comision, respetuosamente, somete á Su Señoria Ilustrisima sobre el asunto de los penitentes, segun pedido.

> C^{lo} [Camilo] Seux
> Ant [Antonio] Jouvenceau
> J. B. Mariller
> A. [Alph.] Haelterman
> MA [Manuel] Rivera

Transcribed by Marta Weigle from the Microfilm Edition of the Archives of the Archdiocese of Santa Fe, New Mexico State Records Center and Archives, Roll 58, Frames 0289–0290. Loose Documents, [1886], No. 8, described by Chavez, *Archives of the Archdiocese*, p. 142.

APPENDIX XIV
Report on Additional Points of Reform for the Penitentes, submitted to Archbishop Bourgade ca. 1900

Puntos de reforma a añadir a las reglas de los Penitentes.

I. Deben los hermanos de la cofradia de Nuestro Padre Jesus, someter las reglas cuanto antes a la autoridad Eclesiastica para su aprobacion.

II. Todos los miembros de dicha asociacion estan obligados en confesar se y comulgar a lo menos una vez en el año.

III. Es prohibido estrictamente a todos los Socios de los varios Hermandades, el flagelar se arrastrar maderos y cruces, usar instrumentos de disciplina, publicamente ni de dia, ni de noche, fuera de sus respectivas moradas.

IV. Los hermanos de N. Padre Jesus deberan de asistir durante los tiempos santos de Cuaresma y de Pasion, a los oficios publicos de la Iglesia, como es el Via Crucis, los Viernes de Cuaresma, ya todos las oficios de la Iglesia, El Jueves y Viernes Santo y Sabado de Gloria. Pueden los hermanos, hacer los ejercicios del Via Crucis, en las Capillas publicas en los lugares en donde no hay parroco, despues de haber tenido un arreglo previo con el cura.

V. No podran ser admitidos como hermanos mayores, o oficiales en la cofradia ni aun como miembros, individuos escandolosos y de mala fama. Es decir que no podran entrar en la Cofradia aquellos que no puedan servir de padrinos de bautismo. En todo caso, antes de recibir nuevos miembros, deben los cabecillos de la asociacion consultar con su parroco.

VI. No pueden los hermanos oficiales hacer prestar juramento en ninguna manera a los que entran en la Cofradia, mucho menos a los menores de edad.

VII. La politica debe de ser excluida dela asociacion que se tiene por religiosa y no reconoce ninguna organizos politica.

VIII. Los miembros dela asociacion de N. Padre Jesus que rehusaran someter se a dichos reglas, despues desu publicacion, seran considerados como rebeldas y desobedientes a la Iglesia, en materia grave, luego la sancion a su desobediencia sera: no admitir les como padrinos de bautismo o de Confirmacion; privarles de la recepcion delos Sacramentos de penitencia y Eucaristia durante su vida, en el articulo dela muerte deberan prometer ante dos testigos, al reformar se y someterse ala Iglesia la pena de ver se privados delos ultimos auxilios y dela Sepultura eclesiastica.

IX. Estas reglas, o puntos modificando reglas y existentes dados por la autoridades . . obligan en conciencia a todos los fieles hijos de la Iglesia. Los miembros del clero diocesano, seglar y regular deben de conformar se en cuanto respecta la administracion de los Sacramentos, a la orden del ordinario. En caso de que existiere alguna desavenencia respecto la observancia de dichos reglos, entre parrocos y fieles, la interpretacion de los puntos en litigacion pertenece al S^r arzobispo quien se debe considerar como Juez final en tales casos. Respetosamente sometido a Su Señoría Mgr Bourgade.

Transcribed by Marta Weigle from the Microfilm Edition of the Archives of the Archdiocese of Santa Fe, New Mexico State Records Center and Archives, Roll 58, Frames 1114–1118. A draft for this version is found on Roll 58, Frames 0286–0288. Loose Documents, [1899], No. 8, described by Chavez, *Archives of the Archdiocese,* p. 148.

APPENDIX XV
Resolutions passed by the Penitente Brotherhood in San Miguel County, New Mexico, May 1894

In Self-Vindication

The following resolutions of self-vindication were passed by the Society of "Nuestro Padre Jesus," out at Agua Zarca, on Thursday evening of last week, first appearing in Spanish, in *La Voz del Pueblo:*

WHEREAS, Recent events have proved the fact that different individuals, by means of deceit and intrigue, have obtained admission into the religious order of "Nuestro Padre Jesus," of which the undersigned are members; and

WHEREAS, The society has discovered that several political demagogues, who are professional office-seekers, have obtained admission to our membership, through false representations and pretenses, and thus abused the good faith and aim of this society; and,

WHEREAS, In our opinion, the society will continue to suffer in its liberty and welfare of its members: And further, it having come to our knowledge that there is a prevailing impression in the community at large that this order has for its object the protection of assassins, thieves and all classes of criminals; and,

WHEREAS, Such charges against the order are false and unjust; and further, it being the desire of all honest and sincere members of this order that the public understand its real character and objects; therefore, be it

Resolved, By all the members in meeting assembled, that we emphatically condemn the nefarious acts of those persons who have thus joined our order; and that we consider such persons as traitors to the avowed principles and honorable objects of our society; be it further

Resolved, that we condemn the actions of such persons as have joined our order for the sole object of political preferment; and that we brand as cowards and intriguers those persons who have made a cloak of their membership in our order to obtain public office; be it further

Resolved, That it is the determined purpose of this society that it shall expel any member who is or may be connected with any crime or violation of law; be it further

Resolved, That it is the duty and to the interest of each of the members of this order to preserve it inviolate for the objects for which it was created, and not to make it subservient to the worldly advantage and advancement of any individual member, or other person or persons; be it further

Resolved, That we offer for the inspection of the public the rules and regulations of our order, that all may be satisfied of their worthy intent, and innocence of any malice or possible detriment to the public weal; be it further,

Resolved, That these resolutions be published in *La Revista Catolica,* and any other papers desiring their publication.

Las Vegas New Mexico Daily Optic, Thursday, May 31, 1894, p. 2, cols. 2-3. Originally published in Spanish in *La Voz del Pueblo,* Las Vegas, New Mexico, Saturday, May 26, 1894, p. 1, col. 4, and entitled *"Exoneracion que se Esplica por si Misma."* La Revista Católica apparently did not choose to publish the resolutions.

The original document was signed by a thirty-three member *"Comision y cuatrocientos más."* Although the "four hundred more" were not identified, the list of "Commission" signatures was published in *La Voz del Pueblo.* The names appeared in this order:

Serafin Baca y Armijo
Jose Felipe B. Montaño y Sandoval
Julian Trujillo y Vigil
Perfecto Baca
Juan Montoya
Benito Martinez
Prospero S. Baca
Ramon Padilla
Juan Isidro Martin
Antonio T. Gallegos
Jose Nazario Arguello
Juan Antonio Archuleta
Jose Eusobio Archuleta
Santiago Archuleta
Juan Gallegos
Tiburcio Tenorio
Florencio Esquibel
Juan Martin

Jesus M. Rivera
Miguel Saccomano
Jose Ma. Chaves
Nicolas Domingues
Juan Ramon Trujillo
Patricio Montaño
Tircio Torres
Antonio Garcia
Vicente Chavez
Juan D. Madrid
Braulio Montoya
Pedro Espinosa
Felipe Maez
Pablo Armijo

APPENDIX XVI
Governor George Curry Pardons Penitente Serafin Baca, 1909

THE TERRITORIAL PENITENTIARY FURNISHES
ANOTHER CHAPTER.

How the President of the Penitentes Was Released From
Imprisonment by the Governor.

A Letter That Fell Into The Hands Of The
Phillistines And Its Sequel.

[A letter on prison stationery is reproduced across the six columns below these banner headlines.]

The above is a reproduction, on a slightly reduced scale, of a letter written to Cresencio Herrera, at Chamita, N.M., and dated Oct. 18, 1908. It was postmarked at Santa Fe, Oct. 22, 10 a.m. and backstamped Espanola, N.M., Oct. 22, 1908, 1 p.m. and Chamita, N.M., Oct. 23, 1908, 1 p.m.

The reproduction of the letter is by a photo-etching process which shows every detail in the printed head as well as the body of the letter. Those of our readers who are able to read Spanish, in which language the letter is written, will not find a translation necessary, but for those who do not read Spanish we print the following translation of the letter:

Santa Fe, N. Mex., October 18, 1908
My dear Mr. Cresencio Herrera and Brother in Christ Jesus:

To the greater honor and glory of God, and claiming the protection of the sorrowful Mother of God, I say thus: May the peace of God be with you and with your fraternity!

Now, brother, by means of these letters according to the rules of urbanity, and the obligation of our society, with fraternal affection, I shall tell you that I find myself in the territorial prison, and recalling at these mements I shall tell you that the executive of New Mexico promised my brothers and friends of the county of San Miguel, Mora and Taos to give me my liberty as soon as the election be over. And such being the case, by the bond of such sacred obligations in which we find ourselves, you should exert yourselves more than ever for the election of Mr. Andrews for the following reasons which exist against his competitor which is Mr. Larrazolo. The reasons that follow—He is the very bitter enemy of our society, for the case is that while defending a Mr. Gonzales in the court of the Fourth district for the killing of our brother Marcelino Seballes the defense that he made was to say openly that the purpose and object of the Penitentes was to protect one another in robberies, murders, and other more deplorable epithets.

And thus it is that I believe that you will not have the courage to support a scoundrel of such vituperation and insult. I count on our organization! With this I beg you to make every effort that you possibly can to show the world that our* are laudable.

With this I remain praying to God for you.

Serafin Baca
President+ of the Council.

*Evidently a word is omitted at this point.

It will be observed that the letter was written and mailed shortly before the last general election. The date of the letter shows that it was written on Sunday and the postmarks show that it was mailed four days later, leaving here on Thursday and arriving at Espanola the same day. Within six months of the date of the letter an executive order was issued pardoning Serafin Baca and four days later the instrument was filed in the office of the secretary of the territory as the following will show:

Territory of New Mexico, office of the Secretary.

Certificate of Comparison. I, Nathan Jaffa, Secretary of the Territory of New Mexico, do hereby certify that there was filed for record in this office at   o'clock   M. on the twenty-first day of April, A.D., 1909,

Executive order pardoning Serafin Baca and also, that I have compared the following copy of the same, with the original thereof now on file, and declare it to be a correct transcript therefrom and of the whole thereof. Given under my hand and the Great Seal of the Territory of New Mexico, at the City of Santa Fe, the capital, on this 16th day of October, A.D., 1909.

Nathan Jaffa,
Secretary of New Mexico.
By Edwin F. Coard. Assistant Secretary.

Executive Office Santa Fe.

Whereas, At the regular December, A.D. 1907 term of the district court sitting within and for county of San Miguel, territory of New Mexico, Serafin Baca was convicted and sentenced to serve a term of three years in the territorial penitentiary; and

Whereas, responsible citizens of San Miguel county have petitioned for executive clemency in behalf of said Baca; and

Whereas, the said prisoner has an excellent record in the penitentiary:

Now, therefore, I, George Curry, Governor of the Territory of New Mexico, by virtue of the authority in me vested, being fully informed in the premises, believe that the said Baca is deserving of executive clemency, and in view of his advanced age, I do hereby grant to Serafin Baca a complete pardon from further service of his sentence; and the superintendent of the territorial penitentiary upon receipt of this executive order properly signed and sealed will act accordingly.

Done at the Executive Office this the 17th day of April, A.D. 1909.

Witness my hand the great seal of the Territory of New Mexico.

(Signed)   George Curry.

(Territorial Seal)

By the Governor:

(Signed) Nathan Jaffa,

Secretary of New Mexico.

[ENDORSED]:

Executive order pardoning Serafin Baca.

Filed in Office of Secretary of New Mexico. Apr. 21, 1909.

Nathan Jaffa,

Secretary.

Compared C. F. K. to O.

It has often been denied that pardons have been issued for political purposes in New Mexico and that this has actually been the case in many instances would be extremely difficult to show, but here is a case that speaks eloquently for itself. There is nothing left to be imagined. The President of the Council of the Penitentes finds himself in the territorial prison and calls upon his friends to assist in the defeat of Larrazolo. He says that his friends were promised his liberty by the executive and he has been at liberty for more than six months. He was sentenced for three years and it is but two years this month since he was sentenced. It seems strange that a letter of this sort would be allowed to go out of the penitentiary, but it is possible that it was sent out surreptitiously. The letter is eloquent in its appeal for Andrews as might be expected from a man who is looking forward to promised liberty from behind prison walls.

The Eagle, Santa Fe, New Mexico, vol. 10, no. 17, Saturday, December 18, 1909, p. 1. A copy of this newspaper is among the E. V. Long Papers in the New Mexico State Records Center and Archives, Santa Fe.

APPENDIX XVII
An Act to incorporate the "Pious Fraternity of the County of Taos," January 30, 1861

Be it enacted by the Legislative Assembly of the Territory of New Mexico:

SECTION 1. That Petrolino Medina, J. A. Martinez, Miguel Griño, Juan de la Cruz Medina, José Miguel Archuleta, Mateo Martinez, Antonio Lucero, Francisco Cortes, Nicolas Sandoval, José Medina, M. S. Mondragon, Joaquin Sandoval, Cornelio Coca, and their successors and all those who are or may be associated with them as members of said fraternity, shall be and are hereby erected and established into a body politic and corporate, in law and in fact, by the name and style of the "Pious Fraternity of the County of Taos," and by that name shall have perpetual succession, may sue and be sued, plead and be impleaded, in any court of law or equity; and shall be able, in law and equity, to take and hold for themselves and their heirs, either by grant, bargain, sale, will, gift, devise, lien, or otherwise, any land, property, tenements, or real and personal estate, and at their pleasure to grant, bargain, or sell, for the use of said fraternity, and generally to do all and singular the matters and things which shall be legal for the well-being and the management of the affairs of said fraternity.

SEC. 2. That the object of said fraternity shall be for the dispensation of charity, and the establishment of all the moral and social virtues, and to provide and furnish all such halls and buildings as may be necessary for the members of such fraternity in their exercises.

SEC. 3. That it shall be lawful for said corporation to have a common seal, the device of which the same shall determine, and at will and pleasure change, alter and renew as they shall think proper, and shall have and exercise all the rights, privileges and immunities necessary for the purpose of the association hereby constituted.

SEC. 4. That said corporation shall have the power to make such private rules as may be necessary for the government thereof, not inconsistent with the constitution of the United States, nor the general laws, nor those of this Territory.

SEC. 5. That all real or personal property now belonging to the said corporation may be claimed in their name, and possess and retain the same for the exclusive use of said fraternity.

SEC. 6. The Legislative Assembly reserves to itself the right to annul or revoke this charter, and the establishment herein created, whenever in its opinion, at any time, the exercise of their institutions and private rules are in conflict with the general laws or the laws of this Territory, or contrary to good morals.

SEC. 7. This act shall be in force from and after its passage.

Laws of the Territory of New Mexico: Passed by the Legislative Assembly, Session of 1860–1861 (Santa Fe: John T. Russell, 1861). The act itself, approved on January 30, 1861, is in Spanish, pp. 75, 77. This English translation appears on pp. 74 and 76.

APPENDIX XVIII
Archbishop Edwin V. Byrne's Official Statement recognizing the Brothers of Jesus of Nazareth, 1947

Archbishop Grants Church Blessing to Penitente
Order in New Mexico

Archbishop Edwin V. Byrne today, in a declaration on the status of the Penitentes, granted this order the Catholic church's blessing and protection, "if the Brethren proceed with moderation and privately under our supervision."

Miguel Archibeque and leaders of the Hermanos have acted to rid them of "excesses and abuses" which have occurred in their practices in past years, the metropolitan says. However, "there are still instances of individual bad lives, as in other societies, and this or that group still makes itself a political football, thus giving a bad name to the Brethren."

Declaring the order's aim is corporal and spiritual penance, he declares such acts "after abolishing whatever excess or abuse there might have been, are not acts of sadism or masochism . . . not so severe or cruel as to injure one's health."

Frowning upon what has been called "Penitente hunting," the archbishop says no polite or cultured person should try to spy upon their meetings.

His statement follows in full:

It has become necessary for us to make a definite declaration regarding the Brothers of Jesus of Nazareth (commonly called the Penitentes), in order to clarify their status both to Catholics as well as to non-Catholics.

These Brothers or Brethren constitute a pious association of men joined in charity to commemorate the passion and death of the Redeemer. This society, like many others in the Catholic church, is part of that church and therefore deserves her protection and guidance so long as it keeps and practices the teachings of the Church.

Its origin is obscure in history. It seems that it began somewhere in the beginnings of the last century when the Franciscan padres left New Mexico by order of the new government of Mexico. No other priests were sent to take their place. Groups among the faithful tried to keep up Catholic practices without priestly guidance, and though certain excesses crept in, it is to these groups of penitential brethren that we owe, in a manner, the preservation of the faith in those hard and trying times.

But why do we make this declaration now? Precisely because many, even Catholics, harbor an erroneous idea concerning this association. It cannot be denied that the association itself is at fault because of certain excesses and abuses in the past. There are still scattered instances of individual bad lives, as in other societies, and

226

this or that group still makes itself a political football, thus giving a bad name to the Brethren.

However, moved by the admirable zeal of Mr. Miguel Archibeque, who at cost of great personal sacrifice has conferred with heads and important members (Hermanos mayores), in order to abolish any abuse there might be and so place the association definitely under the guidance and protection of the Catholic church which they love so much, I, as archbishop of Santa Fe, take them under my supervision to guide them according to directions already accepted by them, and to protect them from ill-instructed persons who consider them as objects of curiosity or ridicule.

Therefore, I declare:

1. That the Association of Hermanos de Nuestro Senor Jesus Nazareno is not a fanatical sect apart from the church, as some seem to think, but an association of Catholic men united together in love for the passion and death of our Blessed Lord and Saviour;

2. That the end of this society is to do corporal and spiritual penance, for the saying of our Lord concerning the necessity of penance for salvation is just as true now as it was centuries ago, and therefore should be no shameful connotation attached to the word penitent; (The saints, like the humble and sweet St. Francis of Assisi, loved by the wild birds and beasts, and whom the whole world still loves and admires, practiced many penances. The Third Order, which he founded for lay people in the world, he himself called "the Order of Penance." And this confirms us in the opinion that the Hermanos are descended from those Tertiaries founded here by the Franciscans in centuries gone by. Certainly there is no connection, as some writers claim, between the Hermanos and those fanatical sects of Flagellants in medieval times.);

3. That these acts of penance, after abolishing whatever excess or abuse there might have been, are not acts of sadism or masochism, as modern wise men wish to say in these days, softened by luxury and comfort; and that they are not so severe or cruel as to injure one's health, for then they would be sins and not acts of virtue; and that these penances must be done in private to avoid scandal, because Christian penance is of itself private and not like that of the Pharisees; hence it follows, that no individual, be he Catholic or not, should interfere with their meetings, just as no one

227

who deems himself polite or cultured would try to break in or spy on the meetings of societies to which he does not belong;

4. That we have the authority and power to suppress this association, just as we can and must suppress any other pious association in the church which goes counter to, or exceeds, the laws of God and His church, or the dictates of reason. But if the Brethren proceed with moderation and privately and under our supervision, meanwhile giving a good example to all as Catholics and citizens, they have our blessing and protection.

Santa Fe New Mexican, Wednesday, January 29, 1947, p. 1, cols. 5–7; p. 7, cols. 4–5.

APPENDIX XIX
Don Miguel Archibeque, July 1, 1883–June 16, 1970

Miguel Archibeque funeral mass held

SANTA FE (AP)—Miguel Archibeque worked as a parking lot attendant in Santa Fe until old age retired him five years ago.

Today, the governor was going to his funeral mass, and the archbishop called Archibeque "a very reliable and positively motivated leader."

A writer-historian who knew him called him "one of the great spiritual leaders of our people."

Archibeque, born in 1883, was the leader—the hermano mayor —of New Mexico's "Penitentes"—La Cofradia de Nuestro Padre Jesus.

In the 1940's he was the leader in reorganizing the Penitente brotherhood and bringing it back within the good graces of the Roman Catholic church.

Ceremonies marking his passing were a combination of Roman Catholic liturgy and the mysteries of the two-centuries-old brotherhood.

The Penitentes conducted a public rosary for Archibeque Thursday evening, then took the body to a morada near the 170-year-old mountain village of San Miguel, where he was born; returning this morning for the funeral at Our Lady of Guadalupe Church in Santa Fe, and burial in Rosario Cemetery.

A standard with a painting of Christ bearing the cross and the words "Concilio Supremeo (Supreme Council)" remained beside the coffin. The brotherhood sang the anguished folk chants that have been passed on from generation to generation for centuries.

The Penitente brotherhood in rural New Mexico is one of the world's last remnants of the religious tradition of pentitente orders in late medieval Europe. Little is generally known about the New Mexico brotherhood or its rituals, although they were popularized by travelers at the turn of the century who emphasized that the Penitentes at that time held "ceremonial Crucifixions."

The Most Rev. James Peter Davis remarked upon learning of Archibeque's death Tuesday in Santa Fe that he "was very instrumental in bringing some very good leadership into the Penitentes."

The archbishop noted that before Archibeque's leadership, "a number of excesses from time to time occurred with regard to their penitential disciplines."

Gov. David Cargo said Archibeque "had a tremendous impact on New Mexico, particularly in the northern part of the state because of his activities among the Penitentes. Few people were aware of his influence.

State historian-archivist Myra Ellen Jenkins said her studies showed Archibeque "was very influential in ameliorating much of the misunderstanding between the Penitentes and the hierarchy of the church."

Writer-teacher Peter Ortega of Santa Fe, who knew the leader, said, "I respected him as perhaps one of the great spiritual leaders of our people.

"He definitely realized the Penitentes were a part of the Spanish-Christian culture. His great life work as a Penitente leader was to make them acceptable to the church without loss of their character, without losing any part of the spirit of the Penitentes in our culture. His contribution in keeping them alive and keeping them respected was very important," Ortega said.

Despite his influence, Archibeque wasn't wealthy. He worked for the state as a parking lot attendant in Santa Fe until he retired in 1965. He had been a resident of Santa Fe 28 years.

Cargo appointed him to the Governor's Approval Commission, which deals with veteran's benefits.

Survivors include six grandchildren, reared by Archibeque —Carmel, Frank, Raymond and George Larranga; and Mrs. Julio Chavez and Mrs. Enrique Rivera.

When Archibeque began his leadership in 1940, the Penitentes were divided, with organizations going their own ways in separate communities of northern New Mexico and southern Colorado.

Archibeque began traveling among the communities and by 1944 had succeeded in unifying all the factions under one supreme council. In 1947 the organization was approved by the late Archbishop Edwin V. Byrne.

The successor to Archibeque as the informal but clearly recognized leader is M. Santos Melendez of Albuquerque.

Through a mortuary spokesman Melendez said Friday the brotherhood would continue as the unified organization created by Archibeque. Melendez estimated there are about 1,700 active members of the brotherhood in dozens of moradas across New Mexico and southern Colorado.

Lujan eulogizes personal hero

Upon the death of Miguel Archibeque, well known Santa Fe resident, Congressman Manuel Lujan Jr. made the following comments to The New Mexican.

"If I were to name the men who have had the greatest influence on my life," said Lujan, "I would think Miguel Archibeque would be high on the list."

"Ever since I was a teen-age boy, Mr. Archibeque had been one of my personal heroes," continued Lujan. "No problem was ever too small for his concern, and he had a way of making you see all problems large and small in the largest text of life itself. His gentle, humble, unselfish nature was an example and inspiration to everyone who knew him."

Mr. Archibeque services held

Miguel Archibeque funeral services were held this morning at our Lady of Guadalupe Church, with interment following at Rosario Cemetery. Members of La Cofradia De Nuestro Padre Jesus served as pallbearers. . . .

The Santa Fe New Mexican, Friday, June 19, 1970, pp. 1, 2.

APPENDIX XX
Constitution and Rules for the Pious Fraternity of Taos County

Reglas y Conistitucions [*sic*] de La Fraternidad de Nuestro
Padre Jesus del Condado de Taos.

I

Nosotros, los miembros de la Fraternidad de Nuestro Padre
Jesus del Condado de Taos Estado De Nuevo Mexico

Desando incorporar La Fraternidad de Nuestro Padre Jesus del
Condado de Taos este dia 27 de Marzo Ano de Dios 1931 y
quedamos en order a firmar esta conistitucion para el Govierno de
Dicha Fraternidad y para establecer y Desaminar la moralidad y
buenas costumbres, asegurar la tranquilidad de nuestras consien-
cias y para probir instituciones uniformes para la regla comun de
la Fraternidad, y para segurar. Los Beneficios Selestiales que trai
consigo la Benebolenia y la Sana Moral para nosotros mismos y
para nuestros hijos y sus susesores, formamos y establesemos esta
conistitucion bajo las aspisias de aquel Supremo Salvador que
continuanmente cuida sobre sus creaturas, en cuyo poder infinito y
lleno de misericordia esperamos humildemente nos ade socorrer,
para andar por las villas rectas del Senor emitando en cuanto nos
sea permetido por su divina majestad Las huellas saludables y
Santa Doctrina de nuestro Salvador universal, Jesucristo nuestra
Vida, nuestra, Guilla y nuestra Luz y es del Tenor Siguiente:

Articulo primero Secion 1 ra

1ra S

El poder superior de la Fraternidad sera inbertido y sometido en
un hermano mayor que sera nombrado por una mayoria de la
Fraternidad y un Segundo hermano sera alludante del Hermano
Mayor los cuales tendran su destino durante la Boluntad de la
Fraternidad y podran ser removidos en cualesquier tiempo por
faltas y mal cumplimiento de sus destinos y deveres.

Secion 2da

Tan luego como un hermano mayor un segundo hermano sean
nombrados prestaran un juramento ante la Fraternidad, de

231

cumplir fiel y legalmente todos los deveras y poderas que le sean encargados por estas reglas de la sosiedad.

Secion 3ra

Sera el dever del Hermano Mayor duidar del buen order y manejo de la Fraternidad cuidar que los miembros de la congregacion cumplan con fiedelidad con sus promesas guarando la continencia y sovriedad que requiere oir sitar y haser compareser a los delincuentes que estrabiandose del horden se entrieguen a tales vicios. que se hagan culpables de algun castigo podra castigar a su albitrio alos miembros viciosos con las penas acostumbradas ala sosiedad. No siendo asesivos ni desusados pero equivalentes al delito reserviran y a el seran derejidos todas las aplicaciones de perzonas que desean ser admitidos a tal Fraternidad y dispondra de la manera que ade ser admitodo a las reglas de la sosiedad.

Articulo Segundo 2do Secion 1ra

Que la Fraternidad no podiendo estar junta en masa por lo estenso del condado sera dividida en las seciones mas conbinientes que la Sosiedad estime y haga para el mayor cumplimiento de sus deveres y descrision.

Secion 2da

Que en cada secion sera nombrado un hermano mayor a gusto de los componentes de tal secion y ellos mismos deveran elejirlo el cual cumplira con los poderes asignados al hermano mayor el el articulo primero secion Tres de esta conistitucion pero asi este como el alludante seran subalternos al Hermano Mayor nombrado conforme al Articulo primero teniendo que avisrale a el de tales nombramientos que se agan quien los conservara para los fines combinientes

Secion 3ra

Que el hermano mayor y en su lugar el segundo Hermano tendran superentendencia sobre todos los hermanos mayores nombrados en cada secion conforme la anterior secion de este acta podiendo jusgarlos cuando sean acusados por enormes faltas y destituirlos cuando la Grabedad de la causa lo pida declarando vacante tal oficio y avisar a la Secion correspondiente para que proseda a cubrir tal vacancia.

Articulo 3 Secion 1ra

Que cuando quiera que los negosios de la Fraternidad . . .

Transcription from the Dorothy Woodward Penitente Papers, New Mexico State Records Center and Archives, Santa Fe. This constitution was filed with the State Corporation Commission of New Mexico, Santa Fe, on April 27, 1931, at 3:10 p.m. It accompanied the Certificate of Incorporation of La Fraternidad de Nuestro Padre Jesus del Condado de Taos, no. 16980, vol. 8, p. 101. Except for orthographic irregularities and the change in approval date, the remainder of the document is identical with the *"Fragmento"* published by Darley in 1899:

. . . Los requieran, los Hermanos Mayores de las diferentes Secciones se renuirán con el Hermano Mayor Principal quien presidirá sobre la junta y una mayoría de dichos hermanos constiuará una competencia para hacer negocios; tal reunión se hará en donde ellos de acuerdo lo determinan en cualquier partido dentro del condado de Taos.

Sección 2a. Que en cada sección había un Celador que será nombrado por el Hermano Mayor de la sección, con previo consentimiento de los miembros de la Hermandad: y que los deberes de tales Celadores serán determinados por el Hermano Mayor respectivo con arreglo á los usos y costumbres antiguos.

Sección 3a. Que en cada sección había un Tesorero nombrado, con consentimiento de los miembros, por el Hermano Mayor correspondiente, quien tendrá en su poder el dinero y fondos pertenecientes a la Fraternidad, y llevará cuenta exacta de los ingresos y gastos, sujeto al arreglo que le sea dado.

Sección 4a. Que había un sello comun de la Fraternidad, el cual será usado en todos lós papeles que pertenecen á la Sociedad y con él se autorizaran todos sus escritos y el cual será designado en los arreglos.

Articulo Cuarto.

Sección 1a. Que esta Constitución será sometida á todos los miembros de la Fraternidad del condado que residen en las diferentes partes del condado y despues que haya sido adoptada por ellos tendrá todavía efecto y fuerza sobre los que la hayan adoptado.

Sección 2a. Que el Hermano Mayor Principal tendrá que mandar una copia á todos las plazas dirijidas á los Hermanos Mayores ó á sus ayudantes quien la someterá á sus correspondientes hermanos, y él le mandará el resultado al Hermano Mayor Principal y si los adoptará serán reconocidos como miembros de la Fraternidad Piadosa del condado de Taos, y gozarán de todos privilegios franquicios que goza dicha Fraternidad.

Sección 3a. Que el estilo que encabezado de todos los papeles, órdenes, peticiones y memoriales será *"Fraternidad Piadosa de Condado de Taos"*, y serán firmados y atestiguados por el Hermano Mayor Principal, ó por cualquier Hermano Mayor de cualquiera Sección.

Articulo Quinto.

Sección 1a. Que los miembros de cada sección, en su respectivo lugar, tendrá el poder de preparar una casa para el acomodamiento de los miembros cuando esten en sus ejercicios, tenerla, repararla, poseerla y adornarla.

Sección 2. Que el Hermano Mayor de la Sección correspondiente podrá reclamar en nombre de la Fraternidad Piadosa del Condado de Taos cualesquiera edificios y pertenencias que hayan sido pertenecientes á la Hermandad desde tiempos pasados y en nombre de la Fraternidad reclamarlas ante cualquiera autoridad civil, usando todos los medios posibles por medio de desembargo ó de cualquier otro modo hasta conseguir la debida y justa restitución; así mismo podrá presenciar cualquiera persona que intente burlarse, perturbe y de cualquier modo estorbe el ejercicio de tal Fraternidad, y que no sea miembro de la sociedad, le demandará ante cualquiera autoridad civil en nombre de la Fraternidad del Condado de Taos.

Sección 3a. Que siempre el Hermano Mayor Principal será nombrado una persona habil y competente, el cual residirá y tendrá su oficina en la cabecera del Condado de Taos en Don Fernandez de Taos como el punto céntrico y conveniente para dirijir y recibir las comunicaciones necesarias y además tendrá en su poder el original de esta Constitución, y todos los papeles pertenecientes á la Sociedad como siempre ha sido costumbre y practicado.

NOSOTROS los abajos suscritos con el fin de sostener esta Constitución comprotemos y obligamos nuestro honor, nuestra fé y nuestro carácter, y sostendremos todos los puntos puestos aquí, para nuestro propio gobierno y dirección, é impretamos el auxilio de nuestro Dios y elevamos nuestros ruegos y suplicamos á nuestro Señor Jesu Cristo para servirle con honestidad, guiados por su justo ejemplo.

En testimonio nosotros los que hemos hecho y adoptado esta Constitución la firmamos con nuestras manos en Don Fernando de Taos en día 23 de Febrero de año de Nuestro Señor de 1861.

"Un Fragmento de La Constitucion Y las Reglas de Los Penitentes," La Hermandad, Pueblo, Colorado, vol. 11, no. 2, April 1899, p. 1, cols. 1–2.

Reglas Para El Gobierno Interior de la Fraternidad Piadosa del Condado de Taos.

La Fraternidad Piadosa del Condado habiendo conseguido una patente de la Asambléa Legislativa del Territorio de Nuevo Mexico establece las siguientes Reglas segun la facultad que les dá la ley para que sean la guía de nuestra Sociedad.

Capítulo Primero.

Los miembros de la Fraternidad Piadosa del Condado de Taos deben saber que la instrucción nuestra ha sido desde tiempos antiguos la devoción de la sangre de Cristo que fué derramada por salvar á nosotros los pecadores, pues de tal modo como Dios al hombre que dió á su Hijo Unico para que se ofreciese en sacrificio por los pecadores; que el objeto principal de nuestro instituto es servir á Dios Nuestro Criador y creer que Jesu Cristo es el Salvador del Mundo; según la doctrina que predicó como consta el Santo Evangelio; guardar los diez mandamientos de la ley de Dios; arreglar la conducta siendo modesto; huir de las riñas, de controversias de pleitos injustos, de tabernas y de todas las tentaciones que el mundo nos pone porque "Que aprovecha al hombre," como dice el Evangelio de San Matéo, "se ganare todo el mundo y perdiere su alma"; que uno á los otros nos hemos de dispensar la caridad, la voluntad amándonos como hermanos en Jesu Cristo, dándonos buen ejemplo unos á otros, socoriéndonos en nuestras enfermedades, angustias y necesidades, perdonándonos nuestras injurias unos á otros, tolerándonos nuestras debilitades mutuamente; seguir la vida humilde y ejemplo que nos dió Nuestro Señor Jesu Cristo, y reconocernos y estimarnos como miembros de un cuerpo que es Cristo Jesus, Nuestro Redentor, y decir como dice el Evangelio de San Matéo, capítulo 11 versos

25-26: "Doy gloria á Tí, O Padre, Señor del cielo y de la tierra porque escondistes estas cosas á los sabios y entendidos y las has descubierto á los parvulos: Así es, Padre, porque así tu agrado.

Por lo tanto debemos acogernos á los ofrecimientos que se nos han hecho por Dios para el bien de nuestras almas cuando en el cap. 11: de San Matéo v.v. 28, 29, y 30 "Venid a mí," dice Cristo, "todos los que estáis trabajados y cargados y yo os aliviaré, traed mi yugo sobre vosotros y aprended de mí que manso soy y humilde de corazon y hallaréis reposo para vuestras almas; porque mi yugo suave es, y mi carga ligera." Y en cap. 12: de San Matéo dice v. 36–37. "Dígoos que de toda palabra ociosa que hablaren los hombres darán cuenta de ella en el día del juicio: Porque por tus palabras serás justificado y por tus palabras serás condenado."

Por tanto con un fervoroso deseo y una intención san de tomar como nuestra la doctrina del Señor, hablemos con San Pablo en su carta á los Filipénses cap. 3: vs. 16–21 "Más en cuanto á lo que hemos ya llegado tengamos unos mismos sentimientos y permanescamos en una misma regla, sed imitadores mios, hermanos, y perdáis de vista á los que así andan segun que tenéis nuestro ejemplo, porque muchos andan de quienes otras veces se dicen y ahora tambien lo digo, llorando, que son enemigos de la cruz de Cristo; cuya fin es la perdición, cuyo Dios es el vientre, y su gloria es para confusión de ellos, que gustan solo de lo terreno mas nuestra morada está en los cielos de donde tambien esperamos al Salvador, nuestro Señor Jesu Cristo el cual reformará nuestro cuerpo abatido para hacerlo conforme á su glorioso cuerpo, segun la operación conque puede sugetar á sí todas las cosas."

Capítulo Segundo.

1a. Los deberes del Hermano Mayor Principal, y de los hermanos de las diferentes poblaciones, serán como estan designados en el primero y segundo artículo de la constitución de la fraternidad.

2a. Que cuando alguna persona desee entrar á ser un miembro de esta sociedad hará su aplicación al Hermano Mayor el cual despues de echar las averiguaciones necesarias relativas á su conducta será admitido haciendo unas declaraciones segun este estilo que consiguen:—Vd declara, bajo la religión Cristiana que profiese que se ofrece, como un miembro de la Fraternidad

Piadosa, que cumplirá y sostendrá la constitución y reglas de dicha corporación y su objeto, que es la caridad y buenas costumbres, y se ofrece como devoto á la sangre de Cristo é imitará á lo mejor de su alcance la perfeccion y modelo de Cristo; que se halla bien dispuesto pertenecer á esta corporación en virtud y amor de Cristo y deseaís verdaderamente seguir su ejemplo, arreglar vuestra conducta por el sendero de cumplir con los diez mandamientos de la ley de Dios con el auxilio de su gracia divina. Declaro y juro.

3a. Declara además Vd que concluido el noviciado y admitido como miembro, abraza Vd esta corporación con gusto y voluntad y sufriréis con paciencia y conferme lo bromoso y aspero de su práctica, y promete arreglar bien su conducta, arrepentiéndose de los desordenes y miras pecaminosas, amar á Dios sobre todas las cosas y esperar sus beneficios profesando vivir en esta Fraternidad esperando en Dios misericordia por medio de Cristo: Declaro y juro.

Entónces el que toma el juramento le dirá es Vd admitido miembro de la Sociedad de la Caritad; pero debe guardar silencio y no dar la gloria de vuestro mérito al mundo, sino es en lo escondido.

4a. Entónces el Hermano Mayor correspondiente junto con el nuevo hermano se hincará de rodillas delante una imágen de Cristo crucificado y hará la oración contenida en la vuelta de página la del libro antiguo y las siguientes oraciones hasta concluirse.

5a. Si se observa que algun hermano se hace escándaloso, cometiendo crímenes y quebranta la constitución y reglas de esta fraternidad y no cumple con los mandamientos será castigado por el Hermano Mayor y Celadores severamente y le requierirán que se arrepienta y enmiendo, explicándole los deberes que ha prometido, y en caso que no le haga é insista en sus vicios será desechado y su nombre borrado de la lista; en caso que despues de estar expulsado y desechado se arrepienta verdaderamente, será admitido otra vez, pero no tendrá ningun cargo hasta despues de un año que corre su arrepentimiento y enmendación acredita con los hechos.

6a. Que los Celadores tendrán facultad de vigilar sobre la conducta de los hermanos y corregirlos cuando sea necesario y, en caso de desobediencia los denunciarán al Hermano Mayor para su correción y castigo.

7a. Que los hermanos y miembros de la corporación obedecen a sus superiores y les guardarán todo el respecto debido, siendo un crímen sí desobedecen.

Capítulo Tercero.

1a. Que la Fraternidad será dividida en las Secciones siguientes, á saber:—

El Primero—de Don Fernando de Taos—constituirá la Sección de Don Fernando, No. 1.

El Precinto del Ranchito constituirá la Sección del Ranchito, No. 2.

El Precinto del Rancho compondrá la Sección del Rancho, No. 3.

El Precinto de la Placita será la Sección de la Placita, No. 4.

La Agua Negra será la Sección No. 5.

El Arroyo Hondo será la Sección No. 6.

2a. Que el Hermano Mayor comunicará á las demas Hermandades de las diferentes plazas y Mora la Constitución y Reglas ahora adoptadas, invitándolas para ver sí quieren organizar bajo la ley, y segun ser respuesta, los que admitan serán recibidas y reconocidas como miembros de la Fraternidad Piadosa.

La Hermandad, Pueblo, Colorado, vol. 11, no. 2, April 1899, p. 1, cols. 2–6. These rules were not included with the Corporation Commission documents. (The first paragraph of *"Capítulo Primero"* has been translated by Richard Grove in George Mills, "Penitentes of New Mexico and Colorado: An Exhibition," The Taylor Museum of The Colorado Springs Fine Arts Center, Colorado Springs, Colorado, Summer-Fall, 1955. This translation has been reprinted by Bill Tate in *The Penitentes of the Sangre de Cristos: An American Tragedy,* 5th ed. [Truchas, New Mexico: Tate Gallery, 1971], p. 2.)

Notes

Part I: A Geographical Sketch

1. H. H. Bancroft, *History of Arizona and New Mexico: 1530–1888* (San Francisco: The History Co., 1889), p. 279.

2. Cultural Properties Review Committee, *The Historic Preservation Program for New Mexico,* 2 vols. (Santa Fe: State Planning Office, 1973), 1:24.

3. Fray Angelico Chavez, "Early Settlements in the Mora Valley," *El Palacio* 62 (1955):318–23.

4. Fabiola Cabeza de Baca, *We Fed Them Cactus* (Albuquerque: University of New Mexico Press, 1954), pp. 1–5.

5. Nancie L. González, *The Spanish-Americans of New Mexico: A Heritage of Pride* (Albuquerque: University of New Mexico Press, 1969), p. 6.

6. See, e.g., Marc Simmons, *The Fighting Settlers of Seboyeta* (Cerrillos, New Mexico: San Marcos Press, 1971).

7. Frances Leon Swadesh, *Los Primeros Pobladores: Hispanic Americans of the Ute Frontier* (Notre Dame: University of Notre Dame Press, 1974), chap. 2.

8. Robert W. Larson, *New Mexico's Quest for Statehood 1846–1912* (Albuquerque: University of New Mexico Press, 1968), pp. 65, 71, 319.

9. See, e.g., Francis T. Cheetham, "The Early Settlements of Southern Colorado," *Colorado Magazine* 5 (1928):1–8; and Myra Ellen Jenkins, *Tracing Spanish-American Pedigrees in the Southwestern United States: I. New Mexico, Texas and Colorado* (Salt Lake City, Utah: Genealogical Society of the Church of Jesus Christ of Latter-Day Saints, Inc., 1969), pp. 8–9. Fort Massachusetts was established on June 22, 1852, and intermittently occupied, while Fort Garland was set up in 1858.

10. Morris F. Taylor, *Trinidad, Colorado Territory* (Pueblo, Colorado: O'Brien Printing & Stationery Co., 1966), pp. 16, 26–27.

11. Cultural Properties Review Committee, *Historic Preservation,* 1:34. Also see González, *Spanish-Americans of New Mexico;* and Cabeza de Baca, *We Fed Them Cactus.*

12. Swadesh, *Los Primeros Pobladores,* chap. 5.

13. *The Old Faith and Old Glory: Story of the Church in New Mexico since the American Occupation* (Santa Fe: Santa Fe Press, 1946), p. 12.

14. J. Manuel Espinosa, "The Neapolitan Jesuits on the Colorado Frontier, 1868–1919," *Colorado Magazine* 15 (1938):67.

15. Ibid., p. 68.

16. See Appendix I.

17. Aurelio M. Espinosa, *The Spanish Language in New Mexico and Southern Colorado,* Publications of the New Mexico Historical Society, no. 16 (Santa Fe: New Mexican Printing, 1911), pp. 24–25. The word "morada" may refer to the physical meeting place of the Penitentes or to the chapter as an organization of Brothers. E. Boyd identifies "morada" as "the Spanish noun for the home, 'la casa de mi morada' the house of my residence, also used for a schoolhouse or building in which public meetings are held" (*Popular Arts of Spanish New Mexico* [Santa Fe: Museum of New Mexico Press, 1974], p. 440, fn. 1). Fray Angelico Chavez also derives "a dwelling place or lodge, from the verb *morar* [to dwell, lodge, reside], and not from the feminine of the adjective 'purple,' as some writers have guessed" ("The Penitentes of New Mexico," *New Mexico Historical Review* 29 [1954]:122, fn. 62). William G. Ritch's notes for 1878 include the entry: "name of place of meeting—Casa morada" (Memo

book, HM RI 2212, vol. 4, p. 326a; Ritch's papers are at the Huntington Library, San Marino, California, hereafter cited as "HM"). This may indicate an early confusion of the noun with the adjective.

18. Bainbridge Bunting, *Taos Adobes,* Publication of the Fort Burgwin Research Center, no. 2 (Santa Fe: Museum of New Mexico Press and the Center, 1964), pp. 54–55; Richard E. Ahlborn, *The Penitente Moradas of Abiquiú,* Contributions from the Museum of History and Technology, Paper 63 (Washington, D.C.: Smithsonian Institution Press, 1968); E. Boyd, *Popular Arts,* p. 459. It is notable that the East Morada of Abiquiu, Rio Arriba County, is listed on New Mexico's "Inventory of Cultural Properties." "This three room adobe structure built between 1820 and 1850 is probably the oldest surviving morada in the state" (Cultural Properties Review Committee, *Historic Preservation,* 2:104).

19. Boyd, *Popular Arts,* pp. 459–60. Other discussions of the general characteristics of moradas are found in Bainbridge Bunting and John P. Conron, "The Architecture of Northern New Mexico," *New Mexico Architecture,* September-October 1966, p. 25; Bunting, "An Architectural Guide to Northern New Mexico," *New Mexico Architecture,* September-October 1970, pp. 35–36; and idem, *Of Earth and Timbers Made: New Mexico Architecture* (Albuquerque: University of New Mexico Press, 1974), plates 13, 17, 21, 47, 63, 64. George Kubler does not treat moradas in his pioneer study because their "architectural style is closer to the domestic architecture of New Mexico than to the churches" (*Religious Architecture of New Mexico* [Colorado Springs, Colorado: The Taylor Museum, 1940], p. viii).

20. Woodward's 1935 map would be the most accurate, although incomplete, available except that she has not specifically identified the indicated moradas in an attempt to protect the Brotherhood from unwelcome intrusions. Dorothy Woodward, *The Penitentes of New Mexico* (1935; reprint ed., New York: Arno Press, 1974), p. 21.

21. Ibid., p. xi.

22. Cabeza de Baca, *We Fed Them Cactus,* p. 72.

23. Vic Lamb, "Penitente Cemetery Near Lincoln," *Albuquerque Journal,* June 11, 1967, p. G-1.

24. Betty Woods, *101 Trips in the Land of Enchantment,* 3rd ed. (Santa Fe: New Mexico Magazine, 1969), p. 122.

25. Woodward, *Penitentes,* pp. xi, 21.

26. S. Omar Barker, "Los Penitentes," *Overland Monthly and Out West Magazine* 82 (1924):180.

27. Thomas R. Lyons and Margil Lyons, personal communication.

28. Jo Roybal Hogue, "The Penitentes: Unique New Mexico Easter Rites," *The Santa Fe New Mexican,* April 11, 1971, p. D-1.

29. E. Boyd, "Penitentes in California," *El Palacio* 57 (1950):372–73.

30. More detailed maps are found in: Anonymous, *The Old Faith and Old Glory* (Santa Fe: Santa Fe Press, 1946); Fray Angelico Chavez, *Archives of the Archdiocese of Santa Fe, 1678–1900* (Washington, D.C.: Academy of American Franciscan History, 1957); Warren A. Beck and Ynez D. Haase, *Historical Atlas of New Mexico* (Norman: University of Oklahoma Press, 1969); and D. W. Meinig, *Southwest: Three Peoples in Geographical Change 1600–1970* (London: Oxford University Press, 1971). Other useful but sometimes inaccurate information is contained in the W.P.A. Guides to Colorado and to New Mexico. The results of the New Mexico Place Names Project are available in T. M. Pearce, ed., *New Mexico Place Names: A Geographical Dictionary* (Albuquerque: University of New Mexico Press, 1965).

Chapter 1: The Germinal Period, 1776–1850

1. H. Bailey Carroll and J. Villasana Haggard, eds., *Three New Mexico Chronicles: The*

"Exposición" of Don Pedro Bautista Pino, 1812; the "Ojeada" of Lic. Antonio Barreiro, 1832; and the additions by Don José Agustín de Escudero, 1849, Quivira Society Publications, vol. 11 (Albuquerque: University of New Mexico Press for the Society, 1942), p. 51. The original clause reads: "yo que cuento mas de edad, nunca supe cómo se vestian hasta que vine á Cádiz" (Escudero, ed., *Noticias históricas y estadísticas de la antigua provincia del Nuevo-México* [1849; reprint ed., West Las Vegas, New Mexico: Our Lady of Sorrows Church, 1972], p. 31).

2. For a substantial account of the final fifty years of Spanish civil administration, see Marc Simmons, *Spanish Government in New Mexico* (Albuquerque: University of New Mexico Press, 1968). Civil aspects of the following period are described in Lansing B. Bloom, "New Mexico under Mexican Administration, 1821–1846," *Old Santa Fe* 1 (1913):3–49, 131–75, 235–87, 347–68; 2 (1914–15):3–56, 119–69, 223–77, 351–80. A sound recent summary appears in Myra Ellen Jenkins, *Guide to the Microfilm Edition of the Mexican Archives of New Mexico, 1821–1846* (Santa Fe: State of New Mexico Records Center, 1969).

3. A good summary of the allegations and defenses is presented in Eleanor B. Adams, *Bishop Tamarón's Visitation of New Mexico, 1760,* Publications in History, vol. 15 (Albuquerque: Historical Society of New Mexico, 1954), pp. 1–19.

4. Ibid., pp. 22–23.

5. *Lamy Memorial: Centenary of the Archdiocese of Santa Fe, 1850–1950* (Santa Fe: Schifani Brothers, 1950), p. 23.

6. Fray Angelico Chavez distinguishes between the two modes of religious vocation thus: "The Franciscans . . . lived in community as members of an Order. As distinct from the house or residence of a secular priest, or the palace of a bishop, either of which can be separate and even distant from the church itself, their communal dwellings were contiguous to and communicated with the parish or mission church which they served. They were not called monasteries . . . but rather *convents,* or gathering-places, for the *friars,* or brethren —who held a position half-way between the *monastic* life (alone or secluded from the world) and the *secular* life (in the world) of the diocesan clergy" ("Santa Fe Church and Convent Sites in the Seventeenth and Eighteenth Centuries," *New Mexico Historical Review* 24 [1949]:88–89). In addition, most friars were paid a *sínodo,* or stipend, from the royal treasury, amounting to some 330 pesos annually. Simmons, *Spanish Government in New Mexico,* p. 107. Secular clergy were to be supported by parishioners' *diezmos,* or tithes.

According to Chavez, friars are properly designated as *Fray (Fr.)* before full religious names only, or *Padre* before first, last, or full names. The practice of calling secular clergy "Padre" or "Father" is peculiar to English-speaking areas in recent times; the proper designation is *el Señor Cura,* Cura, or Don. *Archives of the Archdiocese of Santa Fe, 1678–1900,* Publications of the American Academy of American Franciscan History, Bibliographical Series, vol. 3 (Washington, D.C.: Academy of American Franciscan History, 1957), pp. 5–6 (hereafter cited as Chavez, *AASF*). For a general picture of New World Church administration and rivalries, see, e.g., C. H. Haring, *The Spanish Empire in America* (New York: Harcourt, Brace & World, 1952), pp. 166–93; and Charles Gibson, *Spain in America* (New York: Harper & Row, 1966), pp. 68–89.

7. Adams, *Bishop Tamarón's Visitation.*

8. Eleanor B. Adams and Fray Angelico Chavez, eds., *The Missions of New Mexico, 1776: A Description by Fray Francisco Atanasio Domínguez, With Other Contemporary Documents* (Albuquerque: University of New Mexico Press, 1956).

9. Simmons, *Spanish Government in New Mexico,* p. 107.

10. Fray Angelico Chavez, "The Penitentes of New Mexico," *New Mexico Historical Review* 29 (1954):116.

11. Carroll and Haggard, eds., *Three New Mexico Chronicles,* pp. 50–51. The original

reads: ". . . por consiguiente, se hallan sin cumplir las soberanas disposiciones y lo prevenido en la disciplina eclesiástica. . . . Se hallan sin confirmar todos los nacidos en dichos 50 años; y los pobres que quieren contraer matrimonio con sus parientes por medio de dispensa, no lo pueden verificar por los crecidos costos en el dilatado viaje de mas de 400 leguas que hay á Durango; de aquí proviene que muchos, estrechados del amor, viven amancebados y con familia . . ." (Escudero, ed., *Noticias*, p. 31).

12. Rev. Edwin A. Ryan, D.D., "Ecclesiastical Jurisdiction in the Spanish Colonies," *Catholic Historical Review* 5 (1919):9.

13. Archives of the Archdiocese of Santa Fe, Accounts, Book 62 (Chavez, *AASF*, p. 190). (The Archives of the Archdiocese are available on a microfilm edition, but Chavez's calendar will hereafter be cited in these notes. Roll and Frame numbers may be found in the *Bibliographical Supplement* to this volume.)

14. Chavez, *AASF*, p. 192.

15. Ibid., p. 196.

16. Ibid.

17. Ibid., p. 194.

18. Carroll and Haggard, eds., *Three New Mexico Chronicles*, p. 53. The original reads: "La administracion espiritual se encuentra en un estado verdaderamente lastimoso: nada es mas comun que ver á infinitos enfermos morir sin confesion y Extrema-uncion: y nada mas raro que verles administrar la Eucaristia. Los cadaveres permanecen insepultos muchos dias, y los párvulos se bautizan á costa de mil sacrificios; infelices hay en considerable número, que se pasan sin oir misa los mas domingos del año; las iglesias están casi destruidas; y las mas de ellas son ciertamente indignas de llamarse templos de Dios" (Escudero, *Noticias*, p. 33).

19. Carroll and Haggard, eds., ibid., p. 55. The original reads: ". . . que la piedad cristiana se resiente al ver los abusos que se cometen en Nuevo-México, con el culto y cura de almas; y la caridad prescribe, que un velo se eche sobre muchas cosas que causaria escándolo referirlas. . . . La mies es mucha, pero faltan operarios; roguemos al Señor que vengan sobre ella sus cosecheros" (Escudero, *Noticias*, p. 34).

20. A transcription of the entire document appears in Appendix I. Chavez has translated portions of this manuscript in "The Penitentes of New Mexico," pp. 110–11. Nonetheless, a rough translation of the complete text follows: Beyond a doubt, there is in this Villa a Brotherhood of Penitentes, already in existence for a number of years, but without authorization or knowledge of the bishops, who certainly would not have given their consent to such a Brotherhood, even if it had been asked. The very indiscreet, excessive corporal penances which they are accustomed to practice on certain days of the year, even publicly, are quite contrary to the spirit of the Religion and the regulations of the Holy Church. Among the various things or unsuitabilities which it is possible to bring up, there is nothing which conforms to Christian humility. In order that such practices not be allowed to remain unmitigated, even the construction of a room intended for the custody of instruments of mortification or meetings of the Penitentes, if they should ask, may not be permitted by any Cura. If they sometimes mortify themselves with due moderation, they have a Temple (Church) in which they can congregate. Since it is necessary to close the door on abuses of this kind, which will sometime bring grief to the Holy Church, trusting the conscience of our parochial Curas in this Villa, both present and future, we strictly command that in the future they not permit such meetings of Penitentes for any reason. The Room in which they have kept their crosses, etc., if not the property of a definite individual, may remain in the service of the Holy Parish Church. The aforesaid instruments must be destroyed, although each one may take his own to his house, without its ever again being used by a congregation or Brothers of such a brotherhood of Penance, which we annul and which must remain extinct. All are ordered to strict obedience in this regulation of the Prelate, penance being one of the most acceptable sacrifices which can be made in the eyes

of God. And we furthermore decree with equal strictness that if the Cura of this parish comes to understand that in any other parish of this Territory there are such meetings of brotherhoods of Penitentes, in order to deter them, he should advise the appropriate Cura, mentioning this Decree, for we do not wish other similar abuse in any area of this Territory.

21. A transcription of the paragraph appears in Appendix II. A rough translation follows: At the conclusion of this article, in order to arrest another great ill which could become greater in the future, I prohibit these brotherhoods of penance, or rather, of carnage, which have grown in the shelter of an unlawful tolerance. Each priest or minister will take care that none of these brotherhoods remains in any district of his administration and that nowhere is a storehouse for those large crosses and other instruments of mortification with which some half murder their bodies, at the same time forgetting their souls, which they leave for whole years in sin. Moderate penance, which is beneficial to the spirit, is not prohibited; but totally illegal gatherings incorrectly called brotherhoods are. Each one who is of good faith and desires mortification, not destruction, must take up the usual instruments, but they must take them up in private.

22. Josiah Gregg, *Commerce of the Prairies,* ed. Max L. Moorhead (Norman: University of Oklahoma Press, 1954), p. 181. The first edition of the original two-volume work, which appeared in 1844, includes this passage in chapter 13 of volume I.

23. Patentes, Book 19 (Chavez, *AASF,* p. 155). The document is nearly illegible, but it is possible to distinguish the words "prohiba absolutamente tales reuniones de Hermandad."

24. Ryan, "Ecclesiastical Jurisdiction," pp. 10–11; Chavez, *AASF,* pp. 185, 186.

25. Dorothy Woodward, *The Penitentes of New Mexico* (1935; reprint ed., New York: Arno Press, 1974), pp. 1–16.

26. The full range of these often preposterous theories are reviewed and refuted in ibid., pp. 36–90; and Mary Martha Weigle, " 'Los Hermanos Penitentes': Historical and Ritual Aspects of Folk Religion in Northern New Mexico and Southern Colorado" (Ph.D. diss., University of Pennsylvania, 1971), pp. 39–47.

27. Ross Calvin, *Sky Determines: An Interpretation of the Southwest* (Albuquerque: University of New Mexico Press, 1965), p. 217.

28. Charles F. Lummis, *The Land of Poco Tiempo* (1893; reprint ed., Albuquerque: University of New Mexico Press, 1966), pp. 82–83; A. F. Bandelier, *Final Report of Investigations among the Indians of the Southwestern United States, Part I,* Papers of the Archaeological Institute of America, American Series, no. 3 (Cambridge: John Wilson, 1890), pp. 278–82, 284; Albert B. Reagan, "The Jemez Indians," *El Palacio* 4 (1917):60; idem, "The 'Penitentes,' " *Proceedings of the Indiana Academy of Science, 1904* (Indianapolis, 1905), p. 294.

29. George P. Hammond and Agapito Rey, "The Rodríguez Expedition to New Mexico, 1581–1582," *New Mexico Historical Review* 2 (1927):346. This translation of Gallegos's *Relación y concudió* has also been published separately as *The Gallegos Relation of the Rodríguez Expedition to New Mexico,* Historical Society of New Mexico, Publications in History, vol. 4 (Santa Fe: El Palacio Press, 1927). The "Disciplinant" reference appears on page 42.

30. Woodward, *Penitentes,* p. 70. In addition to the references she cites, see Ruth Benedict, *Patterns of Culture* (1934; reprint ed., Boston: Houghton Mifflin, 1959), pp. 90–91; and Elsie Clews Parsons, *Pueblo Indian Religion,* 2 vols. (Chicago: University of Chicago Press, 1939), 1:467–76, 2:1068–69, 1102–03. Note too George Foster's generalization that "in contact situations marked by disparity in power and cultural complexity, the donor group changes its ways in some degree, but the major changes are found in the ways of the recipient group" (*Culture and Conquest: America's Spanish Heritage,* Viking Fund Publications in Anthropology, no. 27 [Chicago: Quadrangle Books, 1960], p. 7).

31. John J. Bodine, "A Tri-Ethnic Trap: The Spanish Americans in Taos," in *Spanish-Speaking People in the United States: Proceedings of the 1968 Annual Spring Meeting of the*

American Ethnological Society, ed. June Helm (Seattle: University of Washington Press, 1968), p. 149. Also see, e.g., Edward H. Spicer's history of the Spanish programs to "civilize" the "barbarian" Indians, in *Cycles of Conquest: The Impact of Spain, Mexico, and the United States on the Indians of the Southwest, 1533–1960* (Tucson: University of Arizona Press, 1962), pp. 281–333.

32. William G. Ritch, Memo Book, HM RI 2212, vol. 4, p. 326; Elsie Clews Parsons, *Tewa Tales,* Memoirs of the American Folk-Lore Society, vol. 19 (New York: G. E. Stechert for the Society, 1926), p. 168 (also noted in her *Pueblo Indian Religion,* 1:159); Charles H. Lange, *Cochiti: A New Mexico Pueblo, Past and Present* (Carbondale: Southern Illinois University Press, Arcturus Books, 1968), p. 25; Swadesh, *Los Primeros Pobladores,* pp. 120, 225, n. 4.

33. Alice Marriott, *María: The Potter of San Ildefonso* (Norman: University of Oklahoma Press, 1948), pp. 39–51; Mary Austin, "Los Hermanos Penitentes," HM FII-29, Austin Collection, Huntington Library, San Marino, California, p. 4 (hereafter cited as "HM"); Mabel Dodge Luhan, *Edge of Taos Desert: An Escape to Reality, Intimate Memories,* vol. 4 (New York: Harcourt, Brace, 1937), p. 146; Dorothy Woodward, "Notes on Santa Clara Pueblo," Dorothy Woodward Penitente Papers, New Mexico State Records Center and Archives, Santa Fe, 1939, p. 5; Lange, *Cochiti,* p. 25.

34. Marriott, *María,* p. 43.

35. Ibid., p. 51.

36. Inigo Deane, S. J., "The New Flagellants. A Phase of New-Mexican Life," *Catholic World* 39 (1884):303. For a review of other writers with a similar idea, see Woodward, *Penitentes,* pp. 100–102.

37. See, e.g., Rev. Wm. M. Cooper, *Flagellation and the Flagellants: A History of the Rod* (London: William Reeve, n.d.), pp. 102–21; George Ryley Scott, *The History of Corporal Punishment: A Survey of Flagellation in its Historical Anthropological and Sociological Aspects* (London: T. Werner, 1938), pp. 135–44; Johannes Nohl, *The Black Death: A Chronicle of the Plague* (London: Unwin Books, 1961), pp. 134–38.

38. Nohl traces the progress of the Brotherhood of the Flagellants (or the Cross) as follows: "The first town in which the flagellants appeared in Germany, in Lent 1349, was Dresden. Then came Lübeck, Hamburg, Magdeburg, Parchim, Erfurt, Halberstadt, Bremen, Speyer, Würzburg, Strasbourg, Basle, Berne, Metz, Coblence, Aix-la-Chapelle, Cologne, Frankfort-on-Main, Mayence, etc. Other towns which they visited were Lille, Doornik, Troyes, Reims, Bruges, London, Valenciennes, Deventer; also Denmark, Sweden, and Poland" (ibid., pp. 138–39).

39. James Hastings, ed., *Encyclopedia of Religion and Ethics,* 13 vols. (New York: Charles Scribner's Sons, 1951), 6:50.

40. Julio Puyol, "Plática de disciplinantes," in *Estudios eruditos "in memoriam" de Adolfo Bonilla y San Martín* (Madrid: Imprenta Viuda e Hijos de Jaime Ratés, 1927), pp. 244–45; Donald Attwater, *The Penguin Dictionary of Saints* (Baltimore, Maryland: Penguin Books, 1965), p. 336.

41. For a partial list of writers using this metaphor, see Woodward, *Penitentes,* p. 91, n. 127.

42. Sister Joseph Marie McCrossan, I.H.M., *The Role of the Church and the Folk in the Development of Early Drama in New Mexico* (Philadelphia: Dolphin Press, 1948), p. 46.

43. Ibid., p. 39.

44. Ibid., p. 89. Chavez maintains that the Brothers appropriated, preserved, and made more realistic the crucifixion scene of the "old folk Passion Play" ("Penitentes," p. 121). His suggestion that the death cart was also borrowed from such medieval mystery plays will be discussed later.

45. Olibama López, "The Spanish Heritage in the San Luis Valley" (M.A. thesis, University of Denver, 1942), pp. 39–40.

46. For descriptions of the Talpa version, see, e.g., Mary Austin, *The Land of Journeys' Ending* (New York: Century, 1924), pp. 364–69; and Blanche C. Grant, *When Old Trails Were New: The Story of Taos* (New York: Press of the Pioneers, 1934), pp. 243–45. On Tome, see Florence Hawley Ellis, "Passion Play in New Mexico," *New Mexico Quarterly* 22 (1952):200–212. Evelyn Frisbie mentions a community passion play at Cubero, New Mexico, in "Superseding Superstition with Hygiene: In Remote New Mexican Village," *The Congregationalist and Herald of Gospel Liberty* 117 (1932):142.

47. Mary R. Van Stone and E. R. Sims, eds., "Canto del Niño Perdido," in *Spur-of-the-Cock*, ed. J. Frank Dobie, Publications of the Texas Folklore Society, no. 11 (Austin, 1933), pp. 48–49.

48. See objections by Father Zephyrin Engelhardt, O.F.M., "Father Zephyrin and the Penitentes," *El Palacio* 8 (1920):73–74; Woodward, *Penitentes,* pp. 90–97; and Chavez, "Penitentes," p. 121.

49. Woodward, *Penitentes,* pp. 140–46; Chavez, "Penitentes," p. 114.

50. Evelyn Underhill, *The Mystics of the Church* (1925; reprint ed., New York: Schocken Books, 1964), p. 168.

51. Basing much of his discussion on Antonio Rumeu de Armas's *Historia de la previsión social en España: Cofradías-gremios-hermandades-montepíos* (Madrid, 1944), George M. Foster briefly traces these groups' evolution in " 'Cofradía' and 'Compadrazgo' in Spain and Spanish America," *Southwestern Journal of Anthropology* 9 (1953):10–17.

52. Puyol, "Plática de disciplinantes," pp. 245–46, 259. Reference to the 1777 law is also in Woodward, *Penitentes,* p. 165.

53. See, e.g., Puyol, "Plática de disciplinantes," pp. 245ff; Woodward, *Penitentes,* pp. 154–72; George M. Foster, *Culture and Conquest,* pp. 181–85; Gabriel Llompart, C.R., "Desfile iconográfico de penitentes españoles (siglos XVI al XX)," *Revista de dialectología y tradiciones populares* 25 (1969):31–51.

54. Woodward, *Penitentes,* pp. 155–59; Chavez, "Penitentes," pp. 117–19. See also note 122 below.

55. Chavez, ibid., pp. 118–19.

56. Aurelio M. Espinosa, Review of *Brothers of Light,* by Alice Corbin Henderson, *Journal of American Folk-Lore* 51 (1938):448.

57. "Las siete cadaveras, q^e se hallaron exumadas, en la piesa adjunta immediatamente se sepultaran sin permitir q^e ruede otra alguna, en la Iglesia, ó Exercicios, pues para esto se observara, e imitara la practica rectam.^to establecida, en las Escuelas de Christo, de que sea de madera; entendiendose con sumo apresio, que toda exhumacion, parcial, ó total de los cadaveras, no puede haserse sin expressa lissencia de los Illmos. Señores Ordinarios" (Accounts, Book 62 [Chavez, *AASF,* p. 189]). For a translation and discussion of this command, see E. Boyd, *Popular Arts of Spanish New Mexico,* pp. 445–47.

58. Haring, *The Spanish Empire in America,* p. 181. See also historical discussions in Woodward, *Penitentes,* pp. 174–88; and Foster, " 'Cofradía' and 'Compadrazgo,' " pp. 17–19.

59. Chavez, "Penitentes," p. 115, n. 46. The persistence of public flagellation is documented in various sources, including Frances Toor, "Editor's Note on Penitents," *Mexican Folk-Ways* 6 (1930):100–102; Gertrude P. Kurath, "Penitentes," in *Funk & Wagnalls Standard Dictionary of Folklore, Mythology, and Legend,* ed. Maria Leach and Jerome Fried (New York: Funk & Wagnalls, 1972), pp. 851–52; and Robert S. Fetrow, "The Penitentes of Santo Tomas" [Colombia], *Explorers Journal* 51 (1973):164–66. The similarity between New Mexico Penitentes and penitents in the Philippines has been noted by Carl N. Taylor,

Odyssey of the Islands (New York: Charles Scribner's Sons, 1936), pp. 246–52; and Lorraine Carr, *To the Philippines with Love* (Los Angeles: Sherbourne Press, 1966), pp. 217–20.

60. George P. Hammond, *Don Juan de Oñate and the Founding of New Mexico,* Historical Society of New Mexico, Publications in History, vol. 2 (Santa Fe: El Palacio Press, 1927), p. 93. Gaspar Pérez de Villagrá, *History of New Mexico (Historia de la Nueva México),* trans. Gilberto Espinosa (1933; reprint ed., Chicago: Rio Grande Press, 1962), pp. 110–111.

61. Woodward, *Penitentes,* p. 195.

62. Mrs. Edward E. Ayer, trans., *The Memorial of Fray Alonso de Benavides 1630* (1916; reprint ed., Albuquerque: Horn and Wallace, 1965), pp. 21, 211, n. 10; Peter P. Forrestal, C.S.C., trans., *Benavides' Memorial of 1630,* Publications of the Academy of American Franciscan History, Documentary Series, vol. 2 (Washington, D.C.: Academy of American Franciscan History, 1954), pp. 20–21; Frederick Webb Hodge, George P. Hammond, and Agapito Rey, eds., *Fray Alonso de Benavides' Revised Memorial of 1634: With Numerous Supplementary Documents Elaborately Annotated,* Coronado Cuarto Centennial Publications, 1540–1940, vol. 4 (Albuquerque: University of New Mexico Press, 1945), p. 66.

63. Ibid., pp. 44, 100.

64. Descriptions of the *cofradías* and the page references to Adams and Chavez's translation of *Missions of New Mexico* are in Weigle, "Los Hermanos Penitentes," pp. 96–100. See also Fray Angelico Chavez, *Our Lady of the Conquest* (Santa Fe: Historical Society of New Mexico, 1948); and Eleanor B. Adams, "The Chapel and Cofradía of Our Lady of Light in Santa Fe," *New Mexico Historical Review* 22 (1947):327–41.

65. Archivo General de la Nación, Mexico, D.F. (AGN), Ramo de Historia, vol. 313, f. 348–50. Fray Buenaventura Merino's October 14, 1794 report on Santa Fe confraternities was incorporated into this document (Loose Documents, 1794, No. 15 [Chavez, *AASF,* p. 52]).

66. Microfilm Edition of the Spanish Archives of New Mexico, Roll 16, Frame 122 (hereafter cited as *SANM*). Ralph Emerson Twitchell cites this as document no. 1982 in *Spanish Archives of New Mexico,* 2 vols. (Cedar Rapids, Iowa: Torch Press, 1914), 2:497.

67. Woodward, *Penitentes,* pp. 247–48.

68. Chavez, "Penitentes," p. 117.

69. Ibid., pp. 119–20.

70. Ibid., p. 115, n. 46.

71. The history of El Santuario has been traced by Stephen F. de Borhegyi in "The Cult of Our Lord of Esquípulas in Middle America and New Mexico," *El Palacio* 61 (1954):387–401; and "The Miraculous Shrines of Our Lord of Esquípulas in Guatemala and Chimayo, New Mexico," in *El Santuario de Chimayo* (Santa Fe: Spanish Colonial Arts Society, Inc., 1956), pp. 2–28.

72. Chavez, *AASF,* p. 187.

73. Carroll and Haggard, eds., *Three New Mexico Chronicles,* pp. 52–53. The original reads: "Como la religion de S. Francisco ha sido la conquistadora, digámoslos así, y ha sido ella sola en lo espiritual, están los habitantes tan acostumbrados á ver este hábito, que cualquiera otro no seria quizá bien admito. En este concepto, convendrian fuesen los 12 religiosos de la misma órden, y aun el primer obispo. . . ." (Escudero, *Noticias,* p. 32).

74. Carroll and Haggard, *Three New Mexico Chronicles,* pp. 53–54. The original reads: ". . . y las mas de estas feligresias, solo son visitadas algunos dias del año; ¿cuánto no se resentirán los pobres que sufren este abandono, al ver que de sus cosechas y ganados tienen que costear la mantencion de un sacerdote que no vive con ellos, y que ni siquiera les auxilia con los consuelos de la religion en aquella hora postrera, en que mas le necesitan?" (Escudero, *Noticias,* p. 33).

75. Nesta de Robeck, *Among the Franciscan Tertiaries* (London: J. M. Dent & Sons, 1930),

p. 5. S. Hartdegen gives the probable place of origin as Faenze or Florence (*New Catholic Encyclopedia*, 15 vols. [New York: McGraw Hill, 1967], 14:94).

76. A. G. Little, "The Mendicant Orders," in *Cambridge Medieval History*, ed. J. R. Tanner, C. W. Previté-Orton, and Z. N. Brooke, 9 vols. (New York: Macmillan, 1911–36), 6:755.

77. Ibid. See also de Robeck, *Among the Franciscan Tertiaries*, pp. 259–67; and Woodward, *Penitentes*, pp. 112–13.

78. Little, "The Mendicant Orders," p. 766.

79. Edgar L. Hewett and Reginald G. Fisher, *Mission Monuments of New Mexico* (Albuquerque: University of New Mexico Press, 1943), pp. 47–48.

80. Chavez, *AASF*, p. 18.

81. Fray Angelico Chavez, *Origins of New Mexico Families: In the Spanish Colonial Period* (1954; reprint ed., Albuquerque: University of Albuquerque with Calvin Horn, 1973), p. 206.

82. Ibid., p. 308.

83. Chavez, *AASF*, p. 36.

84. Chavez, *Origins of New Mexico Families*, p. 286.

85. Adams and Chavez, eds., *Missions of New Mexico*, pp. 18, 19.

86. Ibid., p. 148.

87. Ibid., pp. 75–76.

88. Chavez, *AASF*, p. 42.

89. See Appendix III.

90. Most Rev. J. B. Salpointe, D.D., *Soldiers of the Cross: Notes on the Ecclesiastical History of New Mexico, Arizona and Colorado* (Banning, California: St. Boniface's Industrial School, 1898), p. 294.

91. Loose Documents, 1778, No. 3 (Chavez, *AASF*, p. 40).

92. Loose Documents, 1801, No. 11 (Chavez, *AASF*, p. 60).

93. See Appendix IV.

94. Woodward, *Penitentes*, pp. 106–119; Chavez, "Penitentes," p. 100.

95. See, e.g., F. Lombard, "Confraternities and Archconfraternities," *New Catholic Encyclopedia*, 4:154.

96. Chavez, "Penitentes," p. 100, n.4.

97. See, e.g., *Revista Católica* (Las Vegas, New Mexico), April 7, 1877, p. 160; Viator, "How a Pious and Useful Body Degenerated into a Sect—A Secret Society," *Albuquerque Review*, April 6, 1878; Deane, "New Flagellants," p. 304; Rev. James H. Defouri, *The Martyrs of New Mexico: A Brief Account of the Lives and Deaths of the Earliest Missionaries in the Territory* (Las Vegas, New Mexico: Revista Católica Printing Office, 1893), p. 13, n. 9; Salpointe, *Soldiers of the Cross*, pp. 161–62; Fr. Zephyrin Engelhardt, O.F.M., "Franciscans in New Mexico," *Franciscan Herald* 8 (1920):177; Padre E. Barrat to Mary Austin, March 7, 1920, HM FII-29; Rev. A. Brunner, S.J., quoted in Honora DeBusk Smith, "Mexican Plazas along the River of Souls," *Southwestern Lore*, ed. J. Frank Dobie, Publications of the Texas Folk-Lore Society, no. 9 (Dallas: Southwest Press, 1931), p. 80.

98. HM RI-1866, p. 3.

99. Memo Book, HM RI 2212, vol. 4, p. 325.

100. Adams and Chavez, eds., *Missions of New Mexico*, pp. 29, 80, 150.

101. Ibid., p. 124.

102. Richard E. Ahlborn, *The Penitente Moradas of Abiquiú*, p. 126.

103. Adams and Chavez, eds., *Missions of New Mexico*, p. 75.

104. An important document reads: "En el centro de la misma Iglesia, esta construida una capillita que sirve de tercer orden, cuya pequeña fabrica está aunque inmediata

independiente de dicha Iglesia, pues para su comunicacion, se dividio para del cimenterio principal, según se advierte, con lo que quedá esclusivo" (Don Ignacio Sánches Vergara, "Plan demostrativo de la Iglesia Mayor de la Capital de Santa Fe," *SANM,* Roll 21, Frame 686). E. Boyd has translated the entire manuscript in *Popular Arts,* pp. 452–54. This report destroys the long-held notion that the south parroquia chapel of San José was continuously used by the Third Order until its concession was revoked by Don Agustín Fernández San Vicente in 1826 (Salpointe, *Soldiers of the Cross,* p. 161). No record of this revocation seems presently to exist.

105. Books of Burials, Bur-50 (Chavez, *AASF,* pp. 237–38).

106. E. Boyd, *Popular Arts,* p. 446. See note 57, above.

107. The original reads: "Ni á la Tersera Orden, ni nada delo que pertenese, se reconocio en manera alguna" (Accounts, Book 62 [Chavez, *AASF,* p. 189]). E. Boyd's discussion and translation of this appears in ibid., pp. 447, 449.

108. See Appendix V.

109. In 1827, e.g., Santa Fe had only 5700 inhabitants, compared with 6500 at Santa Cruz, 3600 at Taos, and 3600 at the rebellious Abiquiu (Ahlborn, *Penitente Moradas,* pp. 128–29; see also Swadesh, *Los Primeros Pobladores,* p. 232, n. 2). Difficulties in Taos are discussed below. A good history of the stalwart, isolated village of Las Trampas and its eighteenth century church is in Bainbridge Bunting, "An Architectural Guide to Northern New Mexico," pp. 37–46.

110. Juan B. Rael, "New Mexican Spanish Feasts," *California Folklore Quarterly* 1 (1942):84.

111. Ibid., pp. 84–87; Cleofas M. Jaramillo, *Shadows of the Past (Sombras del Pasado)* (Santa Fe, New Mexico: Seton Village Press, 1941), pp. 72–73. See also Reyes N. Martinez, "Velorios," May 13, 1936, ms., W.P.A. Files, Santa Fe, pp. 6–8.

112. E. K. Francis, "Padre Martínez: A New Mexican Myth," *New Mexico Historical Review* 31 (1956):267; Chavez, *Origins of New Mexico Families,* p. 317; Ahlborn, *Penitente Moradas,* p. 128.

113. Early, exaggerated accounts of Martínez's involvement with the Penitentes are in Willa Cather's novel, *Death Comes for the Archbishop* (New York: Alfred A. Knopf, 1927), Book 5; and Harvey Fergusson, *Rio Grande* (1933; reprint ed., New York: William Morrow, 1967), pp. 211–39.

114. HM RI-1866, p. 4; Memo Book, HM RI 2212, vol. 4, p. 325.

115. Ibid.

116. E. Boyd, "The First New Mexico Imprint," *Princeton University Library Chronicle* 33 (1971):35–37.

117. Cecil V. Romero, trans., "Apologia of Presbyter Antonio J. Martinez," *New Mexico Historical Review* 3 (1928):339.

118. Loose Documents, 1856, No. 30 (Chavez, *AASF,* p. 123). A transcription of this section reads: "Pongo en conocimiento de V.S.I. que por el penultimo Custodio de N.M. que hubo en ejercicio, y con la aprobacion del Señor Obispo Zubiria en su tiempo, tengo una subdelegacion para recibir á fieles de ambas sexas aqui en Taos en noviciado y darles la protesion en la EnCorporacion de Terceros de S. Francisco de Asis en el orden de penitencia, y aplicar las Misas Cantadas que alcancen de su costa contribucion en la Iglesia de San Francisco del Rancho, los Domingos cuartos de cada Mes. Como esta fue una subdelegacion personal, y no como Cura de Taos, no la entregué el Señor Cura Taladrid . . ."

119. Lorenzo de Córdova, *Echoes of the Flute* (Santa Fe, New Mexico: Ancient City Press, 1972), p. 17. Interestingly, the author's grandfather, a former student in Martínez's school, "took another tack; he became an active, aggressive foe of the *Cofradia.* He organized a *Sociedad* for this purpose. In one of their encounters with members of the Order, he received

a severe scalp wound which nearly cost him his life. Subsequently, he wore his red hair pompadour style to cover the scar" (ibid., p. 18).

120. "Obituario," *The Santa Fe New Mexican,* August 17, 1867, p. 4. According to Woodward, Sanchez's short *Memorias del Padre Antonio José Martínez* (Santa Fe, 1903), is "a bombastic eulogy" which was "written by a Penitente, once an officer" (*Penitentes,* p. 258, n. 21).

121. Chavez, *AASF,* p. 222.

122. Reginald Fisher, "Notes on the Relation of the Franciscans to the Penitentes," *El Palacio* 48 (1941):271. Recent, preliminary investigation of one iconographic source, the Man of Sorrows as depicted by New Mexican *santeros,* reveals that either theory of origin could be supported. "This complex pictorial theme, with its many artistic forms, is expressive of the popularized mysticism and realism of the late Middle Ages that found support in the devotions that were initiated by the Franciscans and that are based on the God-Man and the Passion. . . . Also of significant importance is the fact that the title of the Seville *Cofradía* includes the term *Santa Cruz en Jerusalem.* It should be pointed out, however, that the *Santa Croce in Gerusalemme* is at Rome and not in the Holy Land. . . . In it are venerated a particle of the Cross and other relics of the Passion. In the same church is also to be found an icon that is the source of the western tradition of the Man of Sorrows" (Yvonne Lange, "The Santos of New Mexico: The Man of Sorrows and the Origins of the Penitente Brotherhood," *Europe in Colonial America: Summaries of the Lectures and Suggested Readings,* Williamsburg Antiques Forum, Williamsburg, Virginia, January 27–February 1 and February 3–8, 1974, p. 24).

123. de Borhegyi, "Miraculous Shrines," p. 13. Swadesh suggests this in *Los Primeros Pobladores,* p. 217, n. 20. See also Fray Angelico Chavez, *My Penitente Land: Reflections on Spanish New Mexico* (Albuquerque: University of New Mexico Press, 1974), p. 218.

124. de Borhegyi, "Miraculous Shrines," p. 11; Boyd, *Popular Arts,* p. 361.

125. de Borhegyi, "Miraculous Shrines," p. 17.

126. Chavez, *AASF,* p. 120.

127. Reprinted in Rev. Alex[ander] M. Darley, *The Passionists of the Southwest, or the Holy Brotherhood: A Revelation of the Penitentes* (1893; reprint ed., Glorieta, New Mexico: Rio Grande Press, 1968), p. 18; and Woodward, *Penitentes,* p. 315. Swadesh has also suggested this connection in *Los Primeros Pobladores,* p. 217, n. 29.

128. Boyd, *Popular Arts,* p. 450. This is part of her thesis about the direct relationship between "The Third Order of St. Francis and the Penitentes of New Mexico," pp. 440–51. Boyd proposes that "after the two cults of Our Lady of Light, and Our Lady of Carmel were introduced in 1760, the prominent and well-to-do class transferred its interests and benefactions to these, leaving the Third Order composed mostly of the poorer people" (p. 442). However, many *ricos* asked to be buried in a Third Order habit at least until 1814 (Myra Ellen Jenkins, personal communication). (Note that the 1760 date above is for the *re*-erection of the Confraternity of Carmel, which "had its beginning and founding in the year 1710, with license for it given by the Reverend Principal of the Carmelites, Fray Miguel de Santa Teresa, by his patent of April 3, 1710" [Adams and Chavez, eds., *Missions of New Mexico,* p. 249].)

Chapter 2: Ecclesiastical Aspects of the Territorial Period

1. *The Old Faith and Old Glory: Story of the Church in New Mexico since the American Occupation* (Santa Fe: Santa Fe Press, 1946), pp. 9–10. See also the "official" history by Salpointe, *Soldiers of the Cross.*

2. *The Santa Fe Cathedral of St. Francis of Assisi* (Santa Fe: Schifani Brothers, n.d.),

section IV, part 1, on Lamy (no pagination). See also George Kubler, *The Religious Architecture of New Mexico: In the Colonial Period and Since the American Occupation* (1940; reprint ed., published for the School of American Research by the University of New Mexico Press, Albuquerque, 1972), p. 141.

3. *Lamy Memorial: Centenary of the Archdiocese of Santa Fe, 1850–1950* (Santa Fe: Schifani Brothers, 1950). For a fictionalized account of Lamy's life in New Mexico, see Willa Cather, *Death Comes for the Archbishop.* See also Paul Horgan's recent biography, *Lamy of Santa Fe: His Life and Times* (New York: Farrar, Straus & Giroux, 1975).

4. Chavez, *AASF,* p. 170. See the conclusion and notes 126 and 127, chap. 1, above. Darley, *Passionists,* pp. 14–18; Woodward, *Penitentes,* pp. 312–15.

5. These rules were copied by local priests for moradas under their jurisdiction. Thus, there are copies by Don José Valezy, *cura del Rito* (Loose Documents, 1856, No. 11 [Chavez, *AASF,* p. 122]); by Don José Eulogio Ortiz of Taos in June or July, 1858 (Loose Documents, 1858, No. 1 [Chavez, *AASF,* p. 125]); and by Don Pedro Bernal of Abiquiu on April 6, 1867 (Loose Documents, 1856, No. 12 [Chavez, *AASF,* p. 122]). Transcriptions are included in Woodward, *Penitentes,* pp. 319–21; and Weigle, "Los Hermanos Penitentes," pp. 468–72. See Appendix VI for a translation.

6. Loose Documents, 1856, No. 32 (Chavez, *AASF,* p. 123). A transcription reads: "En breve irán á esa los dos Hermanos mayores de la hermandad con las reglas que yo mismo he formado y que estarán concluidas. V.S. Ilm͠o. puede examinarlas, y si merecen su aprobacion se pondrán en practicar despues de organizada la hermandad donde no me avisará pᵃ reformarlas segun ordenes."

7. Loose Documents, 1856, No. 34 (Chavez, *AASF,* p. 123).

8. Loose Documents, 1858, No. 1 (Chavez, *AASF,* p. 125). For a transcription, see Weigle, "Los Hermanos Penitentes," pp. 467–68. Monsignor Mahoney's translation appears in Appendix VII.

9. Barron B. Beshoar, "Western Trails to Calvary," in *1949 Brand Book,* ed. Don Bloch (Denver, Colorado: The Westerners, Denver Posse, 1950), p. 123.

10. "Penitentes Re-Enact Christ's Suffering," *Pueblo Colorado Star-Journal,* March 24, 1967, p. 8-A, col. 3.

11. Charles Aranda, *The Penitente Papers* (Albuquerque, New Mexico: author, n.d.), p. 48.

12. Newspaper article partially reprinted in E. Boyd, *Popular Arts of Spanish New Mexico,* p. 455.

13. Sister M. Lilliana Owens, S.L., with Rev. Fr. Gregory Goñi, S.J., and Rev. Fr. J. M. Gonzalez, S.J., *Jesuit Beginnings in New Mexico, 1867–1882,* Jesuit Studies-Southwest, no. 1 (El Paso, Texas: Revista Católica Press, 1950), p. 46.

14. J. Manuel Espinosa, "The Neapolitan Jesuits on the Colorado Frontier, 1868–1919," *Colorado Magazine* 15 (1938):66.

15. *Old Faith and Old Glory,* pp. 11–13. The press was moved to El Paso, Texas, in 1918, before the Colorado-New Mexico Mission was divided and dissolved in 1919.

16. J. M. Espinosa, "Neapolitan Jesuits," pp. 67–69.

17. E. R. Vollmar, S.J., "Religious Processions and Penitente Activities in Colorado, 1874," *Colorado Magazine* 31 (1954):177.

18. Ibid., pp. 178–79.

19. Sister Blandina Segale, S.C., *At the End of the Santa Fe Trail* (Milwaukee: Bruce Publishing, 1948), p. 42.

20. *Revista Católica,* vol. 3, no. 14 (April 7, 1877), p. 160. The original reads: "Los Penitentes han ciertamente desfigurado, adulterado y corrompido la idea y reglas fundamentales que recibieran de sus institutores, probablemente los piadosos hijos del grand Patriarca de Asís. En la intencion de estos la vida cristianamente irreprochable

formaria indubablemente la base de las Cofradías. Alguna lijera y discreta mortificacion corporal hecha durante los dias dedicados á conmemorar la pasión del Salvador, seria lo de menos, y solo un ejercicio devote para acompañar con corazon compungido al Hijo de Dios que sube al Calvario." This may be the basis for the assertion by Father Inigo Deane, S.J., that the penitential practice of flagellation originally instituted by the Franciscans for "putting them into intelligent sympathy with the Passion of Christ" came to be viewed not "as the supplementary and medial thing it is, but as the only coin current for discharging all debts of the world to come" ("The New Flagellants. A Phase of New-Mexican Life," *Catholic World* 39 [1884]:304).

21. *Revista Católica,* vol. 3, no. 14, ibid. The original reads: "No podemos dejar pasar sin una palabra de vituperacion el hecho horrible que acaba de llegar á nuestros oidos de la muerte atroz y violenta de uno de esos señores que tienen la osadía de llamarse los *Hermanos de Nuestro Padre* JESUS. La muerte acaeció de resultas de sus locas penitencias."

22. *Revista Católica,* vol. 3, no. 15 (April 14, 1877), p. 173.

23. See Appendix VIII.

24. Loose Documents, 1885, No. 20 (Chavez, *AASF,* p. 141). The original reads: "Ahora con respecte á las sociedades secretas, á todo verdadero fiel cristiano basta saber que la Iglesia la prohibe, para que él se aparte de ellas. Hemos procurado que sea distribuida entre vosotros la Encíclica que el Padre Santo publicó el año pasado sobre este asunto. Naturalmente es fuerte la tentacion que inclina hácia ciertas sociedades, que aseguran algunas ventajas materiales á sus adeptos y á las familias de ellos. No culpamos á nadie por buscar honestamente estas ventajas: mas diremos á nuestros feligreses que tambien en la Iglesia Católica hay sociedades bien conocidas y aprobadas, en las cuales puede hallarse el mismo beneficio material, sin correr riesgo de hacer nada que sea contra su religion. Ya están bien establecidas en varias parroquias de la diócesis y prosperarán mientras quedan sujetas á la autoridad ecclesiástica."

25. Sister Edward Mary Zerwekh, C.S.J., "John Baptist Salpointe, 1825–1894," *New Mexico Historical Review* 37 (1962):1–19, 132–54, 214–29.

26. Salpointe, *Soldiers of the Cross,* p. 163.

27. Ibid.

28. Loose Documents, 1891, No. 6 (Chavez, *AASF,* p. 144). A transcription is in Weigle, "Los Hermanos Penitentes," pp. 481–88. The original version is Loose Documents, [1886], No. 8 (Chavez, *AASF,* p. 142).

29. The original reads: "Las asosiaciones católicas están recomendaras por el Papa Pio IX de Santa Memoria y por el actual sumo Pontifice Leon XIII, han sido siempre protejidas la Jerarquia ecclesiastica como auxiliarios de Nuestra Santa religion, particularmente en nuestro tiempo para contraponer influjo deletero de las Sociedades secretas, irreligiosas inmorales."

30. Loose Documents, 1886, No. 1 (Chavez, *AASF,* p. 141).

31. See Appendix IX. An undated, printed copy of Pope Leo XIII's "Regla" is among the Miscellaneous Church Papers at the New Mexico State Records Center and Archives in Santa Fe. Papal and local attempts at rejuvenating the Third Order were reported in *Revista Católica,* vol. 12, no. 12 (March 21, 1886), p. 135; and vol. 12, no. 15 (April 11, 1886), pp. 174–76. The secular press reported, probably exaggeratedly, a much more vicious condemnation of the Brotherhood (*Santa Fé Daily New Mexican,* April 8, 1886, p. 1, col. 5).

32. *Revista Católica,* vol. 14, no. 29 (July 15, 1888), pp. 341–42. Notes and drafts from these meetings, in Latin, are preserved in Loose Documents, 1888, No. 1 (Chavez, *AASF,* p. 142). Points about the Brotherhood appear under the heading "De societatibus inhonestis."

33. Anonymous, "Los Hermanos Penitentes," *El Palacio* 8 (1920):5.

34. According to Chavez, sections on the Penitentes are incorporated in the *Synodus Sanctae Fidei Prima* (Las Vegas, New Mexico: Revista Católica Printing Office, 1893), Cap.

IX, Par. 1, No. 2, pp. 31–32 ("The Penitentes of New Mexico," pp. 100–101). Honora DeBusk Smith also mentions an 1888 circular in "Mexican Plazas along the River of Souls," in *Southwestern Lore,* p. 80.

35. Loose Documents, 1889, No. 2 (Chavez, *AASF,* p. 143). Also in *Revista Católica,* vol. 15, no. 15 (April 14, 1889), pp. 171–73.

36. *Revista Católica,* vol. 15, no. 17 (April 28, 1889), p. 196.

37. This is also mentioned in Aranda, *Penitente Papers,* p. 54.

38. See Appendix X.

39. See Appendix XI.

40. *La Voz del Pueblo,* Las Vegas, New Mexico, November 7, 1891, p. 1, col. 5.

41. See note 28, above.

42. See Appendix XII.

43. Aranda, *Penitente Papers,* pp. 54–55.

44. *Santa Fé Daily New Mexican,* March 11, 1892, p. 2, col. 2.

45. *Revista Católica,* vol 18, no. 10 (March 6, 1892), p. 113.

46. See note 5, above. Peyron's signature is in Loose Documents, 1870, No. 7 (Chavez, *AASF,* p. 135).

47. Charles F. Lummis, "The Southwestern Wonderland, II: An American Passion-Play," *Land of Sunshine* 4 (1896):257.

48. Florence Hawley Ellis, "Tomé and Father J.B.R.," *New Mexico Historical Review* 30 (1955):218, n. 40.

49. Wesley Robert Hurt, Jr., "Manzano: A Study of Community Disorganization" (M.A. thesis, University of New Mexico, 1941), p. 182.

50. F. Stanley, *The Mora, New Mexico Story* (Pep, Texas, 1963), pp. 8–9. Frank Waters also includes this legend in his novel, *People of the Valley* (Denver, Colorado: Sage Books, 1941).

51. S. Omar Barker, "Los Penitentes," *Overland Monthly and Out West Magazine* 82 (1924):179; Sister M. Matthias Wall, "Contributions to New Mexico Folk Lore" (M.A. thesis, New Mexico Normal [Highlands] University, 1932), pp. 53–58. Darley also mentions "a young priest of Trinidad Colorado [who] like Don Quixote of old, rushed his horse into a procession of them, exclaiming against their folly; but it cost him his parish and position" (*Passionists,* p. 35), so a legend may have been popular within Hispanic tradition in the area.

52. April 2, 1895, p. 2, col. 3; p. 3, col. 3. These are copyrighted by the *Dallas News.*

53. *Las Vegas Daily Optic,* April 6, 1895, p. 1, col. 3.

54. "Los Hermanos Penitentes," HM FII-29, n.d., p. 8.

55. "Los Hermanos Penitentes," *El Palacio* 8 (1920):2.

56. Letter to Dorothy Woodward, February 28, 1934, Dorothy Woodward Penitente Papers.

57. Austin, "Los Hermanos Penitentes," p. 7.

58. Barker, "Los Penitentes," p. 179.

59. James, *New Mexico: The Land of the Delight Makers* (Boston: Page, 1920), p. 298; Darley, *Passionists,* p. 30.

60. Swadesh, *Los Primeros Pobladores,* p. 224, n. 32.

61. Salpointe, *Soldiers of the Cross,* p. 281.

62. Ibid., Appendix VII, n.p.

63. Letter of July 27, 1907, "Contemporary Issues, No. 9-Penitentes," Prince Papers, New Mexico State Records Center and Archives, Santa Fe.

64. See Appendixes XIII and XIV.

65. *New Catholic Encyclopedia,* 12:1064.

66. Porter A. Stratton, *The Territorial Press of New Mexico, 1834–1912* (Albuquerque: University of New Mexico Press, 1969), p. 136.

67. *Old Faith and Old Glory,* p. 13.

68. José E. Espinosa, *Saints in the Valleys: Christian Sacred Images in the History, Life and Folk Art of Spanish New Mexico* (Albuquerque: University of New Mexico Press, 1967), p. 33.

69. For a very brief early history of the Protestant denominations in New Mexico, see Cultural Properties Review Committee, *Preservation Program for New Mexico*, 1:41.

70. Rev. John L. Dyer, *The Snow-Shoe Itinerant* (Cincinnati, Ohio: Cranston and Stowe, 1890); Rev. Thomas Harwood, *History of New Mexico Spanish and English Missions of the Methodist Episcopal Church from 1850 to 1910*, 2 vols. (Albuquerque, New Mexico: El Abogado Press, 1908, 1910); Mrs. Harriet S. Kellogg, *Life of Mrs. Emily J. Harwood* (Albuquerque, New Mexico: El Abogado Press, 1903); Martin Rist, "Methodist Beginnings in New Mexico," in *The 1966 Brand Book*, ed. William D. Powell (Boulder, Colorado: Johnson Publishing, 1967), pp. 75–91; Martin Rist, "Penitentes of New Mexico in the 1870's according to Thomas and Emily Harwood," *Denver Westerners' Monthly Roundup*, January 1970, pp. 3–14.

71. W. G. Ritch, comp., *New Mexico Blue Book, 1882* (Albuquerque: University of New Mexico Press, 1968), n.p.

72. Edith J. Agnew and Ruth K. Barber, "The Unique Presbyterian School System of New Mexico," *Journal of Presbyterian History* 49 (1971):202.

73. Sherman H. Doyle, *Presbyterian Home Missions: An Account of the Presbyterian Church in the U.S.A.* (New York: Presbyterian Board of Home Missions, 1905), pp. 214–15.

74. Martin Rist, "Colorado's First Magazine: The Rocky Mountain Sunday School Caskett, 1864–68," *Denver Westerners' Monthly Roundup*, October 1969, pp. 4–7. See also Robert Laird Stewart, *Sheldon Jackson: Pathfinder and Prospector of the Missionary Vanguard in the Rocky Mountains and Alaska* (New York: Fleming H. Revell, 1908).

75. M. H. MacLeod, *Historical Sketch of the Presbytery of Pueblo and Proceedings of its Quarter Century Celebration* (Pueblo, Colorado: M. H. MacLeod, Publisher, 1906), p. 35.

76. Doyle, *Presbyterian Home Missions*, pp. 215–16.

77. Agnew and Barber, "The Unique Presbyterian School System."

78. Ibid., pp. 200–201; Gabino Rendón, as told to Edith Agnew, *Hand On My Shoulder* (New York: Board of National Missions, Presbyterian Church, 1953).

79. Townshend, *The Tenderfoot in New Mexico* (New York: Dodd, Mead, 1924), pp. 48–53.

80. R. B. Townshend, *Last Memories of a Tenderfoot* (London: John Lane The Brodley Head Ltd., 1926), pp. 101, 104.

81. For example, "The Cruelties of Heathenism in the United States," *Rocky Mountain Presbyterian*, vol. 5, no. 10 (1876), pp. 2–3; Rev. J. M. Roberts, "Home Mission Letter to Children," *Rocky Mountain Presbyterian*, vol. 7, no. 12 (1878), p. 4; Rev. Robert M. Craig, *Our Mexicans* (New York: Board of Home Missions of the Presbyterian Church in the United States, 1904); Robert McLean and Grace Petrie Williams, *Old Spain in New America* (New York: Associated Press, 1916).

82. *Revista Católica*, vol. 3, no. 30 (July 28, 1877), p. 353.

83. Lummis, *The Land of Poco Tiempo*, p. 95.

84. Lummis, "The Southwestern Wonderland, II," p. 265.

85. *Revista Católica*, vol. 3, no. 30 (July 28, 1877), p. 354.

86. *Revista Católica*, vol. 2, no. 46 (November 11, 1876), pp. 545–46.

87. Doyle, *Presbyterian Home Missions*, p. 212. Jose D. Mondragon of Taos County served in the House for the Nineteenth Legislative Assembly in 1869 (Ritch, *Blue Book*, p. 114).

88. McLean and Williams, *Old Spain in New America*, p. 43; MacLeod, *Presbytery of Pueblo*.

89. Darley, *Passionists*, p. 18.

90. MacLeod, *Presbytery of Pueblo*.

91. *Revista Católica*, vol. 3, no. 45 (November 10, 1877), pp. 529–30.

92. Rendón, *Hand On My Shoulder*, p. 75.

93. Ibid., pp. 84–85.

94. MacLeod, *Presbytery of Pueblo.*
95. Stewart, *Sheldon Jackson,* pp. 155ff, 241ff.
96. Laurence F. Lee, "Los Hermanos Penitentes" (B.A. thesis, University of New Mexico, 1910), p. 20.
97. *La Revista Católica,* vol. 16 (1890), issues of: April 20, p. 183; May 25, pp. 247–49; June 1, pp. 257, 260–61; June 29, pp. 304, 305.
98. Darley, *Passionists,* p. 35.
99. Ibid., p. 44.
100. Patricio M. Montano. "Observations on the Penitentes," in "Papers on Spanish Institutions and Customs in New Mexico," ed. Lynn I. Perrigo (Las Vegas, New Mexico: Highlands University, Donnelly Library, 1968), p. 30.

Chapter 3: Secular Aspects of the Territorial Period

1. Cultural Properties Review Committee, *The Historic Preservation Program for New Mexico,* 1:31. The text of Kearny's August 19 proclamation is in Ralph Emerson Twitchell, *Old Santa Fe: The Story of New Mexico's Ancient Capital* (1925; reprint ed., Chicago: Rio Grande Press, 1963), pp. 264–65. The so-called Kearny Code is discussed in Robert W. Larson, *New Mexico's Quest for Statehood, 1846–1912* (Albuquerque: University of New Mexico Press, 1968), pp. 4–5.
2. The Treaty of Guadalupe Hidalgo was signed on February 2, 1848, and ratified by the U.S. Senate on March 10, and by the Mexican Congress on May 26. For a complete text, see Hunter Miller, ed., *Treaties and Other International Acts of the United States of America* (Washington, D.C.: Government Printing Office, 1937), vol. 5. Also see Richard N. Ellis, ed., *New Mexico Historic Documents* (Albuquerque: University of New Mexico Press, 1975), pp. 10–31.
3. For a text of the Organic Act of the Territory of New Mexico, see W. G. Ritch, comp., *New Mexico Blue Book, 1882,* pp. 25–46. Also see Ellis, *New Mexico Historic Documents,* pp. 32–38.
4. Larson, *New Mexico's Quest for Statehood,* p. 65.
5. George I. Sánchez, *Forgotten People: A Study of New Mexicans* (Albuquerque: University of New Mexico Press, 1940), p. 25.
6. David F. Myrick, *New Mexico's Railroads: An Historical Survey* (Golden, Colorado: Colorado Railroad Museum, 1970), p. 11.
7. González, *The Spanish-Americans of New Mexico,* pp. 119–20.
8. Larson, *New Mexico's Quest for Statehood,* pp. 303–304.
9. *Revista Católica,* vol. 3, no. 30 (July 28, 1877), p. 354. The original reads: "Ahora especialmente que los ferro-carriles llegan hasta las fronteras de Nuevo Méjico, seria de gran desdoro á la religion que profesan, si se les viera desnudos y sangrientos por llanos y por montes. Hombres, que no buscan sino pretextos para conmover contra la Iglesia católica la opinion pública, vienen acá á fin de observer y referir despues á los periódicos de los Estados esas locuras; atribuyendo á todo la población católica de este país, lo que no es sino el efecto de extravió de unos pocos mejicanos que hacen consistir en estas prácticas toda su religion."
10. Lummis, "The Southwestern Wonderland, II."
11. Lummis cites a very dubious example of this sort of rumor, claiming a young politician in need of votes for a county race met with the San Mateo Brotherhood on October 17, 1888, and had himself initiated with three gashes on his back, thus securing the required count (*The Land of Poco Tiempo,* p. 106).
12. Memo Book, HM RI 2212, vol. 4, p. 325. Theodore D. Wheaton, from Taos County, served as Speaker of the House in 1851, 1852, and 1853, and as a member in 1860 (Ritch,

New Mexico Blue Book, 1882, pp. 101–102, 107). LaFayette Head, also from Taos, was elected to the Council of 1857, and served as president of the 1858 Council (ibid., p. 105). Swadesh discusses Head's career and possible Brotherhood ties in *Los Primeros Pobladores,* pp. 78–79.

13. Fergusson, *Rio Grande,* p. 220. Warren Beck also makes this claim, comparing the Brotherhood "with the Ku Klux Klan in the South in the post-Civil War period" (*New Mexico: A History of Four Centuries* [Norman: University of Oklahoma Press, 1962], p. 222).

14. Darley, *Passionists,* p. 42.

15. Ibid.

16. Salpointe, *Soldiers of the Cross,* p. 162.

17. "Mexican Grandee with a Harem," *Denver Post,* August 9, 1901, p. 6.

18. "Base Libel on Worthy Mexican," *Denver Times,* August 11, 1901, p. 13. There is presently no record of Montez having been an Hermano Mayor (M. Santos Melendez, personal communication).

19. "Another Cruel Fake in the Denver Post," *Denver Times,* August 14, 1901, p. 5.

20. Simmons, *Spanish Government in New Mexico,* p. 176.

21. Woodward, *Penitentes,* pp. 266–67, 280. Other descriptions appear in Inigo Deane, S.J., "The New Flagellants. A Phase of New-Mexican Life," pp. 305–306; R. B. Townshend, *The Tenderfoot in New Mexico,* pp. 49–52; Mary Austin, "Hymns of the Penitentes," HM EII-5, n.d., p. 4; Mary Austin, "Business at Cuesta La Plata," in *One-Smoke Stories* (Cambridge, Massachusetts: Riverside Press, 1934), pp. 200–210.

22. Viator, "How a Pious and Useful Body Degenerated into a Sect—A Secret Society," *Albuquerque Review,* April 6, 1878, p. 1.

23. Birge Harrison, *Española and Its Environs, 1885: An Artist's Impressions* (Espanola, New Mexico: Rio Grande Sun, 1966), pp. 18–19.

24. S. Omar Barker, "Los Penitentes," 179.

25. Woodward, *Penitentes,* p. 285.

26. Jack E. Holmes, *Politics in New Mexico* (Albuquerque: University of New Mexico Press, 1967), p. 41.

27. Ritch, HM RI 2212, Memo Book, vol. 4, p. 326a.

28. Barton, *The Penitentes of New Mexico* (Boston: Congregational Education Society, n.d.), p. 8.

29. Lummis, *Land of Poco Tiempo,* p. 108; Fray Angelico Chavez, *My Penitente Land,* pp. ix–xi, and elsewhere throughout. For a discussion of this widespread and persistent item of folklore, see Weigle, "Los Hermanos Penitentes," pp. 283–85. See also Chavez, "The Penitentes," p. 106.

30. Ritch, HM RI 2212, Memo Book, vol. 4, p. 326b.

31. Swadesh places the incident at San Pedro (*Los Primeros Pobladores,* p. 76). Darley, however, alleges that a similar action took place at Costilla in 1866 (*Passionists,* pp. 27–28). Barton does not specify either informant or location (*Penitentes of New Mexico,* p. 5). The story was likely current in the lore of the Valley and later inspired an incident in Louis How's sensational novel, *The Penitentes of San Rafael: A Tale of the San Luis Valley* (Indianapolis, Indiana: Bowen-Merrill, 1900).

32. Bourke, "Notes on the Language and Folk-Usage of the Rio Grande Valley (With especial regard to Survivals of Arabic Custom)," *Journal of American Folk-Lore* 9(1896):110.

33. See, e.g., discussions in Jim Berry Pearson, *The Maxwell Land Grant* (Norman: University of Oklahoma Press, 1961), pp. 67–71; Howard Roberts Lamar, *The Far Southwest, 1846–1912: A Territorial History* (New Haven: Yale University Press, 1966), p. 153; Larson, *New Mexico's Quest for Statehood,* p. 138; Stratton, *The Territorial Press,* pp. 177–78; Victor Westphall, *Thomas Benton Catron and His Era* (Tucson: University of Arizona Press, 1973), pp. 118–20.

34. Harwood, *History of New Mexico Spanish and English Missions,* 1:268–69.

35. Lamar, *Far Southwest,* p. 154. The *Santa Fe Weekly New Mexican* tried unsuccessfully to block Springer's election to a Council seat in the 1880 Territorial Legislative Assembly by publicizing the contents of his 1877 affidavit on October 5 and 19, and November 2, 1878. For excerpts from these articles, see Weigle, "Los Hermanos Penitentes," Appendix 15, pp. 498–500.

36. Ritch, HM RI 2212, Memo Book, vol. 4, p. 326b.

37. Swadesh claims that "Haines' statement is illuminated by the assertion of numerous informants that from the 1880's to the 1930's, it was customary in northern New Mexico to exclude a Hispano venirement from district court juries if a Hispano was to be tried on criminal charges, on the mere allegation that both were Penitentes" (*Los Primeros Pobladores,* p. 91).

38. *The Santa Fé New Mexican Review* of April 24, 1884, claims "the members of the Order of 'Penitentes' met them and gave them succor." Jack D. Rittenhouse gives a full account of this incident in *Cabezón: A New Mexio Ghost Town* (Santa Fe, New Mexico: Stagecoach Press, 1965), pp. 45–50.

39. *Santa Fe New Mexican,* December 17, 1898, p. 1. See also George B. Anderson, *History of New Mexico: Its Resources and People,* 2 vols. (Los Angeles: Pacific States Publishing, 1907), 2:597.

40. Robert Johnson Rosenbaum, *"Mexicano versus Americano:* A Study of Hispanic-American Resistance to Anglo-American Control in New Mexico Territory, 1870–1900" (Ph.D. diss., University of Texas at Austin, December 1972), p. 226. See also his Appendix E, "Some Las Vegas *Politicos,"* showing Lopez's assessed property valued at $1600 in 1890, while that of his wife totals $28,150.

41. Robert W. Larson, *New Mexico Populism: A Study of Radical Protest in a Western Territory* (Boulder, Colorado: Colorado Associated University Press, 1974), pp. 35–47. For other views of the White Caps, see, e.g., Lamar, *Far Southwest,* p. 194, and Stratton, *Territorial Press,* pp. 130–31.

42. Larson, *New Mexico Populism,* pp. 67–68.

43. Rosenbaum, *"Mexicano versus Americano,"* p. 266. Commenting on Lopez's and others' defection, Rosenbaum remarks that *"El Partido del Pueblo Unido* grew out of this strange coalition of middle-class Hispanos from both parties, Anglo laborers and lawyers, and some old style *jefes politicos,* founded upon an angry and rebellious mass of *los hombres politicos"* (p. 227).

44. See, e.g.: *Santa Fé Daily New Mexican,* March 11, 1892, p. 2; Milton W. Callon, *Las Vegas, New Mexico: The Town That Wouldn't Gamble* (The Las Vegas Daily Optic, 1962), pp. 175–76.

45. "White Cap Folder, 1890–1893," Official Papers, L. Bradford Prince, New Mexico State Records Center and Archives, Santa Fe. Also cited in Rosenbaum, *"Mexicano versus Americano,"* p. 267.

46. Larson, *New Mexico Populism,* p. 67, citing Walter John Donlon, "LeBaron Bradford Prince, Chief Justice and Governor of New Mexico Territory, 1879–1893" (Ph.D. diss., University of New Mexico, June 1967), p. 239.

47. "Letter to the Editor," *La Voz del Pueblo,* August 8, 1891, p. 1.

48. See Appendix XV.

49. Record of Convicts, New Mexico Penitentiary, vol. I, p. 53. On December 28, 1894, Serafin Baca, no. 791, never before imprisoned, was reported to weigh 142 lbs., to be 5'5" tall, with brown "crossed" eyes, black hair, a dark complexion, a beard, good teeth, size 6 foot, and "1 cut on top of head 2" long/ 1 large lump on back of head/ 1 scar on calf of left leg." Listed as a Catholic, he was born in San Antonio Plaza, New Mexico, worked as a laborer, and was married with seven children. Intemperate in habits and a user of tobacco,

he could read and write and had supported himself since age 18. Both his parents were living, and Mrs. Maria Armijo de Baca of Las Vegas was shown as his nearest relative. (Penitentiary record books and glass negatives of prisoners "before" and "after" admission are in the New Mexico State Records Center and Archives, Santa Fe.)

50. Record of Convicts, New Mexico Penitentiary, vol. II, p. 35. Convict no. 2235 was reported to weigh 158 lbs., be 5'4½" tall, with brown eyes, black hair, a fair complexion, a sandy beard, medium good teeth, size 7 foot, and "Wen on back of head/ Scar from dog bite on calf of left leg." He was listed as temperate in habits. His parents were living, and he claimed seven children, but listed no nearest relative.

51. "Curry Pardons, 1907–10, A-C," George Curry Papers, New Mexico State Records Center and Archives, Santa Fe.

52. Territory of New Mexico, *Report of the Secretary of the Territory, 1907–1908 and Legislative Manual, 1909* (Santa Fe: New Mexican Printing, 1909), pp. 44–45. In 1906, statewide totals for Andrews were 22,915; for Larrazolo, 22,649; and for Socialist William P. Metcalf, 211. San Miguel County cast 2,728 votes for Larrazolo, 1,945 for Andrews, and none for Metcalf. 1908 state totals were: Andrews—27,605; Larrazolo—27,217; Metcalf—1,056. San Miguel County voted 2,890 for Andrews, 2,186 for Larrazolo, and 28 for Metcalf. For other material about "Bull" Andrews's career, see Larson, *New Mexico's Quest for Statehood,* and Westphall, *Catron.*

53. Letter of January 9, 1909, "Curry Pardons," ibid.

54. Ibid.

55. See Appendix XVI.

56. Swadesh, for example, reports that: "an unnamed person, apparently the hermano mayor of Abiquiú, sent a letter to a Las Vegas printer on May 29, 1900, with a proposal for reestablishing contact among the disunited Brothers of Río Arriba County, by referring to him all inquiries concerning the recently published rules of the Confraternity. The writer wished to launch a slate of Democratic candidates for county office to break the stranglehold of Catronist Republicans" (*Los Primeros Pobladores,* p. 217).

57. See Appendix XII.

58. *New Catholic Encyclopedia,* 6:134.

59. For a discussion of "The Brotherhood as a Secret Society," see Weigle, "Los Hermanos Penitentes," pp. 318–24.

60. Josiah Gregg, *Commerce of the Prairies,* p. 181. Thomas J. Steele, S.J., has recently addressed this question, suggesting that: "the statistics relating to the two patrons of Penitente secrecy, San Juan Nepomuceno and San Ramón Nonato, suggest that they were adopted from very early on, and that although the entrance of the Anglo Protestants, the Anglo-French Catholic clergy, and the Italian Jesuits forced the ceremonies to be held outside the villages, it was not the signal for starting to keep certain things secret" (*Santos and Saints: Essays and Handbook* [Albuquerque, New Mexico: Calvin Horn, 1974], pp. 93–94).

61. Woodward, *Penitentes,* p. 272. Mrs. Thomas Harwood claims that some of the new Hispano Methodist preachers "have the cross *tattooed* in their foreheads which can never be erased" (Mrs. Harriet S. Kellogg, *Life of Mrs. Emily J. Harwood,* p. 338). Early in the twentieth century, Lorenzo de Córdova recalls seeing a herder at Valdez who had "the figure of a cross, light gray in color, imprinted in the middle of his forehead." Although he saw only one other man so marked, he notes that "palms or boughs blessed on Palm Sunday were burned and their ashes used as a filler, rubbed into the design of a cross pricked into the skin" (*Echoes of the Flute,* p. 13). Bonney R. Gaastra, describing Chimayo, Cordova, Truchas and Trampas, claims to have talked to a man with "the faint purple cross tattooed under the skin of his forehead" ("The Doorways of Penitente Land," *Architectural Record* 57 [1925]:187).

62. Ritch, HM RI 2212, Memo Book, vol. 4, p. 326a.
63. Chavez, *AASF*, p. 120. See also the "Conclusion" of chap. 1, above, and the discussion in Weigle, "Los Hermanos Penitentes," pp. 227–28.
64. See Appendix XVII.
65. See Appendix XX.
66. Loose Documents, 1869, No. 7; 1870, No. 7 (Chavez, *AASF*, pp. 134, 135).
67. Ibid., 1870, No. 7.
68. Hon. L. Bradford Prince, comp., *The General Laws of New Mexico* (Albany, New York: W. C. Little, 1880), pp. 211–12. See also Woodward, *Penitentes*, pp. 272–73.
69. Record of Societies, Taos County Records, pp. 6–7. This copy is among the Dorothy Woodward Penitente Papers. Other materials from these Taos County Records are listed in Woodward, *Penitentes*, p. 341. The "Sociedad Benevola del Condado de Taos," incorporated December 31, 1881, is also among the Territorial corporation records as file no. 20, The Benevolent Society of Taos, incorporated February 7, 1882, for fifty years.
70. " 'The Penitentes,' " *Santa Fé Daily New Mexican*, March 11, 1892, p. 2, col. 2.

Chapter 4: The Brotherhood in the Twentieth Century

1. Cultural Properties Review Committee, *The Historic Preservation Program for New Mexico*, 1:45.
2. A. David Sandoval, "An Economic Analysis of New Mexico History," *New Mexico Business*, February 1967, p. 15.
3. Cultural Properties Review Committee, *Historic Preservation*, 1:45. See also Marta Weigle, ed., *Hispanic Villages of Northern New Mexico: A Reprint of Volume II of The 1935 Tewa Basin Study, with Supplementary Materials* (Santa Fe, New Mexico: The Lightning Tree—Jene Lyon, Publisher, 1975).
4. Laurence F. Lee, "Los Hermanos Penitentes" (B.A. thesis, University of New Mexico, 1910), p. 20.
5. Mary Austin, "Los Hermanos Penitentes," HM FII-29, p. 4. Italics added.
6. Leo Grebler, Joan W. Moore, and Ralph C. Guzman, *The Mexican-American People: The Nation's Second Largest Minority* (New York: Free Press, 1970), p. 42.
7. Sandoval, "Economic Analysis," p. 15. The figures given in the table are: 1900–10, 67.9%; 1910–20, 10.3%; 1920–30, 17.6%; 1930–40, 24.4%; 1940–50, 29.4%; 1950–60, 39.4%.
8. Jack E. Holmes, *Politics in New Mexico*, p. 10. Figures on persons of Mexican stock (born in Mexico or having at least one Mexican-born parent) are presented in, e.g., Grebler et al., *Mexican-American People*, p. 111. These percentages remain below six per cent in both New Mexico and Colorado from 1910 to 1960.
9. Cited in González, *The Spanish-Americans of New Mexico*, p. 127. Also see, e.g., "Population of the Upper Rio Grande Watershed," Regional Bulletin no. 43, Conservation Economics Series no. 16, Section of Human Surveys, Soil Conservation Service, Region 8, Albuquerque, New Mexico, July 1937; Sigurd Johansen, *The Population of New Mexico: Its Composition and Changes*, Agricultural Experiment Station of the New Mexico College of Agriculture and Mechanic Arts, Bulletin 273 (State College, New Mexico, June 1940); James I. Culbert, "Distribution of Spanish-American Population in New Mexico," *Economic Geography* 19 (1943):171–76; Paul A. F. Walter, Jr., "Population Trends in New Mexico," in *The Population of New Mexico*, Division of Research, Department of Government, University of New Mexico, Pub. 10 (Albuquerque, June 1947), pp. 1–19.
10. In 1950, within a total New Mexico population of 681,187 persons, 381,331 were Anglo, 248,880 Spanish-surname, and 50,976 nonwhite. In 1960, the total population numbered 951,023, with 606,641 Anglos, 269,122 Spanish-surname persons, and 75,260

nonwhites, mostly Indians. Colorado had 1,325,089 people in 1950, only 118,131 of whom were Spanish-surname individuals; and 1,753,947 persons in 1960, only 157,173 of them Hispanos. Further census data may be found in Donald N. Barrett, "Demographic Characteristics," in *La Raza: Forgotten Americans,* ed. Julian Samora (Notre Dame: University of Notre Dame Press, 1966), pp. 159–99; Ernesto Galarza, Herman Gallegos, and Julian Samora, *Mexican-Americans in the Southwest* (Santa Barbara, California: McNally & Loftin, 1969), pp. 79–90; and Grebler et al., *Mexican-American People,* pp. 106–108. Problems in analyzing this data for New Mexico are discussed in William A. Winnie, Jr., "The Spanish Surname Criterion for Identifying Hispanos in the Southwestern United States: A Preliminary Evaluation," *Social Forces* 38 (1960):363–66; and Thomas Weaver, "Sampling and Generalization in Anthropological Research on Spanish-Speaking Groups," in *Spanish-Speaking People in the United States: Proceedings of the 1968 Annual Spring Meeting of the American Ethnological Society,* ed. June Helm (Seattle: University of Washington Press, 1968), pp. 1–18.

11. Grebler et al., *Mexican-American People,* p. 113; Paul Walter, Jr., "Rural-Urban Migration in New Mexico," *New Mexico Business Review* 8 (1939):132.

12. Manuel Antonio Ferran, "Planning for Economic Development of Rural Northern New Mexico, With Emphasis on the Peñasco Valley, Taos County" (Ph.D. diss., University of Oklahoma, 1969), p. 83. See also González, *Spanish-Americans of New Mexico,* pp. 124–28.

13. Ferran, ibid., p. 27.

14. Ibid., p. 29. See also *Low-Income Families in the Spanish-Surname Population of the Southwest,* Economic Research Service, United States Department of Agriculture, Agricultural Economic Report no. 112, Washington, D.C., 1967.

15. Ferran, "Planning for Economic Development," p. 18. See also Marlowe M. Taylor, *Rural People and Their Resources, North-Central New Mexico,* Agricultural Experiment Station, New Mexico State University, Bulletin 448 (Las Cruces, October 1960).

16. "Milder Forms of Penance Replace Penitente Rites," *Albuquerque Journal,* March 23, 1951, p. 11, cols. 2–4.

17. Holmes, *Politics in New Mexico,* pp. 38, 295.

18. Paul Alfred Francis Walter, Jr., "A Study of Isolation and Social Change in Three Spanish-Speaking Villages of New Mexico" (Ph.D. diss., Stanford University, 1938), pp. 201–202; Juan B. Rael, "New Mexican Spanish Feasts," *California Folklore Quarterly* 1 (1942):86; Patricio M. Montano, "Observations of the Penitentes," in "Papers on Spanish Institutions and Customs in New Mexico," ed. Lynn I. Perrigo (Las Vegas, New Mexico: Donnelly Library, Highlands University, 1968), pp. 119–21. For an account of evolving status differences in Brotherhood membership, see Donovan Senter, "Acculturation among New Mexican Villagers in Comparison to Adjustment Patterns of Other Spanish-Speaking Americans," *Rural Sociology* 10 (1945):45–47.

19. See, e.g., González, *Spanish-Americans of New Mexico,* pp. 172–76; Clark S. Knowlton, "Changing Spanish-American Villages of Northern New Mexico," *Sociology and Social Research* 53 (1969):471–72. Statistical data and analyses of "Protestants and Mexicans" throughout the Southwest are found in Grebler et al., *Mexican-American People,* pp. 486–512.

20. Knowlton, "Changing Spanish-American Villages," p. 472.

21. J. B. Johnson, "The Allelujahs: A Religious Cult in Northern New Mexico," *Southwest Review* 22 (1937):132. See also Weigle, ed., *Hispanic Villages,* various refs.; Interagency Council for Area Development Planning and New Mexico State Planning Office, *Embudo: A Pilot Planning Project for the Embudo Watershed of New Mexico* (Santa Fe, n.d.), p. 48.

22. Frances Leon Swadesh, "Hispanic Americans of the Ute Frontier from the Chama Valley to the San Juan Basin 1694–1960" (Ph.D. diss., University of Colorado, 1966), p. 287. This material was not incorporated into *Los Primeros Pobladores,* the published version.

23. Austin, "Los Hermanos Penitentes," p. 7.

24. Letter to L. Bradford Prince, "Contemporary Issues, No. 9: Penitentes," Prince Papers, New Mexico State Records Center and Archives, Santa Fe.

25. Boyd, *Popular Arts,* p. 466.

26. Weigle, ed., *Hispanic Villages,* p. 185.

27. Boyd, *Popular Arts,* p. 466.

28. *The Old Faith and Old Glory,* pp. 22–24.

29. Swadesh, *Los Primeros Pobladores,* p. 225. See also chapter 2, note 63, above.

30. "Church Frowns on Flagellation in Public, Says Archbishop Daeger," *Santa Fe New Mexican,* March 31, 1923, p. 8, col. 4.

31. Woodward, *Penitentes,* p. 247. Austin notes the mitigation of Church opposition in the first decades of the twentieth century: "Writing at this date [early 1920s] the most obvious change that shows itself is the decline of the Church's objection to the order. Two reasons can be urged for this, one of them, decline of the most objectionable features of crucifixion and flaggelation [*sic*], and the other the quiet but obstinate refusal of the Order to fade out under the church's disapproval" ("Los Hermanos Penitentes," p. 7).

32. HM FII-29, Austin Collection, Huntington Library.

33. "Pastor Defends His Penitentes," *The Southwestern Catholic,* September 17, 1921, p. 56.

34. "The Penitentes and the Literary Digest," *The Southwestern Catholic,* September 17, 1921, p. 62. The offensive article appeared in *Literary Digest* 65 (1920):68–71.

35. Austin, "Penitente Hymns," HM FII-41.

36. Engelhardt, "Father Zephyrin and the Penitentes," *El Palacio* 8 (1920):73–74.

37. Engelhardt, "Franciscans in New Mexico," *Franciscan Herald* 8 (1920):176–77.

38. Blanche C. Grant, *When Old Trails Were New: The Story of Taos* (1934; reprint ed., Chicago: Rio Grande Press, 1963), p. 239.

39. *Lamy Memorial,* p. 32.

40. "Archbishop Gerken Preserves Archives," *El Palacio* 43 (1937):103.

41. Holmes, *Politics in New Mexico,* p. 37.

42. Jo Roybal Hogue, "Miguel Archibeque: The King In My Closet," *La Luz,* April 1974, p. 26. See also her biography, "Miguel Archibeque: *El Penitente Supremo Arzobispal,*" *Santa Fe News,* January 15, 1970, p. 2, col. 1.

43. Taylor, *Odyssey of the Islands.*

44. "Boy, 15, Faces Death for Murdering Taylor," *Albuquerque Journal,* February 7, 1936, p. 1.

45. Carl N. Taylor, "Agony in New Mexico," *Today,* February 15, 1936, pp. 2–4, 20–21.

46. "Cries in Cell after Sentence," *Albuquerque Journal,* February 18, 1936, p. 1., col. 6; p. 2, col. 4.

47. Jesse T. Simmons, "The Cross of Blood!," *Headline Detective,* January 1942, p. 30. See also, e.g., Mabel DeLaMater Scacheri, "The Penitentes: Murderous or Misguided?," *Family Circle,* March 20, 1936, pp. 14–16. In this classic article, a guard who objected to Mr. Mario Scacheri's attempts to film a Penitente ritual is described as "a man with the wild, staring gaze of a marijuana smoker." Mrs. Scacheri explains that "marijuana is a narcotic plant which makes men mad, and in Penitente country it is best not to defy it" (p. 15).

48. Letter of April 3, 1936, Miscellaneous Papers of Governor Clyde Tingley, New Mexico State Records Center and Archives, Santa Fe.

49. Charles Lefebure, *The Blood Cults* (New York: Ace Publishing, 1969), p. 148.

50. "Los Penitentes Stage Again Realistic Re-enactment of the March to Calvary," *Albuquerque Tribune,* April 23, 1943, p. 11, cols. 3–4.

51. Barron B. Beshoar, "Western Trails to Calvary," p. 133.

52. "The Penitentes in Las Animas," manuscript in the Charles W. Hurd Collection, State Historical Society of Colorado, Denver.

53. Published biographical materials on Don Miguel Archibeque are sketchy. Born in San Miguel del Barrio (Vado?) on July 1, 1883, at seventeen he was forced to seek work outside New Mexico. His quest took him to Trinidad, Colorado, and then to Wyoming, Idaho, Montana, and Utah, where he worked variously as shepherd, miner, and railroad hand. Apparently, an uncle in Colorado introduced him to the Penitentes, and he entered the Brotherhood during Holy Week of 1910. He returned to New Mexico and married Esquipulita Salazar on November 14, 1916. They had bought a ranch at Palma, in Torrance County, but, in 1922, were forced to seek employment in Santa Fe after the drought. Archibeque began a series of jobs with state and municipal agencies, the last one as parking lot attendant at the Welfare Building. His wife died in 1956, and after his retirement he lived for a time in the Velarde Nursing Home, finally returning to his family in Santa Fe until his death on Tuesday, June 16, 1970. See "Miguel Archibeque Keeps the Faith," *The Santa Fe Scene,* May 13, 1961, pp. 4–7; and the two articles by Hogue cited in note 42, above.

54. Aranda, *Penitente Papers,* p. 11.

55. Jack E. Holmes, notes from an interview on August 27, 1958, in the author's personal files; Hogue, "Miguel Archibeque: *El Penitente Supremo Arzobispal,*" p. 2.

56. Remarks made during a talk, "Penitentes and Flagellants," given at the 29th Annual Meeting of the New Mexico Folklore Society, Santa Fe, May 11, 1974. An unidentified student paper by Joe Lopez, "The World's Greatest Passion Play" (in the collection of the Carnegie Public Library, Las Vegas, New Mexico), also mentions Chavez's involvement with Byrne's final decision, p. 5.

57. "Archbishop Issues Declaration Giving Approbation to Work of 'Penitentes,' " *Santa Fe Register,* February 7, 1947, p. 1., cols. 4–6; p. 4, cols. 4–5. For the text published in the *Santa Fe New Mexican,* see Appendix XVIII. Another translation appears in Aranda, *Penitente Papers,* pp. 2–3.

58. "Holy Week Climaxed Penitente Lenten Rites," *Santa Fe New Mexican,* April 11, 1952, p. 1. Portions of this are reprinted in Boyd, *Popular Arts,* pp. 455–56.

59. "The Brothers of Blood," *Time,* September 1, 1958, p. 46.

60. Hogue, "Archibeque: *El Penitente Supremo Arzobispal,*" p. 2.

61. Holmes, *Politics in New Mexico,* p. 295. The two moradas at Abiquiu are usually cited as classic examples of two-party factionalism. Ahlborn found no evidence for this in the 1960s, noting that "the older members say that the first *morada* merely had become too large for convenient use of the building" (*The Penitente Moradas of Abiquiú,* p. 136). Nabokov mentions rival moradas at Canjilon, Rio Arriba County, but gives no explicit reasons for their factionalism (*Tijerina and the Courthouse Raid,* 2nd ed. [Berkeley, California: Ramparts Press, 1970], p. 94).

62. Barrat, "Pastor Defends His Penitentes," p. 56.

63. Holmes, *Politics in New Mexico,* p. 38.

64. Austin, "Los Hermanos Penitentes," p. 4.

65. Carolyn Zeleny, "Relations between the Spanish-Americans and Anglo-Americans in New Mexico: A Study of Conflict and Accommodation in a Dual-Ethnic Situation" (Ph.D. diss., Yale University, 1944), p. 264.

66. Holmes, *Politics in New Mexico,* p. 46.

67. Woodward, *Penitentes,* p. 292.

68. Ibid., p. 242.

69. Austin, *The Land of Journeys' Ending,* p. 372. Lorenzo de Córdova recalls a less serious incident at Ranchos de Taos when Brothers ejected a noisy spectator from the Tinieblas and tied her skirts over her head (*Echoes of the Flute,* pp. 19–20).

70. "Protecting Penitentes," *Santa Fe New Mexican,* April 4, 1931, p. 4, col. 1. This is

reprinted in Oliver LaFarge, *Santa Fe: The Autobiography of a Southwestern Town* (Norman: University of Oklahoma Press, 1959), pp. 331–32.

71. Letter of November 13, 1933, Dorothy Woodward Penitente Papers.

72. Beshoar, "Western Trails to Calvary," p. 134.

73. B. Ronald Gallegos, "76 stolen santos recovered by NM police," *The Santa Fe New Mexican*, November 28, 1972, p. 1, cols. 1–8. For reports of these thefts, see, e.g., "Second theft of Santos," *The Santa Fe New Mexican*, May 4, 1971, p. A2, col. 3; "Pecos also suffers from santos thefts," *The Santa Fe New Mexican*, March 10, 1972, p. A3, cols. 2–7; and Susan Samuelson, "Stolen santos," *Viva, The Santa Fe New Mexican*, August 20, 1972, pp. 3–5.

74. "New Mass is basically community expression," *The Santa Fe New Mexican*, March 27, 1970, p. A3, cols. 7–8.

75. "Governor, movie star attend Penitente rites," *The Santa Fe New Mexican*, March 29, 1970, p. B8, cols. 2–3.

76. See Appendix XIX.

Chapter 5: The Council Organizations

1. Woodward, *Penitentes*, pp. 273–75. She lists pertinent Corporation Commission files on page 340, and copies of these documents are among the Dorothy Woodward Penitente Papers.

2. Thomas Weaver, "Social Structure, Change, and Conflict in a New Mexican Village" (Ph.D. diss., University of California, Berkeley, 1965), p. 59.

3. Barron B. Beshoar, "Western Trails to Calvary," p. 132.

4. Ibid., pp. 132–33. Beshoar includes the text of this Council's "objectives." For photographs of a Long's Canyon morada, see Robert Adams, *The Architecture and Art of Early Hispanic Colorado*, pp. 74–77.

5. See Appendix XV.

6. Aranda, *The Penitente Papers*, pp. 58–59.

7. Ibid., p. 6.

8. M. Santos Melendez, personal communication. See also Beshoar, "Western Trails," p. 132. Beshoar identifies this *Concilio Ministerial* as embracing groups in Santa Fe, Las Vegas, Santa Rosa, Espanola, La Garita, Aguilar, Sopris, Walsenburg, and other communities.

9. Letter to Mary Austin, HM FII-29, Austin Collection, Huntington Library.

10. Transcripts of Cause No. 13761, Fourth Judicial District Court of San Miguel County, are included in a 1957 student paper by Lucien E. Roberts, "The Penitentes in Court," in "Papers on Spanish Institutions and Customs in New Mexico," ed. Lynn I. Perrigo (Las Vegas, New Mexico: Highlands University, Donnelly Library, 1968), pp. 156–84.

11. "Penitente Chief Denies Politics Cause of Dispute," *Las Vegas New Mexico Daily Optic*, February 25, 1946, p. 1, col. 6.

12. Roberts, "The Penitentes in Court," pp. 149–50.

13. Ibid., p. 148.

14. *Daily Optic*, February 25. Other indications of political ramifications may be found in: "Penitentes Take Discord to Courts," *Las Vegas New Mexico Daily Optic*, February 23, 1946, pp. 1, 3; "Penitentes' Secret Order Takes Fight with Rival Group to Court," *Albuquerque Journal*, February 24, 1946, p. 2, cols. 1–2; "Flagellation, Inc.," *Time*, April 22, 1946, pp. 48–49; Beshoar, "Western Trails to Calvary," pp. 137–38.

15. Roberts, "The Penitentes in Court," pp. 150–51.

16. See chap. 3, ns. 66, 67, above.

17. Loose Documents, 1870, No. 7 (Chavez, *AASF*, p. 135).

18. See Appendix XX.
19. A transcription of this document appears in Weigle, "Los Hermanos Penitentes," pp. 505–507.
20. A transcription appears in Roberts, "The Penitentes in Court," pp. 172–78.
21. Ibid., p. 160.
22. Aranda, *Penitente Papers,* p. 59.
23. See, e.g.: "Prosecutions in Taos Create Grave Situation," *Albuquerque Morning Journal,* March 26, 1914, p. 4, col. 3; George Wharton James, *New Mexico: The Land of the Delight Makers,* pp. 299–300; Woodward, *Penitentes,* pp. 285–87; Fred Lambert, "The Penitentes, A Religious Sect of New Mexico," *True West,* May-June 1963, pp. 31, 59; Lorayne Ann Horka-Follick, *Los Hermanos Penitentes: A Vestige of Medievalism in Southwestern United States* (Los Angeles: Westernlore Press, 1969), pp. 134, 214–16.
24. Woodward, *Penitentes,* p. 286. In a letter to Woodward dated December 21, 1933, Cheetham identified this "Capitan" as Jose Leon Mondragon, leader of another Penitente group comprising some 1700 members. According to him, "the Order was split at that time" (Dorothy Woodward Penitente Papers). The 2300 Brothers he estimates as belonging to the Cordova "faction" must have been those who signed the articles of incorporation filed in 1908 (see "Twentieth Century Councils," above).
25. Lambert, "The Penitentes," p. 59.
26. Woodward, *Penitentes,* p. 287. According to Lambert, one of Cordova's cousins visited him in Cimarron years later and told him that the case "broke" Cordova's power, and that he had moved to Wyoming (ibid.). If true, the effect was certainly not immediate, because Cordova signed the complaint against F. F. Thomas in June 1915 (see below).
27. The defendants, Pablo Rivera, a Penitente, and Genoveva Cordova, were charged with first degree murder in the shooting death of Juan Andres Cordova when the trial opened on May 22, 1922, before District Court Judge Thomas D. Leib. "Sometime after the charges had been made, the District Attorney was quietly advised that, regardless of the evidence, a verdict of second degree murder was all that could be secured in this case. . . . The defendants pled guilty of murder in the second degree, and were, subsequently, sentenced to from 75 to 80 years imprisonment, beginning June 23, 1922" (Woodward, *Penitentes,* p. 284). This plea bargaining may well have been the result of an internal judicial decision of the Brotherhood.
28. Lee, "Los Hermanos Penitentes," 1910, p. 20.
29. Lee, letter to Dorothy Woodward, September 12, 1932, Dorothy Woodward Penitente Papers.
30. "Fired by Penitentes," *Santa Fé Daily New Mexican,* August 4, 1894, p. 4, cols. 2–3. Flynn's article, "Holy Week with the Penitentes," appeared in *Harper's Weekly* 38 (1894):489–90. It is discussed at length in Claire Morrill, *A Taos Mosaic* (Albuquerque: University of New Mexico Press, 1973), pp. 70–73.
31. S.B. No. 24, Chap. 6, *Session Laws of the State of New Mexico* (Denver, Colorado: W. H. Courtright, 1915), p. 21.
32. Dorothy Woodward Penitente Papers. Her account of the case appears in idem, *Penitentes,* pp. 277–79.
33. Henry Wray, "America's Unguarded Gateway," *North American Review* 208 (1918):314.
34. Ibid., pp. 313–14.
35. "A Proud and Loyal State," *North American Review* 208 (1918):487–93.
36. "Alleged Hispano Sentiment and War," Adjutant-General Collection, New Mexico State Records Center and Archives, Santa Fe.
37. *The Santa Fe New Mexico Sentinel,* February 16, 1938, p. 16, cols. 2–3. Mahoney seems to disclaim much direct knowledge of the Brotherhood, concluding his letter as follows: "In

fact, when these articles have been completed, I intend naturally to give my impressions of the Penitentes and having listened to many of the good things that the old priests here in northern New Mexico have to say about this Society I will praise them and not blame them." Both Archibeque's and Mahoney's letters are transcribed in Weigle, "Los Hermanos Penitentes," pp. 510–11.

38. For a note on Spud (Walter Willard) Johnson and his literary activities, see Morrill, *Taos Mosaic,* pp. 133–35.

39. "The NBC Program," *El Grito del Norte,* Espanola, New Mexico, May 19, 1969, p. 11. A copy of "The Most Hated Man in New Mexico" [Reies Lopez Tijerina], an NBC Educational Films production, Tom Pettit reporter, is in the Historical Films Collection, New Mexico State Records Center and Archives, Santa Fe. The brief Penitente sequence at the beginning shows one of Henderson's oil paintings, then a wooden Cristo, and then a death cart. The sound track includes an alabado and the offensive phrases: "religion and violence are in the blood of New Mexico," and "the worship of death." A later sequence claims that land grant leader Reies Tijerina's guards were sometimes Penitentes used to "bloodshed."

40. Melendez, Letter to the Editor, *El Grito del Norte,* June 14, 1969, p. 16.

41. Holmes, *Politics in New Mexico,* pp. 37–38.

42. Aranda, *Penitente Papers,* pp. 14–15, 17.

43. Ibid., p. 20. There is no further reference to any Colorado supreme councils.

44. "Penitentes Choose Hermano Supremo," *The Santa Fe New Mexico Register,* June 10, 1955, p. 3, cols. 2–3. See also Holmes, *Politics in New Mexico,* p. 38.

45. Aranda, *Penitente Papers,* p. 16.

46. Ibid., pp. 14–21. Aranda includes minutes from meetings on February 8, 1953, and January 17, 1954.

47. Ibid., pp. 4, 22–23. Aranda has translated pastoral letters from Archbishop Byrne in 1951 and 1952. Other missives from Archibeque are dated February 12, 1952; August 20, 1958; and October 8, 1959 (pp. 13, 26–27, 31). Letters from Melendez after January 1, 1960, are also included (pp. 32–39).

48. Ibid., pp. ii, 33–38. Roman Aranda, whose father Claudio also served in various San Miguel County council posts, apparently continued as Elder Brother of District 5A until 1964. A letter from Melendez dated January 1, 1960, states that Archibeque's health failed in late November 1959, and solicits aid for the leader (ibid., p. 32).

Chapter 6: The Local Moradas

1. Stan Steiner, *La Raza: The Mexican Americans* (New York: Harper & Row, 1970), p. 4.

2. Lorenzo de Córdova, *Echoes of the Flute,* pp. 22, 38.

3. See, e.g.: Donovan Senter, "Acculturation among New Mexican Villagers in Comparison to Adjustment Patterns of Other Spanish-Speaking Americans," *Rural Sociology* 10 (1945):45–47; Leonica P. Duran, "Los Penitentes," in "Papers on Local History," ed. Lynn I. Perrigo (Las Vegas, New Mexico: Highlands University, Donnelly Library, 1962), p. 70; Swadesh, "Hispanic Americans of the Ute Frontier," p. 216. According to Aurora Lucero-White Lea, herself from an upper-class family, " 'Penitenteism' is the only organization to which a poor, un-lettered native may belong . . . in the society it is he, the *paisano* who wields the power . . . the head-brother is never a higher-up, and in no case may he be an Anglo" (*Literary Folklore of the Hispanic Southwest* [San Antonio, Texas: Naylor, 1953], p. 220). Although Harvey Fergusson refers to the Brotherhood as "an organization of the common man against his masters," the element of class conflict is perhaps not as important as the spiritual commitment involved (*Rio Grande,* p. 118).

4. Austin, "Los Hermanos Penitentes," HM FII-29, p. 4. A less critical attitude is reported for the wealthy Baca family of Rociada, New Mexico. Their son, "Pino had taken part occasionally in Penitente rituals, the rest of the family stayed away from them" (Oliver La Farge, *Behind the Mountains* [Boston: Houghton Mifflin, 1956], p. 98).

5. Lummis, *The Land of Poco Tiempo*, p. 108. See also chap. 3, notes 28 and 29. Cleofas Jaramillo gives her *rico* family's reason for applying this verse: "For a couple of years during Holy Week a flagellant *penitente* with his *acompanador* came to our private chapel and asked permission to go in and make a visit. While the brother of light recited the prayers, the brother lay prostrated with arms extended on the floor before the altar. He got up and stood by the door while flogging himself, and then passed in front of our store on the way back to the *morada*. My family persisted in believing that this was the man who helped himself to one of the fat lambs from our corral and had come to atone for it" (*Romance of a Little Village Girl* [San Antonio, Texas: Naylor, 1955], p. 37). However, it should also be noted that Jaramillo concludes: "The aim of the confraternity was evident in their lives. Their law was to live in peace and in the charity of Christ, prayer to be their support in all their afflictions. Those who were sincere in their rules were religious and scrupulous" (ibid., pp. 40–41).

6. Ibid., p. 40. William Krönig tried the same thing in the Taos area (Rio Colorado?) during the 1850s: "It was the custom for the natives to come into the store and lean their backs to the counter, facing the fire built in the huge fireplace. I would take a measuring stick, run it along their backs and whenever a man flinched I knew he was a Penitent" (Charles Irving Jones, "William Krönig, New Mexico Pioneer: From His Memories of 1849-1860," *New Mexico Historical Review* 19 [1944]:285).

7. Córdova, *Echoes of the Flute*, p. 34. Although his mother had become a Protestant, she returned to Catholicism and was buried in Cordova following services conducted by the Brothers.

8. Swadesh, "Hispanic Americans of the Ute Frontier," p. 275. Also see her revision of this dissertation, *Los Primeros Pobladores*, pp. 189–92.

9. Paul Alfred Francis Walter, Jr., "A Study of Isolation and Social Change in Three Spanish-Speaking Villages of New Mexico," p. 202.

10. Herminia B. Chacon, "The Society of Our Father Jesus," February 6, 1934, ms. among the Dorothy Woodward Penitente Papers, p. 3. Jaramillo, *Romance of a Little Village Girl*, p. 41. Lorenzo de Córdova also notes some amusing consequences of this belief (*Echoes of the Flute*, p. 29–30). For a further discussion of such beliefs and legends, see chap. 8.

11. Carolyn Zeleny mentions this form of inter-ethnic accommodation in "Relations between the Spanish-Americans and Anglo-Americans in New Mexico," p. 264. See also generalizations such as Nathan Miller's that "as a rule secrecy is employed for more effective control over non-members and the uninitiated or for more stringent maintenance of the internal solidarity of the group of individuals who have discovered or built up common interests" (*Encyclopedia of the Social Sciences* [London: Macmillan, 1934], 13:621); and other discussion in, e.g.: Noel P. Gist, "Dogma and Doctrine in Secret Societies," *Sociology and Social Research* 23 (1938):121–30; Norman MacKenzie, ed., *Secret Societies* (New York: Collier Books, 1971); and Robert T. Anderson, "Voluntary Associations in History," *American Anthropologist* 73 (1971):209–22.

12. According to Lucia Cardenas, writing from personal experience: "The members of the Penitente organization regard their memberships with as much pride as any other person would regard his to any other exclusive club or society. . . . Only the chosen go through the initiation. Prospective members must be from families of good reputation and character" (in "History Seminar Papers on New Mexico," ed. Lynn I. Perrigo [Las Vegas, New Mexico: Highlands University, Donnelly Library, 1954], p. 25). See also Swadesh, "Hispanic Americans of the Ute Frontier," p. 90.

13. Aranda, *Penitente Papers,* pp. 50, 55. See also Archbishop Salpointe's 1892 objections to fourteen-year-olds taking an oath, Appendix XII. Lorenzo de Córdova's report would indicate initiation at age ten (see n. 15, below); and Gabino Rendón claims that twelve-year-olds were admitted (*Hand on My Shoulder,* p. 65). During the 1950s, Munro Edmonson, working in a recently settled and only weakly Penitente area of northwest-central New Mexico, claimed that Penitente initiation "takes place much later in life, apparently not earlier than 20–25 years of age" (*Los Manitos: A Study of Institutional Values,* Middle American Research Institute, Pub. 25 [New Orleans: Tulane University, 1957], p. 34).

14. Córdova, *Echoes of the Flute,* pp. 27–30; Aranda, *Penitente Papers,* p. i. Rev. Frank L. Moore claims to have seen at play young boys who "had formed scourges of rope or willows and were lashing their backs, while behind them came the little girls in a long procession, just as they had seen the women following the Penitentes up the sorrowful way" (*The Penitentes of New Mexico* [New York: Congregational Home Missionary Society, n.d.], p. 4). Moore's account may be exaggerated, but there is no other evidence to suggest how or whether children learned to cope with impending Penitente status through imitative play.

15. Córdova, *Echoes of the Flute,* p. 36. Reyes N. Martinez also mentions the custom of having younger boys be " 'entregados a la Sangre de Cristo' (Delivered to the blood of Christ) by their parents" in a manuscript for the New Mexico W.P.A. Writers' Project dated March 26, 1937 ("Sheep Herders Galore," W.P.A. Files, Santa Fe, New Mexico).

16. The basic pattern of instruction and examination prior to initiation is generally documented. Accounts of the actual initiation rituals vary. These rituals overlap entrance rites for any Brother wishing to do penance during Holy Week. They will be discussed in chap. 7.

17. Viator, "How a Pious and Useful Body Degenerated into a Sect—A Secret Society," *Albuquerque Review,* April 6, 1878, p. 1, col. 3.

18. Josué Trujillo, *La Penitencia a Traves de La Civilizacion* (Santa Cruz, New Mexico: author, 1947), p. 8.

19. Swadesh, *Los Primeros Pobladores,* pp. 177–78.

20. Unpaginated ms., HM RI-1866, Ritch Collection, Huntington Library. According to Aurelio M. Espinosa, "the Hermanos Penitentes are men; fifty years ago they admitted women and children into separate organizations, which, however, were never numerous" (*The Catholic Encyclopedia* [New York: Robert Appleton, 1911], 11:635). Female Penitentes are also noted in: Lummis, *The Land of Poco Tiempo,* p. 107; Eleanor Adams, "The Penitent Brothers," *Sunset: The Pacific Monthly* 38, 3 (1917):26–28; and Rev. William E. Barton, *The Penitentes of New Mexico* (Boston: Congregational Education Society, n.d.), pp. 2–4.

21. Wesley Robert Hurt, Jr., "Manzano: A Study of Community Disorganization," p. 71. Dora Ortiz Vásquez notes the existence of organized women Penitentes in Taos who are known as "Las Confradás de San Francisco (Sisters of St. Francis)" in her *Enchanted Temples of Taos: My Story of Rosario* (Santa Fe, New Mexico: Rydal Press, 1975), p. 44.

22. Carlos J. Craig, "The Penitentes," in "Papers on the Southwest: History Seminar Papers" (Las Vegas, New Mexico: Highlands University, Donnelly Library, 1965), p. 94. Severe female penances are mentioned in Lee, *Los Hermanos Penitentes,* pp. 9–10; George Wharton James, *New Mexico: The Land of the Delight Makers,* p. 289; and elsewhere. Anglo informants told Matilda Coxe Stevenson about witnessing a flagellant procession in which women flogged themselves over white cotton dresses (ms. notes dated 1906, among the Dorothy Woodward Penitente Papers). Milder penances are noted in Córdova, *Echoes of the Flute,* pp. 41–42.

23. William Wallrich, "Auxiliadoras de la morada," *Southwestern Lore* 16 (1950):4–10. Wallrich gives no name to these auxiliary groups, but both Patricio M. Montano ("Observations of the Penitentes," in "Papers on Spanish Institutions and Customs in New

Mexico," ed. Lynn I. Perrigo [Las Vegas, New Mexico: Highlands University, Donnelly Library, 1968], pp. 119–20) and Bill Tate (*The Penitentes of the Sangre de Cristos: An American Tragedy,* 5th ed. [Truchas, New Mexico: Tate Gallery, 1971], pp. 20–21) call them *Las Carmelitas.* While this may be the local designation, they should not be confused with members of the Confraternity of Our Lady of Carmel, established at Santa Cruz de la Cañada in 1710. Lorenzo de Córdova, e.g., indicates that this distinction was maintained in Cordova, New Mexico (*Echoes of the Flute,* p. 45).

24. Margaret Abreu, "The Three R's—Plus," *New Mexico Magazine,* October 1959, p. 37; Wallrich, "Auxiliadoras de la morada," p. 9; Swadesh, *Los Primeros Pobladores,* p. 120; La Farge, *Behind the Mountains,* pp. 97–98.

25. Darley, *Passionists,* pp. 14–17.

26. Loose Documents, 1870, No. 7 (Chavez, *AASF,* p. 135).

27. Trujillo, *La Penitencia,* pp. 8–10; Beshoar, "Western Trails to Calvary," p. 125; Holmes, *Politics in New Mexico,* pp. 35–36.

28. Darley, *Passionists,* pp. 30–31; Chacon, "The Society of Our Father Jesus," p. 4.

29. See Appendix XX.

30. Beshoar, "Western Trails to Calvary," p. 126. These are similar to the 1875 by-laws for the Rincones, Colorado, morada published by Darley (*Passionists,* pp. 20–22). Wallrich notes that novices in San Luis Valley chapters were required to take out and maintain an insurance policy. Premiums were given to the Hermano Mayor, who in turn paid the company representative. Another regulation involved compulsory attendance for at least half an hour at all Brotherhood-sponsored wakes ("Auxiliadoras de la morada," pp. 7, 10). See also various rules in Aranda, *Penitente Papers.*

31. See, e.g., Woodward, *Penitentes,* p. 224, fn. 49; Cleofas M. Jaramillo, *Shadows of the Past (Sombras del Pasado),* p. 64. Only one person claims to have been an eyewitness to such a practice. An entry in soldier James A. Bennett's diary for April 6, 1852, notes that at La Joya, New Mexico, north of Socorro, he saw flagellants, cross-bearers, and: "One other I noticed buried, standing upright, in the ground with nothing above the surface but his head. He remained in that position two days and nights" (Clinton E. Brooks and Frank D. Reeves, eds., "James A. Bennett: A Dragoon in New Mexico, 1850-1856," *New Mexico Historical Review* 22 [1947]:87).

32. Córdova, *Echoes of the Flute,* pp. 21–22. Mary Austin suggests a range of penalties: "Gossiping in the twilight with the wives and mothers of the brotherhood, one hears how Tomacito was made to pay for the damages his cow committed against the corn of Pablito, of how Ascensio was required to withdraw his membership from his own morada to one six miles distant because of a too conspicuous interest in the wife of Bartolomé, and how at Questa, after the visit of the national representative of the Anti-Tuberculosis campaign, a penalty of two strokes with the disciplina was prescribed for spitting on the floor" (*The Land of Journeys' Ending,* pp. 370–71).

33. For a good description of traditional funeral practices, see Córdova, *Echoes of the Flute,* pp. 13–16, 34, 48–50. Mutual aid societies are discussed in González, *The Spanish-Americans of New Mexico,* pp. 89–90. Swadesh notes the rapid growth of the *Unión Protectiva,* established in Santa Fe in 1916, following the decline of the Brotherhood in many places (*Los Primeros Pobladores,* pp. 194, 237–38). However, as late as November 1965, Ahlborn witnessed Brothers actively supervising a nonmember's funeral (*The Penitente Moradas of Abiquiú,* p. 124).

34. Quoted in W. Thetford LeViness, "He Carves the Santos—In the Land of the Penitentes," *Desert Magazine,* January 1958, p. 12. For details about the *fondo,* see Woodward, *Penitentes,* pp. 288–89.

35. Hurt, "Manzano: A Study of Community Disorganization," pp. 65–74.

36. Clark S. Knowlton, "Changing Spanish-American Villages of Northern New

Mexico," *Sociology and Social Research* 53 (1969):471. Patricio Montano also ends his essay in this vein, stating that the younger people might be controlled if the Penitentes could regain some of their old power ("Observations of the Penitentes," p. 122).

37. Weaver, "Social Structure, Change, and Conflict in a New Mexican Village," p. 28.

38. Reyes N. Martinez, "Early Settlements, Folkways of Northern Taos County," February 29, 1936, ms. in W.P.A. Files, New Mexico History Museum Library, Santa Fe, p. 3.

Chapter 7: The Rituals

1. The significance of the variation in Penitente worship has rarely been emphasized. Laurence F. Lee stressed this point in a letter of September 23, 1932, to Dorothy Woodward, cautioning that "you must remember that . . . a great many of their activities are according to their own whims and caprice, so there is no uniformity in the practices excepting in the way they attempt to emulate the crucifixion of Christ" (Dorothy Woodward Penitente Papers). Arthur L. Campa also makes this point in a letter of November 26, 1934, to Woodward, stating that "as you know, these ceremonies vary a great deal with personalities, variety being one of the essential qualities of any Spanish ceremony" (ibid.).

2. E. Boyd, *Saints and Saint Makers of New Mexico* (Santa Fe, New Mexico: Laboratory of Anthropology, 1946), p. 67. Photographs confirm this "lighter" impression, e.g., in: Richard E. Ahlborn, *The Penitente Moradas of Abiquiú;* The Editors of *Look Magazine, Look At America: The Southwest* (Boston: Houghton Mifflin, 1947), p. 172; Dorothy Stewart photo in Marta Weigle, *The Penitentes of the Southwest* (Santa Fe, New Mexico: Ancient City Press, 1970), p. 41; Robert L. Shalkop, *Arroyo Hondo: The Folk Art of a New Mexican Village* (Colorado: The Taylor Museum of The Colorado Springs Fine Arts Center, 1969), pp. 21, 29. The "darker" impression of morada chapels is best expressed by Harvey Fergusson in *Rio Grande,* p. 121, an account of 1903 rites; and in Cleofas M. Jaramillo's reminiscence of her childhood visit to an Arroyo Hondo morada (*Romance of a Little Village Girl,* p. 37). See also chap. 1, n. 57.

3. For different versions, see, e.g.: Alexander M. Darley, ed., *La Hermandad,* (Pueblo, Colorado, April 1890), p. 1; Aurora Lucero-White, "The Penitentes," August 29, 1936, ms., W.P.A. Files, Santa Fe, New Mexico, p. 7; Reyes N. Martinez, "La Entrada a La Morada," April 10, 1940, ms., W.P.A. Files, Santa Fe; Aurelio M. Espinosa, *Romancero de Nuevo Méjico* (Madrid: C. Bermejo, 1953), pp. 14–15. Roughly translated, this formula reads: Who gives this house light?/Jesus./Who fills it with joy?/Mary./Who preserves it in faith?/Joseph. Accounts of visits are found, e.g., in: Aurora Lucero-White Lea, *Literary Folklore of the Hispanic Southwest,* p. 222; Córdova, *Echoes of the Flute,* pp. 33–34, 41–42; Reyes N. Martinez, "Curious Practices and Curious Beliefs," March 13, 1937, ms., W.P.A. Files, Santa Fe, p. 2.

4. See, e.g.: Laurence F. Lee's anonymous published version of his 1910 B.A. thesis, "Los Hermanos Penitentes," *El Palacio* 8 (1920):7–9; George Wharton James, *New Mexico: The Land of the Delight Makers,* pp. 285–88; Woodward, *Penitentes,* pp. 229–31; Beshoar, "Western Trails to Calvary," pp. 126–27.

5. Darley reports this pattern in *Passionists,* pp. 15–16, 24–25; and Woodward also includes it in *Penitentes,* p. 225.

6. Reyes N. Martinez, "Early Settlements, Folkways of Northern Taos County," February 29, 1936, ms., W.P.A. Files, Santa Fe, p. 2. Descriptions of the seal vary. "In some *moradas* the cross is cut between the shoulder blades; in others, two crosses are cut, one under each shoulder blade; and, in still others, a cross is formed by making two long, sweeping cuts down the length of the back and one horizontal cross across the center of the back" (Beshoar, "Western Trails to Calvary," p. 126).

7. Jo Roybal Hogue, "The Penitentes: Unique New Mexico Easter Rites," *The Santa Fe New Mexican,* April 11, 1971, p. D-1.

8. Foster, *Culture and Conquest: America's Spanish Heritage,* Viking Fund Publications in Anthropology, No. 27 (Chicago: Quadrangle Books, 1960), p. 158.

9. Ibid., pp. 165–66.

10. *Shadows of the Past (Sombras del Pasado),* pp. 48–53, 72–74, 77–82, 85–87. See also Juan B. Rael, "New Mexican Spanish Feasts," *California Folklore Quarterly* 1 (1942):83–90.

11. Russell Vernon Hunter has recounted his experiences with one such morada patron in "Santa Inez of the Penitentes," *Southwest Review* 32 (1947):275–79. For a systematic and schematic presentation of religion in regional Hispano culture, see Edmonson, *Los Manitos,* pp. 33–44.

12. *New Catholic Encyclopedia,* 8:636, 635.

13. Córdova, *Echoes of the Flute,* pp. 36–38.

14. Weigle, *Penitentes of the Southwest,* pp. 21–24; and Ida L. Frost, "New Mexico," in *The Story of Some Helpers* (Boston: Congregational House, n.d.), pp. 31–32.

15. Mary Austin, *Land of Journeys' Ending,* p. 357.

16. L. S. M. Curtin, *Healing Herbs of the Upper Río Grande* (Los Angeles: Southwest Museum, 1965), p. 171. She also reports an *encerado,* salve, of *oshá* for treating these wounds, p. 140.

17. Ibid., pp. 145–46; Winfield Townley Scott, "The Still Young Sunlight: Chimayo, New Mexico," in *A Vanishing America,* ed. Thomas C. Wheeler (New York: Holt, Rinehart and Winston, 1964), p. 133.

18. Boyd, *Popular Arts of Spanish New Mexico,* pp. 464–65. See, e.g., photos in Lee's anonymous *El Palacio* version, "Los Hermanos Penitentes," pp. 5–8; and the descriptions of various Spanish, Mexican, and New Mexican devices of discipline, items 57–61 of the exhibition catalogue for the *5 Continents Gifts and Purchases,* Museum of New Mexico, International Folk Art Building, Santa Fe, November 15, 1964-September 6, 1965.

19. Reyes N. Martinez, "Odd Religious Practices," undated ms., W.P.A. Files, Santa Fe, p. 7. For photos and measurements, see Ahlborn, *Penitente Moradas of Abiquiú,* pp. 146–47. *Maderos* may sometimes be seen today outside undisturbed moradas.

20. Chavez, "The Penitentes of New Mexico," p. 120. The full range of reported penances has been surveyed by George Mills and Richard Grove in *Lucifer and the Crucifer: The Enigma of the Penitentes* (Colorado: The Taylor Museum of The Colorado Springs Fine Arts Center, 1966), pp. 7–9, 15–17.

21. Martinez, "Odd Religious Practices," pp. 1–2. He also reports the custom of *ir a pedir santos,* to ask for saints. Individuals, usually women, petitioned to carry a *santo* in a procession and "were always given a place of honor in the procession, between two rows of 'penitentes de disciplina,' " p. 3.

22. "The Penitente Brotherhood," in "Papers on the Southwest: American History Seminars," ed. Lynn I. Perrigo (Las Vegas, New Mexico: Highlands University, Donnelly Library, 1948–49), p. 17.

23. Córdova, *Echoes of the Flute,* pp. 39–41.

24. Some alabados were closely associated with penitential exercises. Espinosa gives a version of *Bendice, Señor, La Cena,* which was sung in the morada. Brothers began their flagellation after the line "con el sello de Jesús—te vamos a acompañar/en esta santa morada" (*Romancero de Nuevo Méjico,* p. 245). *Por el rastro de la sangre* was a popular accompaniment to public processions (for versions, see Juan B. Rael, *The New Mexican Alabado,* Stanford University Publications, Language and Literature, vol. 9, no. 3, 1951, pp. 24–29; Espinosa, *Romancero,* pp. 170–81). *Bendito el Santo Madero* was sometimes sung during processions when crosses were dragged (Rael, *The New Mexican Alabado,* pp. 36, 39–40).

25. Edmonson, *Los Manitos,* p. 36.

26. Córdova gives some recipes in *Echoes of the Flute,* pp. 24–26. Jaramillo says that the reciprocal exchange of *charolitas* in Arroyo Hondo took place on Holy Thursday and Good Friday (*Shadows of the Past,* p. 67). Swadesh reports that this custom persists in the San Juan Basin today (*Los Primeros Pobladores,* pp. xvi, 144).

27. *New Catholic Encyclopedia,* 10:1059.

28. Ibid., p. 1061.

29. John E. Steinmueller and Kathryn Sullivan, eds., *Catholic Biblical Encyclopedia: New Testament* (New York: Joseph F. Wagner, 1959), pp. 481–84. Quotations are from *The Revised Standard Version Common Bible: An Ecumenical Edition* (New York: Collins, 1973).

30. Blanche C. Grant, *When Old Trails Were New,* p. 244. This has also been described by Mary Austin in *Land of Journeys' Ending,* pp. 364–69, and in "Native Drama in Our Southwest," *Nation* 124 (1927):437–40. See also photos in Fred Mazzulla, "The Penitentes," *Empire Magazine of the Denver Post,* April 11, 1954, pp. 10–11.

31. For versions of *La Pasión del Señor,* see Mary Austin, "Penitente Hymns," HM FII-41, Austin Collection, Huntington Library; Lucero-White, "The Penitentes," pp. 16–23; Rael, *New Mexican Alabado,* pp. 47–51; Reginald Fisher, ed., *The Way of the Cross: A New Mexico Version* (Santa Fe, New Mexico: School of American Research, 1958), pp. 29–30. *Lloren, pecadores* has been recorded by Cleofes Vigil (*New Mexican Alabados,* Taos Recordings and Publications, Taos, New Mexico, TRP 3) from Rael's text (*New Mexican Alabado,* pp. 43–44). See also Boyd, *Popular Arts of Spanish New Mexico,* pp. 472–83. Richard B. Stark, Santa Fe, is completing an important historical and musicological study of alabados collected in Spain and New Mexico.

32. *New Catholic Encyclopedia,* 14:832.

33. See, e.g.: George C. Barker, "Some Aspects of Penitential Processions in Spain and the American Southwest," *Journal of American Folklore* 70 (1957):138–39; Foster, *Culture and Conquest,* pp. 177–78.

34. *New Catholic Encyclopedia,* 14:833.

35. Loose Documents, 1870, No. 7 (Chavez, *AASF,* p. 135).

36. See photo in *The Santa Fe New Mexican,* August 25, 1958, p. 5; and "The Brothers of Blood," *Time,* September 1, 1958, pp. 45–46. William R. Fisher claims that it was difficult to record this alabado because the Brothers considered it very sacred ("A Study of the Historic Background of New Mexican *Alabados,*" research paper, Department of Music, University of New Mexico, Albuquerque, 1952, p. 47). However, Rael has collected five versions (*New Mexican Alabado,* pp. 70–71).

37. "Oracion y alabado dichos durante las Estaciones," April 10, 1940, ms., W.P.A. Files, Santa Fe. Also among these Files is his undated ms. text and translation of *Acompañadnos todos*—"sung on Holy Friday, during the Via Crucis."

38. Woodward, *Penitentes,* p. 233; Rael, *New Mexican Alabado,* p. 15; Córdova, *Echoes of the Flute,* pp. 38–39, 45. Edmonson also reports much the same pattern (*Los Manitos,* pp. 37, 39).

39. *New Catholic Encyclopedia,* 7:105.

40. "Sound accompaniment was provided by the *matraca* (from Arabic *mitraca,* a hammer) on Good Friday to suggest the hail during the hours of darkness of the Crucifixion. . . . The matraca was like the old English watchman's rattle with clapper and gear of wood. These were used for centuries in Spanish churches during the last three days of Holy Week as a substitute for bells. . . . Although no longer used in American churches, it is said that everyone carries a matraca on Good Friday in Haiti, where the mass noise is described as sounding like a field of crickets" (Boyd, *Popular Arts of Spanish New Mexico,* p. 465).

41. Cleofas Jaramillo, *Romance of a Little Village Girl,* p. 38.

42. Jo Roybal Hogue, "The Penitentes."

43. See, e.g., Beshoar, "Western Trails to Calvary," pp. 145–47; Rael, *New Mexican Alabado*, p. 15; Córdova, *Echoes of the Flute*, pp. 44–45.

44. Jaramillo, *Romance of a Little Village Girl*, p. 39.

45. Leonica P. Duran, "Los Penitentes," in "Papers on Local History," ed. Lynn I. Perrigo (Las Vegas, New Mexico: Highlands University, Donnelly Library, 1962), pp. 57–81. Swadesh also notes roles for "Three Marys" and a Veronica in San Juan Basin observances ("Hispanic Americans of the Ute Frontier," p. 283).

46. Woodward, *Penitentes*, p. 235; photos, pp. 324–26. The account and photos come from Harriet Mayfield, according to her letter of April 29, 1934, to Woodward (Dorothy Woodward Penitente Papers). Mayfield's article, "Devout People Enact Sacred Drama Every Year in Quaint Town," and two photos appeared in the *Los Angeles Sunday Times*, May 31, 1925, part II-a, p. 2, cols. 4–8.

47. Boyd, *Popular Arts of Spanish New Mexico*, pp. 462, 471. Nazario Lopez was the father of noted Cordova woodcarver Jose Dolores Lopez (1868–1938) and grandfather of George Lopez (1900–), now a well-known and skilled carver (in addition to ibid., pp. 468–71, see Charles L. Briggs, "What is a Modern Santo?" *El Palacio* 79, 4 [1974]:40–49). Bourke's entry is in vol. 44 of his diaries, reprinted in Lansing B. Bloom, "Bourke on the Southwest," *New Mexico Historical Review* 11 (1936):272–73. The Trampas death cart and its associated penance is described by Ely Leyba in "The Church of the Twelve Apostles," *New Mexico Magazine*, June 1933, pp. 48–49.

48. Boyd, *Popular Arts of Spanish New Mexico*, pp. 462–64. The name *Sebastiana* is an apparent confusion of La Muerte's drawn bow and arrow with the usual depiction of St. Sebastian riddled with arrows.

49. Ibid., p. 464. Louisa R. Stark divides Muertes into two categories—the earlier Sangre de Cristo figures and the later San Luis Valley ones ("The Origin of the Penitente 'Death Cart,' " *Journal of American Folklore* 84 [1971]:304–310).

50. Alice Corbin Henderson, *Brothers of Light: The Penitentes of the Southwest* (New York: Harcourt, Brace, 1937), p. 35; Leyba, "Church of the Twelve Apostles," p. 49; E. Boyd and Roland Dickey, "Early New Mexican Art: Santos," *New Mexico Quarterly Review* 23 (1953):72.

51. Henderson, *Brothers of Light*, p. 32; Martinez, "Death Makes a Hit," March 13, 1937, ms., W.P.A. Files, Santa Fe; Mitchell A. Wilder with Edgar Breitenbach, *Santos: The Religious Folk Art of New Mexico* (Colorado: The Taylor Museum of The Colorado Springs Fine Arts Center, 1943), p. 40.

52. Thomas J. Steele, S.J., *Santos and Saints: Essays and Handbook* (Albuquerque, New Mexico: Calvin Horn, 1974), pp. 89–90, 197. E. Boyd notes that the contemplation of skulls held in the hand or placed on small altars was popular in graphic representations of "St. Francis of Assisi, St. Louis King of France, St. Rita of Cascia, and St. Rosalie of Palermo, all particular patterns of the Franciscans and their Third Order" (*Popular Arts of Spanish New Mexico*, p. 447). Many of these were copied by New Mexican *santeros*, image-carvers, and were often found in Penitente moradas.

53. Stark, "Origin of the Penitente 'Death Cart,' " p. 310; George Mills, *Kachinas and Saints: A Contrast in Style and Culture* (Colorado: The Taylor Museum of The Colorado Springs Fine Arts Center, 1953).

54. *New Catholic Encyclopedia*, 4:485.

55. Ibid., 4:486.

56. W. G. Ritch, Memo Book no. 4, HM RI 2212, vol. 4, Ritch Collection, Huntington Library, p. 325; "Viator," "How a Pious and Useful Body Degenerated into a Sect—A Secret Society"; Lummis, *The Land of Poco Tiempo*, p. 99; W. Thetford LeViness, "The Penitentes: Brotherhood of the Cross," *Empire: The Magazine of the Denver Post*, April 10, 1960, p. 13. On the other hand, Carl Eickemeyer claims that "not many years ago the victim was fastened

to the cross with heavy iron spikes, driven through the palms of the hands; and there are many old men in the community [San Mateo] today with deep indentations in their hands which have only partially healed" (*Over the Great Navajo Trail* [New York: Press of J. J. Little, 1900], p. 101). Mary Austin reports that both she and Laurence F. Lee were told, at Albuquerque, Taos, Las Vegas, and Abiquiu, that the last use of nails had been in 1908 ("Los Hermanos Penitentes," n.d., HM FII-29, p. 8). More recently, Richard Gardner gives no source for his statement that "George Martin recalls giving medical aid to men who had actually been nailed" (*¡Grito!: Reies Tijerina and the New Mexico Land Grant War of 1967* [Indianapolis, Indiana: Bobbs Merrill, 1970], p. 72). All these are unreliable, however. Beshoar, who thinks nails may have been used on rare occasions, succinctly sums up the question: "I have never found anyone, Anglo, Spanish-American, Penitente, or whatever, who could testify that he personally witnessed a real crucifixion . . . tales are always second, third, or some other hand" ("Western Trails to Calvary," p. 136).

57. Lummis, *The Land of Poco Tiempo*, pp. 100–101; Marc Simmons, *Two Southwesterners: Charles Lummis and Amado Chaves* (Cerrillos, New Mexico: San Marcos Press, 1968), p. 16.

58. No. LC-USZ62-12643, Lot 6254, Reference Department, Prints and Photographs Division, Library of Congress, Washington, D.C.

59. Woodward, *Penitentes*, p. 326.

60. Van Deren Coke, "A Note on B. J. O. Nordfeldt's 'Penitente Crucifixion,' " *University of New Mexico Art Museum Bulletin*, no. 2, Spring 1967, p. 9. See also Coke, *Nordfeldt the Painter* (Albuquerque: University of New Mexico Press, 1972), pp. 58–61.

61. Coke, "A Note," pp. 10–11. Shuster was accompanied by artists Frank Applegate, Willard Nash, and Josef Bakos. Governor and Mrs. Hinkle also attended the rites, and some 100–125 people "almost swamped the old village" (*Santa Fe New Mexican*, March 31, 1923, p. 5, cols. 4–6).

62. Henderson, *Brothers of Light*, e.g., pp. 45–49; *William Penhallow Henderson, 1877–1943*, Retrospective Exhibition, July 21-August 20, 1963, Museum of New Mexico, Fine Arts Museum, Santa Fe.

63. Udell, *The Penitentes* (Denver, Colorado: The Cosmopolitan Art Gallery, n.d.); "In The Dust of The Valley," *South Dakota Review* 7 (1969).

64. In addition to Henderson, see, e.g.: Lee, "Los Hermanos Penitentes," p. 10; Córdova, *Echoes of the Flute*, p. 46. See also Steele, *Santos and Saints*, pp. 50–51, 61–63.

65. *New Catholic Encyclopedia*, 13:1007–1008.

66. Ibid., p. 1008. Biblical quotations are from The Revised Standard Version Common Bible.

67. Córdova, *Echoes of the Flute*, pp. 19–20, 23, 30, 42–44. He calls the Good Friday night services *Los Maitines*, Matins, but claims they are identical to *Las Tinieblas*, pp. 46–47.

68. See, e.g.: ibid.; Henderson, *Brothers of Light*, pp. 50–56; Beshoar, "Western Trails to Calvary," pp. 143–45. In 1840, Frances Erskine Calderón de la Barca reported similar Tenebrae services in Mexican churches, including some involving self-flagellation (Howard T. Fisher and Marion Hall Fisher, eds., *Life in Mexico: The Letters of Fanny Calderón de la Barca, With New Material from the Author's Private Journals* [Garden City, New York: Doubleday, 1966], pp. 203, 336–37). This was a common Spanish practice too.

69. Jaramillo, *Shadows of the Past*, p. 76; Rael, *New Mexican Alabado*, pp. 121–22.

70. William A. Douglass, *Death in Murélaga: Funerary Ritual in a Spanish Basque Village* (Seattle: University of Washington Press, 1969), p. 212.

71. See chap. 2. For accounts of Penitente velorios, see, e.g.: Rev. Vicente F. Romero, "Experiences of a Protestant during the Night of Decoration Day," *The Pueblo, Colorado Individual*, June 30, 1898, p. 2; Córdova, *Echoes of the Flute*, pp. 13–16, 48–50; Jaramillo, *Shadows of the Past*, pp. 75–76; Rae Pittam, "A Penetente Wake," *The Pony Express*, August 1947, p. 11; Edmonson, *Los Manitos*, p. 35; Swadesh, *Los Primeros Pobladores*, pp. 193, 237.

72. Aurora Lucero-White, "El Velorio (The Wake)," August 1936, ms., W.P.A. Files, Santa Fe, p. 4. See also E. Boyd, *Popular Arts of Spanish New Mexico,* p. 448; and Dorothy Benrimo, *Camposantos: A Photographic Essay* (Fort Worth, Texas: Amon Carter Museum of Western Art, 1966).

73. Lucero-White, "El Velorio (The Wake)," p. 3. Reyes N. Martinez reports that "a Carmelite, also, in years past, was never buried in a coffin, but in white linen undergarments, with uncovered feet and his head resting upon an adobe or a stone for a pillow, as an indication of eternal rest and peace" ("Curious Practices and Curious Beliefs," March 13, 1937, ms., W.P.A. Files, Santa Fe, p. 2). Besides Lucero-White, see: James, *New Mexico: Land of Delight Makers,* p. 280; Lou Sage Batchen, "An Old Native Custom: El Indio Viejo," May 19, 1940, ms., W.P.A. Files, Santa Fe, p. 3; and the anonymous *A New Mexico Narrative* (Boston: Congregational Education Society, n.d.), p. 8; for those who associate the practice of coffinless burial with the Brotherhood.

74. Lucero-White, "El Velorio (The Wake)."

75. Lea, *Literary Folklore,* p. 219. See also Edmonson, *Los Manitos,* pp. 59–61, inter alia.

76. Douglass, *Death in Murélaga,* p. 210; Evon Z. Vogt and Ethel M. Albert, eds., *People of Rimrock: A Study of Values in Five Cultures* (Cambridge: Harvard University Press, 1966), p. 237.

77. Mills and Grove, *Lucifer and the Crucifer,* pp. 41–44; Weigle, "Los Hermanos Penitentes," pp. 329–38.

78. The historical sections of Henderson's book are weak due to the lack of available archival and other research materials at the time. Dorothy Woodward, Review of Alice Corbin Henderson, *Brothers of Light, New Mexico Historical Review* 12 (1937):204–206; Witter Bynner and Oliver La Farge, eds., "Alice Corbin: An Appreciation," *New Mexico Quarterly Review* 19 (1949):34–79. See also Weigle, "Notes on the Sources," "Los Hermanos Penitentes," pp. 338–41. Córdova's *Echoes of the Flute* is also an excellent source, some of which is drawn from his W.P.A. mss. of the 1930s, as well as personal recollections in 1971.

Chapter 8: The Legends and the Sacred

1. Jacob A. Loewen, "The Social Context of Guilt and Forgiveness," *Practical Anthropology* 17 (1970):88.

2. *New Catholic Encyclopedia,* 11:83.

3. Ibid., 11:80.

4. John Macquarrie, ed., *Dictionary of Christian Ethics* (Philadelphia: Westminster Press, 1967), p. 20.

5. Father Steele observes that, although this contention is "literally" correct, the rites were actually "quasi-sacramental" (*Santos and Saints,* p. 69). See n. 29, below.

6. Charles H. Lange and Carroll L. Riley, eds., *The Southwestern Journals of Adolph F. Bandelier, 1880–1882* (Albuquerque: University of New Mexico Press, 1966), p. 257; Wesley Robert Hurt, Jr., "Manzano: A Study of Community Disorganization," p. 71.

7. E. R. Vollmar, S.J., "Religious Processions and Penitente Activities in Colorado, 1874," *Colorado Magazine* 31 (1954):178.

8. Stephen F. de Borhegyi, "The Miraculous Shrines of Our Lord of Esquípulas in Guatemala and Chimayo, New Mexico," p. 17.

9. Martinez, "Odd Religious Practices," undated ms., W.P.A. Files, Santa Fe, New Mexico, pp. 3–6; Don Branning, "Behind Closed Doors Simple Villagers Called Penitentes Relive Good Friday," *Albuquerque Tribune,* March 24, 1967, pp. A-1, A-4. See also chap. 6, n. 10.

10. Herminia B. Chacon, "The Society of Our Father Jesus," February 6, 1934, ms.,

Dorothy Woodward Penitente Papers, p. 3; Gilberto Benito Córdova, *Abiquiú and Don Cacahuate: A Folk History of a New Mexican Village* (Cerrillos, New Mexico: San Marcos Press, 1973), pp. 50–51; Reyes N. Martinez, "Unmasked," March 26, 1937, ms., W.P.A. Files, Santa Fe.

11. Lummis, *The Land of Poco Tiempo,* p. 98; Aurelio M. Espinosa, "New-Mexican Spanish Folk-Lore: Parts I and II," *Journal of American Folk-Lore* 23 (1910):407–408; Reyes N. Martinez, "La Morada de los Muertos (The Lodge-House of the Dead)," September 9, 1940, ms., W.P.A. Files, Santa Fe. Espinosa's brother, Gilberto Espinosa, presents an elaborate literary version of their father's story in *Heroes, Hexes and Haunted Halls* (Albuquerque, New Mexico: Calvin Horn, 1972), pp. 13–16. The legend is also part of a short story by Fray Angelico Chavez, "The Penitente Thief," in his *New Mexico Triptych* (Paterson, New Jersey: St. Anthony Guild Press, 1940), pp. 23–54.

12. Juan B. Rael, *Cuentos españoles de Colorado y Nuevo Méjico,* 2 vols. (Stanford, California: Stanford University Press, n.d.), 2:605; Reyes N. Martinez, "Candles by the Highway," undated ms., W.P.A. Files, Santa Fe; Patricio M. Montano, "Observations of the Penitentes," in "Papers on Spanish Institutions and Customs in New Mexico," ed. Lynn I. Perrigo (Las Vegas, New Mexico: Highlands University, Donnelly Library, 1968), p. 124.

13. Espinosa, "New-Mexican Spanish Folk-Lore," p. 405.

14. Lorin W. Brown, "Tales of the Moccasin Maker of Córdova," May 3, 1937, ms., W.P.A. Files, Santa Fe, p. 4.

15. Córdova, *Echoes of the Flute,* pp. 32, 33, 41.

16. Juan Hernandez, "Cactus Whips and Wooden Crosses," *Journal of American Folklore* 76 (1963):223.

17. Victor Turner, *The Forest of Symbols: Aspects of Ndembu Ritual* (Ithaca, New York: Cornell University Press, 1967), p. 95. For a psychological perspective, see Carl G. Jung, "Transformation Symbolism in the Mass" (1942; rev. 1954). This paper is reprinted in various sources, including *Psychology and Religion: West and East,* Collected Works, vol. 11 (Princeton University Press, Bollingen Series, 1969).

18. Arnold van Gennep, *The Rites of Passage,* trans. Monika B. Vizeda and Gabrielle L. Caffee (Chicago: University of Chicago Press, 1960). The French anthropologist's work first appeared in 1909.

19. Turner, *Forest of Symbols,* p. 96.

20. Ibid., p. 100.

21. Victor W. Turner, *The Ritual Process: Structure and Anti-Structure* (Chicago: Aldine, 1969), p. 96.

22. Ibid., p. 134.

23. Ibid., pp. 140–54.

24. See Appendix XX. The quotation is from The Revised Standard Version Common Bible.

25. Turner, *Forest of Symbols,* p. 105.

26. Turner, *Ritual Process,* p. 128. Turner's investigation of the "limen" may be viewed as an attempt to elucidate the insights of the various mystery religions. Interestingly, Brotherhood initiations and their Holy Week retreats are somewhat similar to early Christian rituals at the time they were most influenced by the mystery cults. "By the fourth century . . . the idea that the Christian mysteries are to be guarded from the uninitiated finally triumphs. As Father Hugo Rahner expresses it, 'The mysteries of baptism and of the sacrificial altar were surrounded with a ritual of awe and secrecy, and soon the iconostasis concealed the holy of holies from the eyes of the noninitiate: these became . . . "mysteries that make men freeze with awe" ' " (Mircea Eliade, *Rites and Symbols of Initiation: The Mysteries of Birth and Rebirth,* trans. Willard R. Trask [New York: Harper and Row, 1965], p. 120). Alan Watts claims that: "Prior to the general practice of infant baptism, initiation

into the Christian Mysteries was a tremendous solemnity involving preliminary disciplines, tests, and exorcisms of a most serious kind. . . . In those days the inner Mystery of the Mass was by no means a public rite which anyone might attend. . . . The Catechumens were those undergoing preparation for baptism—being catechized—and because they had not yet received initiation were permitted to attend only the introductory part of the Mass. . . . This custom prevailed so long as Christians were a minority in their society, but disappeared when Christianity had been adopted as a state-religion, and when whole societies were nominally Christian" (*Myth and Ritual in Christianity* [Boston: Beacon Press, 1968], p. 139). In many ways, the Brothers formed a similar minority through much of their existence.

27. See. e.g., Eliade, *The Sacred and the Profane: The Nature of Religion,* trans. Willard R. Trask (1957; English ed., New York: Harcourt, Brace, 1959). Otto's work, *Das Heilige* ("The Holy"), was first published in 1917.

28. "The Crucifixion is ultimately a mystical event representing the whole redemptive work of Christ and its proclamation throughout the world. . . . The cross is the pivotal point of history from which all history, prior and subsequent, derives its meaning" (*New Catholic Encyclopedia,* 4:486).

29. Steele, *Santos and Saints,* pp. 69–70. The quotation is from the end of chap. III, "Santos and Saints," in which he develops this argument fully.

30. See Appendix XVIII.

31. Eliade claims that for religious man: "A territory can be made ours only by creating it anew, that is, by consecrating it. . . . The Spanish and Portuguese conquistadores, discovering and conquering territories, took possession of them in the name of Jesus Christ. The raising of the Cross was equivalent to consecrating the country. . . . For through Christ 'old things are passed away; behold, all things are become new' (II Corinthians, 5, 17). The newly discovered country was 'renewed,' 'recreated' by the Cross" (*Sacred and Profane,* p. 32).

32. The last verses of *Adios al mundo,* an alabado from a Penitente *cuaderno,* copybook, included in Henderson, *Brothers of Light,* pp. 104, 106. Henderson's translation, pp. 105, 107, reads:

Good-by, all this company,
All has been completed;
Put me in the sepulcher
In the earth of forgetfulness.

Of nothing I was formed,
By the hands of the Creator,
And in the universal justice
He will be my defender.

To God I kneel humbly,
Of my faults repented;
He will forgive me
For the wrong way I have served Him.

In God I await to repose,
In God I await consolation,
Trusting in His tremendous justice
He will open Heaven's gate.

I am of my Jesus the brother,
I belong to Jesus and always will,
Because I yielded gladly,
And to Jesus I surrender.

Good-by for the last time,
Those who see me on this earth,
Place me in the sepulcher
Which is truly my house.

Good-by, all those present,
All who accompany me,
Pray a *sudario*
In order to overtake me.

Good-by, all my neighbors,
All, all in general,
Commend my soul to God,
And do not forget me.

The End—Amen

Bibliographical Essay

The bibliographical supplement to this study, *A Penitente Bibliography: Supplement to Brothers of Light, Brothers of Blood: The Penitentes of the Southwest* (Albuquerque: University of New Mexico Press, 1975), contains an exhaustive listing of well over one thousand items (most with annotations) relating to the Brotherhood of Our Father Jesus. Popular and scholarly sources of all kinds were extensively surveyed in an attempt to discourage any further erroneous, sensationalized, derivative accounts of the Penitentes and to encourage accurate, sensitive, primary studies of particular communities and/or periods of history. Since the complete bibliography in the supplement is essential to anyone with a serious interest in the Brotherhood and the Hispanic Southwest, this bibliographical essay summarizes only the most significant resources used in the preparation of this volume.

Four important scholarly studies deal directly with the Brotherhood. Dorothy Woodward, "The Penitentes of New Mexico" (Ph.D. dissertation, Yale University, 1935), recently retyped and reprinted with a short biographical foreword by Myra Ellen Jenkins (New York: Arno Press, 1974), provides the basic historical foundation, although the Archives of the Archdiocese of Santa Fe were not then available to her. The first serious study to utilize these archives was Fray Angelico Chavez, "The Penitentes of New Mexico," *New Mexico Historical Review* 29 (1954):97–123, who proposes an outside origin for the Brotherhood from a penitential confraternity. E. Boyd also draws on archival resources to oppose this view in "The Third Order of St. Francis and the Penitentes of New Mexico," part of her monumental *Popular Arts of Spanish New Mexico* (Santa Fe: Museum of New Mexico Press, 1974), pp. 440–83. Finally, the dissertation upon which this book and the

276

bibliography are based, Mary Martha Weigle, " 'Los Hermanos Penitentes': Historical and Ritual Aspects of Folk Religion in Northern New Mexico and Southern Colorado" (Ph.D. dissertation, University of Pennsylvania, 1971), should be cited in this regard. It was preceded by a short preliminary study, Marta Weigle, *The Penitentes of the Southwest* (Santa Fe, New Mexico: Ancient City Press, 1970). Lorayne Ann Horka-Follick, *Los Hermanos Penitentes: A Vestige of Medievalism in Southwestern United States* (Los Angeles: Westernlore Press, 1969), a 1968 doctoral dissertation at St. Andrew's College, University of London, England, should not be relied on due to insufficient research and numerous inaccuracies.

The following collections, listed in alphabetical order, contain the most important documentary and unpublished materials relating to the Brotherhood:

Archives of the Archdiocese of Santa Fe. Fray Angelico Chavez, O.F.M., *Archives of the Archdiocese of Santa Fe 1678–1900* (Washington, D.C.: Academy of American Franciscan History, 1957), the calendar to the available portion of these archives, may be used as a guide to the microfilm edition.

Dorothy Woodward Penitente Papers. Part of the Dorothy Woodward Collection at the New Mexico State Records Center and Archives, Santa Fe, this private legacy contains invaluable documents, manuscripts, notes, letters, photographs, and published sources, assembled before and since her 1935 dissertation.

Lynn I. Perrigo Seminar Papers. While a professor of history at Highlands University, Dr. Perrigo edited bound volumes of his best student papers on New Mexico folklore and history, which are now kept in the rare book room of Donnelly Library, New Mexico Highlands University, Las Vegas. Copies of these and many other papers about the Penitentes are also in an excellent, growing collection at Carnegie Public Library, Las Vegas, New Mexico.

New Mexico Writers' Program W.P.A. Files. Gilbert Benito Córdova, *Bibliography of Unpublished Materials Pertaining to Hispanic Culture in the New Mexico WPA Writers' Files* (Santa Fe: New Mexico

State Department of Education, December 1972), is an indexed, annotated listing of most of these holdings, which are housed in the History Library of the Museum of New Mexico, Santa Fe, and the New Mexico State Records Center and Archives, Santa Fe.

State Corporation Commission of New Mexico Files, Santa Fe. *Laws of the Territory of New Mexico: Passed by the Legislative Assembly, Session of 1860–1861* (Santa Fe: John T. Russell, Printer, 1861), pp. 74–77, contains the first official Brotherhood incorporation. Other certificates of incorporation have since been legally filed with the Office of the Secretary of New Mexico and, after 1912, with the Office of the State Corporation Commission.

William G. Ritch Collection, Henry E. Huntington Library, San Marino, California. Memo Book No. 4 (HM RI 2212, vol. 4) and fourteen pages of various texts (HM RI 1866) provide valuable nineteenth-century materials.

A completely unauthorized publication by Charles Aranda, *The Penitente Papers* (9601 Robin St. N.E., Albuquerque, New Mexico: Author, n.d.), gives translations and transcriptions of some private letters and Brotherhood documents which had been in the possession of his father, the late Roman Aranda, second Hermano Supremo Arzobispal.

On the whole, annual newspaper articles on the Brotherhood are ephemeral and sensational. Specific incidents are generally reported in the appropriate issues of *The Santa Fe New Mexican,* in existence since 1849. Porter A. Stratton, *The Territorial Press of New Mexico 1834–1912* (Albuquerque: University of New Mexico Press, 1969), is a useful reference. Pearce S. Grove, Becky J. Barnett, and Sandra J. Hansen, eds., *New Mexico Newspapers: A Comprehensive Guide to Bibliographical Entries and Locations* (Albuquerque: University of New Mexico Press with Eastern New Mexico University, 1975), should facilitate future use of such sources. Of particular interest is the Jesuit *Revista Católica,* published weekly in Las Vegas after an initial January 1875 edition which appeared in Albuquerque. Besides reporting Church news helpful for reconstructing contemporary ecclesiastical affairs, some of which involved the Brotherhood, *La Revista* editors constantly feuded with various

Protestant newspapers in New Mexico and Colorado. The most important of these were probably Rev. Sheldon Jackson's *Rocky Mountain Presbyterian,* first published in 1872, and Rev. Alexander M. Darley's two Pueblo, Colorado, newspapers, *La Hermandad* and *The Individual,* which are on microfilm in the Pueblo Regional Library. These and other Protestant newspapers occasionally printed diatribes against the Penitentes. A critical article in the *Albuquerque Review* of April 6, 1878, "How A Pious and Useful Body Degenerated into a Sect—A Secret Society," also contains valuable contemporaneous attitudes toward and explanations of the Brotherhood.

Some of the most useful historical background materials and research aids are in three pamphlets edited by Dr. Myra Ellen Jenkins and published by the State of New Mexico Records Center and Archives, Santa Fe: *Guide to the Microfilm of the Spanish Archives of New Mexico 1621–1821* (1967); *Guide to the Microfilm Edition of the Mexican Archives of New Mexico 1821–1846* (1969); and *Guide to the Microfilm Edition of the Territorial Archives of New Mexico 1846–1912* (1974). Another accurate and recent overall historical perspective is found in Cultural Properties Review Committee, *The Historic Preservation Program for New Mexico,* 2 vols. (Santa Fe: State Planning Office, 1973), part of which has been reprinted in Myra Ellen Jenkins and Albert H. Schroeder, *A Brief History of New Mexico* (Albuquerque: University of New Mexico Press, 1974). D. W. Meinig, *Southwest: Three Peoples in Geographical Change, 1600–1970* (New York: Oxford University Press, 1971), also provides a good overview.

Both Marc Simmons, *Spanish Government in New Mexico* (Albuquerque: University of New Mexico Press, 1968), covering the period from 1776 to 1821, and H. Bailey Carroll and J. Villasana Haggard, eds., *Three New Mexico Chronicles: The "Exposición" of Don Pedro Bautista Pino, 1812; the "Ojeada" of Lic. Antonio Barreiro, 1832; and the additions by Don José Agustín de Escudero, 1849* (Albuquerque, New Mexico: The Quivira Society, 1942), give sound background for the late Spanish and Mexican periods. Three books help with Territorial history: Howard Roberts Lamar, *The Far Southwest 1846–1912: A Territorial History* (New Haven: Yale University Press, 1966); Robert W. Larson, *New Mexico's Quest for Statehood 1846–1912* (Albuquerque: University of New Mexico Press, 1968);

and Robert W. Larson, *New Mexico Populism: A Study of Radical Protest in a Western Territory* (Boulder: Colorado Associated University Press, 1974). Jack E. Holmes, *Politics in New Mexico* (Albuquerque: University of New Mexico Press, 1967), which analyses voting patterns from 1910 to 1964, also includes the only serious study of Brotherhood political activity and reports interviews with the late Don Miguel Archibeque.

A comprehensive bibliography of bibliographic, folkloristic, linguistic, sociocultural, geographical, and other related studies of the Hispanic Southwest, most from the twentieth century, is part of Marta Weigle, ed., *Hispanic Villages of Northern New Mexico: A Reprint of Volume II of The 1935 Tewa Basin Study, with Supplementary Materials* (Santa Fe, New Mexico: The Lightning Tree—Jene Lyon, Publisher, 1975). Both the Tewa Basin Study, covering some thirty communities in Santa Fe, Rio Arriba, and Taos Counties, and George I. Sánchez, *Forgotten People: A Study of New Mexicans* (Albuquerque: University of New Mexico Press, 1940), on Taos County, are basic to understanding Hispanic communities in this century. A recent but uneven synthesis by Nancie L. González, *The Spanish-Americans of New Mexico: A Heritage of Pride* (Albuquerque: University of New Mexico Press, 1969), also presents basic data and summary analyses. The Comparative Study of Values in Five Cultures Project of the Laboratory of Social Relations, Harvard University, explored sociocultural variables in west-central New Mexico, 1949–55. Most interpretations of the Brotherhood are found in Munro S. Edmonson, *Los Manitos: A Study of Institutional Values* (New Orleans: Tulane University, Middle American Research Institute, 1957), and the collection of interpretive essays finalizing the Project, Evon Z. Vogt and Ethel Albert, *People of Rimrock: A Study of Values in Five Cultures* (Cambridge, Massachusetts: Harvard University Press, 1966). A more recent historical and field study of the Chama River Valley and the San Juan Basin, Frances Leon Swadesh, *Los Primeros Pobladores: Hispanic Americans of the Ute Frontier* (Notre Dame: University of Notre Dame Press, 1974), also contains important information on Hispanic culture and the Brotherhood. Only one sociocultural study, George Mills, *The People of the Saints* (Colorado Springs, Colorado: The Taylor Museum of The Colorado Springs Fine Arts Center, n.d.), concentrates on the Penitentes and religious folk art.

Ecclesiastical history is still somewhat neglected for the late eighteenth and early nineteenth centuries. Both Eleanor B. Adams and Fray Angelico Chavez are consistently excellent in their studies of Spanish New Mexican Church history, notably: Fray Angelico Chavez, *Our Lady of the Conquest* (Santa Fe: Historical Society of New Mexico, 1948); Eleanor B. Adams, ed., *Bishop Tamarón's Visitation of New Mexico, 1760* (Albuquerque: Historical Society of New Mexico, 1954); Eleanor B. Adams, "The Chapel and *Cofradía* of Our Lady of Light in Santa Fe," *New Mexico Historical Review* 22 (1947):327–41; and Eleanor B. Adams and Fray Angelico Chavez, trans. and eds., *The Missions of New Mexico, 1776: A Description by Fray Francisco Atanasio Domínguez, With Other Contemporary Documents* (Albuquerque: University of New Mexico Press, 1956; University of New Mexico Press, Official New Mexico American Revolution Bicentennial Publication, reprinted 1975). Three anonymous Church pamphlets, largely written by Fray Angelico Chavez, also contain valuable information about regional Church matters, namely: *The Santa Fe Cathedral*, rev. ed. (Santa Fe, New Mexico: Schifani Brothers, n.d.); *The Old Faith and Old Glory, 1846–1946: Story of the Church in New Mexico Since the American Occupation* (Santa Fe: Santa Fe Press, 1946); and *Lamy Memorial: Centenary of the Archdiocese of Santa Fe, 1850–1950* (Santa Fe, New Mexico: Schifani Brothers, 1950). Jesuit history in the region is explored by J. Manuel Espinosa in "The Opening of the First Jesuit Mission in Colorado: Conejos Parish," *Mid-America* 18 (1936):272–75, and "The Neapolitan Jesuits on the Colorado Frontier, 1868–1919," *Colorado Magazine* 15 (1938):64–73, and in the official volume by Sister M. Lilliana Owens, S.L., with Rev. Fr. Gregory Goñi, S.J., and Rev. Fr. J. M. Gonzalez, S.J., *Jesuit Beginnings in New Mexico, 1867–1882* (El Paso, Texas: Revista Católica Press, 1950).

Neither Bishop Lamy nor his native adversary, Cura Antonio José Martínez, have been sufficiently researched. Paul Horgan's recent biography, *Lamy of Santa Fe: His Life and Times* (New York: Farrar, Straus & Giroux, 1975), should help remedy this lack. At present, the most substantial material on Martínez may be found in Cecil V. Romero, trans., "Apologia of Presbyter Antonio J. Martínez," *New Mexico Historical Review* 3 (1928):325–46; E. K. Francis, "Padre Martínez: A New Mexican Myth," *New Mexico*

Historical Review 31 (1956):265–89; and E. Boyd, "The First New Mexico Imprint," *Princeton University Library Chronicle* 33 (1971):30–40. Archbishop Salpointe himself wrote a history, *Soldiers of the Cross: Notes on the Ecclesiastical History of New Mexico, Arizona and Colorado* (Banning, California: St. Boniface's Industrial School, 1898). His biography, an M.A. thesis by Sister Edward Mary Zerwekh, C.S.J., has been published as "John Baptist Salpointe, 1825–1894," *New Mexico Historical Review* 37 (1962):1–19, 132–54, 214–29.

Protestant church history is even less adequate. Researchers must for the most part rely on highly colored home mission reports and occasional local denominational histories. The Presbyterians were quite influential in the area. A sound historical summary of their schools and missions appears in Edith J. Agnew and Ruth K. Barber, "The Unique Presbyterian School System of New Mexico," *Journal of Presbyterian History* 49 (1971):197–221. *Hand On My Shoulder* (New York: Board of National Missions, Presbyterian Church in the U.S.A., 1953), the autobiography of Rev. Gabino Rendón as told to Edith Agnew, describes the work of an important early Hispano convert to Presbyterianism. Martin Rist thoroughly explores early Methodist Episcopal Church history in "Methodist Beginnings in New Mexico," in *The 1966 Brand Book: Volume 22 of The Denver Posse of The Westerners,* edited by William D. Powell (Boulder, Colorado: Johnson Publishing, 1967), pp. 75–91, and "Penitentes of New Mexico in the 1870's According to Thomas and Emily Harwood," *The Denver Westerners Monthly Roundup* 26 (1970):3–14. Finally, the evangelical groups, many of which succeeded in converting former Brothers, have been least studied, the main exception being an article by J. B. Johnson, "The Allelujahs: A Religious Cult in Northern New Mexico," *Southwest Review* 22 (1937):131–39.

The history of outsiders' interest in the Brotherhood really begins with the highly emotional and inaccurate accounts of two men: Charles Fletcher Lummis and Rev. Alexander M. Darley. Lummis photographed Holy Week rites at San Mateo, New Mexico, in 1888. The most familiar version of his experience and the now-famous photographs appear in his *The Land of Poco Tiempo,* first published in 1893, and reprinted in an illustrated facsimile edition by the University of New Mexico Press, Albuquerque, in

1966. Rev. Darley's fifty-nine-page volume of 1893, *The Passionists of the Southwest, or The Holy Brotherhood: A Revelation of the 'Penitentes,'* which he printed himself in Pueblo, Colorado, was almost impossible to find until its reprinting, together with pertinent photographs and appendixes, by the Rio Grande Press, Glorieta, New Mexico, in 1968. Since 1893, annual journalistic, sensational, and derivative "reports" on the Penitentes have appeared in every imaginable type of publication.

In 1910, Laurence F. Lee, who was familiar with Brothers in the area of San Mateo, New Mexico, submitted a B.A. thesis entitled "Los Hermanos Penitentes" to the English Department of the University of New Mexico. It was later expurgated, but substantial portions of it were published anonymously in *El Palacio* 8 (1920):2–20. Both Mary Austin and Alice Corbin Henderson used material from Lee's thesis. Austin's papers, which include a number of alabado texts and various fragments of articles, are in the Henry E. Huntington Library, San Marino, California. Her most complete published interpretation and account of the Brotherhood is in *The Land of Journeys' Ending* (New York: Century, 1924). Alice Corbin Henderson's description of Holy Week rites at Abiquiu, New Mexico, *Brothers of Light: The Penitentes of the Southwest* (New York: Harcourt, Brace, 1937), remains the most sensitive and beautiful outsider's account, although it is less sound historically. Other notable overviews are by Josué Trujillo, *La Penitencia a Traves de La Civilizacion* (Santa Cruz, New Mexico: Author, 1947); Barron B. Beshoar, "Western Trails to Calvary," in *The 1949 Brand Book,* edited by Don Bloch (Denver, Colorado: The Westerners Denver Posse, 1950) pp. 119–48; and Juan Hernandez, "Cactus Whips and Wooden Crosses," *Journal of American Folklore* 76 (1963):216–24.

While preparing for a 1955 exhibition on "Penitentes of New Mexico and Colorado" at the Taylor Museum of The Colorado Springs Fine Arts Center, Colorado Springs, George Mills and Richard Grove assembled and analyzed sixty-five "eyewitness" accounts of Brotherhood rites in *Lucifer and the Crucifer: The Enigma of the Penitentes,* 2nd ed. (Colorado Springs: The Taylor Museum of The Colorado Springs Fine Arts Center, 1966). This list was revised and enlarged by Weigle in the dissertation (1971) previously cited, pp. 329–41. Mills and Grove also propose various psychological and sociocultural explanations for Penitente practices. Such interpretations have generally been both numerous and unsatisfactory. The most sober and suggestive interpretive remarks have been made by people familiar with regional and ecclesiastical history. In addition to many of the writers cited above, interpretations offered by New Mexican author Harvey Fergusson in *Rio Grande* (New York: Alfred A. Knopf, 1933), and Catholic novelist and historian Paul Horgan in the first volume of *Great River: The Rio Grande in North American History* (New York: Rinehart, 1954), a section entitled "Mortality," pp. 377–82, should be noted. A recent interpretive history and spiritual autobiography by Fray Angelico Chavez, *My Penitente Land: Reflections on Spanish New Mexico* (Albuquerque: University of New Mexico Press, 1974), provides an interesting perspective on the area and, less centrally, the Brotherhood. It was published too late to be fully incorporated into the present volume.

Comparative interpretive material may be found in many fields. The basic reference work for Church history, theology, and ritual is the fifteen-volume *New Catholic Encyclopedia* (New York: McGraw Hill, 1967). The first edition, *The Catholic Encyclopedia* (New York: Robert Appleton, 1911), did contain an entry by Aurelio M. Espinosa, "Penitentes, Los Hermanos (The Penitent Brothers)," 11:635–36, but the new edition merely mentions the Brotherhood in Fray Angelico Chavez's article, "Santa Fe, Archdiocese of (Sanctae Fidei), N. Mex.," 12:1060–66. Flagellation has been widely discussed, for example, in a twentieth-century compendium with bibliography, George Ryley Scott, *The History of Corporal Punishment: A Survey of Flagellation in Its Historical Anthropological and Sociological Aspects* (London: T. Werner Laurie, 1938). Julio Puyol, "Plática de disciplinantes," in *Estudios eruditos "in memoriam" de Adolfo Bonilla y San Martín* (Madrid: Imprenta Viuda e Hijos de Jaime Rates, 1927), vol. 1, pp. 241–66, is a valuable historical and descriptive study of the Spanish flagellant tradition. George M. Foster gives historical and general comparative data in " 'Cofradía' and 'Compadrazgo' in Spain and Spanish America," *Southwestern Journal of Anthropology* 9 (1953):1–28, and *Culture and Conquest: America's Spanish Heritage* (Chicago: Quadrangle Books, 1960). William A. Christian, Jr., *Person and God in a Spanish Valley*

(New York: Seminar Press, 1972), suggests many dimensions for comparison and future exploration.

A number of psychological, anthropological, and historical studies of religion were examined for insights into the Brotherhood. Perhaps the most directly influential of these were the following: Mircea Eliade, *The Sacred and the Profane: The Nature of Religion,* translated by Willard R. Trask (New York: Harcourt, Brace, 1959); Don Yoder, "Official Religion versus Folk Religion," *Pennsylvania Folklife,* Winter, 1965–66, pp. 36–52; Weston LaBarre, *They Shall Take Up Serpents: Psychology of the Southern Snake-Handling Cult* (New York: Schocken Books, 1969); and Victor W. Turner, *The Ritual Process: Structure and Anti-Structure* (Chicago: Aldine Publishing, 1969). LaBarre's interdisciplinary approach to an equally "vivid" religious expression is very heuristic. Turner's discussion of St. Francis and the Franciscans can be fruitfully applied to Brotherhood history.

The fine arts also contain provocative interpretations of the Brotherhood, although outside artists' liberties are often exasperatingly exaggerated. From the outrageous turn-of-the-century novel by Louis How, *The Penitentes of San Rafael: A Tale of the San Luis Valley* (Indianapolis, Indiana: Bowen-Merrill, 1900), until a recent Gothic novel by Mona Farnsworth, *A Cross for Tomorrow* (New York: Pinnacle Books, 1972), the Penitentes have unwittingly supplied either the plot and theme or the "local color" for many good and bad novels. Perhaps the best of these is Robert Bright, *The Life and Death of Little Jo* (Garden City, New York: Doubleday, Doran, 1944), set in Talpa, New Mexico, and the inspiration for an opera incorporating New Mexican Hispanic folk melodies, J. D. Robb, *Little Jo* (Paris: Neocopie Musicale, 1949). One of the most stimulating poems with a Penitente theme is "Men in New Mexico," by D. H. Lawrence, first published in his *Birds, Beasts and Flowers* (New York: Thomas Seltzer, 1923), pp. 166–68. Various artists have painted pictures of Brotherhood activities, and a useful study of one such painter has been made by Van Deren Coke, "A Note on B. J. O. Nordfeldt's 'Penitente Crucifixion,' " *University of New Mexico Art Museum Bulletin,* no. 2 (Spring, 1967):6–11, later included in his *Nordfeldt the Painter* (Albuquerque: University of New Mexico Press, 1972), pp. 57–61. A series of thirteen oil paintings by former Taos doctor Isaac L. Udell are among the most complete and detailed available. Photographs and descriptions of these scenes are published in an exhibition catalogue edited by Morris L. Appelman and I. L. Udell, *The Penitentes* (Denver, Colorado: The Cosmopolitan Art Gallery, n.d.). Udell's illustrated, impressionistic essays about the Taos area during the 1930s are published as "In The Dust of The Valley," *South Dakota Review* 7 (1969):9–105.

The most important expressive forms are of course those preserved by the Brothers themselves. Excellent studies of all these folk arts have been completed or are promised. Richard E. Ahlborn, *The Penitente Moradas of Abiquiú* (Washington, D.C.: Smithsonian Institution Press, 1968), documents the history, structures, and contents of both moradas. A similar, though less meticulous, study is by Robert L. Shalkop, *Arroyo Hondo: The Folk Art of a New Mexican Village* (Colorado Springs, The Taylor Museum of The Colorado Springs Fine Arts Center, 1969). A technical architectural description of the upper morada at Arroyo Hondo is in Bainbridge Bunting, *Taos Adobes: Spanish Colonial and Territorial Architecture of the Taos Valley* (Santa Fe: Museum of New Mexico Press, 1964). Other photographic essays which include moradas are Robert Adams, *The Architecture and Art of Early Hispanic Colorado* (Boulder: Colorado Associated University Press with The State Historical Society of Colorado, 1974), and Bainbridge Bunting, *Of Earth and Timbers Made: New Mexico Architecture* (Albuquerque: University of New Mexico Press, 1974).

E. Boyd's previously cited *Popular Arts of Spanish New Mexico* (1974) is a fundamental resource for any of the arts in Hispanic New Mexico. Since the publication of this final master work, there is a much shorter volume with a number of provocative aesthetic, theological, and sociocultural analyses, Thomas J. Steele, S.J., *Santos and Saints: Essays and Handbook* (Albuquerque, New Mexico: Calvin Horn, 1974). Forthcoming work on the woodcarvers of Cordova, New Mexico, by Charles L. Briggs will also make an important contribution. A brief preliminary study is in Briggs, "What Is a Modern Santo?" *El Palacio* 79, 4 (1974):40–49.

To date, the most useful collection and brief study of regional Hispanic religious music, including the Penitentes, is in Juan B. Rael, *The New Mexican 'Alabado'*, Stanford University Publications,

University Series, Language and Literature, vol. IX, no. 3 (Stanford, California: Stanford University Press, 1951). Former Brother Cleofes Vigil has recorded a number of these alabados for Taos Recordings and Publications, Taos, New Mexico: *New Mexican Alabados* (TRP 3), and *Buenos Días, Paloma Blanca: Five Alabados of Northern New Mexico* (TRP-122). Richard B. Stark of the Museum of International Folk Art, Museum of New Mexico, and St. John's College, Santa Fe, is preparing a needed historical and musicological study of alabados. Meanwhile, some of the flavor of Brotherhood music and ritual is preserved in the beautiful limited edition portfolio edited by Reginald Fisher, *The Way of the Cross: A New Mexico Version* (Santa Fe, New Mexico: Graphic Printing, 1958).

Two recent pamphlets exemplify the sort of works which convey an appreciation for Hispanic villages and the Brotherhood's place in their history and community life. Lorenzo de Córdova, *Echoes of the Flute* (Santa Fe, New Mexico: Ancient City Press, 1972), contains reminiscences and contemporaneous accounts of the Brotherhood in Cordova, New Mexico, and elsewhere in the north-central Hispanic villages. The legend of ghostly flagellants is woven into local folklore and history in Gilberto Benito Córdova, *Abiquiú and Don Cacahuate: A Folk History of a New Mexican Village* (Los Cerrillos, New Mexico: San Marcos Press, 1973). A similar and less skillful but nonetheless informative folklife study, Cleofas M. Jaramillo, *Shadows of the Past (Sombras del Pasado)* (Santa Fe, New Mexico: Seton Village Press, 1941), describes Arroyo Hondo, New Mexico, early in the twentieth century. Hopefully, more such localized, sensitive accounts by native Hispanic New Mexicans will appear in the future to offset the too frequently irresponsible reports by outsider observers.

Index

Abeyta, Bernardo (Brother, El Potrero), 50 51, 183

Abiquiu, N.M.: east morada at, 240n*18;* 1776 flagellation at, 44; mentioned, 4, 6, 46, 47, 169, 173, 184, 250n*5,* 257n*56,* 261n*61,* 283, 286, 287; population in 1827, 248n*109;* secularization of, 22

Abreu, Margaret, cited, 145–46

Acompañadores (Attendants), 144, 148, 172, 179, 184, 265n*5. See also* Brothers of Light

Agua Zarca, N.M., 124

Ahlborn, Richard E., cited, 7

Alabados (hymns): *Acompañadnos todos,* 270n*37; Adios al mundo,* 191–92, 275n*32; Bendice, Señor, La Cena,* 269n*24; Bendito el Santo Madero,* 269n*24; Considera alma perdida,* 165; *La encomendación del alma,* 175; *La Pasión del Señor,* 164, 270n*31; Lloren, pecadores,* 164, 270n*31;* mentioned, 112, 164, 167, 182, 270n*36,* 286–87; *Por el rastro de la sangre,* 269n*24; Recuerda si estás dormido,* 119, 189; sung during exercises, 269n*24;* sung during wakes, 176

Albuquerque, N.M.: confraternities at, 35; mentioned, 3, 6, 21, 56, 78, 117, 136, 138, 179; secularization of, 21; Third Order at, 40, 41, 43, 44

Albuquerque Journal, 107

Albuquerque Review, 80, 82

Alcalde, N.M., 28, 123, 185

Alcaldes, 81, 82. *See also* Judiciary

All Saints, Feast of (Todos los Santos), 157, 158

All Souls' Day. *See* Day of the Dead

Allelujahs, 99–100. *See also* Protestants

Andrews, William H. (N.M. Delegate to Congress), 89, 90, 257n*52*

Annin, J. A. (Presbyterian minister at Las Vegas, N.M.), 70, 72

Antonito, Colo., 185

Apaches, 64

Applegate, Frank, 272n*61*

Aranda, Charles, cited, 62, 142, 278

Aranda, Roman (second Hermano Supremo Arzobispal), 18, 138, 264n*48,* 278

Archbishop's Supreme Council (Concilio Supremo Arzobispal). *See* Councils

Archibeque, Don Miguel (first Hermano Supremo Arzobispal): biography, 261n*53;* death of, 18, 117; mentioned, xix, 8, 17, 18, 98, 106, 109, 110, 111, 112, 124, 135, 136, 138, 142, 165, 264n*47,* 264n*48,* 280; on origin of Brotherhood, 55

Arizona, 6, 8, 53, 58, 67

Arkansas Valley, Colo., 74

Armijo, Luis E., Judge, 126

Arroyo Hondo, N.M., 6, 46, 99, 122, 123, 130, 140, 158, 161, 165, 166, 167, 170, 183, 184, 185, 270n*26,* 287

Arroyo Seco, N.M., 123, 168

Arroz ("rice"), 161. *See also* Penance

Asceticism, 181–82

Ash Wednesday (Miércoles de Ceniza), 158, 159

Associated Press, 107, 111, 116, 117

Assumption ("La Asunción"), 115, 158

Austin, Mary, cited, 28, 65–66, 96, 100, 102, 104, 113, 115, 140, 178, 260n*31,* 267n*32,* 272n*56*

Auxiliadoras (female auxiliaries). *See* Women

Avel, Etienne M. (priest at Mora, N.M.), 64

Ayudantes ("helpers"). *See* Acompañadores

Baca, Manuel Jesus (Hermano del Centro, San Miguel Co.), 126

Baca, Prospero S. (Hermano del Centro, San Miguel Co.), 124, 220

Baca, Rafael (Brother, San Miguel Co.), 62, 211

Baca y Armijo, Serafin (Brotherhood official, San Miguel Co.), 62, 88–90, 124, 209, 211, 220, 256–57n*49*

Balland, C. (priest in Mora, N.M.), 64